THE FREELANCE WAY

Jan Melvil publishing

About the book

Freelancing is by far the simplest approach to doing business on the free market. With very little capital, risk and equipment, you can turn gigs and side jobs into a successful business career, become your own boss and do meaningful, well-paid work.

Yet over time, freelancing may also prove to be quite a challenge for your self-management, for a freelancer is both an expert and a businessperson. Failing to recognize this leads many freelancers to a bitter end, so developing both your expertise and business skills is essential for attaining sustainable professional growth and better profits.

There's just one more catch. You may soon find out that the rules for success written for companies and startups lack relevance for freelancers. Freelancing is so distinct, that what you need isn't just *any* business strategy, but the *freelance* strategy. In other words, you need this book.

The Freelance Way is THE business book for independent professionals. It presents the best available and fully up-to-date freelance know-how, compiled from hundreds of quality sources, including surveys, the latest market data, advice from world-class experts, as well as real-life experiences and stories from hundreds of professionals in different fields and countries, which makes the book highly relevant to freelancers worldwide.

The contents of this volume cover all the basics and best practices for beginning freelancers, as well as advanced career strategies and tools for freelance veterans. There are practical tips for greater productivity, successful teamwork, smart pricing, powerful business negotiations, bulletproof personal finance, effective marketing, and much more.

Regardless if you've been in business for 20 years, or are just starting out, this book will help you to grow, avoid countless mistakes and develop a successful personal business based on your expertise and good name, to live a free, independent, and fulfilled life.

About the author

Robert Vlach is a senior business consultant, specialized in supporting independent professionals and business owners. In 2005, he founded one of the largest national freelance communities in Europe and later, in 2012, Europe's first think-tank for freelancers which meets regularly in Prague and other cities. He has been holding freelancing courses for more than a decade, and has consulted on over 300 business cases with individuals, startups, and companies. Robert lives with his family in the Czech Republic and Spain.

— For details and updates, go to **Vla.ch**

Praise for *The Freelance Way*

"If you want to succeed as an independent professional, it is essential that you educate yourself about running a personal business. You can either learn this the hard way through trial and error, or read this unique book instead. It covers virtually everything you need to know as a freelancer on how to start, manage and grow your business – be it a local or a global one, working remotely. Robert's book is packed with proven advice, tools, stories and wisdom from people who have gone down this road before you. It will undoubtedly help you live and prosper, the freelance way."

— **Steven Pressfield**, world-famous author of *Gates of Fire,*
The War of Art, and *The Legend of Bagger Vance*

"As freelancers, we know *why* we should run our indie careers as a business, but *how* is often a challenge. This essential book delivers actionable advice and practical tips you can use to build a solid business foundation right now."

— **Melissa Joulwan**, author of the best-selling *Well Fed* cookbook series

"Are you an experienced entrepreneur? Then this book will save your ass several times over. Are you a newbie freelancer starting out? It may even save your life! Most people think there are two groups of people out there: entrepreneurs and employees. They couldn't be more wrong. In fact, there are those who are willing to learn and those who believe they know everything. This book is for the first group. *The Freelance Way* is one of the most useful books that I have read on my journey to a free(lance) life."

— **Michelle Losekoot**, freelance writer and digital storyteller with major
brands like Puma, T-Mobile, O_2, Skoda, and Prague City Tourism

"Just because you're a freelancer, you don't have to figure it all out on your own. There is a wealth of knowledge and wisdom out there from people who have succeeded on their own terms as independent professionals – and Robert Vlach puts it in your hands with *The Freelance Way*. The book is packed with practical advice on the challenges you will encounter, from the mundane to the artistic. And whatever your current level of freelancing experience, Robert reminds you and me that there is always more to aspire to."

— **Mark McGuinness**, creative coach and host of
The 21st Century Creative Podcast

"I had the privilege to work with Robert many years before he wrote this book. He is the best business advisor I've ever had and he played a significant role in my career move from the corporate world to freelancing. *The Freelance Way* is a must-read for anyone leaving the corporate bubble and taking back control of their professional identity and destiny."

— **Eva Skornickova**, leading data privacy and GDPR advisor, former diplomat to Canada and top executive in Fortune 500 companies

"*The Freelance Way* is a book you will be returning to… for years, over and over again. It is written for both beginners and established professionals, so as you grow, it will give you new insights each time you read it. This book is a must for every freelancer, regardless of their profession."

— **Michael Petrus**, illustrator and art director, founder of the comic book app Nanits

"Robert's upbeat book about freelancing ends on a fascinating and unexpected twist. Even seasoned freelancers will find this work a great opportunity to go back to their roots and recalibrate their freelance business."

— **Jan de Graaf**, senior business developer and expert on EU exports to China

"*The Freelance Way* is a comprehensive and well-structured masterpiece on freelancing, and rightfully the main go-to resource for independent professionals, entrepreneurs and creators alike. The book sums up years of experience and tons of advice and research, yet it is super pleasant to read. Robert presents a complete roadmap with hundreds of real-world examples on how to seriously upgrade your freelancing toolbox. Going freelance is a lot of fun, but it also brings a lot of challenges. Reading this book will surely allow you to enjoy more of the former and put you in control of the latter."

— **Petr Klymec**, EMEA Expansion Manager at WeWork

"Robert Vlach is one in a million. Friendly, hard-working, fully engaged, but most of all a true professional, who walks the talk. His book is precisely like that. Before I opened it, I wasn't really aware that I was half-freelance myself. I was awestruck by the sheer number of things I could improve on. Ever since, the book has been my go-to business guide. It has helped me a great deal and I am sure it will help anyone who reads it as well."

— **Daniel Gladis**, investor and founder of the EU-based Vltava Fund, best-selling writer

"For Robert, freelancing is not a fancy hashtag. For Robert, freelance means business. His truly eye-opening book is here to help you in setting the right prices, keeping your inbox sane and preventing the most common deadly mistakes."

— **Michal Kasparek**, writer and editor-in-chief at FINMAG.cz

"There's an estimate that freelancers will make up the majority of the workforce by 2027. Do you want to succeed in this new economy? By buying this book, you can make Robert your personal advisor. I don't know anyone who could be a better guide for you on this journey."

— **Peter Fabor**, founder of Surf Office's international network of company retreat venues

"A breathtaking business guide that will take your freelancing to the top. *The Freelance Way* leads you safely through valleys of failure, financial risks and tough business decisions. While climbing higher, Robert teaches you to avoid pitfalls and master the survivor's toolkit to fix problems. Together you cross challenging spots like negotiations, pricing, and marketing to reach the peak of success, a good reputation and clients who appreciate you and your work. Standing there, up on the top, as an accomplished freelancer, you look back and know in your heart: It was worth it."

— **Imre Jernei**, world-class brand designer, founder of the Ziijn studio

"*The Freelance Way* took my business to the moon and back. A very readable and enjoyable book that taught me how to professionalize my work."

— **Eliska Vyhnankova**, senior social media consultant with major brands like Bayer and Johnson & Johnson

"I could have saved myself countless blind alleys and wasted hours; miscalculated budgets for my services; neglected self-presentation; trials of useless tools; accounting and tax-filing errors, if only Robert had written this book 10 years ago, when I left my corporate job and went freelance. *The Freelance Way* is a must-read for all of you, who are just starting to take their lives back."

— **Radek Hrachovec**, a leading loyalty marketing expert, *The Loyalty Magazine Awards* judge

"Robert is passionate about creating and realising individual business stories, taking that inspirational spark and enthusiasm for an idea and making it real. To make it real you need to understand the details and dynamics of doing business. Robert's book is a must read, full of practical and actionable advice, allowing you to discover the entrepreneur in you and to make that passionate idea come to life. I can't recommend this book enough."

— **Maxwell Colonna-Dashwood**, three-time UK barista champion and entrepreneur at Colonna Coffee, author of *The Coffee Dictionary*

I dedicate this book to my dearest Lenka and to our son Richard – not out of fatherly sentiment, but because if he too starts freelancing one day, the age-old principles for doing business successfully will still be unchanged.

Robert Vlach

A note from Jan Melvil Publishing

To buy the e-book, other editions and translations (or if you want to have this book translated into your language) visit our website with all the updates:

www.freelanceway.eu

ROBERT VLACH

THE FREELANCE WAY

BEST BUSINESS PRACTICES, TOOLS & STRATEGIES FOR FREELANCERS

CONTENTS

1 / BUSINESS

Can Business Be Learned?   13

Your Niche in the Market Universe   18
Why is freelance business more than just the gig economy?

A Good Name   43
Why is your reputation crucial for lasting success?

2 / THE PROFESSIONAL

It's a Freelance Life   67
What are the pros and cons of freelancing?

The Foundations of Success   82
What makes a professional a success?

A Business Plan Makes a Career   105
What should be the foundation of your professional and career strategy?

3 / KNOW-HOW

Personal Productivity   137
How can you do it all on time and with no headaches?

Professional IT   162
How to keep your data safe and what tools should you use?

Teaming Up 183
How do you team up and share work with the right people?

You're Only As Good As Your Clients 215
How do you care for your clients and build a clientele?

Pricing 236
How much should you ask for your work?

Business Negotiations 288
What are the best practices for negotiations?

Getting Paid 324
Can you outsmart non-payers?

Websites, Blogs, and Social Media 342
How can you fully harness the internet's potential?

Freelance Marketing 377
Which kinds of self-promotion should you choose?

Personal Finances and Risk Prevention 411
How can you prepare for the worst?

The Freelance Way 435
Where are the limits of professional growth?

Acknowledgments 445

Bibliography 446

Index 449

1 / Business

CAN BUSINESS BE LEARNED?

This is a great question! But it's really three questions in one:

Can business be learned?
If so, then how?
And am I the one to teach you?

Let me answer these, starting from the core of the matter:

Business can be learned, and you can learn it too.

It's not a matter of luck or talent, but a set of skills that lead to lasting prosperity and profit, when fully learned. And what is even better, the key principles of how to succeed as a freelancer are universal and therefore basically the same everywhere.

Yet when I say *learn,* I'm not just thinking of beginners. You can be a top expert but a merely average businessman, still making big mistakes after many years. Furthermore, it's still good to learn new skills, even if you've been freelancing for 20 years – like me.

◉ WORRIED YOU'RE NOT CUT OUT FOR BUSINESS?

I understand your worries better than you may think. I myself believed for years that I wasn't made for business. I was 12 when my parents opened their bakery in 1991. Their business plan was simple and seemingly doomed to succeed: *People will always buy and eat bread.* And they were surely right, but they didn't realize that this sector is capital-hungry while bringing little profit. They used all their assets to buy new equipment, so once they first fired up their oven, there was no going back.

Baking is hard work, as my parents would soon learn. My dad went to work at five so there would be fresh bread on the shelves each morning. My mom worked hard to keep those shelves stocked. As a result, my brother and I didn't see them much at home for the first ten years. Such a large chunk of life sacrificed just to protect their investment.

When I saw how much time and care it took, and how many overnight and weekend shifts were involved in their business, I swore: *I'll never be an entrepreneur.*

I was already studying business at school by that time, but it only strengthened my bias. It had a strict company focus, and as such it fit with the business style of my parents. Freelancing? Forget it! Family and school influences led me to an incomplete – and mistaken – view of business that turned into rejection. And that would have been it…but for a happy accident.

WHO AM I TO SAY HOW YOU SHOULD DO BUSINESS?

In 1999, I headed out to Spain to do some seasonal labor, but I ended up working there for several years as a web development contractor. These were pioneering times, before the dot-com bubble burst, and as a project's lead developer, I had enormous freedom to work whenever and on whatever I wanted. I sometimes even worked seven days a week, my own boss urged me to take a break. I didn't care. That was how much I loved my work.

But every project ends one day, and so a few years later I found myself faced with a decision: either enter into some kind of permanent employment, or put my skills on the open market for other clients. That idea both excited and frightened me, because after all, I had never wanted to be an entrepreneur. But at the same time I longed for the freedom to choose with whom, where, on what, and under what conditions to work. Suddenly I *could* imagine going freelance.

As I gained more experience as a freelancer, the focus of my interests shifted towards supporting my freelancing friends. I created a few websites that successfully promoted their services, which led me to another turning point: In 2005 I founded a Czech national community of independent professionals that is now among the most active in Europe and helps the 150,000 freelancers who follow it to do business better. Then in 2012, I founded Europe's first think-tank for freelancers, which meets regularly in Prague and other cities.

I've been holding business courses for freelancers for more than a decade, putting me in contact with countless professionals from dozens of fields and providing me with a view of what parts of business worry and interest them the most. I've trained nuclear physicists, introverted IT developers, extravagant artists, and ordinary bar owners – and as much as their fields varied, as solo entrepreneurs they had surprisingly much in common.

I've worked an equally long time in business consulting. I have dozens of projects behind me, and over 300 consulting cases. As a consultant, I've gotten to know the businesses of individuals, startups, and companies from all sides, including the dark ones. So I won't be telling you in this book that business is a rose garden.

The results of freelancing surveys, including our own, are another tool that has helped me to better understand this broad subject. I'll be citing some of these, along with other resources and books that can help you in business.

BUSINESS MEANS SOLVING PROBLEMS

My experience has taught me not to think about business too theoretically and generally, because that often leads people astray. Instead I always ask the question:

What kind of business are we talking about?

Are we talking about a certain business approach? A certain profession? A certain person's business? These questions are in order here as well, so let me give you a precise answer:

> This book is about how freelancers do business, work on them-selves and their name, and sell their expertise on the free market. So it's about independent professionals with a publicly declared expertise, profession, or trade – and this is precisely why we as customers hire them.

But freelancing can also be defined in many other ways, and people commonly include into it side jobs that are done to make a little extra money, like tutoring and temporary work, along with gigs acquired through agencies or apps like Uber and Airbnb. This makes sense in some ways, but this book is mainly for freelancers who have a specific expertise and the ambition to do business on their own, or have already been doing so for a few years.

If you've already been freelancing for a while, or you often cooperate with freelancers, you can take this book as an informal audit – search for tips and new ideas, bridge your gaps, check off what you're already doing, and fix mistakes. There are always some left.

If you're still trying to figure out which direction to launch your career, I'll offer you a realistic idea of what freelancing brings to your life, including practical recommendations on making that launch successful.

Learning to do business is similar to learning art, science, or a new language. There are no step-by-step guides, because no such thing exists in the ever-changing and complex world of business. It all starts with basic knowledge and approaches, which I'll definitely describe, but the final goal is to gain the ability to solve new problems.

Business means solving problems. So I'll describe not only the latest know-how and time-tested strategies, but also how experienced freelancers think, and what strategies they apply to stay successful even after ten or twenty years. And along the way, I'll show you so many tempting traps and dead ends that by the end, you'll be able to see them from a mile away. I'll teach you how to track success, catch it, and then bring it home with a victory cry.

You'll also learn how slow-success strategies work, and that being a reliable certainty for your colleagues and clients in our hurried age will clearly give you a strong edge. But as a business this will only work if you can make good use of your advantage.

FREELANCING WORKS ON THREE SEPARATE LEVELS

1. *Expertise* is the core element for doing business in a profession. It's what your clients want.

2. *Administrative obligations* depends on your country and your type of business. It's what your government wants.

3. *Business* includes everything else, and getting better at it is mainly what you want.

Expertise is of course up to you. We are all experts in our professions, and we have to know their specifics. Administrative obligations, especially in areas like taxes, accounting and various regulations, vary from country to country, and more and more freelancers are entrusting them to experts or special applications. Either one is correct. Your actual business is what I'm going to tackle head-on in this book. Together, we'll build firm foundations, then place key business skills upon them – skills like personal productivity, pricing, marketing, negotiation, and financial self-management. And I'll also add hundreds of smart tips.

Naturally no book can be a universal guide for every country, culture, profession, niche, or personal business approach (there are so many). I have dealt with this by taking into consideration the things that are more widespread and commonplace. But don't worry; the main principles apply everywhere, and most of the know-how described here will apply for your specific career.

YOUR FREELANCE WAY MIGHT START RIGHT HERE

You never know when the moment will strike you. Nobody is born to do business and there are countless ways leading up to it – including your own. And then, suddenly, you can't rest until you've started going that way.

Speaking of which, my parents literally couldn't rest for a quarter-century, but their story has a happy ending. After 27 long years, they sold their well-established bakery with its own network of stores at a hefty profit, and now enjoy their retirement alongside their grandchildren. They chose their way freely, and even though it was immensely demanding, they walked it to the end. Freedom has its price.

So now you know my reasons for saying that business can be learned, that ways exist for mastering it, and that I just may have walked one of these ways long enough to be able to help you find your own. Are you ready to step forth?

YOUR NICHE IN THE MARKET UNIVERSE

Why is freelance business more than just the gig economy?

Who comes to mind when you hear the words *independent professional*? I know *my* answer. As a boy I loved two literary heroes: Sherlock Holmes and James Herriot, a veterinarian who visited his clients throughout the Yorkshire hills and had various adventures with them. Both were their own masters, and that impressed me immensely. I wanted to be just as free as they were.

It was only quite recently that I realized to my surprise that these dreams of mine had come true. After all, Sherlock was a self-styled *consulting detective*, and as for Herriot the veterinarian, a small part of my clientele takes me from the city into the mountains. Just like him, I too sometimes set out for house calls along some winding roads. However, instead of animals, I help small businesses and local companies.

But there is a catch. While my consulting business today may *resemble* my childhood dreams, in reality it's completely different. And likewise your idea of working independently as a freelancer should be more than a beautiful dream that dissolves on first contact with market reality.

So I'll start by describing independent professionals' activities from ten different angles, to give you a precise idea that will then accompany you through the rest of the book. Take it as a crash course in the freelance economy.

⊚ EVERYTHING YOU ALWAYS WANTED TO KNOW ABOUT THE FREELANCE ECONOMY (BUT HAD NOBODY TO ASK)

Freelancing is a fascinating market and social phenomenon that I could easily discuss for dozens of pages…but I'll spare you. I know from experience that this mainly interests journalists, economists, politicians, activists, and those of us whose work supports freelancers professionally. But this level can't be skipped completely, as it's the base for important strategies that we'll discuss later.

So my solution for the following pages has been to list only the most important things that every independent professional should be aware of.

1. IN THE BEGINNING WAS THE WORD: FREE-LANCER

It doesn't matter if you say *freelancer, independent professional, contractor* or something else. These terms have minor nuances, but in everyday speech they're interchangeable, just like *freelancing, freelance, a personal* or *freelance business*, and so on. It's all about the same thing, and as we'll see, no universally valid definition of freelancing even exists, and there are far more new terms surrounding freelancing beyond these.

So the term *freelancer* is an entirely customary one, just like the derived words *freelance* and *freelancing*. Its first use, still in the form "free-lancer," is attributed to Sir Walter Scott, who used it in *Ivanhoe* (1820) to designate a medieval mercenary warrior.

2. FREELANCER ≠ SELF-EMPLOYED

One frequent mistake is treating freelancers as identical to sole proprietors or self-employed persons, i.e. as one of the legal forms that business can take on. Many self-employed people are not freelancers. Some of them receive their work from a single agency. Some do business under their own brand (as a company). Some employ other people. And some are really employees masked as the self-employed, which in many countries is an unlawful practice also known as misclassification. In this practice, an employer forces its workers to invoice their work as if they were self-employed, to save on taxes, any national health- or social-insurance payments, sick pay, and other costs.

But the equation is also broken in its other half. Some professionals who consider themselves freelancers aren't officially *self-employed*. Some are employees and only make some extra income freelancing via side jobs or the gig economy. Or they have set up a company so that they can issue invoices for their services. Or they do contracted work that is taxed as occasional income. Or they have themselves hired out on projects as fixed-term employees. Or they combine multiple part-time jobs. Or they have only minor income that doesn't need to be taxed under local laws. Or they bill through their parents, partner, or another person.

While many freelancers do have an official self-employed status, as you can see, these terms aren't interchangeable. For independent professionals, the determining factor is their very *independence* and how they present themselves as experts on the free market. But they choose the legal form for their business depending on what is best in terms of taxes or other issues.

This is nicely illustrated in the 2016 British survey *Exploring the UK Freelance Workforce* by IPSE, which treats freelancers as a sub-section of the wider self-employed workforce and states openly that "there is no official, legal or commonly accepted definition of freelance status which exists in the UK." It thus defines freelancers as "self-employed workers without employees working in a range of managerial, professional and technical occupations," amounting to a total of two million such freelancers, or 42% of the entire British self-employed population and a mere 6% of the UK workforce.

3. DEFINITIONS AND STATISTICS VARY WIDELY; THE BEST TO DATE IS MCKINSEY'S

While Britain's IPSE works with a conservative definition, the American Freelancers Union chooses the opposite approach, with the *widest possible* definition of freelancing. They count everyone with even a *side income* on the free market as a freelancer. Almost 57 million Americans – a third of the entire labor market – fit this generous definition in 2018, according to their *Freelancing in America* survey. This survey divided freelancers into five categories:

1. *Diversified workers*, who combine part-time jobs with other income

2. *Independent contractors*, i.e. "traditional" freelancers with no employer (the quotation marks are theirs)

3. *Moonlighters*, who earn a bit more by freelancing on top of their main job

4. *Freelance business owners*, who have employees but still consider themselves freelancers

5. *Temporary workers* hired through an agency

This ultra-wide definition has its pros and cons. While it makes it easier to follow the trends, it also includes tens of millions of basically stably employed Americans who likely wouldn't call themselves freelancers into the freelance economy alongside "traditional" freelancers.

And indeed you would struggle to find Uber drivers, students occasionally tutoring their classmates, or people babysitting for a few bucks once in a while among the Union's members. The Freelancers Union's members (I'm one of them) are clearly mostly those "traditional" freelancers. Their 2014 *Independents United* report states that a dominant 38% of their members are artists and creatives, 25% are in services and sales, 13% are writers and editors, 13% work in tech and web development, 5% in health care, and only 11% in other fields.

The European Commission (and thus the EU) does not define freelancers. Meanwhile, the European Forum of Independent Professionals state on their site that "independent professionals (often referred to as freelancers or contractors) are highly-skilled self-employed workers without employers nor employees." In an internal document they add, however, that "they are not a homogeneous group and as such, they cannot be considered or investigated as a whole." It couldn't be put better.

Somewhere between the conservative definition, the ultra-broad one, and none at all you'll find the golden mean in the form of the best analysis of the freelance economy to date on both sides of the Atlantic. The extensive 2016 study named *Independent Work* from the McKinsey Global Institute provides a sensitively handled taxonomy of freelancers and a comparison with other research. It makes the sober estimate that about 13% of the American job market is fully freelance (27% including side jobs), and reminds the reader that there were more independent workers in advanced economies in the past than today – up to 45% in the US by the beginning of the 20th century. You can also find additional quality sources of data on the Gig Economy Data Hub.

Yet if you consider yourself a freelancer or an independent professional, don't worry about the definitions. Your self-definition is more important than what box you're placed into.

4. YOU ARE YOUR CAPITAL

Freelancing isn't capital-intensive. The vast majority of freelancers start with a reserve on their bank account and with the equipment they use for their personal needs: a computer, a phone, a car, a home office, etc. How can this be? It's because we are our own true capital.

Yes, we need a lot of capital, but it's *personal* capital, not money or physical assets. It includes expertise, qualifications, skills and know-how, education, tests and certifications, as well as time, practice, experience, strengths, contacts, references, and even our reputation.

The market desires this capital and is willing to pay well for it, especially if you have the required expertise. If you don't have any, or there's not enough demand for it, this pushes prices downwards. A lack of personal capital then means a lot of pain for very little gain. Without qualifications and other characteristics that increase a professional's value (and thus price), the market will wear you down with badly-paid work, and customers will think twice before handing you large responsibilities. Everyone who starts out like this quickly feels the need to learn new skills, specialize, differentiate, and maximally increase their market value.

Naturally you need money to open a cafe, equip a workshop, or buy expensive professional software. And if you are restoring historical samurai swords and selling them to collectors, like one of my clients does, then you'll be breaking every piggy bank in reach just to have a few swords in stock. But these are the exceptions that prove the rule.

Most independent professionals make do in business with who they are and what they know. So don't look at your business as something external – as a firm you can shut down or sell.

You'll find truly *independent* professionals mainly in fields that focus on skill and talent – in creative, media, and technical professions; in marketing, management, and administration; in personal services, education, and consulting. These are often well-paid activities performed by the well-qualified, in many cases primarily as intellectual work or on a computer (so called *knowledge workers*). Less represented are more capital-intensive fields like the trades, leasing assets, manufacturing, or trading.

5. THE HOLLYWOOD MODEL: TOP FREELANCERS COOPERATE

Just because a freelancer is the pillar of their business doesn't mean that they work alone. Not at all. Freelancers cooperate intensively. Those succeeding have constant helpers or partners or an informal support team. And they themselves join the teams of others.

And there are even cases of personal businesses that have blown up to enormous proportions. Globally successful artists, such as Bruce Springsteen, have large production teams around them, and with such a team's support, The Boss earned a remarkable 75 million dollars in 2017.

And it's not just artists. Professor Robert Cialdini is another example; his book on manipulation, *Influence* first came out in 1984 and is still one of the best-selling titles on Amazon. His service company Influence at Work offers training, certification, and workshops, but its heart and face are, of course, Cialdini himself. Just look at what one exceptional book can do!

Interesting things happen when freelancers cooperate on a large-scale. And because most film people are freelancers, the term *Hollywood model* is sometimes used for this division of labor:

"Projects tend to come together quickly, with strict deadlines, so those important workers are in a relatively strong negotiating position. Wages among, say, makeup and hair professionals on shoots are much higher than among their counterparts at high-end salons," writes Adam Davidson in his 2015 article *What Hollywood Can Teach Us About the Future of Work* for The New York Times, and notes: "The Hollywood model is now used to build bridges, design apps or start restaurants."

The great advantage of this model is that a film studio can have far fewer permanent employees than before and only hire expensive experts when it needs them. And the experts are also satisfied, because more productions are competing for their services, and unions negotiate their minimum rates. They earn a lot – but they also have to care all the more about their reputation, professionalism, and expertise. You can see the results in your cinema.

6. WE BEAR THE BURDENS AND HERITAGE OF ANCIENT SMALL-BUSINESS TRADITIONS

What applies to the success of an independent professional today doesn't differ too much from what already applied to the success of a free tradesman back in Roman times. They too had to know their craft, produce quality goods, and care for their reputation to keep their customers, gain new ones, and prosper. They likewise had to know how to calculate their costs and profit, pay helpers, invest in tools and equipment, manage any debts, and place some money in a reserve for unexpected expenses or losses. And naturally they had to fulfill their promises and obligations.

Whether we realize it or not, as independent professionals we are inheritors of small-business traditions whose roots lie in antiquity. Professor Rufus Fears describes Roman livelihoods during the *Roman Peace* under Caesar Augustus around 0 AD in his gripping audiobook *A History of Freedom* like this:

"From Rome itself out to the provinces, there is a strong middle class. Anyone who walks through the excavations of Pompey or Leptis Magna, of any Roman city like Ephesus or Timgad, sees house after house built by people with money and stability," says Fears. He further explains that it was also possible to achieve and maintain a higher social standing because ordinary Romans worked just two days a year to pay their taxes. And that they could also invest their capital: "Capital gains are not taxed, interest is not taxed. You could take your money to a Roman bank (and they existed) and earn 6% interest. There are the equivalents of joint stock ventures. You could buy 10% of a merchant venture going out to Palmyra in the east. Now, it might fail but there's a good chance, because of the Roman Peace, that it will succeed and this will bring you back twelvefold on your investment," adds Fears.

This heritage stretching back over 2000 years (and in some parts of the world even longer) is both a blessing and a curse for us modern professionals, because over that time it has become an integral part of our culture. We all have a clear idea of how an independent professional should behave.

Part of our heritage is the idea that an ordinary person can only excel in one field – a prejudice further strengthened by the medieval guilds, which regulated or directly limited the ways of conducting a business freely. Anyone who alternated trades was perceived and hired as a helper, and certainly not a master of a demanding profession.

In our modern age this opinion is again strengthening with the rapid development of most fields, which increases the pressure to specialize. It's logical to assume that if an expert is to stay up to date, they have to work on their profession 100%. You probably wouldn't want to have your eyes operated on by an editor who does eye surgery as a side job, right?

I'm not saying that you can't be good in two or three different fields. But a customer might see it as a real issue. A professional can certainly be superb as both a cosmetician and a financial advisor, but when you present yourself that way publicly, you probably won't convince many people. It's hard to fight against prejudices, and so most experienced professionals naturally accept this for what it is. They put their main expertise at the fore and the others in the background, or separate them completely.

Thanks to this historical heritage, customers understand that an individual business is based on the efforts of one person, who had to start somehow and learn something, who improves and grows, who has only one reputation and can lose it if they don't work honestly. So it's in your own interest to never destroy the basic trust that your customer places in you, that is, that you are an honest and qualified professional, improving in your field long-term.

7. YOU TOO SPEAK FOR FREEDOM BY DOING BUSINESS

The beginnings of the new freelancing trend can be seen in the West starting in the 1960s, with the rise of a generation worshiping individualism, consumerism, personal freedoms and needs. (Adam Curtis covers this ingeniously in his 2002 BBC documentary film *The Century of the Self*.)

This generation dusted off the ideas of classical liberalism – a political philosophy that defends individuals' freedom as a primary value. And an emphasis on personal and economic freedom and respect for civic rights and private property then leads to greater entrepreneurship.

Freedom is never a given. For example, I was born in 1978 behind the Iron Curtain in communist Czechoslovakia, where doing business was legally limited to state companies only, and you couldn't even open your own hot dog stand, because it would be a crime. After the 1948 coup, the totalitarian state cruelly punished all forms of enterprise – forcing self-employed professionals, property owners, and free-thinking people into poverty, or even jails and labor camps. Later, in the 1980s, shortages of basic necessities gave rise to a shadow economy of underground service providers and smugglers. We only got our civil liberties and economic freedom restored after the 1989 Velvet Revolution, when Vaclav Havel became president.

Havel was one of a handful of intellectuals who managed to preserve the spirit of freedom despite such pressure, to revive it for us all, while also inspiring millions of other people worldwide. Freedom that is not widely applied easily dies. This is why I say that you too speak for freedom by doing business. It's one voice out of many, but all of them together form a lion's roar that not much can suppress.

8. TECHNOLOGIES ARE FUELING THE MODERN RISE OF FREELANCING

Moving on from philosophy, the main cause of the freelancing boom over the last three decades has been the rise of modern technologies, especially personal computers, the internet, and mobile phones. These innovations gave rise to dozens of new fields, and let existing professionals work in an entirely new way, outside their former workplaces, or for a fraction of the cost.

And soon we may see an equally revolutionary effect from the rise of things like 3D printers, artificial intelligence, robotics, automation, or virtual reality.

Not only has the internet connected formerly isolated professionals; it has also lowered the threshold for doing business. Today, online services can make the things you're bad at – maybe marketing and sales – markedly easier. Platforms like Airbnb literally bring the customer to your door and have a fine-tuned business process that covers typical risks for you and is a reliable guide for doing business successfully. All for an acceptable commission.

Online services that pair supply with demand have brought small-business freelancing to tens of millions of people worldwide. This is the globalization of work, in a sense, because in many fields distance no longer plays a fundamental role. And we're still just at the start.

The *Accenture Technology Vision 2017* annual report, for example, predicts that traditional employment will decrease as the practice of hiring external contracted workers on a temporary basis increases, and that every sector will have new leaders with small cores, less bureaucracy, and a powerful ecosystem of experts. Accenture believes that on-demand work platforms will be the primary driver of most economies and will gradually replace corporate organizational structures and management models.

The rise of *e-lancers* who work for customers remotely is already evident today. It's driven by platforms such as Upwork, Freelancer.com, Twago, AngelList, and Toptal. Their share keeps rising, but isn't major yet – a mere 1 to 4% as a primary work source in US, UK, Germany, Spain and Sweden according to *The New Freelancers* 2019 survey.

9. FREELANCING ALSO HAS A DARK SIDE

Unfortunately, freelancing also has its dark side, in the form of the shadow economy and illegal activities in cyberspace. This may also affect you, if, for example, you use Airbnb and a prostitute secretly turns your apartment into a short-term brothel. This exact practice is described by Svetlana Z., a New York based, Russian immigrant, and freelancing sex worker, in her article *Sex Is Sex. But Money Is Money:* "Escorts make $100 a hand job—but entrepreneurs like me? We make $5,000 a night. Welcome to the new economy of the oldest profession."

There are even worse professions. The book *Future Crimes*, by cyber-crime and security expert Marc Goodman, describes the shocking underworld of freelance hackers, who can destroy data, steal identities, or do hit jobs on their client's competition. He writes of *crime as a service* and of how the modern mafia emulates the successful approaches of online startups. But dark sides aside, the future will likely be bright.

10. THE LABOR MARKET IS GOING THROUGH A QUIET REVOLUTION

Already in 1997, Daniel Pink predicted in a visionary article, which later grew into the book *Free Agent Nation*, that the future of the US would be in freelancing. Today we can say that the quiet revolution in the labor market that he predicted is actually well under way.

There will always be people freelancing involuntarily, due to a lack of other options, and this labor destabilization is rightly criticized as a creeping social problem. But surveys show that most freelancers choose freelancing on their own and are in many ways more satisfied with their work than employees. It apparently better matches what they want from life – less commuting, more time with family or friends, flexibility, and the ability to vary their work tempo and choose on what and with whom to work.

The shift in what work style today's professionals prefer has now also been noticed by companies. The *Deloitte Millennial Survey 2017* states that while 70% of the millennials in developed countries prefer the certainty of a permanent job's income, they would ideally combine it with a free-lancer's flexibility. And it notes that the number of companies offering such conditions is rising rapidly. As a result, the number of freelancers may decrease in the future due to the greater attractiveness of working as an employee.

The worlds of freelancers and employees are growing closer, because it's not just companies that are changing their approach to freelancing. Most of society sees it today as a perfectly legitimate career choice and labor-market experts have long been pointing out that this is the result of a shift in white-collar career orientation. The study *PwC Work-life 3.0* speaks of a fundamental change and literally states that "talented employees were seeking freelance and contract work in record numbers." Former British Prime Minister David Cameron put it more elegantly in 2010 in an open letter to British freelancers on their National Freelancers Day:

"I can't tell you how much admiration I have for people who leave the comfort of a regular wage to strike out on their own. It takes a lot of courage – and without that courage this country would be a much poorer place," Cameron writes. "More and more people are choosing freelancing, recognising that it strikes the right balance between work and life in the 21st century."

⬦ THE SIMPLEST KIND OF BUSINESS OUT THERE

Now that we've gone through an introduction to the freelance economy, it will help us to navigate as we go forward. Having a deep understanding of what sets freelancing apart will not only help you to tackle real problems from the right angle, but also to make wiser career choices in the future, when deciding whether to remain freelance or to try something else.

We will explore those differences throughout the rest of this chapter in order to see where we stand as individuals in the broad market universe. After all, there are many approaches to doing business, and freelancing is only one of them – the simplest one:

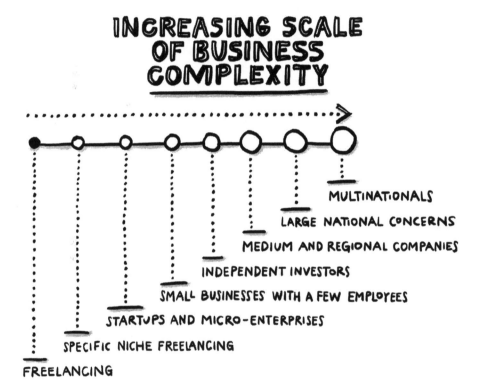

Stepping forth into freelancing, especially via occasional side jobs, can truly be easy. I've heard stories like this one from many professionals in a variety of forms:

> *"I was doing more and more work on the side, until one day I realized that I was actually already running my own business."*

The relative simplicity is visible even more when we compare a typical freelancer to a small company or an entrepreneur with several employees acting as a company:

FREELANCE BUSINESS	COMPANY BUSINESS
Personal and knowledge capital dominate	Large capital needs are common
Often just one-off gigs and side jobs at first	Launched after formally founding the company
You can start or stop almost any time	Preparing the business takes a long time; so does ending it
Acts under their own name	The brand and its creation, protection, and promotion have costs
Safe business without debts	The larger investment often demands full personal engagement
The day only has 24 hours, and clients understand this	Time is just one factor, and multiple jobs can be handled simultaneously
Demand is managed by raising prices	Demand is covered by raising production

Time is obviously the critical factor here. When you do business under your own name, you're making it clear to your customers that you have a limited amount of it, and that makes many things easier.

The customer wants quick (or better yet immediate) service, but they also understand that a translator has to finish their current assignment before taking on an additional large translation, or that a server admin sometimes needs to sleep. A translation agency, on the other hand, takes on orders at any time, because it can delegate them, and every major web host offers 24/7 technical support by having admins work in shifts.

On the other hand, clients expect freelancers to offer flexible and personalized services, which often places us as professionals before difficult choices as to which inquiry to prioritize, or pass on, because you can't always completely please everyone.

Beginning freelancers typically have much more time than those who have been at it for ten years. Beginners have fewer gigs, and between them there is lots of room for enjoying their newfound freedom. But slowly work piles up, and time drains away. If a professional is capable and their work is in demand, inevitably a moment will come when work takes up all of their available time.

What will you do the first time this happens to you?

You'll probably work on your personal productivity. You'll limit downtimes, social media, time in cafes or post-lunch cigars, whatever… In any case, you'll free up previously unsuspected capacity that will enable you to handle up to several times more work.

But what will you do when your calendar fills up again?

This time you're already better organized, handling more work for a growing number of satisfied clients, but your capacities are stretched once again. A further increase in productivity will help you for a while, but never as much as the first time. You're suddenly faced with the decision of raising prices, adding someone to the team, or turning orders down. You have just reached one of the major crossroads on the freelance way.

⊙ HOW YOUR REACTION TO GROWING DEMAND SHAPES YOU AS A PROFESSIONAL

Let's carefully examine this crossroad at the peak of your working capacity and the paths you may take from there, because it will tell us something very important about the nature of freelance business.

If you raise prices, you'll turn away those seeking cheap solutions and suppress that type of demand. But you'll also change your customers' expectations.

You definitely wouldn't expect the same from a massage therapist who asks ten dollars per hour of massage as from one who asks a full hundred, right? And if I pay a talented student a few bucks for some blog articles, I'll overlook a couple of typos that I would never tolerate from a copywriter with a fee ten times higher.

Price affects not only your quantity of work, but also its qualities. If you significantly raise your prices, your satisfied clients likely won't run away, but they'll turn to you all the more for qualified tasks that your cheaper colleagues can't handle. And they'll look more closely at your level of quality and the scope of what they're asking of you. Everyone tries to manage their resources efficiently.

Thus by raising your prices, you'll turn away people seeking cheaper, less qualified work, but you'll also be raising your clients' expectations. In other words, you're not making it easy for yourself. And yes, in order to stand up to these higher demands, you have to further professionalize, study, improve, specialize, and grow.

Pricing pressure often does the most to truly shape professionals, because most of us want to do interesting work for good money, not routine work for peanuts. So a professional has an immense interest in maintaining the standard of living they have achieved and in taking steps that stabilize and improve it. It's in their own interest to strive to be of maximum benefit to their clients and to never disappoint them.

What happens, however, if a freelancer chooses the other path and adds someone to their team? They'll likely try to maintain, or even lower their prices while also increasing their production capacity. They'll take on new helpers, team members, or even employees.

A professional who makes this decision will likely do more managerial work and less expert work. As the work of the team stabilizes, its other members will be communicating with customers and this will push the freelancer to cover this new team structure with a unified identity or brand – in other words, to shift towards working as a company.

In practice it's all more complicated, because a professional can raise prices while also slightly increasing capacity. What is decisive, though, is which tendency dominates.

You can, however, also do nothing, if your demand is stable over the long-term. Yet this is unlikely, because freelancers with satisfied, returning customers who continue to recommend them will logically see rising demand. They would have to fail in some way, or grow against a shrinking market, for demand to stay stable. In general, it is more common for exceptionally skilled professionals to end up taking on more and more work, since unsatisfied customers around them try to get away from their less-skilled competitors. If they then can't keep up and don't maintain quality, people note it, and demand falls again. Understandably, you don't want that to happen.

A freelancer can also react to growing demand by simply rejecting good orders. Yet this is shortsighted. Even for sought-after professionals, it can freeze the flow of recommendations: "That one is great, but try someone else. She's always busy and doesn't take on new clients, not even for good money." Which is a problem if you *do* have time down the road.

The occasional refusal is OK, but if you repeatedly reject relevant, well-paying orders, it can really hurt you in terms of lost income in the future. A sensible entrepreneur won't make this mistake twice. (There are indeed some minor variations to this rule, such as with professional celebrities, and I will comment on them in later chapters.)

So the two good solutions are to increase expertise and prices as an independent professional, or to increase production capacity as more of a company. Neither one is clearly better than the other. Some people dislike managerial work and love their profession, and so they prefer to grow as an independent expert. Others, meanwhile, see expansion as an opportunity and bet on their future success with the overall income growth as a company.

Some surveys indicate that up to half of all freelancers perceive freelance work as only a jumping-off point for a larger business. From experience I can state that it depends a lot on the tax legislation in a given country. If becoming a company is disadvantageous and complicated there, freelancers will tend to avoid it.

Think long and hard about which of these directions you prefer. Many professionals blow right through this crossroad without noticing it, and if later on they notice they're going in the wrong direction, it's then harder to turn around. Or to put it more precisely: you can always expand from freelancing into a company, but the opposite is tough. Shrinking an agency or company back into a freelance business again can take several years.

This book doesn't cover building a company, but it's useful to know this context. Many famous companies, agencies, and studios began with a capable professional who started piling up an ever greater volume of work and clients. Advertising, law, design, or IT development companies arise this way all the time.

Freelancers aren't that uncomfortable either about building up their support teams, but they mainly react to growing demand via pricing and picking clients through smart business negotiations. We will dive much deeper into these topics in later chapters. Now let's explore some other specifics of freelancing.

STUDY YOUR NICHE TO BE AT HOME THERE

Every business has its own demands. Just judging from my comparison of freelancers and small companies, you can probably see that a freelance business requires an entirely different type of know-how for success. Most freelancers don't need to understand HR, wages, or warehouse management.

This applies at all levels. The owner of a small business with five employees almost certainly wouldn't be able to manage a large factory effectively. And Mr. Factory himself probably wouldn't be a successful CEO at a multinational, let alone the visionary for a garage startup.

Even if the public has a tendency to throw all business into one pile, there are really dozens of categories, and we don't have to compare free-lancers with corporations to make it clear that every business has its own needs. Looking at my overview of the relative complexity of businesses, you'll find within it two very different categories of individual enterprise.

Independent investors have acquired some level of wealth and aim to maintain it by protecting it from inflation and hopefully earning interest on it. They need investing know-how and good information, but they'll probably worry less about their daily productivity or pricing. They will need a fundamentally different set of knowledge for their activities.

Incidentally, there are lots of wealthy people in developed countries, and by their side you might find a number of freelancers specialized precisely in supporting them: various asset managers, researchers, chauf-feurs, investment consultants, and more. (Peter Mayle describes this class of professionals with superb wit in his essay collection *Acquired Tastes*.)

Specific niche freelancing represents fields that demand some kind of special business know-how. This can refer to certain demanding, highly regulated trades and occupations, such as doctors and lawyers, or minor franchising, as well as art and professional sports. These end up as practi-cally separate market niches.

Professional athletes enter into special sponsoring and media contracts, where they are once again advised by a specialist or agent. Their business also has to be set up so that they can focus fully on their training and performance. This especially applies to individual sports, where there is also a large imbalance in earnings between the athlete's relatively short profes-sional career and the rest of their life. (Andre Agassi offers an honest view of management in individual sports in his award-winning autobiography *Open*, as does Arnold Schwarzenegger in his monumental *Total Recall*.)

Writers and artists are an equally exclusive group of professionals. They definitely have to earn their living and promote and sell their creations somehow. But far from all of them want to present themselves as commercial artists or, even worse, as entrepreneurs. So people with specially adapted business know-how are put to work in the art world too. For painters and sculptors, for instance, cooperation with an expe-rienced gallery manager can be fundamental; writers may be represented by literary agents; and every other area of art has its own slightly different approach to the market.

Professionals active in the creative industries have a somewhat simpler situation. You can find a number of books and online resources here – for independent illustrators, designers, writers, etc. My favorite blog is

Lateral Action, from the poet Mark McGuinness, today a successful business coach for artists and creatives:

"Everyone knows Shakespeare is the greatest writer in the English language. But did you know he was also a highly successful entrepreneur? The young Shakespeare left his rural home town to seek his fortune in London. In common with many entrepreneurs, he didn't have the benefit of a family fortune or a university education – just his talent, ambition and an enormous capacity for hard work," he writes in his article *The Shakespearean Guide to Entrepreneurship.*

"In the course of his career in the great city, Shakespeare became a shareholder in an acting troupe called the Lord Chamberlain's Men, who beat off fierce competition to become the most famous and successful theatre company in the land. They played to packed houses of paying customers and received regular summons to perform before Queen Elizabeth and King James. Shakespeare rose from the ranks of commoners to the status of a gentleman, taking great pride in the coat of arms he was awarded. And he earned enough money to buy the biggest house in his home town and retire there in comfort. This story doesn't quite fit the Romantic image of the starving artist or the poet wandering lonely as a cloud – but Shakespeare lived 200 years before Romanticism, so perhaps we can forgive him," writes McGuinness with a hint of irony towards the unrealistic ideas of uncommercial charity in art, and goes straight on to deliver a cannonade of business tips inspired by the Shakespearean legend.

Another online resource for creatives, and especially writers, is Steven Pressfield's blog, in which he occasionally uncovers the field's customary rules and gives day-dreaming amateurs a healthy dose of reality. In his article *The #1 Amateur Mistake*, for example, he explains why you should never send successful artists like Bob Dylan unsolicited samples of your creative work. Hundreds of such recordings go straight to the trash so that Dylan can't be accused of plagiarism if he happens to work on an album and unconsciously uses someone else's musical motif that has gotten stuck in his head. Pressfield states that amateurs' greatest mistake is precisely their disinterest in the business rules of the field of art in which they want to succeed.

⟩ UNIVERSAL BUSINESS KNOW-HOW? NO SUCH THING

Business know-how differs not only among businesses of different sizes, but also among individual fields. Knowing this is fundamental.

It's in our best interest, as freelancers, to seek out and absorb know-how that is highly relevant to freelancing *in our own field*. For all other sources, we need to either ignore them, or learn to interpret them correctly. That is, for know-how in a distant field of business to be of any use to us, we need experience and knowledge to be able to adapt it sensitively, just as when a musician transposes a composition for a completely different instrument.

Take for example popular selections of the type *30 Business Tips from 30 Successful Entrepreneurs*. They might be great tips from greatly successful people, but not all of them can serve your needs when they are doing business in various fields, with one owning a billion-dollar business and another a hat-making shop. After all, you wouldn't go to the dentist for new eyeglasses. And the same applies to books, which are often primarily focused on companies or startup businesses.

Using the right know-how in the wrong place is a common freelancer business mistake. And these tend to be mistakes with unpredictable results. For instance, I once met a professional who built websites, but left customer support to other freelancers, a bit in the spirit of outsourcing services. In practice, however, there was no contractual agreement on who had final responsibility for the sites, and when a fundamental problem appeared, neither side took responsibility for it. The result was an angry customer and a ruined reputation.

Or there was a senior developer who hired a sales representative – who then went on to send out sales proposals in his name, but full of mistakes and unfounded nonsense. Once again it was a good idea taken from the business world, but inapplicable in practice for freelancing, where the customer basically expects to communicate directly with an expert, and not with the halfwit who run errands for him. (Naturally if you're a world-famous author with a literary agent that is an entirely different situation.)

Misapplied know-how is also common among, for example, foodie freelancers making small delicacies. These enthusiast-craftsmen are often worrying about brands, slogans, domains, responsive websites, and elaborately designed packaging before they even have three paying customers. Perhaps they should be improving sales and their product or production process, leaving the brand-building until later when they are dealing with more customers?

Another frequent mistake among professionals is that even though they are doing business entirely on their own, they mask their activities under a company-like brand in an effort to gain a dubious advantage, and it ultimately looks laughable. Customers then tell each other with a wry smile: "It's named the Hercules Group, but really it's just Bob Smithers from the next town over."

So choosing appropriate know-how is a fundamental habit that you should pick up to prevent serious mistakes and wasting resources. These aren't fatal mistakes, but they'll definitely put you off-track.

Experience has made me skeptical of the abilities of ordinary freelancers to adapt business know-how intended primarily for startups or companies. It's not just about the individual procedures here; it's also about the needed skills. Company practice regularly draws from the advanced abilities of a whole team, while freelancers usually have to handle most steps themselves, or manage their own team – which itself requires managerial skills and money.

One tenth of them perhaps can handle it, but for the rest it's best to turn directly to appropriate sources where this know-how has already been adapted for freelancers.

⊙ FEELINGS CAN'T BE MEASURED

There is also one more divide between business by companies and individuals: people are beings of flesh and bone, while companies are not. Companies are born of the cooperation of many people and groups, whose interests and opinions often differ dramatically. An owner surely views their company differently than an ordinary employee, while management, shareholders, unions, and the State also have their say.

So that all of them can agree somehow, the language of numbers dominate in company dialogue, giving it a sensible, objective basis. So we have record profits? The unions demand a wage increase. That is rational and fair. This is why companies measure everything, and great key performance indicators are in their logical interest. A good company is a fine-tuned, well-oiled machine that is also being pushed towards greater efficiency by its competition. And nobody is playing on its feelings.

As freelance professionals, we have an undeniable advantage over companies in that we can manage our business based on both measurable indicators and subjective feelings, whether others like that or not. And not only *can* we do it, we *do* do it – a lot. The top ranks in all surveys of freelancers' motivations for freelancing are held not by money and material security, but by purely emotional values such as independence and freedom, time flexibility, and the ability to do what they enjoy, work anywhere, be their own master, and have their future in their hands. Finances are taken into consideration, but generally not in first place.

So when you ask independent professionals where they see the benefits of their status, the variety of their answers will surprise you. Some emphasize fulfillment from work well done, others the unrestricted possibilities for professional growth, learning new things, or their reputation and the respect it brings within their local or expert community. These are all things that, while hard to measure, can be felt and experienced.

And there are also professions that, while poorly paid, provide such a strong feeling of satisfaction that people stay in them even when more commercial work would pay much better – for example literary translations.

The ability to balance emotional and performance standpoints is a luxury unknown to even many agency or company owners, including family businesses or partnerships of several owners. You can't measure the feelings of freedom or pride, but for us independent professionals they are just as tangible as a balance sheet or an annual report.

Thus, if you want to introduce some kind of corporate know-how into your freelancing, always remember that large companies must think and act differently. Their management is rooted in achieving measurable objective goals – in terms of money, performance, or profits, not feelings. And if someone isn't performing, they're replaced, and things move on.

We, however, can't cut off the emotional side of things so easily. On the contrary, it's in our fundamental interest to work and live a balanced and satisfied life, because we are irreplaceable for our business.

⊙ WHERE TO SEEK ADVICE, AND THE IMPORTANCE OF MENTORING

If you're thinking seriously about doing business, I recommend cooperating from the start with an experienced accountant or tax advisor who can present references from other freelancers, ideally in your field. Then you'll get not only quality service, but also a number of practical tips for your field – what can reasonably be billed, how to bill abroad, typical amounts for advance payments, how to deduct the costs for a home workshop or a car, etc.

The status of accounting and tax advisors can vary from country to country. Usually how it works is that accountants handle freelancers' normal financial paperwork, while tax advisors are more expensive and can advise you on everything around taxes, or both.

The services of these qualified experts are not at all expensive, considering that they help to transfer know-how and best practices across a range of fields. And that is very beneficial, especially when you're new. Beginners often look at accounting services as a cost that they can save on by handling the administrative work on their own through an invoicing or accounting application. But these services can also be a great aid and investment into launching a business.

A good accountant is a treasure. Having one doesn't just mean getting rid of boring administrative tasks. A good accountant will also be eager to talk with you and advise on doing many things smarter and better. A good accountant will be a friend. So choose one carefully and don't be afraid to check out two or three recommended experts and see which one sits better with you on a personal level.

If you're working in a field that is somewhat regulated or that faces larger risks than ordinary services, it pays to supplement your accounting or tax advisor with a consultant specialized in meeting regulatory requirements. This can apply for work safety, health, etc. Every field has its specialists.

Law and consulting services can be several times more expensive than accounting services, but there are many reliable lawyers who aren't expensive. In the US and several other countries, there are also subscription platforms like RocketLawyer that offer templates, contract editing, etc. in addition to their legal consulting.

The services of the more expensive consultants can be priceless if a brief consultation saves you a ton of future problems and worries. This is why in general I recommend consulting mainly on those decisions where you fear a risk and those that can affect your business – and life – for several years to come.

For beginners, choosing a business consultant is harder than finding a lawyer or tax advisor, because this is a less-regulated market. But I can tell you one trick that works among us consultants. Seek a consultant recommended by other, senior consultants, ideally in the same field. After all, consultants are best at judging the expertise and work quality of their peers, especially if it is someone they occasionally meet on assignments. Sometimes you can also connect with experienced yet affordable consultants through membership in your local chamber of commerce or other business communities.

Consulting is a service like any other, through which you pump time-tested know-how and another expert's smart recommendations into your business. This is especially beneficial in fields that are far removed from yours, such as accounting, law, technology, etc.

But it's not so common to hire consultants from your *own* field. And yet this too can be a wise option when a more experienced peer is offering consulting and you're just starting out. More common within a field is *mentoring*, where an experienced professional leads or inspires a junior in some way.

Mentoring is about the informal transfer of experience, including various tricks and customs that experienced professionals know, but almost nobody publicly talks or writes about. While in the past this transfer took place naturally and spontaneously, from a master or teacher to an apprentice or pupil, today expert education is the domain of schools and educational institutions, and it's not a sure thing for professionals to have mentors.

A mentor isn't a consultant. They are a professional who is farther along than you and whom you view correspondingly. At the same time, they should be someone who can be not only a professional model, but also a role model and a psychological support.

A mentor's role is thus informal, but important. They offer an opportunity to talk about things that are uninteresting for the people around you or close to you. And since this is a private connection between two people, mentoring can take on many forms. Some people have their parents as mentors in a family firm, for others this may be a long-term relationship with someone more experienced in business.

In any case, mentoring is advantageous for both sides, because the mentor assumes the status of an authority and gains an important ally for the future.

You can certainly encounter paid mentors (it's sometimes called *business coaching*), but the informal and unpaid kind is paradoxically often more worthwhile. I personally probably wouldn't ask someone to be my mentor or business coach. These relationships arise and work better based on a shared interest, friendship, and sympathies. The initial impulse can be reading a book or taking an interest in someone's work, article, or lecture. Or it may be someone from your local professional or coworking community.

Find a mentor. I mean this seriously. This is one of those things that likely nobody is advising you to do, and you might be afraid to do it yourself. Your mentor doesn't have to be a celebrity in their field; an experienced colleague whom you respect for what they have achieved is enough.

I think it's best to respectfully contact that person, explain that you're just starting out with freelancing in the same field, and ask if they would be willing to devote a little time to you someday and answer a few questions or advise you. The word *mentor* doesn't even have to come up and there is no long-term commitment in it for either of you.

Even if someone turns you down at first, don't worry needlessly; sooner or later, someone else will help. There is far less rivalry among freelancers than there is among corporate clans. Collegiality and willingness to cooperate, support, and help all dominate.

CHOSE WISELY AND LEARN FROM THE BEST

But a little skepticism is in order when absorbing know-how in fields that are still growing, such as IT and digital marketing. The seemingly endless demand and tidal waves of work and cash inevitably reduce the need to develop business skills, create reserves for bad years, and generally build one's business robustly to make it resistant to risk.

In a field that is constantly rising, every second entrepreneur can look successful. Just look at their price and status! But a rising tide lifts all boats, and as Warren Buffett says, only when the tide goes out do you discover who has been swimming naked. You don't tell a good entrepreneur by how well they're doing when the whole market is rising, but by how they handle hard times.

Also, be wary of people, who are great only in hard-selling themselves and their advice, but have no significant history in selling or managing anything else.

So I would advise a cautious stance regarding business tips from people who have little experience and, even if they act successful, have never had to handle major business problems. Short-term success can be about chance or good market conditions. It can also be about real strengths, but only time will tell.

Of course it makes sense to listen to anyone who wants to share their experience. Just be sure to think about how their (or your) business and the whole field could look after a few years of recession. The most valuable tips come from people who have made it through the ups and downs of the market.

When I say that, in your own interest, you have to carefully choose relevant sources of business information, this is triply true for the web. Try finding a few freelancers from your field who have been writing a long time about their business, because their experience and conclusions will likely be quite relevant for what you're doing. You can sift through them to find field experience that probably won't be as well-described elsewhere.

With general blogs for freelancers, quantity unfortunately pushes out quality. Some of them spew out low-quality content outright – *10 Tips on Doing This*, *5 Steps to Achieving That*. Honestly, reading these articles is a waste of time. The Freelancers Union blog is solid, as are the occasional freelancing articles published in the better business media. But they are hard to dig out. Sometimes you'll find a truly valuable article or tip, but the overall quality to quantity ratio is just sad.

"When you're studying internet marketing, and in fact any field, prefer quality over quantity," writes Jindrich Faborsky, the organizer of

Europe's successful Marketing Festival. "What do I mean? The internet is full of articles, videos, and e-books, and the goal of most is not to educate, to provide new information, but to make money, get email addresses, or at least to bring in visitors from search engines. In my company and at the university, I see how marketers grow, and I notice how real growth arrives only for those who can distinguish beneficial content from spam. Only for those who study quality content and learn from true experts, and who ignore the 99% of information that's worthless, irrelevant, or unfounded nonsense."

Language plays an important role here too. Globally oriented sources for freelancers and experts are mostly in English and may be less relevant in some local contexts. Learning another world language (or even less widely spoken one) could therefore be a great, unexpected benefit. It may enable you to access other quality sources, giving you a much broader perspective in almost any field, not speaking of multiplying your opportunities.

Out of the general books for freelancers, I would recommend *The Freelancer's Bible*, written by the Freelancers Union's founder Sara Horowitz in 2012, which is a distillate of years of experience and contact with countless freelancers. Books for freelancers in specific fields can be very beneficial (just look for *freelance writer, illustrator, designer, developer*, etc. on Amazon), as well as good books on specific business areas such as negotiations, sales, or time management (I mention some of the best ones within this book).

Books can also go into greater depth and explain difficult matters much better. When I can choose, I personally prefer them over short blog posts or podcasts. If you are looking for something in between these options, check out the titles from The Great Courses or MasterClass where leading global experts and professionals share key insights from their experience and know-how.

Last but not least, turn to training from experienced independent professionals who have started offering training courses alongside their practice. Their courses often serve freelancers best, because they are working from their own findings on freelancers' needs. Courses like these can bring you both expertise and the benefit of meeting another successful professional willing to share their business know-how.

There is lots of information out there, an almost unlimited amount, but only a fraction of it is truly relevant for you. So choose the best and ignore the rest, or sift through it finely. And regularly ask your colleagues what works for them. Mistakes that comes from applying inappropriate know-how can really hurt. And not just financially. They can damage a freelancer's greatest treasure – their *good name*.

1. The ability to orient oneself in the freelance economy is useful for every freelancer.

2. An independent professional works on themselves and their good name within a clearly defined area of expertise.

3. We are the inheritors of ancient small-business traditions, and these govern client expectations.

4. Freelancing is the simplest approach to business out there. But it's not easy.

5. Independent professionals grow primarily in their expertise and price. The alternative is expansion.

6. Freelancers, unlike companies, can emphasize their feelings and other immeasurables.

7. One frequent mistake is to apply know-how from other types of business to freelancing.

8. The most valuable know-how comes from freelancers in your field.

9. This is why it's important to have a mentor, a good accountant, a lawyer, and possibly other advisors.

10. When it comes to business tips, be choosy and quick to ask your colleagues what works for them.

PRACTICE

I have attached some practical tasks and suggestions to the end of each chapter in order to help you to put the advice from this book into practice. While there are a much greater number of best practices mentioned in most chapters, these closing ones may help you to start off with something easy, useful, and applicable for most freelancers.

✓ Check out the latest *Freelancing in America* survey.

✓ Research quality sources on freelancing in *your* field, starting with surveys, books, courses, lectures, blogs and podcasts. Then focus on the best three or four only, to limit the time invested as well. Ideally, do this in each language you know.

✓ Look for a good accountant or tax advisor to discuss your freelance business. If you're facing larger risks or uncertainties, consider also talking to a lawyer or other advisors.

✓ Find a mentor – an experienced freelancer in your field, who you trust and admire, and who would be willing to tell you a thing or two that often no one ever writes about.

A GOOD NAME

Why is your reputation crucial for lasting success?

So you've settled into your role as an independent professional and know your place on the market. However, to have the full picture, you need to understand your position in society and in your field. This is the most important secret ingredient, which some people pursue in vain their whole lives. Let's go find it, starting with the three reasons for caring about your good name.

I. A GOOD NAME IS THE KEY TO BETTER CLIENTS

Alongside expertise and reliability, having a good name is a decisive factor in acquiring lucrative orders and clients that an incompetent professional will never see.

Would you want a new website from someone who was still designing gardens a year earlier and sold insurance door-to-door before that? I wouldn't. As customers, we know perfectly well that demanding work demands expertise and years of practice. This is why we don't do it ourselves. We perceive a lasting interest in a profession as an important sign of quality. We don't want "experts," who started only yesterday. We want the real ones.

The conservative, wealthy customers who move the money on mature markets would never hire anyone with a meaningless reputation for a meaningful job. When a client has money, little time, and no taste for annoying problems that others are supposed to solve, they also won't gamble on cooperating with someone untested. They'll prefer to pay more for the work of an experienced expert for whom they've received a recommendation, in order to ensure good results without nasty surprises.

In dominant freelance fields and specializations such as language services or marketing consultations, a well-established professional's good name often rings truer than an agency brand. Their customers realize that work from both senior experts and incompetent juniors can be sold under a company brand, and that it's sometimes unclear which of them will handle their order, while a freelancer is always one person. Adults rarely change much, while companies do, and their existence is often shorter than leading experts' careers.

II. A GOOD NAME IS A SOURCE OF SATISFACTION

There is a difference between doing average, routine, or otherwise unattractive work, and doing work that excites others so much that they say so.

If you do top-notch valuable work that delivers, your colleagues, customers, and others around you will tell you so, and you'll feel good. Can you imagine any better prevention against burnout, cynicism, or feeling depressed and useless?

We humans are social creatures. Recognition from both friends and strangers is a psychological need. Here Dale Carnegie aptly comments in his *How to Win Friends and Influence People* that even the most successful and rich businessmen yearn for recognition and harmonious relationships with others. Money and power alone aren't happiness.

III. A GOOD NAME LENGTHENS YOUR CAREER

In your youth, you don't see the importance of a good name as much as a professional who might have retired long ago, but doesn't have to, thanks to their reputation.

Young people have an advantage on the labor market over long-term employees in their fifties and above, especially if the latter lack qualifications and an established name within their field. If they lose their job, they often become a cheap commodity on the labor market.

Things are so much better for a professional who has been working ten or twenty years on themselves and who is widely recognized as an expert. In advanced economies, independent professionals' careers often hit their peak well into their sixties. Or even later.

Take for example Warren Buffett, who is almost ninety and still manages Berkshire Hathaway, one of the world's largest corporations. Or Clint Eastwood, who is over eighty and still directs award-winning films. Or the Japanese sushi master Jiro Ono, who at 93 is still determined to improve his small business, the Tokyo sushi restaurant Sukiyabashi Jiro, which has three Michelin stars to its name. (If his story interests you, watch the documentary *Jiro Dreams of Sushi,* one of the most beautiful movies ever about a trade.)

But my actual favorite is the elderly barber who cut my hair in Campeche, Mexico in 2004. I had gone in search of a barbershop that stayed open during the siesta, and found only his. All the shop's bits and pieces, including him, looked so old that I couldn't help but ask how long he'd been doing this. His answer really got me: He was over 90, and had been cutting hair since he was 10, when he started as an apprentice – so, 80 years straight since 1924. His hands shook gently as he told me that his work had changed a lot over that time, and that his livelihood had been complicated the most by the spread of AIDS, since customers no longer wanted a straight razor shave.

Probably few people want to work that long, but if you enjoy it and stay healthy, why not? If an independent professional stays in shape and doesn't stagnate, they can do excellent work even at an advanced age. Where an ordinary employee is out of breath, thinking about retirement, and on paper can hardly match up to the younger, bulldog competitors determined to climb the narrow corporate ladder, an independent professional is just catching their second wind. They're thinking about how to best make use of their reputation and experience after fifty, and their income can also still increase. A good name is like an elixir that miraculously lengthens careers.

A GOOD NAME TAKES YEARS TO BUILD AND THEN BRINGS CONSTANT BUSINESS

Freelancers' career dynamics are basically the opposite of those for employees, who can rise quickly while they're still young. As a freelancer, meanwhile, you have to master both your own expertise and business as such, which also includes dozens of other skills that a company employee will never need to know. And mastering all this can take quite a while.

When you're starting out in freelancing, you go about your work aimlessly, nobody knows you, you don't know how to do business, and good jobs are hard to find. But the advantage is that if you keep at it and earn a name for yourself, you'll have work for life.

There are professionals who have never invested a penny into promotion, and yet customers are insisting on having their services and gladly waiting in line. A good name is the best advertisement, but still, many professionals miss its fundamental importance.

One renowned clockmaker told me that even when he had been working in that profession for over a decade, experienced clockmakers still treated him like a greenhorn: "Old clockmakers know well that it takes decades before a clockmaker earns their reputation by repairing unique timepieces large and small. Some of these wait a quarter- or half-century for restoration; the clockmaker gathers experience slowly and laboriously. Today, when I've been doing this job for 34 years, they treat me as an equal, which I recognize by the fact that they recommend me themselves," he says.

Working hard for, say, twenty years before more experienced colleagues start to respect you and unreservedly recommend you is an extreme example. In most fields it's roughly half that time, and in dynamic ones even less. In any case, you might not feel the benefit of your reputation in business for the first few years.

There's a huge difference between when a few friends recommend you and when it's then hundreds of people who have encountered or heard of your work over the years. If you acquire greater renown through good work, over the years this will be thousands, or through the media maybe hundreds of thousands of people who will know who you are and what you do, even though they have never met you personally. And this enormously increases your chances that clients you're not yet even dreaming of will approach you.

A good name's cumulative effect is overwhelming, and it's no exception for it to gradually eliminate the need for any self-promotion. A professional who has work for two years to come and who is constantly struggling with a lack of time loses the need to advertise themselves further.

So a good name is the key to long-term success, but its slow growth over time keeps many freelancers from seeing this simple truth. This is why some of them act the way they do – they rush orders, sometimes lie and speak badly of others, and are unreliable; they won't do everything for customer satisfaction. A good name is also a bit ethereal in that its creation isn't entirely under your control. All you can do is to try to provide first-rate work and advance your name a bit here and here. Are you up to the challenge?

A GOOD NAME IS WHEN CLIENTS ASK FOR YOU, NOT FOR A SERVICE

When a customer turns to multiple suppliers, they thoroughly compare your offer with others. For them, you're a number, a row on a spreadsheet, nothing more. Whereas demand based on a personal recommendation looks completely different. Customers want you, as a person, not some silly spreadsheet. But it's even better if they already know your work and have heard the best about it from all sides, or even want to be connected with your work and your name, which has a unique market position.

Here we have arrived at the definition of what precisely a good name means for freelancers:

> A good name is an established association of quality between the professional as a person and their area of expertise.

This established connection can work in two directions. In the basic direction, it means that in connection with you, people remember what you do and that you do it well: *You → a certain area of expertise, and quality.* This association arises first. In the opposite, stronger direction, meanwhile, the way it works is that when there is word of your profession, people remember you as a high-quality expert: *An area of expertise → you as a top expert.*

Who do you think of when you hear the words *The best talk-show host? The best marketer? The best coach?* This direct quality association between a profession and a specific person is called *top-of-mind aware-ness* – the first position, occupied in your mind by the top professional in the given field.

And we don't have to be talking about the best in the world. These associations also work locally, or within your circle of friends. Most of us have an idea of who bakes the best bread around, or who is the best dentist in town. And likewise you probably know whom to turn to for babysitting or small home repairs, right?

So a good name is a stable quality connection between you and what you do:

> one person = one area of expertise

No thinking required. Done! A is B. *You're that profession.* Period. I don't think about it; I call you. The pillar of your freelance business is you and your personal capital, remember?

⊙ YOU'RE NOT JUST A NAME, YOU'RE A PERSON

I know of three other professionals who are named Robert Vlach, just like me. One is an American photographer, the other came to one of my courses, and the third even uses the same coworking space as me. But still nobody gets us confused, because we look different and we each do something different. We also have different social circles, different personal and professional histories, and different social media profiles. In short, the public can easily tell us apart.

My definition of a good name deliberately mentions the professional as a *person* and not their *name*, because it really does involve the whole person.

In practice people in your field who share your name are not a problem, outside of occasional misunderstandings. More serious confusion can come if you don't have a website or any social media profiles and you're impossible to find compared to other namesakes in your field. Nevertheless you don't really have to worry about shared names.

Occasionally you'll find a professional who changes their name because of this, but this mostly applies to the arts and show business. These are aimed at the general public, making uniqueness valuable. For example, the author Stieg Larsson changed his name from Stig, so that readers wouldn't mistake him for his friend Stig Larsson, who was already well known as an author before him. And Winston Churchill, upon agreement with an American with the same name, signed his books as Winston S. Churchill to prevent confusion.

But the most common real issue is name changes for women. The more successful a woman is as a professional, the more reasons she has to not change her surname after getting married, or rather: it's in the financial interests of the whole family. Changing your name can confuse your customers and make you harder to find on the internet. It doesn't have to be such a problem, but if your name is itself an established brand, be careful about changing it. If you marry, you can temporarily use both names; this is a common practice in business.

Various professional nicknames used instead of or alongside a name are one fascinating phenomenon here. For mysterious personalities like the street artist Banksy or Bitcoin's creator Satoshi Nakamoto, we don't even know anything other than their nickname.

For artists, especially, nicknames and pseudonyms are commonplace, as they're part of the artist's self-styling. Some even use pseudonyms for various parts or stages of their work. The best-known example in recent years is J. K. Rowling, who wrote four detective stories as Robert Galbraith and kept the author's true identity secret for some time after the first book was released.

But if you're not working as an artist, it's better to avoid nicknames and stick mainly to your name. A nickname may sometimes catch on and stick to the bearer, but this can be hard to predict. It's probably exciting to build up your brand under the nickname *Killer* at twenty, but will you still bear it proudly at forty? Nicknames grow old, and in time they can become more comical than cool. Other nicknames can be hard to pronounce abroad, or can sound insulting or silly in other languages.

Using nicknames can also be complicated in certain media, where they'll be calling you by your real name, as well as in other official and formal matters, where addressing you as *Killer* simply won't be an option.

A professional nickname is a personal brand that coexists alongside a professional's normal name. So when you do want at all costs to use a nickname you've thought up, it should be a well-considered part of your image, taking in mind all of these circumstances and complications. And remember: your real name, unlike a nickname, will never gather dust or rust.

A GOOD NAME IS AN UNSPOKEN AGREEMENT ON YOUR QUALITIES

Enough on a professional as a person. What about the other half of the equation? That is their area of expertise, which for independent professionals is often also at the core of their business.

This is about what we *do* as freelancers. Some people are clockmakers, some are barbers, others coach, others translate books. In short it's the main area of expertise that people associate with you as a person. And it's not important here exactly what people call it.

"When my grandmother asks me what I do, I say I earn my living by writing. When my parents ask what I do, I say I earn my living by writing on the web. And when people around me ask, I say I'm a social media copywriter and content marketer," says Michelle Losekoot of her gradated elevator pitch. As a freelancer, Losekoot's jobs have included managing the official social media profiles with millions of fans for Prague as one of Europe's biggest tourist spots.

It's natural that she explains her work differently to her grandmother, the media, and her peers. We describe our area of expertise differently in various contexts, but that doesn't mean we don't know what it is. Not at all.

Sticking to your trade, area of expertise, and profession is a key prerequisite for building up a good name, which is the result of hundreds and thousands of conversations that other people have had about you and your work over the years. This is so important that I'll repeat it:

> A good name grows when people talk about you and your work over a long period of time.

People and their fates are the most frequent contents of our conversations. When you head out to dinner with your friends, you'll probably mainly talk about other people. Who has done what, who has aced what, and maybe who is cheating on whom…or cheats at their work.

Just open any tabloid and you can clearly see what ordinary readers care about the most: the lives of celebrities, sports (more people), politics (people), animals (OK, not people) and pop culture (stars above all). People and more people.

But there is a catch. With so many people, you won't be the only one to be talked about. In fact, you'll only be an occasional topic. If your work isn't very visible or interesting, all the worse – it will take many long years before your work as a professional comes to be known by a broader circle of people. This leads to another fundamental conclusion:

> Since people will only discuss your work occasionally, it's important to be consistent and persistent.

"Hey, Janie, remember how you raved on about that piece of furniture some carpenter next door made for you? Can you give me his number?" This is what people do. It can sometimes take years from the first mention to the actual payoff on a recommendation like this. And the more seeds you sow, the more you'll reap.

I see this myself – I often get newcomers who first read an article of mine ten years ago, but have only just now started freelancing and see my course as a good first step.

It's essential to stick to one field, because if you're hawking insurance one year, mocking up websites the next, and cobbling furniture after that, the result will be distrust and uncertainty as to what you do. And what if people recommend you for insurance after you've already been designing websites for a year? Nobody will hire you for web design just because they have heard praise about your grasp of insurance conditions and exceptions.

If you change your main area of expertise in mid-career, don't count on automatically bringing your good name along with you. Yes, people appreciate it when a nutritional counselor helps with improving their diet, but that doesn't mean they'll hand them their money if they become a financial advisor overnight. Expertise is the compass for most customers, and especially for the more demanding, better paid activities, they think hard about whether you have the knowledge, experience, and references needed for them to entrust such important work to you.

Sticking to one profession and area of expertise fortunately doesn't mean that you have to do the same thing all your life. Your overarching expertise remains roughly the same, but your specializations, your core business, skills, and current selection of services can gradually shift towards what is attractive for you as a professional…and for the market. We all evolve and our fields do too, so it's not that common for a person to do the same thing throughout their freelancing career. In ten or twenty years, most of us will probably be learning new skills that hardly even exist today, and there will be new specializations or professions, some of them within your field.

You can visualize this as concentric circles: 1. Your *Circle of competence* represents the sum of everything you know and can do, well or at least a bit. 2. Your *Expertise* is a key competency linked to your good name (e.g. writing). 3. Your *Specialization* or *Profession* is what you focus on and how your colleagues likely perceive you (e.g. web copywriter). 4. Your *Core business* is the part of your specialization that you sell to clients and that currently supports you the most (e.g. social media copywriting and consulting).

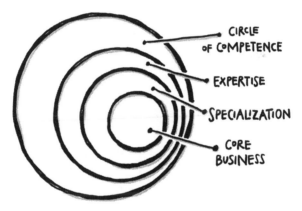

A broadly defined expertise offers plenty of space for changes. If you steer your career so that it externally makes sense and has continuity, you don't have to worry about losing trustworthiness. You should expect, however, for your colleagues and customers to spend some time finding the right place for you in their projects after each of your major changes.

For example in the IT sector, a person can start as a programmer, move on in a few years to making web pages, after a few more, narrow that focus down to digital marketing, and ultimately find a role as a marketing strategist. When I think about it, I went through a similar evolution myself, when I shifted from developing web services to founding an online freelancer community and supporting freelancers' businesses, which meanwhile relates to my field of studies.

Coming full circle in a career like this, recycling previously acquired skills in another field, is not at all uncommon among freelancers: "I worked for eight years as a media professional, mostly as a radio presenter and broadcaster, and I had a degree in communications too," recalls Imre Jernei, who left this job 13 years ago to reinvent himself as a brand designer. "I was able to draw on a lot from my previous media experience, especially when holding lectures and talking about brand communication and tone of voice."

Shifts like these are OK and they'll likely to be understood when other people talk about your work in retrospect. They'll perceive your past experience as a big plus, proof that you take a wide view of your subject.

Meanwhile, a reckless or too radical change of expertise can lead to justified doubts about your professionalism. As I've mentioned before, historically people who frequently changed professions were perceived as mere helpers, not experts to be entrusted with difficult tasks. Even today it's still hard to recommend someone like this for anything, because who knows what they'll be doing tomorrow.

So a good name is a clear consensus, an unspoken agreement that forms hand in glove around you as a person and your expertise. The more faithful you are in the long term to your field and profession, the better. You can still seek lucrative market niches. You can still specialize further and acquire new skills. You can still move towards more attractive clientele. You can still develop some side jobs and projects, even in other fields. All this is natural, even desirable, in career development. Just don't change your main area of expertise on a whim, so that you don't lose the trust you've earned.

We have discovered another paradoxical difference between personal businesses and companies. While a professional who states that they can handle nine trades is viewed with suspicion and looked down upon, we tend more towards admiration for entrepreneurs who have launched several companies in different fields one by one. Theoretically they could both be equally competent. But while for the independent professional we expect a focused interest in their own field and coherent growth, for which we are glad to hire such a person and recommend them to others, for a company owner we mainly appreciate their ability to build and manage the company as a whole. We don't expect them to perform their professional activities exclusively on their own, even though that often may not be far from the truth.

Never try, as a freelancer, to offer a scope and range of services that competes with a company, because you'll never be able to sustain yourself in such an unfair fight. If you find switching professions and fields positively fun, you basically have four workable options:

1. Present yourself as a generalist with one deep expertise that you can clearly communicate externally and develop as the core of your business. So all your secondary activities will overlap somehow with your main area of expertise.

2. Present yourself as a two-field professional with a stable combination of fields. For example, massage therapist and photographer, this might work; or copywriter and graphic designer, why not. (We'll explore this in detail in the later chapter on business plans.)

3. Develop various projects, side jobs, startups, or whatever you want to call them, apart from your main area of expertise. You could potentially even do this with other professionals, but always separately.

4. Steer your business towards a company approach to separate out and manage each activity under a distinct brand.

As you can see, freelancing too can be somewhat scalable. An established expert can easily maintain their main area of expertise for decades and meanwhile invest their remaining time into a dozen side projects.

Always try, however, to make your activities comprehensible and trustworthy from the outside. The more it looks like a coherent, interconnected, and thoughtful whole, and the less like a chaotic tangle of entirely unrelated activities, the better it will be for you. The time angle is also important. In the long-term view it must be clear that you're firmly focused on several areas, rather than just being a jack of all trades, master of none. Then it all can more or less work, even for conservative customers.

In any case, you should invest your good name, time, and other precious resources with deliberation into only those projects that won't threaten your trustworthiness and main business. By joining up with someone who doesn't deserve your trust, you're not only running the risk of being disappointed, but also of ruining your reputation. So seek out opportunities that are ethical and that supplement your professional profile well.

⊚ AT WHAT AGE CAN YOU STILL CHANGE YOUR EXPERTISE?

Changing one's primary area of expertise is, for some people, a question so important that I have to stick with it a little longer. Often in my consulting practice I see people changing their profession in mid-career due to burnout or some type of life crisis.

Opinions on the reasonability of such a dramatic change vary even among career coaches and consultants. I'll take the liberty here of mainly stressing the business angle.

If you work and do business for years in a field and you're doing relatively well, always think carefully before starting a new career in another profession just because you need a change. It can be achieved differently, and with a smaller loss of income, than by starting elsewhere from zero.

You can truly change a lot, from your specialization and pricing to your own approach to life and habits. Feel free also to do pet projects on the side that bring you joy. But always think twice before throwing away ten or more years of practice in some field. While I'm not totally against it, there are unfortunately many cases when these career changes fail. This is why I advise caution and considering minor adjustments at first.

The second note concerns age. There are professions that basically require a formal education (e.g. doctors, architects, and lawyers), and there one can only submit to these requirements and study as needed. In most other cases, however, switching professions up to about age thirty or the time you start a family is more or less OK.

Some people state that a professional should settle on a field as soon as possible, ideally during their studies, because the path to the top is long. But you'll also encounter experienced professionals who really found their area in their 30s, and switched among all sorts of things before that. They still had time enough to make their names. Universality, overlaps among fields, and experience and interests that piled up naturally during years of searching can also have great value.

Also, the span of our productive age is constantly increasing, and if I'm not too wrong, in time it won't be an exception to freelance until seventy and beyond, even if at a significantly slower pace.

Your personal reputation can even outlive you if you create something truly exceptional. This also applies to family businesses where the younger generation sticks to the trade. Then your name stays, so to speak, in the family, and customers will expect a certain continuity, in short, that the parent has passed on the family tradition to their child, or the grandparent to their grandchild.

⊚ BEING RENOWNED AND KNOWN IS NOT THE SAME

In one of her interviews for Harry Potter fans, J. K. Rowling revealed that the only character in the novels that she truly wrote based on a real person was the narcissistic magician Gilderoy Lockhart, the author of the book with the truly charming name *Magical Me*. In Lockhart she perfectly captured the archetype of a self-centered poser who presents himself as being much better than he really is. He thinks up fairy-tale successes and takes credit for the achievements of others to deceive those around him.

These people exist. Their existence is proof that you can fool some of the people some of the time. But no lie lives forever, and sooner or later the truth will be revealed. Ordinary people can often be deceived, but not experts. In almost every field you'll run into people who may be known, because they invest lots of time into self-promotion. But these people aren't renowned – as everyone knows, except them.

And likewise there are professionals, and quite a few of them, who are excellent and successful at what they do, but outside of a narrow circle of colleagues and customers nobody knows them, because they don't care about self-promotion. Their good reputation isn't connected with being more widely known.

Think about it a while. A good name grows gradually, and it's nothing less than your image in the minds of many people. It genuinely takes a long time for this image to stabilize and crystallize. It forms slowly, but its value is all the more prominent and permanent.

You can't hack your way to a good name. If you try to, you might become known, but not renowned.

⊙ WHY A GOOD NAME ISN'T THE SAME AS A PERSONAL BRAND OR THE IMPORTANCE OF HAVING A GRANNY

Having a good name is a phenomenon as old as humanity. Even our distant ancestors spoke about who was an agile hunter, who was the best tracker, who was hot-tempered, who was a liar, a thief, or lazy. And this principle of individuals being judged by their tribesmen hasn't changed fundamentally over all these thousands of years. It's still important for us to know who is the best at something, who is useful – or dangerous.

So personal reputation is hardly a modern phenomenon. It doesn't have anything to do with marketing, or with personal branding. It's shaped slowly and only by other people talking about you doing something well and being a pleasure to work with.

What is personal branding, then? Put simply, it's a systematic effort to improve a professional's public image. In other words, it's marketing.

If you hire a specialist in personal branding, they can advise you on how to better describe what you do, how you should pose for pictures, how to dress, how to do your website, or what to say to the media or write on social media networks to get the final effect you want. A personal brand is the result of this process. It is your altered, improved image.

So far so good. If personal branding helps you to unify your professional image so that you can be more trustworthy for clients and clearly communicate what you're doing and what you're the best at, with it all feeling natural and unforced, bravo! But don't confuse a good name with a personal brand, because these are two entirely different things that may be, but don't have to be, in sync.

A *good name* is a slow social consensus that quietly and justly weighs you and your work, successes and failures, on the scales of public opinion. The result is renown and positive acceptance of your work by customers and colleagues (and often even competitors).

Whereas your *personal brand* is the outcome of marketing processes. These aid your self-styling and the spread of this altered image. Ideally they lead to a better level of knowledge of you as a person and to a better public understanding of where you excel. In the worst case they bring nothing, or make you known but not renowned.

A GOOD NAME	A PERSONAL BRAND
Produced mainly through good work	Produced by a marketing strategy
Other people speaking about you	You speaking about yourself
People around you shape it	You yourself actively shape it
Arises freely and spontaneously	Created in a controlled, targeted way
You influence the result only through excellent work	You have the result partially under control
Feels authentic and trustworthy	Feels suspicious if it's overdone
Costs you nothing	Cost quite a bit of effort and money
Tends to strengthen and grow over time	Often fades over time without regular care
Requires no special management	Becomes outdated if it's not updated
Can have a lot of inertia	Can have a quick and strong impact
Is a synonym for renown and reputation	You can be known and still not renowned
Presents no great risk on its own	A badly built brand can damage you
Stops bad-mouthing mainly through its weight	Outshouts bad-mouthing and even takes it into account
Is a phenomenon as old as humanity	Is undergoing a boom

In practice a good name and a personal brand are rarely in perfect harmony. Which doesn't mean, however, that such harmony shouldn't be sought. And yet if you have to choose between building a good name and a personal brand, I definitely recommend focusing on your good name and leaving your personal brand for later, or only fine-tuning its basic attributes. I'll be coming back to this in my chapter on marketing.

Energy invested into greater expertise, work quality, and satisfied customers brings a greater long-term yield without further costs, not to mention internal satisfaction. And also, experienced clients are looking for quality, not bells and whistles.

Another potential argument against a distinct personal brand lies in the fact that the smarter part of the public can tell authentic personalities from those whose images have somehow been significantly externally altered. How would you like the Dalai Lama, for example, with a styled-up face, a pro logo, and the claim *Escape Samsara Once and for All?* Naturally I'm exaggerating, but at the same time I'm saying that an authentic personality has more weight and influence than any calculated style.

Likewise professionals from whom expertise, force of personality, and experience naturally radiate will typically be valued more by their colleagues and customers than mere actors playing a role. The public simply places more value in authentic personalities who do good, act humbly and naturally, and don't pay excessive attention to their self-promotion.

They have an apt saying for this in Spain. If you praise yourself too much, they impatiently ask you: "Don't you have a granny?" By this they mean, that those who don't have a granny to praise them to the skies have to do it themselves. It's similar with personal brands.

⊙ YOUR REPUTATION BONUS, AND HOW NOT TO BLOW IT

For people to recommend you, they have to naturally find out that you and your expertise stand behind a given piece of well-done work. This needs to be clear enough for you to be credited with a *reputation bonus.*

Note how much harder ordinary employees have it. When they ace something, it's generally presented as a success of their boss, their team, their company. The company has paid for it and is (logically) reaping the fruits, while the employee as the architect of success receives only some credit in the form of a bonus or their coworkers' recognition.

The situation is completely different when the same employee massively messes up. Their boss and company distance themselves, and it's suddenly the mistake of the one specific person who is solely at fault. A scapegoat will be found; you know the drill.

The two situations described above are simplified, but they still illustrate a typically invisible process wherein an employee repeatedly loses their reputation bonus, while their reputation penalty is calculated reliably. It's no wonder that their reputation account is basically exhausted, or even in the red, after age fifty. Nobody knows them, nobody especially cares about them, and even if they surely have a few nice successes behind them, someone else has long since taken the credit for them.

Today more and more top employees are becoming aware of this extremely disadvantageous position. With the shortening of the average time spent at one job and the certainty of a permanent job long gone, these experts are trying more often to independently build up their good name outside their company as well. They might do this by presenting their results, lecturing at conferences, publishing, and making and establishing contacts.

Some professionals can even be so exceptional that they overshadow any brand with which they come into contact. This applies to star chefs, for example. Gourmets come for them, not for the restaurant, no matter how renowned and well-known it may be.

All right, this happens to employees, but can a freelancer blow their reputation bonus? Unfortunately yes: when their work is hard to see. One typical problem lies in orders mediated by an agency, where a translator, for instance, doesn't communicate directly with the end-customer. E-lancers who acquire customers only over closed platforms, such as Free-lancer.com or Upwork, are in a similar position; their rating is encapsulated there and rarely radiates out.

A lawyer or consultant under a non-disclosure agreement faces a similar problem. And what about a project manager or an independent researcher who lets themselves be hired for major projects for several months to years and whose work is drowned in the depths of corporations or institutions?

In all these cases you'll have to help your good name out a little. If your results can't speak for you, it's desirable to find a way to comprehensively explain to people what work you do, where they can encounter it, and that it matters to you. Work from the fact that your reputation is the sum of all your orders, personal or professional activities, projects, publications, or education. Your relationship to the professional and freelance community is also of enormous importance. These professionals form their opinions of you firsthand, and then convey it to their other colleagues.

Adam Grant's book *Give and Take* is a plentiful source of ideas for supporting a good name effectively by helping others. Grant uses many sources and examples to explain that three basic relationship strategies exist:

1. *Takers*, who try to take something for themselves out of most situations,

2. *Givers*, who meanwhile tend more to give and share, and

3. *Matchers*, who act reciprocally, mutually aiding Givers and punishing Takers.

Grant goes on to state that when it comes to success, Givers finish last, because everyone wipes the floor with them. But finishing in first place, meanwhile, are (drum roll, please) Givers as well! Or more precisely, Rational Givers, who like to give, but are also able to detect even masked Takers and are practically immune to them.

Grant's defense of benefaction and selfless giving to those who don't abuse it presents an ideal strategy for functioning in modern networks and connected communities. Here you'll more easily uncover problematic people, but will not always be able to gain reciprocally from stable personal relationships long-term, because people move more often. Demanding immediate repayment is then less advantageous than helping rationally and having faith that you'll be rewarded in return somehow. For example through your good name.

When you add it all up, if you have the disadvantage of your reputation not being recognized on its own, by simply doing your work in an excellent way that is evident enough on its own merits, then it's good to actively bolster your good name to some extent.

Professionals who place their business under a brand for any reason form a special category here. In that case I would recommend that you ask yourself two questions: Is using a brand necessary? And if so, can I also sufficiently build up my good name alongside it? The coexistence of a brand and a name is usually very beneficial for both partners.

THE MORE MISTAKES, THE MORE HUMAN

Having a good name does not mean that you have never made a mistake. We all do. The mechanism by which a good name rises is so gradual, and so spread out over time and people, that it can address the existence of mistakes quite well.

If the dominant agreement is that you do good work, that doesn't mean that nobody will have the opposite opinion. They can envy you and can even bad-mouth you, but all of that typically has only a limited reach and long-term impact if your other customers are satisfied with you and you also have the respect of your peers. A good name is a long-term consensus, not a barometer for the shifting of moods.

The best prevention against defamation is to simply not do bad things – don't make enemies, bad-mouth your colleagues or clients, attack the weak, hate on people just for the fun of it, because this can all easily end up turning against you. Being kind is an art, as paraphrased in the title of Stefan Einhorn's book *The Art of Being Kind,* which has helped me personally to find a balance between harmless conformity and public criticism of everything.

It's a question of ethics. There are times when a critical review in the public interest is certainly needed and beneficial. Constant attacks for fun, far less so – but we each have to find the right balance. Some professionals build their whole brand around shouted, sharp criticism, and it works for them. I'm thinking of the former host of Top Gear Jeremy Clarkson, for example, and the Michelin top chef Gordon Ramsay, and the essayist and philosopher Nassim Taleb. But these are exceptions.

For most of us, being friendly is the best prevention against being bad-mouthed. It doesn't mean being invisible. Lean more towards being beneficial for people, and regularly let the skeletons out of your closet.

"It takes 20 years to build a reputation and five minutes to ruin it. If you think about that, you'll do things differently," says Warren Buffett. That means that you must avoid serious mistakes and behavior that is fundamentally unethical. You can get away with some things unseen for years, but when the truth comes out, real problems will unfold and the situation can get out of your control. Your loss of reputation can then even be permanent. One sad example is the scandal around the comedian Louis C.K., whose starry career (including the release of a new film) was halted in 2017 when a number of women accused him of making totally inappropriate sexual advances. There were other equally devastating #MeToo revelations, and it's clear that the stigma sticks.

But I'm also talking here about deceiving customers, fraud, tax evasion, fake degrees, and major mistakes that do damage to clients. I'm talking about breaking confidentiality, stealing clients from colleagues, and seriously unprofessional and uncollegial behavior. While it may formally apply in business that what isn't forbidden is allowed, that definitely doesn't apply to your good name.

When you make big mistakes and they become known, you'll surely hear about it. The small mistakes are the tricky part. While employees have a manager supervising them, whose job is to evaluate their performance and provide feedback, freelancers have nobody like that above them. When a customer becomes very unsatisfied, they'll likely tell you or indicate it somehow. But they won't take the trouble of sharing *everything* that was wrong.

Many freelancers are known to be problematic to some extent – but other people rarely tell them. It's more comfortable, after all, to seemingly part ways amicably than to confront the harsh truth that their approach simply didn't meet expectations. Yes, it might be hypocritical and cruel, but it's also very common. Nobody wants conflicts, and least of all the customer, who expected a problem-free and comfortable course for the job, without worries, and instead had to monitor quality, give reminders of deadlines, or grit their teeth while hearing quite arrogant comments.

Bad suppliers aren't needlessly told that they're bad, because that just brings further emotional stress, and it also worsens future relationships. I spoke on this topic with a entrepreneur who organizes large international events for thousands of participants, and he complained that four out of five suppliers aren't able to meet his expectations. And he simply handles this by turning to someone else the next time, because it's not his job to teach them how to do business.

So what do you do? Two things. Above all, *don't overlook negative signals.* Few people share their latent dissatisfaction directly, so learn to read between the lines. What does that irritated tone on the phone mean when you've missed a deadline twice – the colder communication – the stronger emphasis on the need for clear terms for the next order? These signals generally mean something, and yet it's very convenient to overlook them and pretend nothing is happening. If you're not sure, go over it with a more experienced colleague or your mentor. They may immediately know what's up.

The second measure is the choice of true professionals. It lies in *asking for open feedback:* from customers after an order, or when part of a bigger job is finished, from your project manager and the colleagues who worked with you on a project, or the people who buy your product, and more. Not speaking of creative fields, where ongoing feedback can be a vital part of the creative process.

The trick to getting good feedback lies in the fact that when you actually ask for it, you'll get honest answers often. This is because the person you're asking can see that their opinion truly interests you and that you're ready to accept any criticism. So don't dig in your heels and object when it comes. Instead, *listen* to what they tell you, and thank them in the end. You asked for it yourself, and even if it's unpleasant to hear it has enormous value for you. If the criticism is justified (and sometimes even if it's not), then think about any immediate compensation you can offer.

And one more piece of advice: Don't come for feedback scared, like a cow to the slaughter. Be positive and open. Start by thanking them for their cooperation and praising what went well. Leave any critical points for later, or don't mention them at all if you don't feel that the other party wants to hear them. The fact that *you* want feedback doesn't automatically mean that everyone does. And when it turns out satisfactorily overall, don't forget to ask for a testimonial.

IS A GOOD NAME REALLY THAT IMPORTANT? DEFINITELY!

I've devoted a whole chapter here to a good name and the difficulties of building it. I'll tell you why. In one survey we asked 2,300 freelancers what helps them the most towards achieving success. Their most frequent answer? *A good name.*

We also asked how new clients reach them. The first six ranks were occupied by *personal recommendations, contacts, a website, a good name, social media,* and *networking.* Similarly, in the *Freelancing in America 2018* survey, *friends and family, social media, previous freelance clients* and *professional contacts* occupied the top four spots as the most typical sources of freelance work. Note how these are almost all various forms of social bonds – strong or weak, personal or online, but they're always other people recommending you, talking about you, or just passing on a contact.

As a freelancer you're never alone. You're surrounded by family, friends, acquaintances, colleagues, customers, and other people who have heard or read about you. You're sitting right in the middle of a giant web of interpersonal relationships. People in your closest and broader surroundings will sometimes try to understand what you do best, and will pass this information on. Make it easier for them.

KEY IDEAS

1. A good name is an unspoken agreement on your qualities. It comes from other people talking about you.

2. It manifests as an established association of quality between you and your area of expertise. In both directions.

3. A professional's reputation is shaped over years, thus a major change of expertise later in your career can be problematic.

4. A good name is the most important long-term prerequisite for freelance success.

5. It's the key to better jobs, a source of satisfaction, and even a lengthener of careers.

6. It will relieve you of the need for paid advertisement and ensures a constant influx of opportunities and orders.

7. A good name is when clients directly ask for you, as a person, not just a service.

8. Good names are a phenomenon as old as humanity. They aren't personal brands.

9. When your work isn't very visible, it's right to work actively for a good name.

10. You have to look after your good name; unethical behavior and mistakes can damage it.

PRACTICE

✓ Let's be clear: What is your main area of expertise? Is it the same work most people associate with you? And what do you call your profession or specialization?

✓ List everything you've been doing professionally over the last 5 to 10 years. Try to tell it as a coherent story to see whether it all fits into a single narrative.

✓ Try to remember everyone that has recommended you recently to others. Thank them for doing so and if it is appropriate, ask what they value most about you.

✓ Do people know about your best work? Let's see. Recall your major outputs (clients, projects, gigs, etc.) and think if you can present them better, share your know-how, etc.

✓ In the next three gigs at least, ask your customers for some open feedback and if there is anything you can improve upon for next time.

2 / The Professional

IT'S A FREELANCE LIFE

What are the pros and cons of freelancing?

Freelancing is in fashion, but you'll rarely hear the whole truth about it. So let's take an open, honest look at how things work in freelancing.

Thus far we have mainly been concerned with the market conditions and forces that act on our businesses from the outside, but our internal life is just as important, and sometimes also just as powerful. All of the human creations we see around us were once just someone's dream. In almost every one of us, there sleeps the potential to make the world better. Thoughts are that powerful.

So the next three chapters will aim at a professional's core. We'll look at the subjective pros and cons and a professional's personal prerequisites, as well as powerful career strategies that support long-term satisfaction and success. With these, our basic foundations will be complete.

⊙ GOOD IN THEORY, RIGHT?

Want to know what it's like to freelance? Watch the musical parody *It's a Freelance Life* on YouTube, and you can skip the rest of this chapter.

But more seriously. Overall, freelancing has a lot of what makes work fulfilling and fun. This is supported by some theoretical models, such as Self-determination theory, which emphasizes the importance of autonomy (independence), competence and good interpersonal relationships. Others meanwhile emphasize variety (nobody likes routine) and a balanced relationship between invested effort and reward (your skills, not your boss or pay scales, determines your rewards). Freelancing gives you a healthy serving of all of this.

But even freelancers themselves confirm in surveys that positive factors win out. The McKinsey study *Independent Work*, for example, states that "free agents reported higher levels of satisfaction in multiple dimensions of their work lives than those holding traditional jobs by choice, indicating that many people value the non-monetary aspects of working on their own terms." Meanwhile, in the *2016 Field Nation Freelancer Study*, 95% of freelancers said that they love, like or are satisfied with what they do on a daily basis (in our own survey it was even 97%). In short, high satisfaction is characteristic for independent professionals, in part because of the previously mentioned consideration of unmeasurable feelings.

But there are two catches here. First, few surveys ask those who weren't succeeding or were not very happy about their lives as freelancers about why they quit. Deloitte focused on these drop outs in their *Evolving Workforce* survey and learned that a full 67% of Americans who have worked as independent contractors would not choose to do so again in the future. That certainly sounds like more than a few!

The second catch lies in the fact that not even prerequisites that look good on paper can guarantee that some little thing won't get you in the end. Even if everyone around you is doing great in freelancing, we all face different challenges.

So you need to pay particular attention to the limitations of yourself and your field, such as education, market saturation and cycles. And it's definitely good at the start to list the points that you see as the main pros and cons, or risks, and if you don't find any antidotes on your own or in this book, then go over them with someone more experienced.

❯ THE ADVANTAGES MOST OFTEN MENTIONED IN SURVEYS

- independence and freedom
- time flexibility
- mobility and working from anywhere
- doing what I enjoy
- being my own boss
- working for my own benefit
- being able to pick projects
- variety in life
- respect and a good name
- professional growth
- good relationships
- comfort and satisfaction
- more money
- more time

The ordering and precise naming of these advantages vary among sources, but the main positives mentioned are always the same – they're the ones in the top half of the list. Money is certainly important, but freelancers rarely mention it in the top ranks (except for the ones who have freelancing as a side job, and the other benefits are secondary for them).

I believe that most of the advantages mentioned above speak for themselves and don't need a long description. Independence and freedom are basically a part of our freelancing DNA. As business professionals we can work when, where, and with whom we want. Nobody can tell us what to do, because we are our own bosses. We don't have to act against our wishes or convictions.

Personally, I strongly empathize with everyone for whom freedom is as important as it is for me. I may be wrong, but this rare agreement in basic values may just be one of the pillars of the strong collegiality among freelancers that I see so often.

Working for one's own benefit, that is, your ability to profit in the future from everything you think up or create, is worth a closer look. Employees have it very different here: the fruits of their labor go to their employer. A freelancer, meanwhile, can create a work of lasting value, like a book, app, innovation, patent, new method or technique, etc. This intellectual property can be a lasting and massive source of income if you're able to protect it. This is also one reason why it's problematic to compare the immediate incomes of employees versus freelancers – or even among individual freelancers. They can have completely different structures or distributions over time.

However, the list of advantages above is by no means complete. These supplementary answers by freelancers in our survey are great illustrations: *I see a higher meaning in it. / I have a good feeling of dignity, confidence, and self-awareness. / I don't have to make the moral compromises that bothered me when I was an employee (custom articles for big advertisers, writing meaningless bullshit). / I'm not a part of the internal politics of a company, I have distance, and when I don't want to, I don't have to; I preserve my mental health.*

THE DARK SIDE: DISADVANTAGES MOST OFTEN MENTIONED IN SURVEYS

- income swings and financial uncertainty
- loss of work-life boundaries
- irreplaceability
- uncertainty and stress
- looking for clients

- tendencies towards workaholism
- loneliness
- tough beginnings
- high taxes and insurance payments
- weak support during parenting and illnesses
- problems with non-payers
- complicated administration

Here too the items near the top of the list are the most-mentioned. The unpredictability of income (and the financial uncertainty that this brings) dominates every ranking and is the most frequently listed reason why people who freelance part-time don't go full-time. We'll cover all the negatives and challenges that top this list in detail later on.

The problems at the end of the list are not as universal, because they are often due to a particular country's laws and market conditions. While they often enjoy attention in the news and politics, freelancers worry less about them than the items at the top. High taxes, debt enforceability, complicated paperwork, corruption, etc. are not, of course, just minor issues. But they tend to poison the business climate in a given country overall, rather than choking individual freelancers.

⊙ ARE WE TO BLAME FOR OUR MONEY TROUBLES?

As a freelancer you can have all the ideals and values you want, but if the money isn't working out, you'll stop cold fast. Getting your business into the black should be a priority when you're starting out, no matter how much you might say it's not about money.

I mean: OK. Maybe you really aren't doing it so you can buy nice things, but you still have to cover your costs and obligations; that is an entirely different matter. To this extent at least, money has to take first place, because a business in the red or running on other people's money won't last long. An entrepreneur has to get their finances under control ASAP.

While an employee knows their income and can more or less count on it and adapt their regular monthly spending to it, freelancers have a radically different situation. It's no wonder that these swings stick out above all the other negatives. And expenses also fluctuate in ways that are worrying. In months when you're paying taxes or paying for expensive equipment, costs can exceed the average of the previous months by several times and cause a good deal of financial stress. When a temporary drop in income comes at the same time as exceptional expenses, this can be a critical situation. It can really cut into your financial reserve, and things are that much worse if you don't have one.

Financial insecurity is not, however, just the result of unpredictable outside factors and income swings. Most freelancers' financial self-management is weak; often it's purely intuitive or entirely missing. For example, in the *Freelancing in America 2017* survey, only two out of five freelancers on average stated that they understand their finances, which also corresponds with my experience from consulting. Finances are understandably the most frequent reason for going out of business. If you can't pay for food and rent, you'll have to find your bread elsewhere.

The good news is that the problem with income swings is solvable. The bad news is that it requires fighting on multiple fronts at once – boosting your marketing, pricing, productivity, and (although I know this isn't the nicest thing to hear) also financial discipline and planning. I'll get to all of that further on in this book. And though things can't be fixed from one day to the next, if you focus on the problem, then you'll only be threatened with stormy seas, instead of occasional financial tsunamis. In the end, you may just gently rock back and forth on transient financial waves.

⊛ WHERE DOES WORK END AND LIFE BEGIN?

Another frequently stated disadvantage is the blurring of the boundaries between work and one's private life, especially if you're working from home. From an employee's standpoint, this can look like a rather exaggerated problem, but when you add in one or more children, a partner who also wants their peace and quiet, and endless housework, it suddenly becomes a time bomb. Its merciless ticking has driven quite a few freelancers beyond the edge and wrecked relationships and families.

Just because it's rare and easy to avoid (if you know how) this doesn't mean nobody is bothered by it. How does something like this happen? Sneakily and easily, as the story that one graphic designer told me illustrates.

He and his wife both worked hard from home with pleasure, often on the weekends too. It was OK until their first child was born. The worries and crying increased, but the work didn't decrease, and, furthermore, the deadlines were tougher and tougher to meet, until one day he collapsed from it all and ended up in the hospital. That was a turning point. As soon as he had bounced back a bit, he and his wife put their heads together, took a calendar, made a daily schedule, made arrangements regarding childcare, and started keeping their weekends clear and caring for their mental health. "In the end we learned that the solution is surprisingly easy; it's just that it hadn't occurred to us before to do something like that. It was only my collapse that drove us to do it," he said.

This story is noteworthy in how, besides the ways in which work and life became intertwined, it also touches on the risk of workaholism. These are essentially two sides of the same coin. If you're single and you work at home, you'll probably call the problems with work overload workaholism or loneliness. While if you're sharing your home with a family, you'll see the problem more in terms of work-life separation. The problem is basically one and the same – but what is the solution?

My basic advice is simple: If working at home doesn't suit you, find a shared office or somewhere else where you're among people. Coworking spaces (there is a global list of them at Coworker.com) can be found in every big city today, and also in many smaller ones. You can visit them daily or as you need; they usually offer a range of price plans. In any case, these are spaces where freelancers meet, connect, and make contacts, and they're one reason why loneliness and isolation are more and more a problem of the past.

Being part of a coworking community is a great benefit indeed and there are even global ones like WeWork (over 600 locations worldwide as of 2019), or Impact Hub (16,000 members in over 100 countries). Networks like these may help you to grow professionally, expand your business with local companies and startups, or serve as a home base when travelling. Their vision reaches far beyond providing just an office space.

And who knows what the future will bring? "Coworking isn't a product, it's a feature," claims Peter Fabor, founder of Surf Office's network of company retreats, in his insightful 2019 article *The Rise of Free Coworking*. He argues that there is a growing number of places that offer their coworking space for free – such as innovative public libraries providing table space, books, printing and fast internet access, as well as sponsored coworking spaces, hotel lobbies, and cafes.

Freelancers love cafes, and if there is one down the street where you can work for a long time uninterrupted, that's great. Besides drinks and maybe a bite to eat, they also offer a pleasant social space, so that you don't feel alone.

The cafe buzz is so stimulating and addictive for some people that there are even apps and websites like A Soft Murmur, Coffitivity, and Noisli where you can play recordings of cafe sounds (or rain and storms) into your earphones. However, you can also work in absolute silence thanks to noise cancelling headphones. Not every model will suit you, but to start with you might try the popular Bose QuietComfort product line ($250 to $400).

Another interesting trend that expands on the idea of coworking is community coliving. Here, I've been impressed by the project Soho Solo Gers in Gascony in southwest France, which is trying to get big-city professionals back into the depopulated countryside. They can choose from a selection of available properties in 50 communities with populations from 100 to a few thousand. Ah Sweet France!

On the other hand, not everyone can or wants to work at a coworking space or in a cafe. Some freelancers have lots of calls or need absolute quiet. Most of them still work at home, and their use of coworking facilities is smaller than is generally assumed. This is also true for remote workers in general, where according to the *State of Remote Work 2019* survey only 8% work primarily in coworking spaces, while 84% work mainly at home.

So how do you set things up at home so that work…works? Think in advance: *Where and when will I be working? Will I be bothering my loved ones? How much stuff can I store at home? Will I be meeting my clients at home, or somewhere else? Can I store expensive equipment or confidential client documents at home safely? Will my work computer be safe from my children?* It's good to have some kind of starting plan or vision and discuss it with other household members before you roll out the field tent for your big battle for freedom and business.

If you work from home often, then you can't rely on your family's peace as a given. So make some basic rules clear to each other and set up reasonable boundaries between your work and home life, which will be in everyone's interest to respect. I also recommend considering home help, especially if you have children. A family member can help, as well as friends or someone from your neighborhood. Or you can turn to an online platform such as TaskRabbit to arrange housekeeping. Services like these can cover routine housework and even babysitting, walking your dog or running errands for you, and thus considerably increase your work performance. So we'll look at this in detail in our chapter on personal productivity.

Even if you're basically OK with working from home, I recommend having other options mapped out too – including an offer of a unoccupied workspace at an office where a colleague works. That makes it much easier to relocate when there is an issue at home. Then once your children are well and your house guests are done visiting, you can return back to your old rituals.

Now I'll go back to my original question: where does work end and life begin? The right answer is: *Precisely at the line that you set. Nobody else can do it for you.*

⟩ MOM AND DAD ENTREPRENEURS

Work-life separation problems naturally take on whole new dimensions when your first child is born. Just like in acting, double roles in business life are very demanding.

Most freelancers are entering uncharted territory when they start a family, especially if they're working from home. If they neglect preparations, they can face an extremely frustrating year instead of a wonderful time in their family circle, with their baby, and with the extra support they need.

Mom and dad entrepreneurs (sometimes called *mompreneurs* and *dadpreneurs*) have considerable responsibility towards their children, as well as towards their clients. And the latter expect the same high quality, reliability, and professionalism as they do from childless professionals.

This is a situation for which you'll need some rather different business know-how and in which you can't use advice from people without children, nor from grandparents and parents if they've never freelanced with children at home. Freelancing parents need to know dozens of practical tricks to keep their business from collapsing due to burnout and a lack of time or sleep. It's simply a second full-time job, even if it does have the definite benefit that you'll see your children grow up and can be with them more.

I recommend preparing for a freelancing parenthood several months in advance. Think about what you can delegate, to what extent your partner will be involved in childcare, when and where you'll be able to work in peace, and what needs to be changed for that to happen.

Find someone who will be able to come to your home to help. If no friends or family members are able to help you for free, then the costs of help, errands, cleaning, and babysitting can run wild. It's not unusual for mompreneurs or dadpreneurs to initially spend most of their earnings to cover these considerable costs, if only to stay engaged in their work. This is why it's sometimes said that parenthood makes people better entrepreneurs, by forcing them to optimize their business and cut things down to the profitable core.

Find out about any parent centers and baby-friendly coworking spaces in your area as well, or any other communities and projects for *parentpreneurs*, and visit them too. It's definitely beneficial to meet other freelancers who have already been through a similar challenge before you and for whom things at home seem to be going fine.

Childbirth is logically a bigger challenge for women – things will depend all the more on how well their partner can support them. But in many countries mompreneurs are on the rise, and for example according to the British IPSE, their numbers rose by a dizzying 79% from 2008 to 2016.

IRREPLACEABILITY IS LIKE A DAGGER FROM THE DARK

Another frequently mentioned freelancing disadvantage is irreplaceability. And while an expert may well be irreplaceable for their clients, everyone deserves a vacation occasionally, to renew their strength and expand their horizons, if they want to stay on top of things.

Irreplaceability is all the more treacherous for how it can strike when you least expect it. As long as you're young and healthy, it's quite reasonable to expect you won't get sick soon. But the longer you freelance, the more certain it is that your life (and business) will encounter exceptional circumstances that will test *all* of your preparations, reserves, and willingness to face fateful trials.

Irreplaceability rarely concerns just one area. So don't face it as one whole, but as a set of problems, and focus on each one separately. Your daily regime and your physical and mental health are important. Meanwhile good processes and delegation – and maybe agreements with colleagues who can cover for you – can help. Also, for exceptional situations, it might help if a close family member has signature rights for your bank account with a cash reserve.

If you act now to manage your irreplaceability well, it will come in handy not only when things are at their worst, but also when you're building up your business – when an exceptional opportunity appears on the horizon, and you need to free yourself up for a big job.

For example, during the months when I was writing this book, my business was able to run itself, having been delegated to completely reliable colleagues as much as possible. I only left myself a small amount of time for consulting and for activities where I had to be there personally. This is the advantage of having a well-coordinated team and of turning repeated workflows into processes. I'm just as replaceable as any of my helpers. And they are autonomous enough that they work not only with me, but also with their own clients. We are not existentially dependent on each other.

DIGITAL NOMADS AND WORKING VACATIONS

One of the least pleasant consequences of a freelancer's irreplaceability is that taking a decent vacation is expensive. Freelancers never have paid vacations, which means double costs – for the trip itself, and for the money lost during the time when you're not working.

This is no small matter, and in *King vs. Sash Window Workshop Ltd*, the European Court of Justice recently took the side of a misclassified self-employed developer who sought compensation for thirteen years of ungranted vacation. But most of us have multiple clients, and so we'll definitely have to pay for our weeks of rest ourselves, and time them during the low season, or when our clients are on their own vacations.

This situation has improved a lot thanks to digital nomadism and the growth of working remotely. You've surely heard about digital nomads before. Simply put, this is the combining of work and travel, or more precisely for typical freelancers, the combining of work and vacation.

You may be saying to yourself: "Ha, a *working vacation* is a contradiction." And I understand. For decades we have been conditioned to think of work and vacations as direct opposites: a vacation is where work is not, and vice-versa.

But like many things in freelancing, this too is a little different than is the norm for employees. Combining work and travel isn't just *possible*; it's one of the best solutions for the problems of irreplaceability, the lack of long vacations, and more.

So how does it work in practice? You just pack up your work laptop and your phone and head out on the road. And now watch this. It's not so important if this means spending the spring in south Asia, the summer visiting your grandpa's cottage, going to a conference in London for a week in October, or traveling in winter to meet me in Las Palmas de Gran Canaria (or other popular nomadic destinations on NomadList. com). What is important is that you're changing your environment and leaving your daily routine, meeting new people, clearing your head, and changing your ways of thinking.

How many hours per day or week you'll work is up to you. If you're heading somewhere for just two weeks, then you'll probably work less and relax more. You may just limit yourself to important emails, urgent work, and a call here and there. If you have the motivation and temptation to go outside, you will prioritize paid work and other important tasks and only cut time spent on your personal development, or procrastination.

The effect on your income will depend mainly on how much of your working time is realistically billable and how much is spent doing non-essential organizational tasks. You might be pleasantly surprised at how little time you need to keep an established business afloat if you set priorities well. And you don't really have to worry about the temptation of rushing your work. I know dozens of digital nomads, but not a single one who would ignore their responsibilities just because of where they were at any given moment.

You may protest that working a little or not at all is a hell of a difference, and you would definitely be right. But here the second big advantage of nomadic vacations comes into play: their length. While a vacation normally lasts only a week or two, with lots to finish before you leave and many emails and a backlog of jobs to handle on your return, a nomadic vacation can last a month or even two, and so the length compensates for the reduced relaxation. This also eliminates the task fever and backlog-chasing before and after, because you stay more or less on the job.

The new environment, experiences, and people and all the bathing and sunbathing fully compensate for the fact that a professional always has one eye on their work. You don't lose touch with your clients and you may be doing a good bit of work, yet meanwhile you get some great relaxation, and what is most important, at the end you feel practically as rested as when coming back from a traditional vacation. This is so non-obvious and counterintuitive that it took a very long time for digital nomadism to really catch on among freelancers. A professional has to experience it to believe it.

I'm not saying that it works for everyone and every field, but for surprisingly many people, it does. Also, you can still alternate between traditional and nomadic vacations.

And to bring this topic even more back to reality, I want to stress one thing: for every digital nomad who flies out towards some exotic place and posts beach and travel photos on Instagram, there are at least a dozen freelancers who work from a variety of locations and take their work with them to their parents on the weekend, to clients, to cafes, onto the train, or into the park, and don't call themselves digital nomads or write about it on Facebook. Working remotely is a completely ordinary part of their freelancing lifestyle, and they have no need to present it, define it, or name it.

If you've got discipline, you can work from anywhere. And if you forget everything that you've heard about digital nomads and just call it work mobility or working remotely, the fact remains that the freedom to work from anywhere is great. For us independent professionals it's one of the few ways to give ourselves a solid vacation without bleeding our reserves dry. And it's not just for freelancers who do everything on a computer. Not at all. I've met lawyers, real estate brokers, teachers, and consultants making use of nomadic vacations to develop thoughts, concepts, and plans.

But nomadism also has its downsides. These mainly apply to perpetual nomads. If you work on the road for most of the year, some customers may find such cooperation unpleasant, because it means communication and time-zone troubles.

The solution goes beyond the mastering of the necessary technologies. This topic is covered in *Remote*, a book by the founders of Basecamp. One of its co-authors, David H. Hansson, answered my question on what would be his advice for freelancers working remotely who want to be more customer-oriented and are looking to prevent problems with conservative clients:

"Trust is really the question in most cases, more so than remote-ness or not. So how can you build trust? The best way is simply to deliver excellent work. A customer may not be comfortable signing on to a long-term remote contract on day one, but could you do meaningful work on a one-week contract instead to build the trust? Failing that, could you show them other engagements where you delivered excellent work remotely? Could you offer to be on-call for an in-person visit if there are material problems? There are a lot of ways to build trust and mitigate risk that can help the case."

⊛ UNCERTAINTY, STRESS, AND TOUGH BEGINNINGS

Uncertainty and risk are unfortunately both a part of business, even for us freelancers. What looks on the outside like a success is often acquired by hiking a very narrow path over steep slopes. Stress is a pest, and not just for beginners. For example, a few years back, newspapers reported on the suicide of the top chef of the world's best restaurant l'Hotel de Ville on the edge of Lausanne. He evidently couldn't take the pressure and high expectations connected with that kind of status.

The level of stress and the risks you can bear are a matter of upbringing and inborn nature. Also of regimen and how much sleep and exercise you get. And lastly the culture of your country or community. Some nations love enterprise, while others love certainties.

Either way, we can only influence our own stress resistance to a certain extent. As for me, I'm a person who can't handle uncertainty well. I can still remember how extremely stressful is was for me to start freelancing many years ago. Thoughts about what was awaiting me on this unknown journey definitely kept me up a few nights. In the end, my will towards freedom of enterprise was stronger than my fear of it, but I have to confess here, so that you understand, I can relate to what you might be going through. There exist ways to overcome even a strong inborn aversion to risk, like I had.

I have clients and friends who play their business like a role playing game, run it on debt, and are paying off a mortgage on top of that, and still sleep well. But someone like me wouldn't take to that kind of situation very well. That's why I do business differently, conservatively; I don't borrow money, I work with my own capital, and I avoid unnecessary gambles. I know and respect my limits.

I'm also helped by my awareness that collegiality and good relationships dominate among freelancers, as well as a willingness to share their experience and help each other in small (but sometimes also big) matters and keep each other afloat. I've experienced enough in life to know that this is rare and shouldn't be taken for granted.

Also the longer I do business, the more aware I am of how relative terms like risk, insecurity, luck, and chance really are. For example, who faces the bigger risk: an employee who could suddenly lose their job due to market crises or an employer's problems, or a freelancer who may suffer constant income swings and occasional uncertainty and stress, but also serves dozens of clients that they'll never all lose at once? And isn't it better in the end to be in touch with risk and uncertainty? And to taste them daily in small doses to strengthen your immunity, rather than falling prey to a false sense of security from having a regular income until one day the cup of risk overflows?

One thing is sure: risks, uncertainties, and probabilities often aren't what they seem to be. This realization has helped me a lot in welcoming a certain degree of uncertainty, no matter how much it may seem to be against my nature. It seems better to me to know my risks and face them than to pretend that none exist. I think this is a better frame of mind overall for starting your business.

The very fact that you *can* start out in business doesn't mean however that it's always the best choice. Quite the contrary. Sometimes temporary stability in employment can be better than swimming in the crashing waves of business at the wrong time. The right timing, deliberation, and respect for risks make for a good captain and a good entrepreneur.

In the next two chapters I'll say far more about the characteristics of successful professionals, and also about how to sail out and set the right course to minimize your uncertainty and risk. I'll start with the thing that interests people the most: *What is success, and how to achieve it?*

KEY IDEAS

1. Overall, freelancing has excellent prerequisites for you to be fulfilled in work and life.

2. We know its main advantages and disadvantages, thanks to surveys. But we all see them differently.

3. The advantages are dominated by unmeasurable emotional factors and the subject of independence and freedom.

4. But finances are still important, and you won't get far without making a profit.

5. The disadvantages are dominated by income swings, often partly caused by a lack of financial discipline.

6. The loss of work-life boundaries is also a problem; typically when working from home.

7. When you have children, freelancing requires even more planning and preparation – and creativity.

8. It's good to map out alternatives like doing work at a coworking space or pleasant cafe.

9. Freelancers are also troubled by their irreplaceability. But like other problems, this is solvable.

10. Uncertainty, stress, and tough beginnings are solvable too. *With a little help from my friends...*

PRACTICE

✓ If you are just starting out, make a full list of your personal pros and cons for freelancing and check them over throughout reading this book. Treat it as a part of your entry audit.

✓ Go to Coworker.com and try a few coworking spaces nearby. And while you're at it, explore cafés, public libraries and other potential working spaces as well.

✓ If you work mainly at home, take a fresh look at your present arrangement whether it can be improved in terms of work-life separation, getting some household help, etc.

✓ Think of how you can improve your irreplaceability at work and try to make at least two or three steps to reduce it (e.g. describe key workflows, or find a decent replacement).

✓ Try to be more location independent with your work by extending your limits one by one. Buy some lighter hardware, move your work to the cloud, and get your clients used to your new setup. It may enable you to travel more and to take on clients from elsewhere.

THE FOUNDATIONS
OF SUCCESS

What makes a professional
a success?

The word *success* dominates business and motivational best-sellers like no
other. I use it too, so I'm aware of just how…*bendable* it is.

What is success? Let's find a meaningful answer. I'll also try to convince
you that such a vision makes sense as it outlines the personal prerequisites
of long term success for an independent professional. This will include
talking about slow success strategies and certain characteristics that might
not have even occurred to you in connection with success.

THE SALESMEN OF SUCCESS

A few years ago, one translator came to one of my courses for freelancers.
Her tension was instantly visible, and she revealed her reason why only
after the session ended: "I was ready to leave immediately if I heard the
word 'Kiyosaki.'"

Shortly beforehand she had gone through a period of crisis in which
her former boyfriend had forced Robert Kiyosaki's books on success upon
her, and she had lost faith in herself. Afterwards she wrote me this on the
subject:

"I had gradually lost faith that what I'd built up for my benefit based
on me and my vision – a small independent business – was really 'it.' I had
a growing thought, one also supported by my partner at the time, that I'd
actually stagnated in my development at the start of my career, that I was
working far below my abilities, was ignoring my potential, and meanwhile
should be aiming for a higher goal: a company with employees who would
do my work for me, with me just managing it. It literally made me feel
guilty, and I began to feel I was wasting my life just by doing what I like
to do."

Sadly she is not the only person whom Robert Kiyosaki and similar
salesmen of success have indoctrinated with their personal – and for

most people unachievable – visions of success. Not to bash motivational reading, but things really aren't as simple as they sometimes say they are in books.

When you see a romantic movie with a modern-day princess and a millionaire on a white horse, you understand it's just a fairy tale. But why is it so easy to take the bait in the case of the tall tales of business? It may be because the emotional aspects of romance hit people closer to home than business, where it's harder to tell what is and isn't realistic.

What worked for the author may not work for you. Even if they didn't glamorize *anything*, three major factors play against your riding their recipe on to success:

1. The author may be suffering from survivorship bias, selfishly overlooking that lucky circumstances may be the root cause of their success where thousands of others with similar strategies failed. So it's always good to ask how many entrepreneurs the author based their conclusions on. If it's only their own story, seek your advice elsewhere.

2. Also, even if a given strategy worked well when it was written, the market is changing, and what worked thirty years ago won't work today. Globalization, the internet, remote work, automation, and hundreds of other innovations are progressively changing the rules of the game. Certain principles, such as maintaining a good name and emphasizing quality and reliability, will likely never change – but others will.

3. Even the best business strategy diminishes proportionately as more people start to follow it. For the biggest of the best-sellers, these can even be, let's say, millions of potential competitors. And there is a hell of a difference between being the first, the hundredth, or the millionth on the market.

Certainly, in the years that I've been supporting entrepreneurs, I've also met some who were helped by these motivational best-sellers. Nevertheless, much larger are the hordes of those who read these texts and became slaves to mammon and dreams of a work-free future. However, when your main motivation is to milk every opportunity rather than to do honest, beneficial work, eventually customers will figure that out and won't be impressed.

If you have a healthy amount of motivation that is in line with your customers' needs, books can hardly hurt you. But otherwise the risk of infection with unrealistic or outdated dreams is high. So watch out for those who'd sell you castles in the sky, providing a key…but somehow no ladder.

In business it's best to work on your own vision of success, and not let anyone force one on you. Nobody can tell you what your business should look like in ten or fifteen years, because only you can see and walk down that path. And yet you also can't do business without a vision – and a beginner will have trouble formulating one. So what do you do?

⟩ SETTING THE BAR FOR SUCCESS

One preconception about freelance work is that only the best will succeed. Yes, certainly not everyone will gain fabulous riches, but here is what you *can* do:

> You can do honest work for good money in a field you enjoy and understand.

Freelancing isn't a lottery where some people win the jackpot sometimes, while others are left out in the cold. When starting out, you have two options. Either to not worry about success and just try and go with the flow, or to form some fairly clear conception, then measure and adjust your approach based on that.

The second option is safer, because strategic thinking, along with having a future outlook, really does eliminate many of the mistakes that a beginner is otherwise almost sure to make. This mainly applies to the first two or three years, before you gain real business experience and learn where your boundaries are. On this basis you can gradually build up a personal definition of success that will be yours alone.

Rather than describing the staggering possibilities and successes you'll surely achieve if you follow this or that recommendation, I'll propose an alternative model. Set a lower bar to start with instead, and as your confidence grows, you can raise it yourself all the way to the sky. As you will see, not even that threshold is low enough that everyone can cross it.

In my recommendations below, I've incorporated the elements of success that are in my view critical for beginners, yet also achievable:

SUCCESS =

HOLDING ON FOR 2 YEARS
+ EXPERTISE +
+ A GOOD NAME
COOPERATION +
SATISFACTION
+ PROFITABILITY

Holding on for 2 years means making it through the most critical period. Beginners often don't have enough work, experience, know-how, or reserves. And they make mistakes. They also have to master the ABCs of business (or as I prefer to call it, the alphabet of business) in a relatively short amount of time and cover at least their costs of living. Some freelancers suffer from a feeling that they have accomplished nothing if their business more or less works after two or three years. But this is a mistake. Many personal businesses (and even many companies) shut down in the first year or two, or never get off the ground and are in the red. Merely getting one to fly just above the ground – to be in the black – takes vast amounts of self-control and discipline. If you manage it, you're among the successful minority.

The number of failed freelancers can't be calculated. We would have to be able to precisely define not only freelancing, but also what qualifies as an attempt at freelancing – for instance, is it that dream side job that failed miserably? Nevertheless my rough estimate is that about half of all freelancers give up within two years. But this isn't about hard crashes to the bottom. They simply pack up and continue to work as employees. Surveys are one sign of the high fluctuation, as beginning freelancers make up a significant and numerous group, while there are relatively fewer veterans. For example, the *Freelancing in America 2018* survey states that 74% of freelancers are newcomers who started within the last four years. In other words, only a quarter of the freelancers persevered for five or more years.

Beginners are often surprised by the humbleness of freelance beginnings. But humble is how it goes. You should understand that it's basically a marathon. You can't become bitter and lose your patience when you don't succeed immediately. A top professional matures with time, and you can't rush any part of that. Aim for a safe start and a sure takeoff instead.

Expertise is what the customer (and thus the market) is paying you for most of all. So another condition for success is the ability to find and clearly define your core expertise. If after a few months you find that you didn't hit the bullseye on your expertise (or core business and services), that is precisely what your initial protective period is for: putting together and fine-tuning something that ideally will be able to support you for the rest of your life. Few will get it all right on the first try.

A *good name* is a part of it. Right from the start, do work so good that your enthusiastic customers spread the word about you.

Cooperation with colleagues and the broad professional or freelance community is the second such bridge to success. Nobody really ever recommends isolated freelancers.

Satisfaction means that when you place the pros and cons of your business onto the scales, the result should definitely be a plus. If you have to overcome problems – and these will come – it has to be fun. Freelancing isn't the type of business where you pour blood on the altar of success for years. If you don't feel like you're in your own skin, something is definitely wrong, and you can be sure that others will sense it as well.

Profitability, a financial reserve, and having your debts under control, or better yet being debt-free, is the right initial goal for your financial self-management. Don't borrow to launch your business either, if the only thing you need is a clear head, a computer, a phone, and a desk. Create a reserve in advance instead, and think before spending every time.

Not even one out of ten freelancers masters the above points satisfactorily. It's not because the bar is set too high. The problem is more about their lack of goals and vision. Many of them don't know what to focus on and wander endlessly without results.

We could give a whole number of alternative formulas for success. The briefest folksy definition I've ever heard sounded quite vague: *If you're makin' a living, you're makin' it.*

Sara Horowitz writes in her *Freelancer's Bible* that the best freelancers 1. are empathetic in their analysis of what their client needs, 2. have matched their skills towards those needs, and 3. have distilled it into a pitch of utter simplicity.

Amy Gallo provides other recommendations in her article *How to Become a Successful Freelancer*, written for the Harvard Business Review: 1. Reach out to your existing network, 2. Make new connections, 3. Determine your fee, 4. Find a good accountant, 5. Familiarize yourself with the legal issues, 6. Have your paperwork in order, 7. Get the word out, 8. Set your schedule, 9. Be prepared for the dry spells

In our survey we asked 2,300 freelancers what helps them the most towards success. Their most frequent answers were 1. a good name, 2. professionalism, 3. 100% reliability, and 4. contacts – the first two were both mentioned by over 60% of the respondents.

⊙ WHERE SUCCESS IS BORN OR HOW TO GROW TRUFFLES

So now you know how I would suggest you think about success at the beginnings of your career. I can understand that this probably isn't what most people would be daydreaming about, but it's an achievable goal that you can gradually reshape into your own grand vision. And one of my stories is connected with precisely this:

We love Switzerland, and we love to go there. We have friends in a village nearby Lausanne who are entrepreneurs. Barbara runs a small and renowned bakery with several employees, and her husband helps the local winemakers with their paperwork. And this family has a dog who is trained to find truffles.

Truffles are mushroom delicacies that grow few inches underground. You won't find them without a trained dog or hog. A dog is better, because they won't eat the truffle – and that would be quite a loss, since for even a handful of truffles, you can get a few hundred francs (think dollars or euros) in certain local restaurants. They buy them and turn them into wonderful treats. And a thinly-sliced fresh truffle laid onto buttered bread is delicious as well.

Hunting for truffles is a nail-biting experience. You head out for a walk with your dog to a secret place where they grow, and after a few hours of excited sniffing and digging, you come back with some treasure – large or small.

You never know in advance how this kind of hunt will end. A truffle can grow to a variety of sizes. It's usually only the size of a walnut, but there are also large truffles that are auctioned off for thousands of euros. The most valuable truffle ever was sold a few years back in Italy for $330,000, and it weighed 1.5 kilograms. It's no surprise that a truffle-hunting dog pays for *itself very well and is among a family's most valued members. Literally. All the relatives make sure to take it for walks.*

One day Barbara mentioned in passing that her family planned to start growing truffles. We couldn't figure what she meant. After all, truffles are so expensive precisely because they can't be grown! They can only be found – with luck, knowledge, and systematic preparation (a dog).

A month later when we stopped by Barbara's again on the way home from France, we couldn't help but ask what she meant by her words about growing truffles. She flashed a little smile and explained her plan to us:

"It's simple. We have a property where truffles could do well. We'll plant leafy trees over there, and in twenty or thirty years, if we're lucky, some truffles will grow there!"

Naturally their chances with this kind of cultivation are small, but their potential gains are large. Barbara's plan perfectly illustrates the Swiss way of thinking and doing business. Not sprinting for quick profits, but rather going after systematic improvements and smart investments that can benefit all generations to come.

The results aren't at all assured, but the forest has other uses besides just providing rich soil for growing truffles. More than anyone else, the Swiss are aware that to reach a great success in the future, you sometimes have to sow seeds years in advance. And when the harvest time comes, you never know how large a truffle is hidden underground. It might be a marble worth some extra cash, or a monster that brings your business to a completely new level.

This truffle story also wonderfully illustrates the key business principle that major entrepreneurial success is rarely straightforward or sure. It's not a plan you just come up with and expect to follow for twenty years without any majors twists and turns on your way towards piles of gold. Exceptional success is always partly about luck and circumstances – but it is also about hard work and dozens of small decisions that you have to make wisely without having a way to know where they'll take you.

When super-successful businessmen who are sincerely self-critical give interviews, they repeatedly emphasize the deep importance of not only luck, but also hard-headed diligence and gradual improvement. (Malcolm Gladwell, for example, straightforwardly presents this dynamic in his fittingly titled *Outliers: The Story of Success*.)

The Swiss way of thinking is similar to that of the top independent professionals. They spend their whole lives getting better at what they do. And once they decide what to spend their valuable time or capital on, they do it with not just a five-year outlook, but a whole-career outlook. In their efforts to increase their autonomy and prosperity, they work with probabilities and opportunities, not certainties.

And what's more, the market fluctuates, and as freelancers we are among its most flexible participants. We can, so to speak, plant a forest here or there. We can also influence what we take with us on our journeys, who we'll set up cooperation with, in what direction we'll grow and learn, and in what condition we and our business will be. These are all bets on success.

Personally, I'm skeptical of books and people trumpeting a direct and certain path to success or singing another siren song of gain without pain. Successful people do business in a smart way, this much is true, but generally they work hard for their success and create profits in proportion to their value for customers. Their goal is not to *not work*, but indeed to *work* to the greatest effect possible.

The riveting biography *The Richest Man Who Ever Lived* shows that this has been so since the dawn of modern commerce. Within it, Greg Steinmetz describes the life and times of perhaps the richest man in history, the German businessman Jakob Fugger (1459–1525). Fugger had more riches and political influence than all the popes and princes of his era, than the competing clans of Venetian bankers, than the modern Rothschilds and Rockefellers, and yet he worked hard right up until his death and lived modestly for his means. Similarly to our contemporary Warren Buffett.

Entrepreneurship is simply work like any other, and sometimes it's even quite a grind. This brings us to the skills and characteristics that make for a successful professional or entrepreneur.

◉ THE ALPHABET OF BUSINESS

At debates and trainings, people often ask me what skills a beginning freelancer should pick up first. The possibilities, both online and offline, are always growing, and freelancers themselves express a strong interest in education in surveys.

The simple recommendation here is: *First focus on the alphabet of business* – i.e. the set of basic knowledge and skills without which you can't do business without major complications, or at all. In large part it's described in this book.

Are you having a dilemma about whether to learn how to invoice and prepare accounting documents for filing your taxes or to go to a course on reading body language instead? Contact your accountant and learn how to invoice! Wondering whether to improve your business negotiations or get rid of your shyness by taking improvisation classes? Go for the negotiations. Are you unsure about whether to first bring order to your work tasks and organize or to attend a creative writing course? Prioritize better personal productivity, because it directly influences your reliability for clients.

Education in your field and filling in the gaps in the alphabet of business should in short have priority. These are holes in your armor that give away your amateurism. And a theater improvisation course won't help you if you don't learn how to defend yourself against non-payers. Shakespearean quotes probably won't do it…

It takes a few years to really get the basics down, but this is an investment with lifelong returns. Gaps in the alphabet of business are among freelancers' most frequent errors. They typically reveal themselves as a professional being usable as an expert, but useless in business. *They don't know how much to ask, so they work for peanuts. They can't organize their work and miss deadlines. They don't file their taxes correctly. Or they're always criticizing their clients behind their back, just like they did among their colleagues when they were still an employee.*

The alphabet as a set of essential knowledge and skills is one thing, while the grammar – a professional's behavior – is another. One example above was about criticizing clients, and this is a classic example of business illiteracy. There is a difference between discreetly warning a colleague about a dishonest client, and complaining about a client just because the work is hard, they are not easy to please, or they just want the best for their money – how dare they! Informing colleagues is definitely fine, but bad-mouthing clients or peers is not.

I personally would *never* cooperate with a professional openly slandering their customers and colleagues. First, it doesn't even interest me. Second, cooperation with such people is risky, because they are indiscreet: they'll often blab secrets. Also, they would most likely bad-mouth *me* as well behind my back and I don't want that. Confidentiality is something I expect automatically from reliable partners, and bad-mouthing is a clear sign that this so-called professional has a problem with it. It also tells me that they are poor at solving problems and conflicts.

In nearly all cases, complaints are just a monologue on one's own incompetence. If someone complains that their client has "huge quality demands, but doesn't understand the issue," I hear: "I can't work with client expectations and explain my services to them." The same goes for:

He's always changing the assignment and doesn't know when to stop. (= I don't have a good system or contract to set the scope of work.) He talks weirdly and frowns at everything. (= I judge people by their faces, expressions, and God knows what else.) With all this, they're telling me: *I have a problem with the client...and I don't know how to solve it.*

Say only the best about your clients and colleagues in front of people, or say nothing. That is the best starting advice I can give you on this. We choose our clients, and we should work in their interest. Naturally they're not perfect – and we aren't either. Their position is weaker in that they often don't understand the matter at hand, and yet they have to explain and define their assignment all the same. An experienced professional will gently apply their authority to *lead and educate* such a client, and *not* write them off as annoying and unqualified to take the lead. Clients expect that despite any differences, we'll respect them, lead them towards growth, and tactfully overlook their problems or faults.

Knowing and shaping these and other client expectations is hard, which brings us to reliability as the king of disciplines for building a professional's success.

⊙ RELIABILITY AS A PREREQUISITE FOR SUCCESS

What do you think of when you hear the word *reliability*? I generally get answers like: *They meet deadlines. What they say, goes. They keep their word. They do the work as assigned. They're on time. When they say they'll call, they call.*

All of these answers are correct. In the normal sense of the word, we understand reliability as *keeping one's promise or obligation.* So it means timeliness, and keeping deadlines, promises, agreements, contracts, and the agreed scope of work.

But this obvious, *explicit* reliability is just the beginning.

Imagine the following situation: During some long-term work for a client's company, you inadvertently learn internal information. The client trusts you and *relies* on your silence, right? It may not be explicitly mentioned in the contract, nor have you talked about it directly. But it's a part of the professional approach that the client expects and assumes.

Or here's another situation. A carpenter is helping to build a house and notices that another party hasn't done their job properly: they've installed the stack pipe at a bad angle so that waste water couldn't freely flow out of the building. The carpenter could act like he didn't see anything and mind his own business. But the customer is *relying* on the fact that a trustworthy worker will point out important facts that could threaten the construction project.

Here is an example from the area of communication: When the client sends you an important email with questions about ongoing cooperation, they *rely* on your reading the message and responding to it without delay. They likewise probably expect that you'll call back if they haven't been able to reach you.

Flexibility in communication, discretion, as well as not withholding information about important facts – these are three examples of *implicit* reliability. Unlike *explicit* reliability, it's not based on a written or oral agreement or a promise, but on client expectations and the responsibility of a professional. It's given by social conventions, business customs, and ethics – and for some fields (medicine, law) some type of formal codex as well. This is exceptionally important, so I'll repeat it:

> There are two levels of reliability: 1. the explicit level, which we're all aware of and which lies in keeping one's given word or honoring agreements, and 2. the implicit level, which lies in fulfilling that which is expected of a true professional.

Each one represents an important challenge; how well (or poorly) you handle it basically decides how well you'll do as a professional.

⊙ RELIABILITY SAYS IT ALL WITHOUT WORDS

Keeping your word, agreements, a level of quality, or promises may seem simple, and yet freelancers repeatedly fail here – and it's definitely not because they don't care about their work. If they didn't, they would end up at the edge of the market or outside of it very quickly.

We generally try to be reliable, but then fail to be. Sometimes we underestimate the difficulty of a job and miss a deadline or don't deliver the promised quality. Other times, we forget to write a task into our calendar, and suddenly it was due yesterday. Or our product isn't working as it should, and the customer returns it. Or in the morning we promise to deliver something by evening, and then during the day so much work is dumped on us that we just can't do it. Or our child gets sick, someone has to stay home with them, and work come to a standstill. The common denominator is obvious:

| Unreliability in the sense of unfulfilled obligations, deadlines, or tasks comes from mismanaging the complexity of business.

Business is a complex activity containing up to dozens or hundreds of different kinds of tasks and activities that all come together to give the seemingly simple results that the customer is paying for.

So reliability is a simple indicator with a very complex background. Unreliability indicates that this time around, the professional hasn't steered their business right. They promised something they couldn't fulfill. They didn't leave enough reserve time. They failed at keeping track of the tasks. They didn't check the final product. They ignored a task's urgency. They couldn't overcome the complexity and it got the better of them in the end.

The solution is to limit outside negative influences and to have a system and order. You have to do your one thing – your core business – superbly, in a stable way, even in a storm.

Through long-term reliability, you tell your clients that you have your business under control. It's an extremely important signal that speaks volumes without your needing to say a word. Moreover, what you *say* is a side issue. You can promise anything and insist you're dependable, but the customer still knows the truth quite well. So the huge significance of reliability is that it *can't be faked*. It's either there or it's not.

Through reliability, you say: *I've got my business under control. I've thought of everything, and I've got everything in order. I work systematically. My work has predictable quality results. I check my work and don't let anything low-quality out the door.*

The customer can't see into the guts of your business, into all the thinking and organizing to keep things in order. They don't poke around in your computer or check how clean your workshop is. They only see the results you delivered on their order, and thus how well your results match up with your promises.

If a professional can't even call when they promised or send a decent business proposal, how can the client have any certainty that they will handle a tough job well? Unreliable professionals are inconsistent on *many* levels, and even an outsider can tell something is wrong. Potential clients form their impression of your reliability quickly based on small and seemingly insignificant perceptions, which work together to decide how much they will want to pay for your work. And defective goods have a very low price on the market.

❯ WE'RE NOT BORN RELIABLE

In all my life, I haven't met even a dozen 100% reliable professionals. This extreme rarity has two main causes. First, reliability is not once and for all. It's a never ending challenge, because the complexity of business has a tendency to grow over time. Experienced freelancers do more and work on harder projects, and often several at once.

But above all: reliability, discipline, and organization are not human nature. Nobody is born reliable. On the contrary, to become reliable, we have to overcome significant amounts of internal resistance and our own selves.

One hundred percent reliability is rare because it's demanding, and thus also expensive in its own way. If you don't achieve it, it's not a tragedy. Most people are unreliable to some extent, and that fully corresponds to the pitfalls of this challenge and to the fact that we're not machines, nor can we predict everything.

So take all of this positively, as an area for growth. You see, customers love dependable professionals. Running into a professional with whom cooperation goes smoothly is a blessing. You don't have to watch them; whatever they promise, they do. This is such an uplifting and unique experience that you generally find yourself needing to spread the news, that is, to spread their good name. And if you're truly crazy about them, cooperation generally won't end with the first order.

Conservative customers test their new suppliers. They don't believe them much at first, and give them something small as a test. Then they send something larger. And sometimes it ends with that dream project that they have been waiting for years to assign – waiting for a reliable professional who is worthy of the work. The unreliable one *won't even know* about this dream job and will keep on toiling over bad ones.

And so precisely handled gigs can lead to big and important projects. Smaller, unannounced test projects are the best filter against incompetent suppliers. I estimate that up to half of my clients naturally think and act in this conservative way. And I would recommend that the other half do the same.

Reliability saves customers costs on order management. After all, even a solid professional needs to be watched and managed if they sometimes fail. And this is an unwelcome responsibility that we're all very glad to put aside for the 100% dependable ones.

Unreliable professionals make us, as customers, stressed out. Instead of being able to enjoy flawless cooperation and feel cared for like a baby, we deal with excuses and conflicts and have to constantly check up on them, push them, and boss them around.

⊗ MEETING UNSPOKEN EXPECTATIONS

Keeping deadlines or promises is hard sometimes, but at least you know that you failed. Understanding what the client is expecting and relying on automatically is a more difficult challenge. You have to know your way around business customs, etiquette, and ethics, and also develop a sensitivity for preventing problems before they arise.

The assets that clients rely on among us independent professionals are too many to list in full. But here are some common ones: *Quality. A pro-customer approach. Going beyond just the task description. Responsibility and admitting mistakes. Quick resolution of any problems with an apology and compensation. Confidentiality and discretion. Attention to detail. Due diligence. Prevention of conflicts of interest. Pointing out important facts. Honesty. Compliance with laws and regulations. Flexible communication and availability. Knowledge of a field's unwritten rules. Frugality. Proper behavior and dress. Loyalty. Boosting the client's independence…*

From this list alone it's clear that you can struggle with expected, implicit reliability for years before achieving any confidence that your approach is basically fine, with no serious mistakes. What helps is contact with more experienced colleagues or a mentor. It's precisely from them that you'll learn best about what normal prices look like, or a typical business proposal in the field. Since isolated self-taught freelancers handle all this themselves, clients can sometimes end up thinking they're from another planet. Steven Pressfield explains this clearly in his piece *The #1 Amateur Mistake*:

"The first obligation of any individual aspiring to a career in any field is to do his due diligence. Educate yourself about the business side of your chosen vocation. Buy books. Read articles. Listen to podcasts. Find out how the business works. What are the protocols? How is business conducted?"

When everyone knows what is expected of them, work goes much more smoothly. The problem comes when someone doesn't know that they don't know. And that often happens where new technologies come into our professional lives.

Once during a small research project, I emailed several expert witnesses from the official public registry. Some of them answered that same day, most within a week, a few of the rest in a month, and the others not at all. With that I was done, I thought. But then an answer came after a half-year, after two years, and then one after a full five years! That last one was sent by a man who was by then retired, who said he found my message in his unanswered email. Who cares if his answer reached me at the speed of a message in a bottle? He had the feeling that he had done the right thing. I couldn't believe my eyes, but then I realized that for him and his generation, email communication might be too new to know its unwritten rules.

And actually, not all freelancers see these rules the same way. The experienced ones often say that it's best to respond to an email inquiry immediately, because it creates a great first impression and increases the likelihood of sealing the deal quickly. When we surveyed freelancers on this, 16% of them really did state that they answer immediately, even within an hour, and 45% generally on that same day. The rest within one, two, or three or more days. Everyone evidently perceives an acceptable response time differently.

And this isn't just about email. Every new communication technology brings with it a certain change in customs. This has affected, one by one, cell-phone calls, text messages, Skype, discussion forums, social media networks, messaging on Facebook and other instant messengers, and collaborative applications like Basecamp or Slack. With each new platform, unwritten rules of communication arise over time, and you should know and respect them if you don't want for others to take you for some kind of country bumpkin.

Social media networks are one good example. The first generation of users perceived them as their personal, private space, where clients would surely never go. But over time this viewpoint turned completely around, and so today networks and the profiles on them are perceived as a core part of one's public professional image. They are even home to those who once belittled Facebook and other social media.

Or take video calls. "Just a few years ago it was normal that, when I was organizing an important event for corporate clients from Germany or Holland, their managers came to look at the individual locations personally; they wanted to check how the tables would be laid out, talk to the owners, etc. And today? Nobody wants to waste precious time, and what we can handle remotely over Skype, we do. When it's needed, we film and send a video; it all goes much faster than before," says top event manager Eva Hermans of her experience with the rise of teleconferencing calls in the EU.

New technologies are seeping into our work lives and habits. Customers expect that we'll know how to use them, and also expect some reasonable degree of availability, which is an important topic that I'll cover in detail in the later chapter on clients.

The fight with your own unreliability has many levels, and their shared goal lies in consistency, comprehensibility, and predictability. You can't, for example, publicly advertise something on the web and then say something else to clients face-to-face. You should always meet the obligations put forward by your public presentation; this too is part of your reliability – and also a task for your personal branding.

Likewise watch out for promises that you make on the fly that your customer can easily take as a given: *I will call you this afternoon. It'll cost about a thousand. I'll send it by the end of the week.* Is that Friday, Saturday, or maybe Sunday? Weigh your words, and factor in a time reserve.

When you have the opportunity to cooperate with professionals who really are dependable, watch how they do it. The result may look simple, but the way to it doesn't tend to be all that easy. In the background you'll find checklists, processes, and established work procedures, project management, or some kind of integrated system that is the product of gradual improvement and simplification.

Long-term reliability is, in any case, the best indicator of how well you manage your business, whether you are its master, or whether it bosses you around. Anything below the level 3 on the following scale therefore means that you have a serious problem – clients are likely to stop recommending you and won't be willing to pay higher than average, if they are not already angry enough to be looking for a replacement (level 5).

1. **absolute reliability** on both the explicit (promised) and implicit (expected) levels

2. **full explicit reliability** with minor deficiencies in implicit expectations

3. **rare failures** in explicit reliability under intense pressure (during the peak season, etc.)

4. **minor failures** in explicit or implicit reliability, but only in tasks of lesser importance

5. **regular failures** in explicit and implicit reliability in tasks of small and great importance

Now that you rated yourself on this scale, let me just add that according to my consulting practice, many professionals and businesses tend to grade themselves a level higher than where they actually belong according to their clients, when we asked them as well.

No matter what your real standing is at the moment, let me present you with a challenge to wrap up my pitch on the importance of reliability. We all live in an unpredictable world of chances and risks, where certainties are very hard to come by. Being one for your customers and colleagues under any and all circumstances makes a huge difference. And even if your only takeaway from this book were that reliability is a key prerequisite for your freelance success, as long as you truly are able to turn that into practice, it will inevitably transform your entire business for the better.

◉ RUN DUE DILIGENCE ON YOUR STRENGTHS AND SKILLS

There is an old saying that goes: *Don't open a shop unless you like to smile.* That describes pretty well the intuitive truth that it's better when your business rests on your strengths.

I'll come back later to a number of topics opened up by this discussion on reliability, but for the rest of this chapter, I'll cover a few more key personality-related prerequisites for a professional's success. After all, it's safer to go into business with the knowledge of what you're good at and what you're dangerously bad at, than to prop up your whole business on those weak points.

As for personality traits, there is no reason to fear that you don't have what it takes to do business. Naturally there is, for instance, a big difference between introverts, extroverts, and ambiverts (somewhere in-between), but no personality type is predestined for business success or failure. It's more important to choose a field and style of business that corresponds with your nature.

The people who I advise about business never stop surprising me. Some of them start with all the on-paper prerequisites for success, but they give up in, say, half a year. And others, from whom I would never expect it, go from one success to another. Business sometimes brings great personal transformations, and you can never predict with complete certainty how a first-time businessman will deal with the new situation. It is as if the encounter with the unknown, uncertainty, and the direct consequences of our own actions has awoken our hidden potential.

You can start by writing up a list of skills and dividing them into those that you personally prefer and those that can be useful for you, for example, because they'll be easy to cash in on when you need more income. I run similar audits with professionals who are considering leaving a corporation to freelance and don't have a grasp of their skills' market value. For some this is very high, for others (like the art of avoiding work in a corporation), almost zero.

You can approach your audit of your strong and weak personality traits similarly. There are a number of ways to achieve this: 1. self-discovery and introspection, 2. cooperation with a therapist or coach, 3. analysis of your past successes, 4. a specialized test like *StrengthsFinder 2.0*, and lastly a method that is *entirely* direct, which makes it my favorite, 5. ask the people who know you best and who are honest (or cheeky) enough to tell you where you shine and fail. The answers may surprise you or even shock you, but they will definitely help you to better understand your strengths so that you can build on them.

PERSISTENCE, GRIT, AND HARD WORK

So now we have looked at how reliability is the result of being able to handle the complexity of doing business, which is (among other things) caused by the fact that projects and gigs don't simply arrive one after another when it would suit you best. Sometimes they come in bunches, and when your time reserves run out, sometimes you really need to push. Sara Horowitz puts it bluntly in her *Freelancer's Bible*:

"Don't turn down work. That's just a rule of being a freelancer. OK, let me amend that. Turn down crappy work and work that doesn't fit your freelance portfolio, assuming you've got plenty to do and dough to live on. But you shouldn't have to turn down good work just because the job's too big to do alone, you don't have some of the needed skills, you'll be on vacation, your life is nuts, or you promised your mate you'd stop working until midnight every night," writes Sara and explains further, that a good manager will always find a solution or share the work with others.

I'm not saying that you have to take this literally. It's more of a principle, and I'm mainly putting this quote here in contrast with the articles that claim that turning down (good) work is the right thing to do. Personally I'm not convinced of that, because all too often among my clients, I see a direct connection between a stagnating income and turning down work during their high season.

When you chop off the tops of your income peaks like this, it can come back to hurt you a lot financially. If you also tell everyone that you're not keeping up, then even your satisfied clients will stop recommending you, just to be sure that you'll have some time left for them!

Fields and markets, as well as whole economies, oscillate in cycles and have seasonal swings. The top of the season during an economic boom can bring up to several times as much income as weak periods. There is a big difference between a professional who refuses work after a certain point and one who keeps a sufficient time reserve, sets prices correctly, has a work system that is prepared for these swings, and is able to temporarily handle a lot more work – in short, to step hard on the gas, which can lead to record revenue. Refusing and relaxing, meanwhile, can mean robbing yourself of, say, half your profits.

And it's not just about money. The ability to temporarily work extra-hard will come in handy for you for large and transformational projects as well. With full self-investment, we can sometimes achieve things that we couldn't do in our normal mode. But all things with moderation; pushing hard should be a capacity reservoir, not a year-round way of life.

SPEAK AND WRITE TO THE BEST OF YOUR ABILITIES

One key way to prove that you are a solid player is to superbly express your professional opinions. No matter whether you are writing texts for your website or emails for customers or presenting a solution proposal at a meeting with clients, you are relying on your writing and speaking skills. So it makes sense to develop them.

Rhetoric isn't just the ability to stand before people and thrill them with your presentation. It's a universal skill that includes prepara-tion, building your arguments, self-expression, knowledge transfer, and performing. Getting better is more often about practicing regularly rather than taking a one-time course.

From my own experience I can recommend the public speaking clubs of Toastmasters, a non-profit organization with over 350,000 members and 16,000 clubs in over 140 countries. I founded one of their European clubs, and I can confirm that their system for development is very effec-tive. Over the years of my service as a club member and president, I've witnessed a number of great personal transformations of people with stage fright into great speakers.

Toastmasters is unique in that its clubs don't have an instructor. You get a basic manual at the start with ten speaking projects, and you improve yourself thanks to feedback from others. You gradually focus on a variety of aspects of speaking, but you choose your topics yourself. I've often used my club speech as preparation for a speech at a conference.

Each club is different, with varying approaches and atmospheres. If you have several of them around you, visit them all and choose. After attending for a year, you'll see a huge difference. You can also get involved in contests between clubs (and battle your way up to the world finals) or combine your membership with other sources and courses.

Like speaking, writing lets you formulate and spread your thoughts. But at its core it's an entirely different skill, as confirmed by the fact that not everyone who can thrill an audience writes well, or vice versa.

Nearly every guide to better writing stresses two principles: Read a lot, and write a lot. It makes sense. If you don't read, that narrows your grasp of language usage and vocabulary, and if you also don't often write, the result will be evident from the first glance. This is not what you want.

To improve, ask your colleagues for a tried and tested creative writing course, or agree on paid or reciprocal coaching from an experienced copywriter. Then you can go over the texts you write together and improve them, no matter whether that means sales emails, articles, or social media posts. Posts are especially useful for learning because you get immediate feedback, such as hearts, claps, and likes. You can see what works right away.

As far as reading is concerned, read articles and blogs, but don't forget about books. They're still the #1 intellectual medium, because they explain and transfer complex ideas as a whole. Being well-read improves an expert's ability to perceive their field and the world in context.

CRITICAL THINKING VS. INTUITION

We are drowning in information. Critical thinking, as the ability to work with information and correctly evaluate it, has thus become an increasingly essential professional skill, especially among knowledge workers.

Experts who can handle analytical thinking and logical argumentation and work with sources – verifying and analyzing them – are in short supply. Everyone can toss off some random thoughts. But extracting the important insights from the flood of data, thinking about it critically, and finally formulating a comprehensible recommendation or conclusion, that is what clients unwittingly want.

Few people want to be overwhelmed with administrative tasks and make dozens of minor decisions. And people who don't think about their work are walking disasters whom you have to constantly watch to make sure they don't do something wrong. That is extremely demanding and tiring, so when you encounter a professional who is able to *think* for you and even better than you, that is a definite win.

Critical thinking isn't a resume item, but it's reflected in all of your work. And it doesn't require a high IQ. It's more a set of skills that you can master – and thereby significantly reduce your error rate. It's thoroughness in thinking and applying approaches that lead to more reliable or cautious conclusions.

As perhaps the best introduction to critical thinking out there, I'd recommend Steven Novella's audiobook *Your Deceptive Mind*. He makes the point that to think well, one has to know the numerous limitations, biases, and defects of the human mind.

Nobel Prize winner Daniel Kahneman goes over these in detail in his famous *Thinking, Fast and Slow*. If that is too demanding for you, then I recommend the wonderfully easy to read book on Kahneman and Tversky's research *The Undoing Project*, by Michael Lewis. While it's a biography, he describes many principles in a more comprehensible way than Kahneman himself.

To see just how broad this problem is, check out Wikipedia's List of cognitive biases. Our brains like to simplify things. Instead of slow, careful thinking that costs a lot of energy, we use various intuitive shortcuts. These sometimes lead to the goal, but often also to colossal mistakes. So quick thinking tends towards predictable mistakes, which Kahneman has famously documented. His conclusion is simple:

> Know your limitations, and in important things, don't depend on fast thinking.

Two vivid examples of the limitations arising from bad thinking in individual entrepreneurs are *survivorship bias* and *confirmation bias* (defined by Wikipedia as the tendency to prefer information in a way that confirms one's preconceptions). And you have surely encountered the *planning fallacy* (the tendency to underestimate task-completion times) and the *Dunning-Kruger effect* (the tendency for unskilled individuals to overestimate their own ability and for experts to underestimate their own ability).

Fast thinking also includes intuition, which is somewhat overvalued among spiritual and artistically oriented businesspeople. While a gut-feeling can definitely help you to pick up subtle signals in everyday social interactions or to read what feels wrong under some very familiar circumstances, it also has a strong tendency to fail in situations that are entirely new…such as starting a business!

Intuition can whisper that you should buy a new car or an expensive piece of equipment, to open up your cafe or hire your first employee, but until you have your decision underlaid with a rational consideration or a model calculation, my advice is: don't do it. I've met many entrepreneurs who listened to their intuition only and were losing money left and right.

⊙ STRAIGHTFORWARD BEHAVIOR AND PROFESSIONAL ETHICS

Which professionals or entrepreneurs are visible without advertising and always have a full workload? The simple answer: *Those with nothing to hide.*

Have you ever met a craftsman or other professional who acted honestly and with pure intentions to help you? And not only acted, but kept their word and did top-notch work? If so, then I'm sure it was an intense experience. Meeting a person like this evokes strong positive emotions. That is what we want as customers. Quality, sincere interest, and fair behavior without any hidden motives. We are willing to pay for that and recommend it.

Straightforwardness simply works. It's among the best entrepreneurial strategies, but despite this it's relatively rare. Why? Because lots of professionals have something to hide: *Little things. Internal insecurity. Lack of knowledge. Disorganization. Cut corners. Indifference. Lies of convenience. Pirated software. Tax fraud.* All sorts of things can be hidden behind the facade of formal professionalism.

A professional who acts openly and straightforwardly has nothing to hide. Such people are proud, respected, and successful, with wonderful personal integrity and internal strength. They will tell you their opinion without hesitation just to help you out. They don't play games, and they don't build any walls around their work. On the contrary, they excitedly and gladly talk about it and protect nothing but perhaps their privacy and key know-how.

Secretive behavior is a big problem. Some clients tell me in their different ways: *We want to be seen and to sell stuff. But we don't want to be too visible in the process.* They want something that in reality they do not want. A paradox. No wonder it's not working for them.

Ethical, straightforward behavior has a fundamental influence on professionals' long-term success, because it's a source of internal satisfaction, and it also turns us away from cooperation with people – colleagues or customers – who don't share these values. And as we'll see in the next chapter, in many unsuccessful freelancers this type of strategic thinking is entirely lacking.

KEY IDEAS

1. It's important to start with a realistic vision of success.

2. Here's one suggestion: Holding on for 2 years + Expertise + A good name + Cooperation + Satisfaction + Profitability

3. Phenomenal business success is rarely linear. It can't be planned out for years in advance.

4. The greatest killers of freelance success are gaps in one's alphabet of business.

5. Of all the personal prerequisites, *reliability* is the most important. In the Olympics of freelance success, it is the ultimate discipline.

6. Reliability has two levels: explicit (promised) and implicit (expected)

7. One's business should be built on one's strengths and skills. And that demands an audit.

8. Writing and presentation skills are useful everywhere in business – not just for books and podiums.

9. In our information age, critical thinking is rising radically in value. Intuition isn't enough.

10. Other important prerequisites: Grit. Honesty. And professional ethics.

PRACTICE

✓ If you're just starting out, write down realistic business goals and priorities to turn your first two years into a freelance success. Use my formula from the beginning of this chapter as a template to start with.

✓ Looking beyond your main expertise, what are your other valuable skills and personal traits? Is there something you can improve on, or use when you need extra income?

✓ Rate yourself honestly on the 5-level reliability scale (level 1 for the 100% reliable), possibly asking your trusted colleagues or clients to do so as well. If you score below level 2, analyze it and try to improve.

✓ Challenge yourself to be more proficient in writing and public speaking. Sign up for a course or a Toastmasters club, have someone evaluate your outputs, and practice often.

✓ Get familiar with the essential professional ethics for your field, as well as various cognitive biases you are prone to as an expert. Read Wikipedia's List of cognitive biases or try using the MyCognitiveBias.com browser extension for a while.

A BUSINESS PLAN MAKES
A CAREER

What should be the foundation of your professional and career strategy?

Do you think a business plan is a structured document that uses lots of spreadsheets and attachments to describe how to start a business? Well, in freelancing, think again.

The vast majority of freelancers don't have a *written* business plan at all. Still, that doesn't mean it isn't important for us. It is! We generally carry it inside ourselves as a vision that leads to our goals, not only at the start, but throughout our whole career. So a professional or career plan would be a better name. It's a cornerstone of our career strategy.

⊚ PINPOINTING YOUR CORE BUSINESS

The first reason why a plan like this is important is that it lets you clearly define your area of expertise – and your core business within it. In addition to the professional as a person, this second element, your area of expertise, is also an essential part of a good name and clearly defines you within the market. A seemingly simple definition can come from years of thinking and the longer you refine it, the more brief, fitting, and clear it will be.

One easy test is the *elevator pitch*, i.e. your brief introduction to a stranger. Can you explain what you do quickly? And does everyone really understand it…or is the more frequent reaction you get a confused expression?

Their understanding is a primary condition to be met if they are to spread the word and tell others what you do. It's best if you can express it in 10 words or less, not a minute-long monologue. Then you're not only being clear, but also brief, which is definitely a major plus.

In connection with the search for the best expression of the core of your business there is also a holy grail in the form of an innovative name for your profession that will become widely used through you as a top-of-mind expert in a new field. I don't mean pop-culture nicknames like *guru*, *ninja*, or *evangelist*, but real profession names for a new era such as *creative coach, intimacy coordinator, decluttering consultant, sustainability expert* or *data journalist*. If the name fits and it's catchy, then your name will spread along with it.

However, thinking up a pioneering name is no small task. But you can meet this halfway by watching the development of professional terminology worldwide, thinking about alternatives, and gradually refining how you call your work. And also take a look at the O*NET OnLine catalog of professions.

⊗ KEEPING YOUR ATTENTION AND INVESTMENTS FOCUSED

A clear expression of your area of expertise, specialization, and core business is a foundation you can return to at any time when you're trying to decide which way to go, especially when things are complicated, tense, or confusing. It will keep your attention from fragmenting into too many activities and directions.

You only have a limited amount of time and money to invest into your business. There is a huge difference between investing long-term in one direction and one flagship expertise, no matter how broadly you define it, and throwing away hours and dollars in all directions. Just like with a good name, it's imperceptible in the short term, but a long-term investment brings a powerful cumulative effect. By having a clarified plan you are saying *I'm doing this, I'm building this, I invest my time and resources into this.*

When a business has no clear plan or core, colleagues and customers often see it as unstable, risky, and disorganized. As if the professional was doing something else every day, or working on several areas at once – poorly. A business like this may simply be fueled by opportunism and be oriented towards quick profits, but more often it's just the result of running aimlessly between too many activities.

I've even met freelancers who picked up more and more professions over the years until they had a half-dozen. Most of what this sort of professional invests into their business comes to nothing. That is the misery I see in it. A business like that is just sad.

Now, you can object that opportunistic switches of profession have their advantages, because you can go dig where the gold is. But that only works when you're young and can still dig the fastest. As you age, the importance of professional reputation grows. Expertise wins out.

Meanwhile the business of a freelancer with a clear plan is visibly goal-oriented, coherent, and reasonable; in short, a sensibly built business. Everything more or less fits together; we can see a wonderful synergy among individual activities, and together it all makes a lot of sense. Such professionals are *readable* – other people know what they do and how they can help. This readability comes not from chance, but from concerted effort.

A stable focus also speaks of your force of personality. It's proof that a professional can focus on something long-term, choose carefully, think things over in depth, and do them well. For us as customers, seeing a business like this is a sign of the quality we can expect to get.

Even though for most freelancers a professional plan is something internal, in reality it radiates out of you in lots of different ways, and especially as the years go by, it's very obvious if you have it or don't.

By the way, there is no harm in writing it down either. Some freelancers keep a document with visions or goals, come back to it repeatedly, and gradually clarify their outlook and strategy for the coming years. If you are that type, then don't hesitate to write down how you see your freelancing. It will also come in handy if you want to consult with someone about your business.

But watch out – if your business needs a large initial investment, then you should definitely opt for a conventional business plan. Don't take risks; talk to consultants and invite people who understand the fields in question to read over it. Yes, it will cost you money, but it may save you 100 times as much. I'm a fan of simple plans that fit on one sheet of paper, but only for business projects without large capital demands.

EXPERTISE: SINGLE OR DOUBLE?

The vast majority of the freelancers who see long-term success can be divided into two groups. They have either a single area of expertise (the T-type below) or two (the A-type):

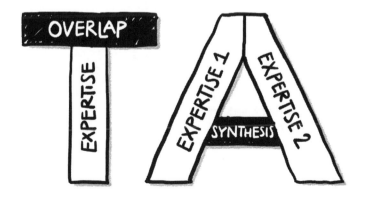

The professional with a single area of expertise works long-term in one field and deepens or expands their expertise over time. But they also have what I call overlap that goes way beyond, into related fields and various hard and soft skills, including the business alphabet. (The concept of T-shaped experts was actually popularized by *Valve's Handbook for New Employees*, but it applies to us freelancers as well.)

Secondary skills without deep expertise aren't worth much. But expertise without overlap isn't enough either. Professionals with overlap score points because they are easier to work with: They perceive clients' needs better. They are team players. They communicate well. They avoid conflicts. They can take criticism. They are open, and they negotiate better. They don't debate trivial matters just before a deadline. They make sure they take care of their reliability, performance, and good name.

The professional with two areas of expertise is active long-term in two different fields. They develop these areas evenly over time, and strive for a reasonable synthesis between them, with the help of other knowledge and skills. Experience has shown me that two-field experts *can* be stable long-term. And they are also fairly transparent and trustworthy for their customers, as long as the professions don't place heavy demands on continuing education.

One advantage of a two-field focus is that when this kind of professional finds customers seeking both skills, they have an unbeatable advantage over their one-field competitors. What can also be an advantage is the division of their risks into two areas of income – and the covering of seasonal swings if those two fields have opposite seasons. But this advantage is deteriorated, on the other hand, by the splitting of your focus and the investment into two separate lines of business. If you invest thousands of hours and loads of money into both of your areas of expertise, up to half of that investment can be wasted if you leave one of them in the future.

The double expertise is quite common among artists and creatives, who like to expand on their gifts and talents, such as being a writer and a visual artist too. One wonderful example of a two-field focus is Meghan Markle, who married into the British royal family in 2018. Before she went into acting full-time, she was also making a good living freelancing in calligraphy – she taught her own courses and also, fittingly enough, produced her own wedding invitations.

Two-field professionals represent less than one tenth of the dependable freelancers I know. But they are professionals whom I respect, because they do their work well. However, over the years, many of them abandon the two-field approach and turn towards one field or the other. The market's pressure to specialize and the need to invest long-term in one direction are just that strong.

The popularity of the two-field approach has grown thanks to the internet and the rise of a variety of online platforms for sales and professional services like Airbnb, Upwork, and Etsy. These make it easier to build up a strong secondary income alongside your main business. Mixing fields is especially popular in the US, and surveys show that its popularity is rising.

However, if you are in a truly demanding, dynamic field that is known to take all of one's time, you might not want to promote your two-field focus.

It can sometimes be hard for two-field professionals to present themselves without looking strange. Some of them have two separate web presentations, two versions of their business card, etc. Others seek to strongly synthesize and present their approach as a plus. Or on the outside they prioritize just one field and only run the second for a limited clientele. The two-field approach is also certainly an acceptable compromise if you don't know yet which way you want to orient yourself professionally.

SIDE JOBS, LITTLE BETS, AND OTHER TIME-TESTED STRATEGIES

There are several time-tested and safe ways to start freelancing. By far the most common are side jobs – during employment, university studies, maternity leave, etc.

Other commonly mentioned entry points into freelancing include: working for free for family or friends and trying to go more professional; problems at work and wanting to be your own boss; business connected with the subject of your studies; or working as a contractor for a single large client.

Relatively more rare, meanwhile, are those who go freelancing with some kind of unique idea and the determination to bring it to life; this is another difference from the world of companies and startups, where smart ideas that utilize gaps in the market are commonly (and rightfully) held up as exemplary. Innovation is still important in freelancing, but freelancers tend to grow towards it gradually, during their careers, rather than its being there at the start. By making their knowledge deeper and their professional identity clearer, they increase their innovation potential.

It's definitely a plus if you can distinguish your business with an idea or innovation right from the start. But expertise is more important. An idea can fail, and maybe nothing will go as you expect, but customers will never stop hiring your for your knowledge and skills. Let's go back to those popular side jobs, and it will immediately be clearer how it works.

Side jobs during employment or university studies represent by far the most common and safe, and perhaps best, way to kick off freelancing.

Naturally fields where you need prior training, certifications, or practice and where business ties in closely to the subject of studies are an exception. According to The Economist, this applies to up to 22% of the current American job market (compared to just 5% in 1950).

For less regulated professions though, side jobs are enormously popular. They typically take on the form of *little bets* – one-time gigs or projects with which you map out the terrain, your market potential, and your real possibilities. Is it not a good match? You don't enjoy the work? Is it badly paid? You don't see any future in it? You don't have what it takes? Then just safely take a step back.

That's how Basecamp partner and co-author of *Rework* David H. Hansson described it in his answer to my question on what would be his rule to follow from day one for someone making the switch from being employed to going freelance:

"I'm generally not a fan of big audacious leaps of faith. I like to make sure the ground is stable before trying to run a marathon on it. Thus, I would try to run a freelance business on the side with smaller projects until I knew that there was something there. That I had a marketable profile, that I enjoyed doing the work as a freelancer, and that I at least had some business lined up before I quit my job. Now this may well not be compatible with every employment contract. If it's not, then I'd still try to line up some deals before going solo. It'll be stressful enough to make sure the work is there after you've cut all ties. It shouldn't have to be stressful on day one."

Sometimes you can reach an agreement with your original employer for a retainer, even after you leave to freelance. It takes a bit of diplomacy, but it's nothing exceptional, and in practice both sides can benefit from it. A brand new freelancer can then have at least minimal income assured at the start, from a client that they already know as an employer, and meanwhile the employer doesn't lose an experienced person overnight – they can still benefit from the knowledge the person would otherwise have taken with them.

The magic of little bets lies in how you can make a fair number of them without taking risks. You can try out different types of work or even related fields until you hit on something good. A start like this can be pretty easy. You aren't worrying about strategy, a business plan, a website – none of that. You just try out a small gig and see what comes of it.

How do you manage to get such gigs? Simply. Through a freelancing acquaintance, a friend, family, or your favorite non-profit, through an agency or somewhere on the web, if you find a project that makes sense and visibly wants support. Joining in on it externally, on a contract, or as a part-time job is often possible (and welcome).

At first glance, such work might seem small, but the income can be quite attractive. Even for a beginner it's not impossible to quickly work your way up to large rewards if you focus on a sought-after area of expertise. Try to sell what you're good at. Find your most valuable skill and try to cash in on it as best you can. Or try to find a valuable skill and master it. It may not work out, but you surely know other things too, and this is why little bets exist – so that failures don't have to hurt too much. The risk is small, the potential is big, and the start is very simple if you don't complicate it much.

But right from the start, watch over the formalities and the tax liabilities from your side jobs properly. In some countries, even a relatively small income can require a license for self-employed status, so I advise caution in advance. Informing yourself ahead of time on the possibilities is good, but talking to an expert is better. An experienced accountant or tax advisor will definitely suggest several easy solutions for your specific situation.

I'm also saying this because beginners with no business background can really be put off when they browse websites on taxes. These (unintentionally) strengthen the prejudice that business is all paperwork, accounting, and tax filings, but this is simply not true. Beginning freelancers, especially, spend only a fraction of their time on this. With a good application and an accountant behind you, it will be neither a barrier nor an exceptional cost.

HOW CAN YOU TELL THAT YOUR BET PAID OFF?

Easily: *You got paid. You got positive feedback. You've got a good feeling and the urge to continue.* A follow-up order is also a confirmation and a good indicator you are going in the right direction. Clients want to keep working with you, and it's clear there is an interest in your product or service.

By the way: I rarely launch a new service until I feel constant demand for its introduction or see a gaping hole in the market. For me, signals that a real long-term demand exists are an impulse to devote myself to the problem in more detail and think about the new things I could bring to it. It doesn't necessarily have to be something people are asking for. It's enough when it all fits together – which I can usually tell after, indeed, several little bets.

No matter whether the business is at its very start or in a very advanced phase, we always have countless possibilities for which way to go next. Some entrepreneurs may have the gift of unfailing foresight, but the rest of us have to walk our way to success by gradually trying what works and what doesn't. In the advanced phases of our businesses, we are often restricted by the need for continuity and consistency – for our new projects to fit into our existing ones reasonably. A beginner has the advantage of not needing to worry about this. They have more freedom to experiment than an established entrepreneur does.

You may be saying to yourself: where will I find the time for side jobs and maybe starting a business on top of everything I'm already doing? In the same place I found it when I was writing this book. Open your calendar or daily planner and start thinking, playing with your schedule and crossing things out.

You probably have to go to work or school, exercise, and spend time with loved ones. But you can cut back on games, TV, and social media. Put your TV or console in the basement for half a year, and get started! I'm not saying you have to do it forever. That is what little bets are for: you spend a certain bit of time on them and see what you can do.

J. K. Rowling once got this question from a fan on Twitter: "How did you find time to write with young kids? I have a one year old." And her answer? "I gave up housework. It wasn't much of a sacrifice, to be honest." That's a perfect description of the mindset of someone who has decided to temporarily reorganize their priorities to create room for a side job they believe in. And what a side job Harry Potter was!

⬗ LEARN TO BE ECONOMICAL

Advising you to tighten your belt and make time during your studies or a regular job may sound cliche. But doing this forces you to be economical with your time right from the start and to optimize your income per hour to earn a living.

The same goes for money. Turning even a small revenue into a profit is an art that an entrepreneur has to learn. And it's much safer to learn it on small sums than to immediately come into large amounts of money, whether from debts, investors, or family savings. Freelancers who survive tough beginnings where they have to count every penny get an important life lesson – one that isn't by any means just for freelancers. A capable entrepreneur knows how to make money even in tough times.

Being economical is a valuable skill that you can't find just anywhere. People who are lucky in business from the start or who work in a stably growing field rarely have it. I often get a chance to look at their finances; they have huge incomes on the one hand, but huge spending on the other. As if they never thought of how things might one day go wrong.

This beginning period where you are struggling for each hour of paid work and are glad for even the smallest earnings represents a stage of evolution where we as entrepreneurs learn to make do with little. We then remember this experience and all its related skills, which we can apply in the future when we are optimizing and saving much larger amounts.

An entrepreneur who has survived such a period with a few memorable scratches is aware that profit isn't primarily there for buying luxuries. They create profits as a defense against future problems, poverty, risks…in short, for worse times. They create them for further investments in the future. They create them to secure their family's well-being.

The first two or three years are like a child's early development, in that this is precisely where the foundation for your business identity comes from. You then carry those first lessons around with you for the rest of your business life.

In a 2005 television interview hosted by Marek Eben, Bill Gates answered the question of whether, when he walks into a store, he ever thinks: "That's expensive." – "Definitely," he replied without hesitation. "Your idea of what's reasonable and what you're willing to pay for is shaped when you're young. When you're young, you always have a certain budget, and you want to spend your money reasonably, and that stays in your head your whole life. When I was young, I had limited funds." (abridged)

⊙ WORKING FOR FREE: NEVER FORGET YOU'RE THE BOSS

Working for free for your family, friends, or acquaintances is a relatively frequent way of entering into freelancing, but I have to admit I'm not a big fan. It's abused all too often, especially against unassertive people and soft negotiators, which is sadly most of us.

Having a purchasing price of zero leads to the wasteful use of the fruits of such labor, and can even make a client unwilling to give the professional the fair feedback that they would otherwise give them as a satisfied, or even unsatisfied, customer. If someone doesn't want to lose a willing slave, they will have a vested interest in manipulating them – as a result they will even praise a substandard output just to stay in good standing, or belittle something done well to keep the still developing professional from growing wings and flying off onto the free market.

There are even whole fields that have seen terrible price deformation from work for free and for peanuts. This often applies to creative professions like writing, photography and graphic design. The @forexposure_txt account on Twitter documents the sheer arrogance of some such free-work offers, and I recommend taking a look.

Some might object that this is just the free market, supply and demand, in short both sides' exercising their free will. This is surely true, but then you have to be all the more careful when you are entering into such a market and free work is not something unfamiliar to you. My main recommendation, then, is:

❚ Be a boss.

The other party you are working for here isn't your client, but the recipient of your charity, no matter how many times they state that they will pay you in experience gained, exposure, a web link, undying fame, who knows… If the service in return isn't truly major, then it's still through your charity and not theirs that the work is taking place at all. This leads to two principles:

1. *Dictate your conditions and set your boundaries.* If these are your first jobs, then only keep them until you have gained the desired experience, skills, references, or contacts.

2. *Be choosy about who and what your work supports.* For clients who do business for profit alone, this doesn't make much sense, while for non-profits and projects that are just starting up, it usually does.

If you stick to these recommendations, working for free will probably bring you more joy than headaches. But there will definitely still be moments of ingratitude; prepare yourself. Working for free is safe territory for rational givers, but a minefield for anyone who trusts blindly and gives themselves away to scoundrels.

Even work for free represents a side job or a little bet on starting a business. With one basic difference: where there is no income, the paperwork falls away, as does the need to legalize your income. For many people, the experience from the course of such an "order" and the possibility to help someone has more value than the relatively small income they would get – especially after taxes and the costs to file them.

But your reward can also be payment-in-kind. So, what would you do for a coffee?

⊛ FROM ZERO TO ONE

Back when he was still an employee at an international IT firm, Daniel Gamrot started developing an intense interest in work efficiency and topics related to it. That led him all the way to organizing a personal productivity course *for coffee*.

"It felt wrong to offer it totally free. My first sessions mostly took place in a cafe somewhere, and I like coffee, so it was a clear choice," is Dan's explanation of how he hit on this original proposition. "Also I'm an introvert, and the thought of saying something to a large group some-where made me break out in a sweat. Talking to a few people in a cafe was a much better start."

Dan's caffeine parties received huge acclaim thanks to his precise preparation, and his star rose rapidly. He soon started giving courses in other cities (now it was "for a ticket and coffee"), and of course this was on top of his work. He got up every morning at five to get in a few hours of labor on his own courses and projects before heading to his full-time job.

When he started getting his first requests for giving lectures at compa-nies, he raised his prices and started taking days off of work, which he then made up on the evenings and weekends. And he only went full-time and broke away once uniting his self-employment with his employment truly became unbearable.

Today, Dan is considered by his peers to be among the very best, and his income reflects that. He has a clearly defined core business as a "personal productivity trainer," he's a certified Evernote consultant, and he publishes and gives lectures. (He seems to have overcome his shyness.) How long did it take him from his first course to this point? Less than four years, filled with hard work.

Dan's story illustrates well how it can make sense to work for free, and why some professionals choose precisely this road as the most viable. But I would also stress Dan's reliability and honesty, diligence, persistence, and willingness to work particularly hard for a period of time.

His story also illustrates how work for free can paradoxically help to set an optimal price based on growing demand. Dan started out from zero, and his current prices as a top expert in the field are nothing other than a result of his constantly growing expertise, good name, and demand. That helps him to set his prices correctly from the bottom to the top so that it reflects all circumstances.

❯ THE MONOGAMOUS PROFESSIONAL

The well-walked paths to freelancing also include contracting work for a single large client. And actually, I myself started out this way.

From my own experience I know that the contractor's dependence on the client can in some respects look like employment, and precisely due to this, it tends to be attacked as misclassification. If your contracting work is wrapped up in long-term projects as self-employment too, then I definitely recommend checking your work setup with a lawyer or tax advisor. They will either help you to comply with what is needed for a legitimate business, or advise you to take on an employment contract for any truly long project.

In any case, this way of starting out has its pros and cons. One doubtless advantage is the certainty of regular income and the temporary suppression of the need to develop your business as such. This route typically means work tied to some sort of long-term project. The contractor works for months without large swings and can devote themselves to paid work fully and grow all the more quickly as a professional. They bill most of their working hours to the client, and truly only a small amount of energy goes towards managing their business. Sometimes the advantage is also the possibility to choose when and where to work. And if their agreement doesn't include exclusivity, then the independent contractor can also have multiple clients and do small gigs on the side.

The disadvantage, meanwhile, is the dependence on one main source of income, which leads to a much weaker position in price negotiations. The other party at the very least suspects that you don't have much room to develop other business opportunities, and can put more pressure on the price. The optimal counter-strategy in such a case is to be irreplaceable, or rather so good that they can't find a replacement easily. In other words, to work on yourself.

The logical disadvantage for such a freelancer is the weaker social and legal protection they have compared to employees. Under the law, an independent contractor is a person doing business, with all the obligations and disadvantages that it brings. So an illness or vacation means unpaid leave.

These close relationships with just one firm or client can sometimes work for even several years if they satisfy both sides and leave room for further development. But other times, contractors can soon get the feeling that the tight bond is choking them. They themselves seek a road to breaking free of this commitment and gradually supplement their sole job with other income.

Unlike employees, a contractor is independent under the law, and if they're not under some extremely strict contract, they genuinely have a great deal of freedom to work and do business as they see fit, and the client has to respect that. It mainly bothers those that see the independent contractor as an outsourced employee, but that in itself is a bad sign – not to mention that it can also be a problem for the authorities.

If your cooperation with one large client is set up in a reasonable way and leaves you room to take other gigs, then it can be a safe runway for taking off. For that matter, taking a bird's-eye view of the common roads to freelancing I have mentioned, most of them let you focus first on building your expertise, which is the most important part in your mix of skills, while you gradually develop your feel for doing business.

For both contractors and dissatisfied employees, it's better to have your full departure into freelancing prepared and thought through, because that way you minimize the risks and don't see such a drastic drop in income. If the transition is as smooth and well-considered as it was for Dan Gamrot, the short-term drop in income can soon be filled in with rapid growth thanks to the better prices for your time that was previously tied up in employment.

Some freelancing professionals love to alternate between freelancing and employment, or some temporary work in different parts of the world to gain experience. This makes their career a combination of freelancing and employment stages. If they stay in the field, it definitely won't harm their reputation; it will just make it more difficult to offer some kind of continuing support to their long-term clients.

❯ THE DESIGNER OF YOUR OWN CAREER

Let's move on now from the absolute beginning, where you are trying to find and define your area of expertise, into the phase where you already know all that. Now we can start talking about your *career strategy*, which in freelancing is an extension of your business plan and says how you want to develop long-term as a professional. Strong careers grow in small steps, and there is a lot of work and hard thinking behind them. The fact that a professional doesn't have a crystal-clear vision five years in advance, but instead tries various approaches, planting a seed of possible future success here and there, is again a form of little bets – slow and gradual improvement.

In the chapter about a good name, I argued against repeated changes of profession, and here I'll add one more reason why it's not a good idea. I simply don't believe in miraculous mile-long steps forward, or that teleporting like this will land a professional where they want. Yes, they might land in a million-dollar mansion, but they will much more likely land in a deserted wasteland or an overcrowded suburb.

I'm skeptical about dramatic changes of professions, because I've seen very few done successfully, and too many where people missed the mark and spent loads of energy going there and back. And it's no wonder. Teleporting is expensive. If navigating the market is difficult for a professional who has been at it for twenty years and can better read its trends and foresee the consequences of their actions, what is the likelihood a newcomer will get it right on the first try?

I recommend that you watch your career growth so you don't end up *having* to take mile-long steps to be where you should have been years before. The market is constantly advancing under your feet, and perceiving this tectonic motion is a part of your career strategy. You don't have to change professions. But you should grow over time and learn new valuable skills in order to stay ahead of the curve in your field.

I once had a client who ran a desktop publishing studio. He started out in the 1990s and he was doing great. But then the home printing boom came. Even though he modernized his equipment and was doing better work thanks to his experience, his profits dropped year after year. He was simply improving on something that was already falling out of favor, resisting the market's call to alter his rather narrow specialization and grow his expertise in new directions. By the time he reached out to me, he was already almost broke.

This is precisely what happens when the market shifts under your feet. If you aren't moving with it, in a few years you may be standing not in its profitable center, but at its rather icy edge. The fact that you are still doing the same thing, and maybe doing it better, guarantees nothing here. If demand and customer preferences have moved on, it's a huge mistake to ignore that and to keep running your business as usual.

⊗ GROW YOUR SKILLS, NOT YOUR EGO

Cal Newport uses the phrase *little bets* quite a lot in the best recent book on career strategies, *So Good They Can't Ignore You*, with the fitting subtitle *Why Skills Trump Passion in the Quest for Work You Love*. It's aimed at all professionals, no matter how long they have been at it.

The key idea in Newport's book is that the popular imperative *Do what you love* is a bad career strategy, because the market wants true skills, not our enthusiasm. You can be an enthusiastic dancer or opera singer, for example, but if you don't have talent and years of toil with a skilled teacher behind you, you will hardly get very far.

Newport stresses that the *Do what you love* strategy is also very problematic because too many people love the same things, such as art, entertainment, food, travel, etc. And that is a problem, because to succeed on the market, doing what everybody else is doing is not terribly strategic.

He recommends an opposite, a rather counterintuitive approach – develop demanding, valuable skills and make use of the feedback loop that often makes us fall in love with the things that we do exceptionally well. He also adds many great tips on how to identify promising skills that you can perhaps expect to fall in love with, and which activities, on the other hand, to avoid (for example, an endless routine is unlikely to be fun). He also advises on how to apply support strategies so things work long-term, how to strengthen your autonomy and independence, whether at work or when freelancing, and gradually maximize and make the best use of your potential.

Valuable expertise supported with relevant skills, experience, and in some cases educational background is what is really decisive for clients. They don't hire a professional for their enthusiasm and smile, but for what they can really do. Eagerness and a cheery disposition are nice, but only if your work is high-quality and done well. And really, an enthusiastic handyman who chops up half your house and causes more problems than they solve is more likely looking to get killed than praised.

So building valuable and valued skills is an important part of independent professionals' career strategies. Although your core business leans heavily on your main area of expertise, you have enormous room to develop further over time towards activities that are in higher-demand and better-paid.

Field training can have a major influence on your future income, especially in professions that are regulated and require licensing, as The Economist points out in its article *Occupational licensing blunts competition and boosts inequality*. Those that stay unlicensed, earn considerably less than their more-qualified colleagues or never make it past a certain income threshold at all.

The tempo you choose is up to you, and it's definitely not about opportunistically trying to jump on passing trends. No. A true professional watches the market, thinks things over for a long time, and then, sometimes, takes action.

Dozens of business plans reach me for review each year, and few of them map the market – what are the prices, what is being sold, what is in decline, where is the market going, what are the trends like elsewhere in the world, and what is the competition offering. Often the reason is enthusiasm, the love of one's own ideas, and an unwillingness to confront them with the market reality. But it truly is essential to do that.

Improve your command of high-demand skills and add new ones that will help your career. Top freelancers are constantly learning, and that is more than a phrase. They read, take courses online and in person, go to conferences, use mentors or consultants…in short, they push to evolve nonstop. Because they have confirmed for themselves that developing and learning new skills has a positive effect on their satisfaction, independence, and income.

And in the end, skills always need to be kept up through use. So it's not about having as many skills as possible, but about developing the ones you use the most often in practice, the drivers of your income. This is why I sometimes sacrifice a half-hour of my time just to write up a killer eBay offer. Copywriting needs training.

When you set up the foundations and a decently conceived mid-term strategy for your skill development, this makes room for the long-term strategies that we'll refine through this chapter and the second part of the book. Take it all as a couple of selected tips on what you can focus on in the future.

❯ DON'T SETTLE FOR A SHADOW CAREER

Cultivation of high-demand skills doesn't mean that a professional should only use reason to steer their career towards well-paid work, while suppressing their desires completely. A good career strategy integrates these two domains into a harmonic whole, so neither your soul nor your wallet suffers.

An approach of pure reason that ignores deeper ambitions and dreams is ultimately just as risky as rushing excitedly ahead. We are complex beings. We have our dreams, desires, and ambitions. So we should at least listen to them and seek to unite our rational and emotional interests.

Just as Cal Newport warns against expertise-free career amateurism in his *So Good They Can't Ignore You*, you should also watch out for the other extreme, i.e. suppressing the feeling that in the long-term you aren't doing what you want to and *should* be doing.

Turning Pro, Steven Pressfield's wonderful book on professionalism, offers an explanation. Our fear of leaping into the unknown, into bold projects, can trap us in a *shadow career*, where a person may be successful, but not fulfilled and happy:

"Sometimes, when we're terrified of embracing our true calling, we'll pursue a shadow calling instead. That shadow career is a metaphor for our real career. Its shape is similar, its contours feel tantalizingly the same. But a shadow career entails no real risk. Are you getting your PhD. in Elizabethan Studies because you're afraid to write the tragedies and comedies that you know you have inside you? Are you working in a support capacity for an innovator because you're afraid to risk becoming an innovator yourself? If you're dissatisfied with your current life, ask yourself what your current life is a metaphor for. That metaphor will point you toward your true calling." (abridged)

Working in a shadow career means to keep on working at something that remotely *reminds* you of suppressed desires and dreams, but doesn't fulfill you in any way. In short, you have simply settled for something small and gave up before being confronted with the first big challenge or barrier. And since a person can easily get used to this situation, it can become chronic.

We all know well what unfulfilling and joyless work does to a person. They either seek fulfillment elsewhere, in hobbies, family or friends, or they ride on towards frustration and burnout without being aware of where the problem lies. That then leads to a sudden awakening where twenty years later, the person remembers what they really wanted to do, and suddenly wants to make up for the lost time.

Pressfield hasn't just named the problem; he also offers a solution. It's in the very name of his book, *Turning Pro* – that is, becoming a professional. In Pressfield's formulation, professionalism means focusing your whole self on your set goal, never letting up, and working without fear.

His recommendation on *avoiding a shadow career* is meant to prevent one from being stuck in a comfortable state of limbo just because the road ahead isn't clear. This is especially true when you suspect inside that you should be *doing something* – not in haste, but by using a tactical approach towards your goal, step by step.

⟩ THE VALUE OF FINDING A PROFESSIONAL CALLING

A professional calling is an extra something a professional does – out of their conviction, for colleagues, for the field, or for the public. It's a calling they have taken on as their own, or set them on a warpath to change the world. A professional calling is the victory arch rising above the transactional level of day-to-day gigs, where you will likely spend most of your time, but which are visible to few.

And I would like to convince you that having a calling is neither crazy nor worthless, and can be a key pillar of your career strategy.

Neil deGrasse Tyson has devoted his professional life to raising science awareness and popularizing astronomy. Sheryl Sandberg, as a successful top manager, fights for the need to support and empower women. Joel Greenblatt, as an experienced investor, has written three books on investment for ordinary people. Richard Dawkins was constantly confronted with creationism as an evolutionary biologist, and so he set off to openly criticize religious fundamentalism. As an illusionist, James Randi was fed up with people trying to pass off stage tricks as supernatural powers, so he started revealing their lies in his One Million Dollar Paranormal Challenge. Sara Horowitz founded the Freelancers Union to support freelancers' development and cooperation. While doing business in Russia, Bill Browder experienced persecution and the murder of a close business partner, and his fight against Putin (described in his great *Red Notice*) directly led to US financial and visa sanctions on the Russian actors behind such human-rights violations.

If you know any of these professionals, then it's most likely precisely thanks to their calling – something they decided to do has influenced or touched many people, including you. So there is a difference between cooperating with a hundred people on ordinary jobs and breaking out of this tight shell to do something that can help everyone.

My professional calling is to help independent professionals. Has it changed my life and my career? Absolutely. To its very foundations. And meanwhile, in the past many people hinted that I was out of my mind and an idealist for doing this. That I should only care about my family and money. Both of these are important for me, but I don't see any conflict here. On the contrary, my calling has become a part of my identity, helps me find motivation, and has fulfilled my ambition of doing something big for other people.

A calling has great importance, on two levels:

Outward facing, it's an understandable, repeating theme. People can't see the work you do for clients, but if you do something more, above and beyond that, that is visible from afar. Your professional calling is usually connected with a story, and people (and the media) generally want stories more than anything else.

So a reasonable professional calling plays a significant part in publicly profiling a professional, and strongly boosts the reach of their good name. It becomes a part of their life story. It helps other people to place you and approach you with relevant work and offers.

Inward facing, meanwhile, a calling like this prevents burnout. It's a topic you can come back to often when you are tired of your routine and of projects that feel like clones. You have multiple positions you can switch among freely.

But there is a catch: Nobody can point you towards your professional calling. Not even ten mentors and dozens of insightful books. It's a mystery how some people hit on one, and others don't. Most professionals grow into one gradually, often unconsciously; it's not a cold calculation – which, after all, people would quickly see. It's better to let things flow freely. A calling comes from inside and is tied to your character. Still, your feeling of good intentions or results will mainly grow with feedback from other people.

Sometimes an open-ended job is what clarifies a professional calling. These are personal or work-related projects of an experimental nature through which you expand your scope or stretch your boundaries.

Naturally you can do fine work that stays fulfilling even without a calling. It's definitely not a condition for satisfaction, success, or a good name. But still, it's something that can have by far the greatest impact and reach of anything you do as a professional.

In his remarkable book on positive psychology *Authentic Happiness*, Martin Seligman mentions three approaches to work separated by their level of personal engagement: 1. a *job* as a necessary evil for making a living; 2. a *career* as a one-sided approach to work with the goal of moving up and increasing one's salary and competency, and 3. a *calling*, work as an affair of the heart, enjoyment, a path towards self-actualization and fulfillment.

Bob Dylan described it similarly in an interview for Rolling Stone, where he answered the question of how he would describe his calling: "Mine? Not any different than anybody else's. Some people are called to be a good sailor. Some people have a calling to be a good tiller of the land. Some people are called to be a good friend. You have to be the best at whatever you are called at. Whatever you do. You ought to be the best at it – highly skilled. It's about confidence, not arrogance. You have to know that you're the best whether anybody else tells you that or not. And that you'll be around, in one way or another, longer than anybody else."

DON'T AVOID CONSULTING

Senior professionals' activities involve consulting quite often. My goal here isn't to describe it from A to Z, but I'd like to explain how it fits into the career strategies of freelancers who don't primarily work as consultants, and how consulting can be integrated into what you do in freelancing. It's not a topic for outright beginners, but I recommend you take note of it.

As a professional gains experience, raises prices, and builds their good name, they also tend to work for a few important clients. With a reasonably-built client portfolio, this is the road of many senior professionals, and also a logical result of price growth – over time, a professional finds a few clients who have no problem paying more for better services.

However, a narrowed clientele can have the side effect of making you repeatedly deal with the same problems. Some freelancers even become experts on a single client! Variety disappears, and with it, the fun. And you might also get stuck in place and lose touch with developments in your field. There are several ways to avoid this: lecturing, educating and being active in the professional community, or indeed, professional consulting.

Consulting is great for its relatively small time demands: even extremely busy professionals who would have trouble fitting in large orders can do consulting. A one-time consultation doesn't obligate you to keep on consulting in the future. And this independence is symmetrical, because respect-worthy consultants strive to make their clients independent.

In consulting, what is important is expert analysis and providing know-how, best practices, and recommendations on the problems or background materials the client presents. This is why consulting is typically billed by the hour. (For professional consultants, by the man-day as well, although that likely won't apply to you at the start.)

So you will have only a few hours to get to the core of the problem and present solutions, recommendations, criticism, etc. By doing this, you are training your professional judgment and gaining experience at a rate that would be unthinkable in long-term projects.

If you have read or seen any of the adaptations of Sherlock Holmes, you surely remember how, as a consulting detective, he constantly employed his brain on small problems when he wasn't working on some large case. Holmes is a fictional character, but the parallel is real.

People with the expert-plus-consultant combo are in very high demand. They have got one leg anchored in their client projects, so they are consulting on a thing that they do daily. And their other leg deftly handles consultations small and large, which further expands their already rich experience. And if they give good advice, they are going to be recommended as advisors all the more.

I as a consultant myself have, over the years, gone through hundreds of consulting cases, and I guarantee you that you will be learning constantly even if you have a thousand cases behind you. Accumulating consulting experience can't be compared with other growth stimuli, because you are in direct contact with practice in all of its many forms.

And that has other advantages too. Since you pass on the most important parts of your experience, knowledge, contacts, and capabilities during consulting so quickly, your earnings can be multiples of the amounts you make for normal work.

Even though consulting is normally billed by the hour, it's not about the time. If a consultant takes a few hours to pass on know-how that they refined over the years, the value they deliver is information, expertise, and insight. Hourly billing is only a customary method or tool for reasonably monetizing this business transaction. This is why consulting fees are so high sometimes. It's not about a few hours; it's about the years of practice before that.

Consulting prices are further influenced by the fact that the consultant also needs time to think about the assignment. And when I go to walk in the park for two hours to freely think over my clients' problems, that is unpaid time. So the mental capacity you set aside is also reflected in the consulting fee.

What we are touching on here is the very important question of what consulting really is. Professional consulting (with the exception of continuous consulting support) should contain two elements:

1. *The analysis itself,* where you study the assignment and the background materials, ask about various things, measure, do your own research or surveys, and evaluate and explore the overall context.

2. *Conclusions,* and thus clear recommendations, hypotheses, development scenarios, critical reviews or personal meetings – in short, consulting outputs in a form that is appropriate to the assignment and the agreement with the client.

Analysis and the conclusions from it form consulting's two-stroke engine. (This doesn't apply to totally trivial questions with simple answers; every consultant or expert receives loads of these, but I wouldn't even call them consulting.) There are two convincing reasons for analyzing even minor consulting assignments in an appropriate depth and scope:

1. The problem may be badly defined on the client side. The consultant has to make sure that they know the whole context, haven't missed important facts, and have a true, complete picture. Just as your doctor has to ask about seemingly unrelated things, a consultant has to verify circumstances to ensure they have complete, correct information. Many clients come with a certain problem or hypothesis, but soon turn out to have their problems rooted elsewhere. And like a doctor, a consultant shouldn't treat false problems; they should treat the true root cause of the client's troubles.

2. A consultant should consciously switch into a mode where they think and assess the assignment carefully and without cutting corners. Thinking fast leads to easy mistakes, even for leading experts in a given field.

Don't trust people who head out with you for coffee and, without doing any preparation or deeper thinking, they just toss out some advice and bill it to you as consulting. That is highly unprofessional, because it's very easy to overlook something, not think things through, not ask about important facts, and then give harmful advice. And then there are the dozens of biases and cognitive errors typical for fast thinking. As an unpaid consultation, why not, but the asker should know that it doesn't have much in common with consulting.

> A chat over coffee is a chat over coffee and not professional consulting.

I don't want to say through this of course that a consultation can't be somewhere in a cafe or outside in a park at a client's request. This is fine, but a thorough, methodical approach is what is important.

A consultant should also be independent and free of conflicts of interest. In short, they shouldn't recommend solutions from which they have hidden commissions or from which they will otherwise profit. They should inform the client of every possible conflict of interest. Watch out for people who take commissions on what they are recommending to you.

They can't be objective, because financial incentives influence their judgment subconsciously too, even if they're not aware of it.

Another important principle if you ever go into consulting is that you have to know your circle of competence for consulting and not step outside it. Every consultant should know their limits. If the assignment is uncertain, then always make sure in advance that it definitely is within your area of expertise. Don't walk blindly into unclear consulting orders; that would really be stupid.

A consultant who oversteps or over-values their competence is skating on thin ice and can harm their client greatly. So a respectable consultant doesn't push their way into places where they don't belong. When they are outside of their competence, they admit it and are able to recommend a trusted colleague.

Creative consulting outputs are another key topic. There is a difference between a task lying in a critical review of a presented marketing plan and a seemingly similar task whose goal is to create a marketing plan. That can take several times longer.

The larger the creative element, the more demanding and less predictable the time-frame for the work is. So I prefer to recommend to beginning consultants that they first cut their teeth on simpler assignments and reviews.

If the last few paragraphs have made you feel the weight of the responsibility that is connected with offering consultations, then they have hit their mark. But they shouldn't turn you away either. Clients have their own minds, and the final decision and implementation is up to them. As a consultant, you typically aren't responsible for the work of others, but for advising on matters that you truly understand, to the best of your knowledge and conscience, without withholding key facts and conflicts of interest. The client is paying for your expertise and advice, but in the end they have to decide based on their own judgment.

A consultant is actually a sort of hired extra brain working on the client's side, and ideally making their decisions more intelligent. They help the client to factor in a much broader range of circumstances and experience, to overlook fewer mistakes, and to create more smart ideas. A consultant never dictates anything or acts from a position of unquestionable authority. On the contrary, through their approach they should continuously support and educate the client.

Another reason not to be afraid of consulting is that starting can be quite safe. Just wait and be sure you have something to share. Every established professional has their area of expertise defined clearly. If you are really good, then less experienced colleagues may well already be coming to you for advice. This is a good opportunity and a signal things will work.

Feel free to advise them for free at first, but try to give your consulting a more formal form. Reach agreements on the time invested (the scope), and try involving both analysis and a formulation of conclusions in a well-considered document or final meeting into your work. In short, try to keep it real. That way you experience the whole process. And be sure to ask for feedback. There is also the possibility of providing free consulting for non-profit organizations, if you know of any and want to help them.

You can start offering paid consulting once you feel at least somewhat comfortable in this role. Don't be afraid to start with a low price if you don't feel totally confident. That way you indicate you are a junior who still has reserves and yet can already help clients a lot.

You can also offer consulting when your supply of time has run dry, and you can't take a whole order: you can still help the inquirer with preparing the task, recommending other suppliers, approaching or selecting them, etc. Offering consulting is better than just refusing and passing lucrative orders on to less demanded (and thus often less capable) colleagues. Ultimately, many clients will be asking you because of your experience and thus won't be totally against it when a less-experienced colleague handles the routine part of the order after going over it with you.

Things can get more difficult when you are both consulting and working on an assignment, for example consulting on a web project while also being hired as one of its contractors. In cases like these, I would advise you to create more formal boundaries for the consulting part to prevent any misunderstandings and conflicts of interests, while also making it clear to the client how they should work with your outputs. One good solution might be to finish the consulting part first and then leave it up to the client whether they also want you to join as a contractor. After all, they may prefer to keep you on as the consultant who prepared the project in the first place.

You should at least have consulting terms and conditions, perhaps with explicit restrictions and financial limits for your liability, and ask clients to approve their agreement with them. Or if you want to be extra-careful, cooperate with a lawyer to prepare a contract. Consultants need contracts more often than regular clients do. The client personally picks a consultant whom they strongly trust, and so they rarely insist on a strict contract. The consultant, meanwhile, can have such a need if they feel that there are uncertainties and risks that they want to get under control.

Here it depends a lot on the field you are working in and on the options for supplementary insurance, as you may find among accountants and lawyers for example. But don't worry unnecessarily; you are liable towards clients for your work in ordinary orders as well; you just may not be as aware of it. So start out with small consultations in the very center of your professional expertise, where you have 100% certainty. That is where the risk of failure is the lowest.

To wrap up, here are four principles that you should uphold as much as possible as a consultant – a sort of codex: 1. Reliability, 2. Independence, 3. Non-disclosure, 4. Honesty. These should apply for all freelancers, but for consultants they are taken more seriously, because consultants truly know a lot about their clients, and their work acts as a foundation.

Within a career strategy, consulting resembles a fulfilled calling: it can push you ever-forward. Why should everything you have learned over the years be reserved for just the few customers with whom you work frequently? It's beneficial for all of us when you draw from your experience and knowledge via consulting and use them somewhere new.

BUSINESS WITHOUT BORDERS

The globalization of services affects everyone – freelancers too. Today freelancers from throughout Europe are standing on the edge of the European Age, and the EU itself is becoming more and more like the US in its cross-border cooperation. Yet American freelancers, too, are serving a much larger market than before, thanks to progress in communication technologies and tools for working remotely.

When I speak today with European university students, many of them are studying abroad or will seek work there after leaving school. Young developers prioritize work for foreign startups in Silicon Valley or London, and some of them aren't even very interested in work back home. And as digital nomads, we can work practically anywhere.

Everywhere in the world, a professional's geographical reach is increasing, just as it did twenty years ago due to the rise of cell phones and the internet, which made it easier to cooperate remotely within single countries. Today the borders between countries are melting away in a similar fashion, and freelancers are at the cutting edge.

At least consider if entering the international market makes sense and what you can do in this direction: *Learn another foreign language? Try cooperating with a foreign client? Fill out your LinkedIn profile in other languages besides English? Put up your portfolio on Behance or Dribbble? Sell photos on microstock websites? Register on Upwork, Freelancer.com, ProZ or other job markets? Become a cross-border contractor for a year or two? Bet on a simple app like Airbnb and start housing visitors from around the world?*

These simple strategies often work better than sophisticated plans for conquering world markets. The in-depth interviews that I've had with globally active professionals have clearly shown me that direct, uncomplicated approaches work best (for now). And that success here has the same needs as it does at home: quality, expertise, a good name, and contacts.

I myself have worked abroad long enough to appreciate what it means for a professional. You significantly expand your professional horizons and your future possibilities. It's not just about money; it's about shifting your business to the international level and towards the clients that are active upon it. The global market offers many times more opportunities than any local economy, even the American and European ones. So expanding your scope makes sense.

If you are creating your business and career plan today, and your business doesn't *have* to be local, then international cooperation should definitely not be dismissed. It's just a plan, we are talking about options and possibilities, not certainties. And if you have a plan open to the world, then in your local freelancing community you will almost certainly meet professionals who have this road behind them and will gladly advise or show you the way.

At the start I recommend that you focus on countries that you are culturally close to and where you understand the language and mentality. Try first to get a test assignment. Your beginning period isn't about money, but about gaining experience. You are getting used to a different work style and different demands. It will be tough, but it's in all probability the future of freelancing. Restraining yourself within the local market will be less and less advantageous, a bit like as if you only worked for clients in and around your city today. That makes sense for barbers, but much less so for graphic designers.

❯ MEET YOUR LUCK HALFWAY

Some people believe in luck, others in fate, but this isn't important. The fact is that unpredictable events of huge importance play a fundamental role in life and in business. Nassim Nicholas Taleb writes about this in his book *The Black Swan*, and among its lines, he also mentions a number of ways to meet luck halfway.

He argues that even though luck is unpredictable, that doesn't mean you can't work on it. He claims that what is important is to be aware of what kind of world we and our business are *really* living in and to adapt our strategies to that end. He wants you to "not be a turkey," to not be rocked to sleep by the seeming certainty that you've got things taken care of, so that you don't wake up one day as the main course at Christmas dinner. So: how can we as entrepreneurs reflect these random influences?

We can suppress the negative influences or bad luck (or risks) via risk prevention and strengthening the core of our business. The better your business runs, the more coherent and stable it is, the easier it will withstand future tremors. In the long term they are unavoidable even if you don't know where they will be coming from.

As for good luck, on the other hand, you can lure it into your life, for example through increased exposure to interesting ideas – reading more and meeting more people who hold unconventional interests, who travel, or who are otherwise inspirational for you. In their company you come across strong stimulating ideas more often.

Steven Johnson develops this idea in his book *Where Good Ideas Come From*, and he points out that key innovations have more frequently appeared in the cities, where different cultural and social influences are layered one over the other. In contrast with our romantic conceptions of isolated ingenious inventors, isolation is poorly suited to serendipity and innovation.

The first thing that we as freelancers can definitely do is to limit our risks and increase our exposure to happy accidents. But this alone is not enough. When an opportunity arrives, we have to be capable of picking it up and holding it in our free (and hard-working) hands, or otherwise it will fail to develop, die, or directly run through our fingers and perhaps be grabbed by someone else.

To care for an opportunity in this way, we have to be independent and have some kind of reasonable time and capacity reserve. A professional who is stuck from dawn to dusk in administrative tasks and for whom countless commitments have cut their freedom of choice down to which shirt to wear to a meeting, will be passed by one opportunity after another at the speed of a bullet train.

People tend to underestimate the role of independence, because we don't know its true value until we put its potential to work. Is it worth thousands? Hundreds of thousands? Millions? Nobody knows, and so it's no wonder that many people prioritize a full workload, sure money, and long-term orders that they perceive as a foundation for security. But unfortunately by doing this they are robbing themselves of one of the most valuable things that freelancing can give us, and this is precisely the freedom to make fundamental day-to-day decisions.

Freedom is also tied to income. If income is low and costs are high, a freelancer has to work constantly even when they don't want to. Every promise, every contract, every debt, every partnership is an obligation, and these, as you know, restrict freedom. But that is fine; we do have to meet our obligations. It's mainly about not selling off all of our independence, so that we still have some left.

In practical terms it means *to reduce your intake of commitments* – to realize for every commitment that it exists at all, and why. Is it necessary? Is there a sound reason for it? And is such a commitment being fairly rewarded? If I give a client exclusivity, saying I won't work for competitors in the field for five years, won't it ultimately cost me more than what I'm getting out of it now? Am I not, as a contractor, tied too much to one place, one project? And when I guarantee fixed prices, am I not losing the freedom to adjust them in case of growing inflation, demand, or my skills?

The fundamental importance of independence in business is an entirely overlooked topic. No wonder, so many professionals have rather unlimited tolerance toward their thickening web of liabilities, commitments and dependence in general, such as:

Hastily made promises and contractual guarantees. Debts that are payable long-term that create a strong dependence on the debtors. Close partnerships or contract-bound cooperation in an association. Poorly thought out outsourcing of core business. Unclear ownership of projects, domains, etc. Accepting subsidies that bring conditions and obligations. Reciprocal services and barter. Promise of future payment-in-kind where you don't know yet what that repayment will be. Excessive links between work and private life.

And this isn't a complete list by far (for instance, loans are missing). It's only here to illustrate how independence quietly suffers even within relationships that are generally viewed as beneficial. Meanwhile most of them can also be set up so as to not strengthen dependence; you just have to focus on that.

For me personally, to reduce and control my intake of commitments means admitting the exceptional value of my time reserves and the freedom to act without having to beg for permission or yield to anyone.

So when I'm thinking about my own career strategy, independence always comes first. My business has experienced so many turns of good fortune by now that on the one hand I'm cautious and pay attention to careful risk prevention, but on the other hand I'm also deliberately open to happy accidents – I read books, take an interest in the world, meet with great people, and keep the independence and time reserve I need for things that might come and that definitely won't come twice.

KEY IDEAS

1. For freelancers, business plans are informal. They are more of a career or professional plan.

2. The foremost importance of a plan is to clarify your declared expertise and the core of your business.

3. Clarifying your expertise protects you from splitting your attention and investment.

4. A reasonable two-field focus isn't a problem, but few will persist in doing so. The market likes specialists.

5. When starting off, a strategy of little bets is best. Working for free, on the other hand, can drain you.

6. A freelancer's career strategy is founded on acquiring and cultivating professional skills.

7. In addition to building your reputation, having a professional calling is among the major strategies.

8. If your head is full of knowledge and experience, consider offering paid consultations.

9. One rising trend among freelancers across all global borders is to cross those borders.

10. Take care of your independence by reducing the intake of commitments and increasing your exposure to happy accidents.

PRACTICE

✓ If you are just starting out, prioritize side jobs as the safest way to try freelancing for real without actually having to commit yourself to a career that you still know little about.

✓ Set a long-term schedule to map new developments and trends in your field and market. Plan for acquiring new valuable skills, but make sure to satisfy your emotional needs as well.

✓ When consulting or giving any serious professional advice, try to employ slow, analytical and critical thinking to prevent biases and reckless short-cuts. And respect your limits.

✓ Consider getting one new foreign client as a goal for the next year. Try at least three ways of finding one – e.g. approach a foreign agency, ask peers, or register on Upwork.

✓ Try to estimate your real independence, i.e. how free are you to do what you want on a daily basis. If it is low, reduce your unnecessary commitments to restore your freedom.

3 / Know-how

PERSONAL PRODUCTIVITY

How can you do it all on time and with no headaches?

If *success* is the most popular word in motivational literature, in the related genre of managerial reading, it's likely *productivity*.

It's vital for us freelancers as well, for three main reasons.

The first is money. More productive professionals can have incomes many times higher than those who don't know how to manage their time and performance. The second reason is reliability, which comes from better self-management. And the third is your own sense of satisfaction and to have more time for relaxation or your family, because a balanced system of personal productivity should take these into consideration as well.

NO SYSTEM TO RULE THEM ALL

But first the bad news: *There is no quick and simple solution.*

Freelancing takes on so many forms that it's unthinkable for one personal productivity method to work for everyone. Even worse is that every guru promotes and advises something different. Their methods sometimes contradict each other, and even the best systems only work for certain things. Every job is different. A craftsman has to manage their time differently from a programmer, who needs to fully concentrate and is totally exhausted after five or six hours, and differently from a project manager, who is constantly switching contexts and flexibly reacting to their team's needs.

The problem is that as freelancers, we are sometimes all of these at once. We are the boss, the expert, and the handyman, all in one. Thus the freelancers with the best productivity are generally those who have developed *their own system* out of the fragments they have found, studied, or observed elsewhere.

So the correct solution is your own palette of approaches, tools, and strategies that you have picked up and adapted to your current needs. You need a bag of tricks and on top of that three aces up each sleeve to handle every situation without losing control. And that won't be easy, because an exceptionally clever and resourceful enemy stands against you.

⊚ INTERNAL RESISTANCE

If I had to name the one book that helped me the most with personal productivity, it would be Steven Pressfield's *The War of Art*. Not to say that other authors haven't written interestingly on this as well. But Pressfield, as an artist, introduces a bold new idea on top.

The creative and personal freedom that we gain as freelancers smashes our usual routines. It brings us into an archetypal battle with our own laziness and inability. In the past you may have blamed others when you really didn't want to do something. But business freedom also brings with it the responsibility for results. It's the definitive end to all excuses.

Exceptional work is never a copy of anything that anyone created before you. It's born of steady effort. Countless hours of seeking functional solutions and walking down blind alleys. True sweat. And maybe also the risk that you won't be understood. Such work is defining for a professional, but there is also a great deal of toil and daily effort behind it.

But a long, long process like this is sometimes also unpleasant, painful, and exhausting. It goes against our nature, and at least a part of our being knows that very well. It doesn't want to work hard on things whose end is hidden in the mists of uncertainty and doubts. What also maybe isn't wanted is the loss of the illusions about what we could manage *if...* Well, you can't lose if you don't try.

And here Pressfield delivers an ingenious artistic parallel: that our *lazy me* not only doesn't agree with the decision to do exceptional work, but even tries to cleverly sabotage it. He calls this internal destructive force *Resistance*.

"Resistance cannot be seen, touched, heard, or smelled. But it can be felt. We experience it as an energy field radiating from a work-in-potential. It's a repelling force. It's negative. Its aim is to shove us away, distract us, prevent us from doing our work."

Resistance isn't picky. It works against every creator, no matter what their focus or profession. But it has countless faces and forms, from ordinary procrastination to self-blame or concessions:

"Resistance will tell you anything to keep you from doing your work. It will perjure, fabricate, falsify, seduce, bully, cajole. Resistance is protean. It will assume any form, if that's what it takes to deceive you. It will reason with you like a lawyer or jam a nine-millimeter in your face like a stickup man. Resistance has no conscience. It will pledge anything to get a deal, then double-cross you as soon as your back is turned. If you take Resistance at its word, you deserve everything you get. Resistance is always lying and always full of shit."

No, this is not one of the sunnier books in a successful entrepreneur's library. In some spots it has the strong aftertaste of dense, concentrated truth.

Pressfield observes that creators blame failures on either themselves or various outside causes. They never think to see behind them a single thing – an intelligent, inventive, and determined force fed by their own fear. An internal shadow pulling strings in the background and setting traps. Like the main villain, like Professor Moriarty vs. Sherlock Holmes:

"Resistance is like the Alien or the Terminator or the shark in Jaws. It cannot be reasoned with. It understands nothing but power... Resistance's goal is not to wound or disable. Resistance aims to kill. Its target is the epicenter of our being: our genius, our soul, the unique and priceless gift we were put on earth to give and that no one else has but us."

Resistance as an artistic metaphor is more understandable than dozen of psychological studies that another author might cite without giving you the courage to send off that bastard once and for all. Pressfield's lesson is to see one single enemy behind every expression of Resistance. To become aware that when you make a resolution to do something difficult, you will have to fight an even match against yourself. And what treatment, then, does Pressfield prescribe?

First, distinguish the symptoms in time and act against them immediately. We each have our own, different expressions of Resistance. It may be procrastination, underestimating ourselves, perfectionism, paralyzing fear, hypochondria, states of insecurity and anxiety, seeking out the reasons why it won't work...in short, there are as many forms of Resistance as there are traits in human nature.

The second part of the treatment is even better, because it works even when you misdiagnose. *Discipline.* No matter how you feel, unsure or full of doubts, far from the goal or lost in a labyrinth of dead ends, you have to get back to work, focus on today's goal, and turn up the heat: "I power down. It's three, three-thirty. The office is closed. How many pages have I produced? I don't care. Are they any good? I don't even think about it! All that matters is I've put in my time and hit it with all I've got. All that counts is that, for this day, for this session, I have overcome Resistance," Pressfield writes.

Every day counts, and a professional is dead serious about their work. Unlike the days when they floated aimlessly as a newcomer, now they know their way. And you can do it to.

What is beautiful about *The War of Art* is that even if the reader isn't a writer struggling to finish their first novel, they intuitively get what it's about. Resistance is so natural and common that (with some exceptions) we all have it in common, no matter whether we write, build websites, compose music, or heal people.

Starting out my chapter on personal productivity with Resistance is important: you need to be aware that external circumstances aren't the only thing keeping us from doing challenging and meaningful work.

❯ WHY DO WE DO IT?

At the age of ten I started going to a new school, where the computer room got me excited. I soon had paper notebooks full of my own programs in Basic. Yet my classmates surrounded the computers too, and during the day it was hard to get on to them. But then I learned that we could also visit the room in the morning, before school. Things went so far here that I learned on my own to wake up early and ride out before dawn to wait in front of school. I sat there, freezing, on a low railing until the custodian came to unlock the darkened building, turn on the lights, and let me inside so I could have time to play something or program for an hour or two before class. And that went on day after day for two or three years.

This experience paid off for me many times over later in life, because it showed me that when I really want something, it makes sense to follow a regimen. With the right goal, it's easier to accept professional discipline and take it as a part of the adventure, not as a limitation to your own freedom.

So the question *Why?* and the answer to it directly influence our productivity as such.

In companies, the goal is often to give employees a full workload. Since the company is paying them, it naturally tries to lead them and motivate them to handle as much as they can. Otherwise the employee may be a sunk cost – and so many are.

But in freelancing, productivity oriented towards filling up your working time isn't sensible. You should leave a reserve and independence for any opportunities that come your way by good luck. A work overload drains your reserves, leads you to make frequent mistakes, and increases the risk of burnout, health complications, etc. That is why it's better to set up your approach to productivity so that you work less, but with greater concentration and efficiency.

If you're working nonstop against your wishes, it's usually the result of bad or neglected pricing that results in elevated demand. Raise prices and cut back your offerings to the core business you have already clarified. Working whole days and racing from deadline to deadline for pennies is nonsense. Try to look on the bright side: *There is interest in you.* In the chapter on pricing, I'll talk much more about raising prices, and above all I'll explain how to raise them in a way that supports your growth, not client loss.

So the two starting prerequisites for raising personal productivity are that you should 1. factor in your lack of discipline and the need to overcome inner resistance, and 2. be clear about why you are focusing on personal productivity in the first place and what your goal is.

In an older article, *The Most Important Piece of Career Advice You Probably Never Heard*, Cal Newport advises: "Fix the lifestyle you want. Then work backwards from there."

You don't have to identify with the goal of working less with more productivity, but you should have some kind of idea here, because otherwise it's very easy to fall prey to working inefficiently, or too much. Your answers can then lead to an individual personal productivity system that will suit you fully and correspond to your needs. Let's start with the three main principles that you should lean on in practice.

1. PRIORITIES

No personal productivity system can exist without clearly set priorities. A professional who doesn't have them will either fly randomly from task to task, or just put out fires.

Setting priorities means that you are clear on what is important to do today and this week. But that also means having some clear idea of what awaits you this month, this season, or this year. And all this has to be in harmony with your deeper, permanent priorities, such as your good name, expertise, reliability, ethics, and professional calling. I'll skip this level here, as you already know it by now.

The planning of yearly priorities is the level on which your main developmental changes will happen and where you can plan out a vacation and needed relaxation thoroughly. Yearly goals help in the fight against burnout and loss of motivation, especially if you're working on a certain project for years. They are also ideal for planning development projects that can push you forward. These might be a new service, founding a blog, moving to a better location, increasing your qualifications, etc.

You surely get various ideas on new things you can do, and it's truly beneficial to think these over in depth at least once a year and pick out the very best one as your focus for the upcoming period. Some people do it regularly at the end of the year, others after achieving their previous goal. If you have never done this kind of yearly planning, you might also appreciate the free e-book *YearCompass*, with its cleverly composed checklist to prevent you from forgetting certain things by accident.

The month, quarter or season level, meanwhile, is better planned via your digital calendar. If that calendar can offer you a clear month-level overview and some kind of work with colors, then it's entirely enough for setting even large working blocks and priorities. Meanwhile for setting your priorities in the coming weeks and days, you will generally use either a daily planner or a to-do list.

There are many possibilities, but a good system should let you see your priorities for the next year or two, for the upcoming weeks or months, and for this specific day or week.

When I head out to work, I have to know in advance what my day's primary goal is, rather than only learning it after hunting for tasks in my memory, email, or notes. And I also have to know my deadline for a given task so that I can manage follow-on tasks on time as well.

The more demanding the work you will be doing, the less you can rely on an intuitive sorting of priorities. Under the stress of work, we have a greater tendency to forget or underestimate a given job's scope, and the result is unreliability and a dissatisfied or outright angry customer.

But having a system doesn't mean your life has to be ruled by your daily planner, phone, or some app. You can fully adapt your work with priorities according to your abilities. There are people with an exceptional memory for whom it's enough to go through a list of priorities or tasks for the next day each evening, and then they never forget anything. Others can't even take one step without a daily planner and a to-do list. What matters are the results.

Just watch out that you keep your priorities under control. Always ask yourself if a given task is needed. Many people turn pointless things into tasks that then stress them out. It's often better to handle one-minute tasks immediately, because the organizational energy needed for keeping track of them can be larger than these very tasks. And learn to cross things off as well. Once a week, go through your to-do list and cross off two or three low-priority tasks that you would probably never get to anyway.

There is even a curious personal productivity concept out there that is essentially based on priorities alone. Stephen Covey describes it in his book *First Things First*. It's over 300 pages long, but its main idea can be expressed in one sentence: *The main thing is to keep the main thing the main thing.* Thumbs up to Covey for trying to promote prioritization to being the sole principle in personal productivity. Still, completing important tasks certainly has priority, but unfortunately this linear approach is not always correct. You'll soon see why.

2. BIORHYTHMS

We are people, not machines. We don't deliver constant performance with a set rotation speed. Our performance over time varies dramatically in partially predictable cycles that I'll simplistically call *biorhythms* here. So as not to complicate things, I'll start right away with a few examples:

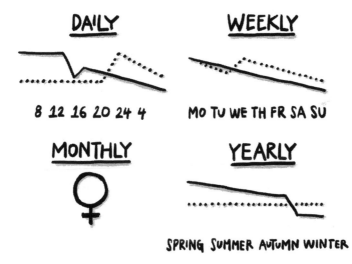

The course of your *daily biorhythm* is very individual. Some people work well throughout the morning, where their productivity is at its maximum for a few hours. Then they go for a quick, but perhaps not easily digestible lunch, followed by a slowdown and then in the afternoon a smaller productivity peak before the arrival of evening fatigue. So in this biorhythm it would make sense to handle priorities right away in the morning and take advantage of how you can handle difficult tasks faster, smarter, and with more creativity and fewer mistakes during your late-morning peak. During your slowdown phase, this work would take longer, and the results might not be as good.

Up to here, Covey's recommendation for starting with your main tasks make sense. But then you have freelancers whose daily biorhythm takes a completely different course. They are night owls. They like to work in the evening, and their performance peaks when the whole world goes quiet. I have quite a few friends who work, or worked, this way. They get up late in the morning. After breakfast (or going straight to lunch) they handle things they have been putting off, reply to emails or maybe even work a little, but they leave their main work for their evening biorhythm peak.

Then you have the early birds, who get up even before dawn, and when other people are just waking up, they already have a major part of their daily tasks completed. Some people say that they like to start working just after waking up, before their brain realizes it's working. You will also find freelancers who like to enjoy a long pause (or siesta) at midday, so they work in the morning and then at night.

The nature of different biorhythms and *chronotypes* is explained in great detail by Daniel Pink in his book *When*. And the remarkable book *Daily Rituals*, subtitled *How Artists Work*, also shows just how many different biorhythms there are. Its author, Mason Currey, describes the ordinary days of history's extraordinary people – artists, writers, scientists, etc. He describes their daily rituals, when and how they worked, how they relaxed, what helped them concentrate – everything that he could find in the available biographical sources. When you read through these dozens of brief bios, you can't help but notice that perhaps the greatest successes came from the creators who worked day after day, often up until late in life, and with surprisingly small swings in their habits and the quality of their work. *Daily Rituals* is thus a sort of biorhythm compendium.

Just about everyone who has ever been a student knows *weekly biorhythms*. On Monday you're still charged up from the weekend, while on Friday you're mostly just waiting for freedom. Nobody says you have to work five days a week from Monday to Friday. Freelancers don't have to and often don't do so. Most freelancers at least sometimes work on the weekends and holidays. And if you don't like working five days in a row, you can, say, take Wednesdays off and have Thursday as a mini-Monday. And what you can't handle in four days, you finish on the weekend. If that feels right for you, then why not?

A *monthly biorhythm* is an exclusively female matter (at least as far as I know), and it's naturally related to the menstrual cycle. Some women take it into account in advance and plan for some extra relaxation, fewer meetings, or a longer reserve for finishing large orders.

We don't all experience a *yearly biorhythm* with equal intensity, but for many people it's just as important as the daily one. Some can't stand the summer heat and fall into a state of lethargy. And some share my yearly chronotype and thus have trouble with the European winter. For many long years, I handled this by delaying all of my difficult work until the spring and beyond. Then one day I had the idea that I could eliminate this winter drop in energy by relocating to somewhere warm, and since then my family and I have been flying each winter to Las Palmas de Gran Canaria, the island of eternal spring, close to the North African coast.

Knowing your optimal daily (or even yearly) biorhythm and integrating it into your own system of work productivity is fundamental for freelancers. If you manage to organize your work so that you face the most important and demanding work tasks during the best part of your day, when you can concentrate fully and nothing can disturb you, then the productivity jump can be truly dramatic – especially compared to the situation where you waste the best hours of the day on meetings, browsing social media, procrastination, emails, distracting phone calls, etc. These delays will leave your toughest work until your slowdown, and by then it's hard to handle. Which is extremely frustrating.

I, for example, can handle demanding work roughly two or three times faster and better during my late-morning peak than at the end of my work day. Not to mention that certain work is so difficult that I wouldn't even be able to do it properly during my slowdown. That is why I reserve my best time for such work while also avoiding any distractions. And if I manage to group my most demanding tasks and priorities into the peak phase of my daily biorhythm, that gives me the extra good feeling that comes from the fact that I control my work and not the other way around.

There are also professions where fatigue prevention is a matter of safety and health. This applies, for example, to professional drivers and construction trades where the risk of an accident rises with fatigue.

The difference in performance between the peak and the slowdown of one's biorhythm is different for everyone. It's related to your age, the work you do, how well you stay in shape both physically and mentally, perhaps how much you have already worked on your biorhythm optimization as such, and more. And you can improve it to the point where your productive peak lasts longer and your downswings are smaller, because you feel better overall. Many strategies exist, yet you will have to learn for yourself what works best for you. But I'll at least mention the most common approaches.

Firstly, you can observe which mode suits you best. A daily biorhythm that peaks during a rested morning state is a cultural custom, but some other pattern may sit better with you. The only way you will hit on it is by testing to see what works best for you and perhaps also for your family, clients, and co-workers. Keep them in mind as well.

When you change your daily regimen, let it settle for a few weeks, and watch how it affects your work. You have to test it on a full sample of daily situations. A new biorhythm generally only reaches its peak after it has been repeated for a while. Your body likes regularity, and you can achieve an ever-better flow via a reasonable amount of discipline.

Stabilizing your optimal biorhythm can even lead you to fixed working hours, which many professionals flee from to freelance. Some of them learn over the years that they do need a fixed regimen, and even create support rituals to help them maintain it. For example, one freelancer described to me how his workday starts with a walk around his house. Another told me that even though she works at home, she wakes up in the morning, sends her children off to school, and then changes her clothes and gets ready as if she were heading off to work. When her children get back from school, she changes her clothes again, and that ends her work for that day.

It's interesting how some people on the other hand don't like regularity and instead try more to work in the blocks where their work energy and attention culminate on their own – right when they are in the *mood* to work. And there is no visible regularity in it; they simply base it on how they feel. This can work well, but there is the risk that, when every workday looks different, it's much harder to plan work long-term and match the peaks with priorities.

Sleep, regimen, and exercise all also enormously influence your biorhythm.

Sleep is a hugely underestimated factor. Getting too little sleep reduces not only your physical and mental performance, but also your immunity, ability to regenerate, accelerates aging, and a number of other health factors, as Matthew Walker describes in *Why We Sleep*. One fact he gives about natural sleep biorhythms is that early birds are about 40% of the population, night owls about 30%, and the remaining 30% have their peak somewhere in-between, with a tendency toward the evening. He also points out that most people have a natural drop in attention early in the afternoon. Walker says that the reasonable foundation is eight hours of quality sleep, and that if you're often tired at work in the afternoon, you should try napping after lunch. And as Daniel Pink suggests, for most people, shorter 10 to 20 minutes naps work best.

Nutrition can influence how long after breakfast the energy for your body and brain holds out, how you feel after lunch and how long it takes you to digest it. There are heavy foods that I would never eat during a normal working day, because it would kill my afternoon. We all know best which foods we like, and which ones make us feel good. So this isn't about eating salads and sipping juice; it's about watching your own metabolism and working out the basics on what foods help you prosper. Healthy eating also affects your overall energy level and well-being.

Alcohol and other drugs naturally have a large influence as well. I personally don't drink liquor at all, and when I'm working on something tough, I skip beer and wine too. Coffee or tea, on the other hand, can be pleasantly stimulating, along with legal smart drugs, whose popularity is growing. Then there is the extreme, shocking for some, of microdosing LSD to increase creativity, which Silicon Valley yuppies are experimenting with, as The Economist describes in *Turn On, Tune In, Drop By the Office*.

Exercise is another important factor affecting our creativity and performance. Exercise as often as possible, especially if you are spending most of your time on a computer. Walks, yoga, fitness training, sports, switching between sitting and standing work…all of that helps you to stay in shape. Everyone who does mental work should know about the close connection between exercise and mental condition. Exercising your brain isn't a contradiction; it's a fact.

In his book *Spark*, the psychiatrist John Ratey sensibly describes the influence of regular intensive exercise on mental health, and exercise as the ideal prevention against restlessness, procrastination, and mood swings. If you prefer a more artistic presentation, then I would also recommend *What I Talk About When I Talk About Running*, by writer Haruki Murakami, about his sports transformation. Equally great is Christopher McDougall's endurance bible *Born to Run* in which he argues, among other things, that our health and running are closely interlinked.

In your work with biorhythms, your first priority should be to realize that you have them and that you can work with them. By experimenting and improving your habits, but also by surrounding yourself with good people to reduce stress and conflicts, you can gradually reach a much calmer course for each day. Then you will know precisely which part of the day is holy and should be reserved for work that you want to, and have to, concentrate on fully.

It's also worth noting that you can produce a fully functional minimalist personal productivity system just by joining carefully planned priorities with an optimized biorhythm. A combination like this is often enough in professions where orders come basically one after another and the business itself isn't especially complex. Then you just need to know how much important work you need to handle on a given day, and have your optimum time reserved for it.

For most freelancers, however, this biorhythms and priorities combo won't be enough, because their work is complex and can include dozens of unrelated activities, not to mention teamwork, communication, or even managing people and whole projects. Here we can't leave out the third principle in personal productivity: the actual productivity toolkit.

3. YOUR TOOLKIT

Sir Walter Scott's medieval *free-lancer* was a mercenary who hired out his abilities to a variety of lords. So he had to be armed for various combat situations, for battles and campaigns both short and long. Similarly the modern freelancer has access to an arsenal of approaches, tricks, and tools enabling them to adapt to any kind of tactical situation.

They choose these tools based on their profession, the type of gigs they do, and purely personal preferences. Some people feel comfortable with heavy two-handed project management with which they can slice the largest of projects into manageable stages. And others, meanwhile, prioritize the knives of a spy: small single-purpose tricks and lifehacks to ease their daily work.

Sadly nobody can tell you for sure in advance what tools are ideal for you. You have to try them out for yourself. So it's great to educate yourself, talk to your colleagues about what works for them, and perhaps also use the services of a personal productivity consultant one time. But the final choice is always up to you. Freelancers' answers in our survey show the large variety in methods and tools as well – the list also includes descriptive examples:

69%	calendars and planners – *these help me organize my work and keep a good overview*
65%	notes – *on my phone, in a notebook, or small paper notes; I don't rely on memory*
55%	a to-do list – *I keep track of what to do and in what context*
38%	first things first – *I prioritize what is truly important*

28%	a healthy lifestyle – *I'm in shape, I eat healthy, and I work in harmony with my biorhythms*
26%	every day counts – *I try to do some kind of important, fundamental work each day*
26%	discipline and regularity – *I know how to work hard and have more or less stable working hours*
24%	a registry of clients – *I keep and actively use a precise registry of my clients*
23%	fighting procrastination – *I have a procrastination issue, and I'm working to solve it*
21%	measuring work time – *I measure and analyze it (Toggl, Pomodoro, a stopwatch, etc.)*
20%	business minimalism – *I know how to chop away everything that is unimportant and get to the core of the matter*
17%	keeping records – *I have an organized archive of documents, ideas, and notes*
16%	mind maps and sketchnotes – *I think visually and these help me be creative*
15%	project management – *I know how to work in a project team and manage projects for both myself and my clients*
13%	workplace ergonomics – *my workplace supports my performance in every way*
11%	a systematic approach – *I have processes / checklists / spreadsheets / procedures / GTD for everything*
5%	a personal assistant – *I make use of regular outside help for cleaning / child care / errands*

I would like to use this and the next two chapters to describe the most useful out of the options mentioned above. Experienced freelancers will try a lot of things over the years, but will generally have settled on using just a couple of tools that suit them best. But the time spent on experimentation isn't wasted. You will come back to certain tools in the situations that directly call for their use.

Let's first go through the simple tricks that you can use right away. Then we will add a few practical aids, as well as a handful of advanced recommendations that do take a bit of time and effort to apply. No list can be complete, and I also don't want to overwhelm you with hundreds of tips. So I have mainly picked out the ones that have proven themselves to freelancers in practice.

EVERY DAY COUNTS

Out of all the simple options, I would like to first stress the principle that *every day counts*. This tells me that every day, I should do something important that visibly moves me forward with a particular job or in my own business. The idea is to not let the day drown in small administrative matters and to reserve time and thoughts for some important step.

Now, administrative tasks *are* important. But a day where you manage to do a visible piece of good work gives you a completely different feeling than one chopped up by errands, minor tasks, and phone calls. No matter how much you check off on your daily to-do list, you can end up feeling you didn't do anything real. And feelings are important.

I even kept my work diary in a Google doc for years. For every entry, I wrote down the date and summarized in a few words the important thing(s) I did on that day.

The advantage of a written diary was that I could then spend 15 minutes a month over tea on a recapitulation. I added a new entry with the month and year instead of the date, and listed just the main things that moved me forward that month.

Even if you document every day like this, it won't take you more than a few minutes per day. Meanwhile the benefit is huge, because you are adding your own check-up level on top of your daily agenda; you can then use it to make sure you are objectively going somewhere. Your Life in Weeks and the similar application Life Calendar have a similar goal. They visualize the number of weeks left in an expected lifetime as a special motivation to spend those remaining weeks wisely.

The present is what is important. Things don't always work out, but this day, what I do today, is what counts. Every big project or success is built on a long series of steps. And instead of blaming myself for yesterday or worrying over what I'll do in a half-year, I focus fully on my step for today. I believe it will give me a solid foundation for my steps to come.

WORK REVIEW

My diary-keeping was a part of my regular daily work review. That is another simple and useful habit you can cultivate: *Spend a few minutes every day going over the work you have done and planning your work to come.*

Some people do their reviews at the end of the workday, others as a part of their morning ritual. The result in any case is that you have ticked off finished tasks and set up priorities for the next day.

You can also include *cleaning out your inboxes* into your daily review – handling unanswered calls and emails, replying to received messages or notifications, organizing your to-do list and so on. But this takes a little more time. So how some freelancers handle this is that during their daily review, they only take care of necessities, and then handle the rest during a weekly review, typically at the end of the work week – they set aside an hour or so to deal with their week's backlog and to schedule the course of the following week.

You can think of these work reviews as a sort of minimum maintenance time that you have to devote to make your personal productivity system run without problems. But it's all up to you what will or won't be a part of it. Again, it's a check-up on your workflow from a higher perspective and a way to make sure your priorities aren't swinging off-course.

⟩ GROUPING TASKS

There is a difference between taking care of minor tasks over the course of a day or a week, and assigning them a sensible block of time based on their degree of urgency. Handling tasks as they pass through your hands fragments your working time and disrupts the compact work blocks that you could otherwise devote to fully focused work.

Multi-tasking, switching contexts between different activities or projects, is very difficult and tiring for the brain, and it worsens your concentration and thinking. Add to that social media, phone calls, and procrastination, and you have easily robbed yourself of a few hours of efficient work. *Per day.* This is why it makes sense to group tasks into compact blocks.

Some tasks such as emails accumulate in one place on their own, and so grouping work on them into one block is fairly simple. But other tasks, like errands or purchases, don't pile up like this, and so to group them, you need to record them somewhere. A calendar isn't a very good fit, because this kind of tracking isn't tied to time. In short you want to write down errands somewhere on the side and handle them when it suits you. A to-do list will help – either a physical one in a notebook, or in an application like Todoist or Google Keep.

The advantage of Todoist and similar applications is that one task (e.g. "buy boxes") can go into both its own corresponding project (e.g. "Moving the Office") and a relevant context (the label "Errands"). Meaning when the time comes, you can open the Errands context in your to-do list and run errands for, say five projects at once.

A perfect candidate for grouping into blocks is also the whole range of administrative tasks: invoicing, payments, correspondence, etc. By merging all this, you can make it quicker and more efficient. This is no small thing. For some professionals this area takes up to a third of their working time, and that makes it worth optimizing. When you get it down to one tenth, you can congratulate yourself.

A less known lifehack related to task grouping is to take your work with you for a long walk. In warmer weather, I do it at least two or three times a week: I prepare some notes and documents in my phone, charge the battery, pack my earphones, and head out for a stroll in a park, or by the ocean. There I read, think, make notes, or take care of three or four long calls at once. Not only am I out in the fresh air enjoying a walk for several hours as a welcome exercise, while also occasionally stopping to grab a coffee, but I also think better and focus more easily on a single group of tasks when I go for a walk.

Sometimes I make use of this habit to first study all the background materials for a project or a gig that I'm working on, and then leave it to my subconscious to generate new ideas during a walk or my leisure time. It works surprisingly well, partly because walking leads me to slower thinking and deeper ideas naturally. Walks also help me to relax and decompress after a long, busy day, making it easier for my brain to process all the residual stress, emotions, thoughts and information, as well as to slow down before the evening.

STEP-BY-STEP MANAGEMENT

Planning without experience is comparable to cooking in your head using ingredients you have never seen and imagining how the final meal will taste.

One good foundation for our own developmental projects and beginning freelancers is *step-by-step management*. It lies in thoroughly applying two simple principles:

1. Don't work on multiple problems in a project at once; put them in order in logical steps.

2. Mainly pay attention to the current step, especially if you can't see far ahead.

In my consulting, I regularly meet freelancers who are paralyzed by the difficulty of the plans or projects that they have set up for themselves. They are working on five tasks at once, which amplifies their uncertainty and only leads them to further postponing things. This type of stuck-in-a-loop thinking is typical for beginners – they think twenty moves ahead, where the precision of their guesses amounts to zero, while they overlook simple steps that could immediately increase their ability to get moving.

It's smarter to set a manageable nearby goal or task that you can realistically imagine and leave the further planning for later. In the case of a business plan, that can mean first heading out for some test work for two months, and only then drawing up plans for your own cafe. For creating your website, it can be an introductory consultation with a web consultant that you then tie into with another step that has much greater certainty.

For beginners, narrowing your progress down to a single next step is an advantage. If it doesn't work out, then just like with little bets, they can safely take a step back without having to halt five other activities in motion. By narrowing their focus, they can profit from the information that even missteps provide. And that gives their plan clearer, realistic contours.

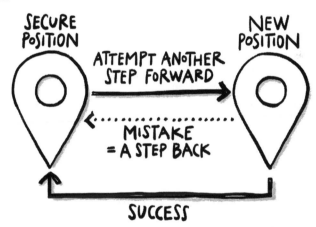

The essence of the method lies in reducing complexity: *Get rid of everything that is uselessly complicated, too theoretical and remote. Repeat it until you have an indivisible foundation.* And the next step is exactly that. Here is how I manage my non-urgent development projects:

1. *I evaluate the situation.* I think through alternative scenarios. If things aren't completely clear, I wait. Sooner or later I reach a conclusion on what the right next step is.

2. *I secure my current position.* Like a climber, I don't take unneeded risks, and I hold on to support points. I gather my strength, breathe in and move on.

3. *I put everything into it!* I punch Resistance in the face until I've finished the task. I let the new situation stabilize, and I evaluate it again. If it didn't work out, I can go back a step safely; otherwise, I secure my new position. Later, the whole process repeats again.

If I want to plan out a development project like this into multiple steps in advance, I once again try not to make things too complicated. Instead of a complex plan, I define a sort of *critical path* as the shortest sequence of steps needed to reach the goal.

⟩ PRACTICAL AIDS

I'll wrap up my list of basic tips that you can start with right away with some practical aids.

A *digital stopwatch* will serve you for basic measurement of your working time before you choose one of the more advanced methods for measuring via a specialized app.

A *kitchen timer* can be used for dividing up your working time into indivisible time blocks, using the Pomodoro technique. You wind your timer up to 25 minutes (1 pomodoro) and get started with focused work on *one* task. Once it rings, you take a short break, set the timer again, and continue where you stopped. After the fourth pomodoro, the pause is somewhat longer. The goal is to help you stay focused while also taking the necessary breaks.

Paper notebooks and *planners* are still holding their own as an alternative to purely digital tracking. The goal remains the same: to get your ideas and tasks out of your head and not to rely solely on memory. Besides the classics such as Moleskine products and the Bullet Journal system of paper task management, which you can keep in any kind of notebook, we are also seeing the rise of hybrid projects like Rocketbook, which lets you easily transfer notes to the cloud – and even erase pages using your microwave or a sponge.

Sketchnoting is about taking notes in the form of sketches and illustrations, as Mike Rohde explains in his *Sketchnote Handbook*. It's useful for notes from meetings, conferences, and classes, and as a kind of training for creative professionals.

Mind maps are perhaps the most popular method for visually describing and structuring notes or ideas. They have the form of a web branching out from the base topic (for example, Preparing My Presentation) into other subtopics and details. The advantage of mind maps is that, compared to ordinary text and nested lists of bullet points, they better represent the hierarchy of importance, and they interconnect topics naturally, via association. They can be produced in apps like XMind or Coggle, but also drawn by hand on any sheet of paper.

A *magnetic white board* is useful for both team meetings and for long-term planning that you want to always have in front of you. Sometimes special magnetic wall paints are also used – these let you write with markers and attach neodymium magnets – and out of the digital alternatives, I would name Limnu and Mural.

DEEP WORK

Lastly, I will add a few advanced tips that do take a little more time to apply, or a deeper change to your own personal approaches or habits.

Deep Work is a catchy neologism, and it's also the name of a book by Cal Newport whose goal is to get professionals back into fully focused work. He states that work that is unfocused and interrupted isn't worth your time – especially in our distracted age of emails, phones, messengers, websites, and notifications that constantly fight for your attention. But he doesn't just complain. On the contrary, he offers a radical solution in the form of long time blocks devoted to 100% pure, distilled, professional work done with full attention.

But he also warns: Watch out, it's easier said than done. You might find his bag of tricks necessary to squeeze at least a few hours of deep work out of your busy weekly schedule.

Newport opposes the conventional view, that creative and managerial work modes differ radically, in that while creators absolutely need immersion to produce their best work, managers can't afford it. He objects that deep work represents the peak of our intellectual output, no matter whether we are creators or managers, and as such can't be easily commoditized or replaced with AI, like we increasingly are seeing in superficial work. He thus sets the ability for deep work as one a prerequisite for success in our current conditions.

Newport actually won me over with his mention of Carl Jung's work retreat. Since we operate Retreat.cz as a comfortable house for deep work of developers and creative professionals in the mountains halfway between Prague, Krakow, and Vienna, this topic is truly close to me.

In culturally advanced countries, it's common, for example, for writers to use houses adapted for long-term writing where they have everything they need for calm work, with a minimum of distractions. You can browse a worldwide network of these art residences at the Res Artis website.

MINIMALISM

Most work minimalists agree that you need to simplify and think about what is essential, and this kind of philosophy is in full harmony with productivity. But in other ways the definitions and individual approaches can vary quite a bit.

The bible of team minimalism is *Rework*, which illustrates the principles of lean business. Amazon founder Jeff Bezos has said of its authors that they have rewritten the rules of business from the ground up. Among the influential apostles of personal minimalism you will find authors such as Tim Ferriss with his *The 4-Hour Work Week*, Leo Babauta with his *Zen Habits* blog and books like *Focus* or *Zen to Done,* and Cal Newport with his book *Digital Minimalism.*

However, personal minimalism can also be damaging. In a market environment, the approaches of hermits, such as staying permanently disconnected from your phone, email, or the internet and the resulting unavailability, can strongly handicap you. Not to mention trying the patience of clients, who really don't keep messenger pigeons anymore. Disconnecting is also a non-solution, because it reduces your exposure to happy accidents and new opportunities.

The philosophy of minimalism leads us to thoughts on life and social priorities. Does it make sense to toil away and earn more money – and borrow money too – to buy a luxury car, a big house, a spacious office, or some other status symbol? Minimalism says that you don't need any of that if you don't really want it. It puts simplicity, reduced stress, satisfaction, readiness for action, health, family and relationships at the top of the pyramid of needs and argues that in the end, all this gives us more utility.

GETTING THINGS DONE

Another technique that has left a deep, lasting trace in freelancers' work habits is *Getting Things Done* (GTD for short) by David Allen. It's an integrated personal productivity process, and even though I haven't yet seen two people that use it the same way, it serves many professionals around me as a foundation to build upon.

The core of GTD lies in organizing tasks based on certain rules and on principles we all partly already know, like: *Don't keep anything in your head. Split big projects into manageable tasks. Do little things right away. Delegate. Perform frequent reviews. Use inboxes.* And so on.

An *Inbox* is a kind of temporary storage where information or tasks pile up. It can be your email inbox, assigned tasks in a project management application, a paper organizer, or a virtual tray or inbox with still-unsorted tasks in your to-do list. The basic innovation in GTD is recording and sorting tasks in inboxes with the goal of minimizing stress and the amount of time it costs you. This can be illustrated via work with emails.

Inbox zero is a rule that views your email inbox like every other GTD inbox. It says that just like we don't leave any post in our mailbox, it's not good to let unhandled email rot in your Inbox. If you leave messages there a long time, they quickly become disorganized, and you are constantly going through the very same messages and saying: *Not yet on this one, maybe yes on this one*, and so on. It's inefficient, and you also thereby increase the risk that you won't answer a truly important message in time. The *Inbox Zero* rule tells us that it's better to handle all the emails in your Inbox regularly – delete or archive them, sort them into folders, or answer, postpone, forward, or delegate them.

I asked this system's creator, David Allen, if there's a GTD tool that he would recommend for freelancers, and his answer cuts to the core of the matter:

"Everyone will need some tool to implement GTD; but in my experience, there is no best one. Now there are literally hundreds of list-management tools available, most of which were built off the GTD methodology. They're all just list managers, with a plethora of different bells and whistles. The best one is whatever one you will actually use – and that can range from Post-it's on pages in a loose-leaf notebook to Excel spreadsheets to customized versions of Salesforce online."

If you feel the desire or need to try an integrated approach to self-management, GTD is a clear first choice. Even if it doesn't suit you completely, it can lead you towards a foundation for further improvement, and as David stressed when answering my direct question, it will still be GTD:

"Many people mistake GTD as something that has to have all the suggestions in the book in some format; and most people think of GTD as a 'system' instead of a 'systematic process,' which it really is. Anything that 'customizes' GTD or says it goes beyond it is simply saying that for some people in certain circumstances that systematic process may look like X, Y, or Z. Of course. Whatever gets something off someone's mind, that creates more cognitive space and freedom to be present and put your attention where you want it, with no distraction, is GTD. If you could hire 40 people to follow you around, wherever, to whom you could trust off-loading any ideas or potential future reminders about anything and walk you through whatever thinking you need to be doing about anything, at the appropriate time, you don't need any tool or additional process. That would be GTD, as well."

Nevertheless, GTD isn't made for managing projects and team activities – that is the domain of project and process management, which we will get to in the chapter on team cooperation.

⊗ PERSONAL ASSISTANCE

For now, the use of personal assistants isn't too widespread among free-lancers. But I would like to convince you that this is one of the biggest trump cards in strengthening your personal productivity, which will let you devote more time to productive work, rest, or your family.

We can define personal assistance as help with activities that aren't necessarily related to our work alone, but are more generally tasks that need to be done or handled. We can distinguish three basic forms of assistance: 1. a full-time personal assistant, 2. a virtual assistant, and 3. household help for cleaning, errands, childcare, etc.

A normal freelancer will hardly ever be able to utilize and pay for a full-time *personal assistant*. These are better employed by celebrities and elite professionals, who are drowning in requests and need someone on the front lines.

Virtual assistants are much more common. This is either a virtual assistance service that you pay for by the hour, with one assistant sometimes replacing another, or long-term cooperation with a single freelancing virtual assistant, which is perhaps ideal for deepening and building up trust. The less anonymous and impersonal the service is, the better.

A virtual assistant can, for example, take care of plane tickets for you, reserve meeting rooms or accommodation, perform online research, prepare invoices, visit photo banks to choose pictures for social networks, and do other time-intensive work that doesn't require such high qualifications that you need to pay a fortune. An intelligent virtual assistant will definitely save you lots of work, and since this is a classic example of on-demand work, you will only pay for it when they are really working.

But watch out for situations where your virtual assistant is interacting with clients in your name. The problems of virtual assistance often appear in the line from assistant to customer. You have to make sure that your assistant can't access confidential information without being bound to some kind of confidentiality agreement, and that you have gotten the client's consent for a third party to have access to such information. The exact way that you cover it in the contract is up to you.

And naturally if your assistant is communicating or acting in your name, you should pay extremely close attention to the level of this communication so they don't harm your name. I have even met professionals who delegated key competencies to assistants so incompetent that I lost all trust in them.

A virtual assistant is an inseparable part of your personal image, even when all they are doing is calling a hotel to reserve a room – not to mention correspondence with clients and business partners. If they are involved in this kind of communication, I recommend monitoring and running it via an address tied to the role (e.g. office@yourdomain.com), not to their name. Then in your contract, reserve the right to check this correspondence. If your assistant is representing you or your brand, take some time at the beginning of your collaboration to clarify your expectations in order to match any communication to your style and persona.

How can you find such an assistant? First look around you. Someone may be offering this service in your local freelance community or coworking space, or maybe you know a trustworthy person who is computer-savvy and who has the room and desire to help you out after some brief training. You can also use catalogs like Upwork and Freelancer.com, but keep distance in mind. It's good when your assistant is in a nearby time zone and understands your culture, especially if they will be speaking in your name. Someone from around the world may be cheap, but awful.

And let's add that in the long term, AI in the form of systems like Amazon Echo, Google Home, and Apple's Siri may partially replace human personal assistants.

Household help is perhaps the most common form of assistance for freelancers. This can be regular cleaning, handling errands and purchases, occasional babysitting, walking dogs, etc. You can delegate the activities that you don't like to do or that your business doesn't leave time for. Or it can be more financially advantageous for you to focus on work and pay for help that is significantly cheaper than your hourly rate.

My partner and I are both in business, and we have agreed that we do need such help. We have a great housekeeper who visits us three times a week to clean, iron, make minor purchases, run errands, and when it's needed, make lunch or watch our son for a while. All this has helped tremendously to keep us satisfied at home. She generally comes on weekday mornings, which means no invasions of our privacy. We are happy to have her.

Since your home helper has access to your private world, I definitely recommend not settling for a compromise, but instead searching until you are truly satisfied, no matter whether that means someone around you or an online professional service. On-call microservices like these, including errands and shopping runs, are growing fast, but the supply varies from country to country, so search or ask other freelancers what local services they use. It's by no means an exception to have to try out two or three before you find the one that is right for you.

In addition to help from a housekeeper, we also use a handyman for minor repairs and maintenance. This also is a relatively cheap service that saves me from worries and buying expensive power tools that I would only make use of once in a blue moon. In the US, for example, the already-mentioned TaskRabbit is popular, as are Amazon Home Services, Handy.com or Thumbtack.

I definitely recommend that you experiment with personal assistance. But I'll add in one breath that the beginnings can be tough, and you have to know precisely what you want to get out of it so that you don't just end up bringing in more problems and raising your costs. Reliable help, however, is priceless.

KEY IDEAS

1. Higher personal productivity fundamentally affects your earnings and long-term reliability.

2. Your goal should be to work less with higher productivity, not to have a full workload.

3. If you are working nonstop and don't want to, it's time to raise prices. There is visibly an interest in you.

4. No quick and simple solution for everyone exists. You have to build your own system.

5. You should take your internal Resistance into account and arm yourself with discipline and the right forms of motivation.

6. When building your personal productivity system, lean on priority management and biorhythms.

7. The third pillar is tools – basic and advanced, including your personal IT.

8. Try to do something solid every day, and review your progress regularly.

9. Learn to work systematically in large blocks, instead of mixing everything together.

10. Other people can also help you with personal productivity, so look into delegating tasks, personal assistance, and more.

PRACTICES

✓ Try to specify what are the main objectives and priorities for your personal productivity system. Review and rework your current practices to match these goals.

✓ Besides tracking your work priorities, focus on finding and optimizing your perfect biorhythm. To start with, get enough sleep to be fully rested for each working day.

✓ Try hard to do something substantial each day, but don't blame yourself if you fail. Every day counts. Set daily priorities. Write a brief diary. Do daily and weekly reviews.

✓ Group similar tasks like calls, errands, emails, or administrative tasks to boost efficiency. Protect your peak times and reserve a few hours for deep work at least once a week.

✓ If you are not used to it, start experimenting with personal assistance. Research your options first and then try to delegate at least 3 tasks per month, either at work or home.

PROFESSIONAL IT

How to keep your data safe and what tools should you use?

You may have a number of personal and purely professional reasons for caring about personal IT, but three are key for business:

1. *IT generally has a fundamental impact on your personal productivity.* Most freelancers spend most of their working time on a computer or a phone, and so even minor optimizations pay off. Not to mention that certain apps and approaches will help you work faster and better. Today you can have your whole business under control and in your hands through your phone.

2. *Your clients want it.* To keep from slowing your clients down, you need to know tech at least as well as they do. They don't want to wait a week for your reply or to teach you the basics. The spread of computers, the internet, and mobile phones has been one of the driving forces behind the freelancing boom for decades, and mastering new technologies is still a clear advantage today.

3. *IT innovations will almost certainly influence your profession's future.* In most fields, saying no to technology has long been unimaginable and keeping an eye on technologies is an integral part of career strategies. Also, as freelancers we are able to adapt more quickly than slow-moving corporations. Furthermore, technologies help us with our marketing, networking, education, and more.

However, we must be the masters, not slaves, of our tools. Having email on your phone is fantastic…until it becomes its own source of stress, as definitely can happen. You have to have your tools fully under control and never let them influence your workflow in a way that you don't want. You should have the feeling that your personal IT is helping and supporting you. You and IT should never be enemies.

⊘ PRIORITIES AND LEVELS FOR PERSONAL IT

Personal IT, just like personal productivity, is mainly about choosing your own palette of tools based on your own set of general rules, principles, and priorities. You may have any number of these, but the most important of them will be probably health, safety, and simplicity – so that your personal IT can be low-maintenance.

Simplicity is key, because personal IT is made up of more levels over time. A personal computer and a phone, including the apps on it, are a foundation that you obviously can't do without. But you also can't forget ergonomics, various websites and web apps, social media networks, cloud-based work, gadgets for personal or home use, and in some cases, even your own app or tool development.

Wait a second. Me? Develop? Don't worry, nobody is forcing you to learn how to code home-made web pages, program apps, perform data analyses, or write Excel macro scripts if you don't want to. But it's good to not automatically be *against* learning advanced IT skills if they can save you time or solve a specific problem.

You will usually build up your personal IT approach on an existing foundation. You have probably already decided on your own whether to go with Windows or Mac, and with an Android phone or an iPhone – and I don't want to push any options here. These are all comparable, and for most of us, they are also something we are used to. So when I talk here about improving your personal IT, it doesn't mean throwing your existing IT away, only that it makes sense to gradually improve it and replace the outdated parts.

Staying up to date will definitely also pay off in other ways. In the next five to ten years, innovations in automation, AI, robotics, 3D printing, or cryptocurrencies may significantly influence your field. The career and technological changes that you undertake today are going to influence who will you be as a professional ten years from now. Thus it does make sense to follow developments and read deep analyses or book-form summaries like *WTF* by Tim O'Reilly. Some predictions may be wrong, but progress will keep marching on.

If your head is already spinning from all of these possibilities, don't despair, and don't stick it in silicon. Some of the levels I'm going to mention may not even affect you. And I won't even go over which computer to buy and why. Instead I'll focus on the above priorities and typical sore points.

If you spend most of your working time at a computer, your health will need to be a fundamental long-term priority. The first level that you will have to focus on is the environment of your office or work space.

In the cold months when people keep the windows closed, or year-round if you are working in a poorly designed building, probably the most important thing is to ensure the constant supply of fresh air. High carbon dioxide levels don't just mean worse concentration, but also less sleep and relaxation. With high CO_2 concentrations, you will see drowsiness, grogginess, loss of focus, and even headaches. So fresh air is the foundation. Gadget-lovers can buy a CO_2 gauge with notifications, such as Netatmo or AirVisual Node.

But what if you don't want to even have to think about it? The grandiose solution, mainly for new construction, is air recuperation. It constantly renews fresh air from outside without any heat loss by using a recuperator. Another much simpler solution is a smart thermostatic radiator valve that lets you keep a room's temperature constant no matter how much air you are letting in. These automatically regulate the heating based on the temperature you set and the daily program, and some can even be controlled via the internet. One extreme alternative is to install a window-mounted system that either regularly lets in fresh air on its own at set intervals or is connected with a CO_2 sensor over an interface like IFTTT.com and lets in fresh air accordingly.

Ventilation may also reduce the concentration of toxins that are released into interior spaces by furniture, carpets, air conditioning, building materials, etc. People in the 21st century spend up to 90% of their time in enclosed spaces and if these are unsuitable, they may be exposed to health risks associated with sick building syndrome.

But in good weather, you can also work outdoors. The increased mobility and battery life of laptops and the availability of quick internet connections today let you easily work not just in your garden, but even in a forest gazebo or in the middle of a city park.

One freelancer I know worked for several months on the beach in the shade of palm trees, with a view out onto the ocean and a light surfboard as his desk. Another friend that freelances as a developer loves to ride bike trails, and he programs at the rest stops, or sometimes during hot summer days he takes his work up with him on mountain hikes.

If you work outdoors in daylight often, it's good to have a notebook with a matte display, because a glossy one throws a lot of reflections even when light isn't hitting it directly.

Along the same lines, it's good to avoid sharp and tiring contrasts such as working at night on a glowing monitor without other lighting, or under direct sunlight. For sensitive people, evening exposure to intense blue light from LED monitors can even lead to sleep disorders, which is why both Windows 10 and macOS have built-in support for nighttime shifting of a monitor's light towards warmer colors.

⊗ WORKING ON A COMPUTER WHILE STANDING UP

Daily sedentary work can increase the risk of health complications: obesity, circulatory system diseases, depression, backaches, etc. You can sit in front of a computer for five years and feel no negative symptoms. But it adds up. After ten, fifteen or twenty years, people usually feel the consequences. However, there are ways to avoid chronic problems.

The typical recommended form of prevention is to take regular breaks and alternate between sitting and standing while working. While standing, we can easily step back and do a few squats or take a few steps around the room or move to the beat of the music. But standing all day isn't healthy as well, so it is important to change the position according to how you feel your body's needs.

The 2018 Finnish meta-analysis *Workplace interventions for reducing sitting at work* says: "The use of sit-stand desks seems to reduce workplace sitting on average by 84 to 116 minutes per day." Sounds good. Still, the available studies are relatively unreliable, and it isn't clear yet how much the reduced amount of sitting time is reflected in improving people's health or well-being. Also, it seems that the reduction in sitting is larger initially and decreases over time. So ultimately, this is about how you feel and the strength of your habits. If you try alternating between sitting and standing, and it feels really good to you, then this will probably be more important to you than the vague conclusions of the currently available studies.

The cheaper models of electrically adjustable work desks include one offered by IKEA (the Bekant sit/stand model for $419), as well as dozens of others from manufacturers who you can easily Google and compare on the local market. The cheapest models start at $300, but the more expensive ones cost up to $2000, the biggest difference being usually in the design and the overall quality. In any case, I recommend a desk with memory settings for two or three stored positions. It will save you a lot of time.

Using an adjustable table helped me from having major back pain. I tried sitting in all kinds of ways, from gymnastic balls to ergonomic chairs, but nothing helped until I started working standing up. Today I sit on a typical wooden chair and I don't have any problems.

⊘ HEALTHY HARDWARE

Let's move on from your desk and your work space to your computer itself. Laptop ergonomics are very good by now, especially for business laptops with a good display technology and keyboard – including a number pad if you frequently type numbers.

However, professionals who use a mouse or a keyboard all day long can still run into trouble. Unfortunately typical mice and laptop keyboards aren't made for such extensive use. They don't leave your hands in the best positions, and if you have to work all day long, you may start experiencing a strange feeling in your fingers, palms, or wrists. It usually means nothing, but it can be a warning sign for the start of carpal tunnel syndrome, which can develop into wrist problems that require immediate treatment.

Fortunately there is ergonomic hardware out there made precisely for long shifts at a PC. There is a large pack of companies making it, but Microsoft has always led that pack. Their ergonomic mice and keyboards have seen years of refinement. I used to have problems with wrist numbness, and they disappeared when I started using a Microsoft Sculpt ergonomic mouse. The Sculpt is special in that its support surfaces angle out towards the side, and so your hand rests comfortably on the outer edge of your palm, with a naturally straightened wrist and your forearm resting fully on your desk.

Tension headaches are another widespread problem that can be caused by holding your head wrong while using your phone (so called *text neck*) or computer (*forward head*). The hunchbacks around me swear by exercises or by a gadget called Alex+ (Upright is comparable), which vibrates to let them know that they are sitting in a twisted position and need to straighten up. And you may also be helped by the affordable folding device by Nexstand, which raises your notebook's display to eye level.

⊘ THE PRINCIPLES OF PERSONAL IT SECURITY

IT security is gradually becoming one of the top priorities, because more and more of our data is entering the internet – the cloud and web or mobile apps. So I recommend that, as a freelancer, you follow at least these ten principles:

I. *Safe passwords and a password manager.* Don't use simple, easy-to-guess passwords, and above all don't use the same password for multiple services. Never store passwords on paper; instead use a password manager – a digital "password safe" made for precisely this purpose. Prioritize the tried-and-tested ones. The cloud-based LastPass is used widely, as are 1Password, Dashlane and the trusted open-source KeePass. You can also use your browser to store your passwords for minor online services. Chrome, for example, synchronizes passwords over Passwords.Google.com, while Safari under macOS uses the Keychain system app.

II. *Two-factor authentication* or 2FA. Gmail supports this, along with all of the other Google services, as well as Facebook, Dropbox, Apple iCloud, LastPass, etc. Turn it on, and then for future major logins (the first login on a new device, etc.) you will need to enter both a password and a unique code sent via a text or a special phone app such as Google Authenticator. That way, if your password is lost or compromised, that won't mean an instant security breach.

III. *Auto-lock for your computer and phone.* Set up your phone, your work tablet, and your computer to require a new login after brief inactivity. Then if anyone gets near to your unattended device, the risk of their getting into it is significantly lower.

IV. *Legal, up-to-date software.* Pirated software can contain harmful code or put you at risk due to its lack of updates. By paying for software, you are also supporting its creators' work and livelihood, making it much more likely they will keep it safe and up-to-date.

V. *A watchful eye on "free" apps and programs.* Some are on a secret quest to pump data from your phone or computer and track your location and online behavior. Others display distracting ads or lack technical and customer support, or are so poorly written and maintained that they represent a security risk. If you really need it to be free, prioritize time-tested open-source freeware. And when installing apps and games on your phone, watch out for which permissions they request. Why should a battery saver app, for example, need your location or contacts?

VI. *An antivirus or security package.* Your operating system will generally have basic protection built in, but while on the Mac it's enough to just turn on the system firewall, on Windows most users will also install security suites such as Norton, Avast, or ESET (my personal favorite). They provide many functions, including firewall protection against network attacks, anti-spyware checks, etc. But unfortunately, they won't protect you against attacks utilizing *zero-day* vulnerabilities, typically within your browser. Thus it's recommended that you increase your browser's security by blocking ads and disabling Flash and Java applets by default and only running those you want, on-demand.

VII. *Backups to disk and to the cloud.* You should always have the ability to restore your data if you lose your computer or your physical backup, for instance after a break-in or fire. Apps like CrashPlan (Code42) enable exactly this, by periodically backing up data from selected folders to a safe cloud and meanwhile also letting you create these same backups on an external disk. Macs have a built-in tool for this called Time Machine that turns an external disk into a dependable backup; it also automatically backs up selected data to iCloud. If you already have your data in a cloud, you will probably want to back that cloud up too; for the most-used Google cloud you can do this using Google Takeout and Google Vault.

VIII. *A safe phone with the latest patches.* The safest of all is to have an iPhone with iOS, which, as one benefit of being less open than Android, better handles updates for its old models. With Android, prioritize a clean system without added manufacturer apps (bloatware) and with regular updates. The Google Pixel premium line gives you this, but so do some cheaper Android One alternatives. You will definitely also be safer if you can log in using a fingerprint reader or facial recognition, because someone watching you use your phone can catch your PIN or gestures, or read them from the marks on your display.

IX. *Online services that let you recover your data.* Whenever you decide to entrust your valuable data to an online service, make sure that you can later download it in a common format. Respecting this *data-liberation* principle is a sign of trustworthy online services.

X. *Common sense and caution.* Be careful in every respect, especially when it comes to your work with logins and passwords. The most important ones should only be known to you. It pays to be a late adopter, that is, to adopt new technologies only once they are proven and multiple people around you are using them. And to be a power user, that is, to invest time into mastering the technologies that you use every day.

The above personal IT security principles are a sort of universal foundation for all ordinary users, as outlined by Paul Minar, my colleague and go-to IT consultant. But if you are working with sensitive information or clients' personal data, your degree of security should be much higher still, and in that case I would recommend taking into consideration a few extra principles:

- *Protection against monitoring and password capture.* Whenever you connect over a public or unsecured WiFi network in a cafe, coworking space, or airport, you are facing the risk of being monitored by an attacker, who can, in the worst case, even obtain your login data. Likewise your mobile operator can spy on you as you are surfing. The solution is to encrypt your connection over a trustworthy VPN app such as Freedome, Encrypt.me or ProtonVPN. You simply install it in your computer and phone and have it encrypt all traffic between you and your access VPN point. But watch out; your VPN provider should be widely respected, transparent, and traceable, because all of your network traffic will be flowing through them. Otherwise it's just one more risk.

- *An encrypted disk and phone.* Much of the data can be extracted from an unencrypted phone even without the system password, and so it's wise to encrypt your sensitive data storage. Apple iPhones do this automatically; while on some Android phones it has to be turned on manually. This doesn't seriously reduce a phone's performance. On your computer, I recommend encrypting your whole drive; macOS has the FileVault system tool for this, while for Windows, there is BitDefender or the open-source VeraCrypt. And when you are discarding an old computer or phone, don't forget to erase it thoroughly using a simple utility such as Eraser or the more advanced Darik's Boot and Nuke.

- *Safe messaging.* Neither SMS text messages nor the common messenger programs are truly safe; they lack sufficient encryption, making it easy for your operator, government agencies, and hackers to monitor your communications. If you want to use a messenger for confidential work communication, then I would advise you to visit SecureMessagingApps.com and take your pick. Although I prefer Signal, there are several safe choices. And if you want to have super-safe email as well, then the Swiss-based ProtonMail should satisfy your needs.

- *Legal knowledge and work with IT consultants.* IT security is complicated, just like all of IT, and state involvement in it is growing. Especially in the EU, the demands on professionals who work with personal data have been increased greatly since General Data Protection

Regulation (GDPR) rules were put in place. So although I understand tech fairly well, I still cooperate with an advisor whose knowledge goes deeper. That way I don't waste time choosing new hardware or solving problems – there is no shortage of those when it comes to IT. And I also eliminate the risk of making mistakes out of ignorance.

Also, here is one bookworm's tip: For a head start read *Future Crimes* by Marc Goodman, who is very gifted at guiding users towards reasonable caution online.

Now I'll explain the advantages of the strongest cloud platform including several security angles, to kick off the overview of apps and services that will take up the rest of this chapter.

⟫ STEER CLEAR OF FREE GMAIL

Do you use Google's free Gmail as your main work email? Do you have an email address like your.name@gmail.com? Are you using Google services like Calendar and Drive for your shared cloud documents? And did you know that Google doesn't offer standard customer support for free accounts?

Is this a problem? It can be. If worse comes to worst, you can lose access to your data.

If you forget your password but you have set up your account in advance so that you can regain access if needed, it's likely that nothing serious will happen. Google will let you recover it via a backup email or phone number. This procedure is fine-tuned and functional, with a rich configuration.

However, a forgotten password can be an unsolvable problem if your account is set up poorly. A colleague of mine is a certified Google Partner and handles dozens of cases per year where users have lost access to their free Gmail account and can't get it back. The problem is generally that Google can't verify the legitimacy of the access request due to basic mistakes made by the user, who for example:

- didn't set up any renewal options such as a secondary email or telephone number (*"Why would I give Google my telephone number, they would spam texts at me"*)

- couldn't answer the question about the labels they used most often (they didn't use any)

- didn't know a password because it had been changed by a third party (an angry spouse or a laid-off employee who had access to a shared Gmail account)

- forgot the password to a long-since forwarded Gmail account that still receives important emails (and nobody knew the information needed for recovery)

Or the unfortunate situation where your computer might be compromised and your account starts sending out suspicious messages, leading Google to block it. The same can happen if someone acquires access via your password or a logged-in browser, computer, or phone, and abuses your Gmail account for illegal activity. This happens rarely, but you should know that in this kind of extreme case, you can permanently lose access to your email and data.

Losing access to your email is a much larger problem than locking yourself out of your house. The chance that you will regain access to an account for which automated recovery has failed or which has been blocked due to suspicious activity is low. Google support won't help you, because their support services are reserved for paid G Suite accounts only.

Losing access is more painful the longer you have been using a free Gmail address and listing it on your website, your business cards, or elsewhere. Imagine the hundreds of emails that will hit your blocked account to which you will never be able to reply. Nor will their senders learn that you didn't receive their messages – you won't hear about them (there is no way you could) and they won't receive an answer.

For a beginner who has been freelancing and using Gmail for hardly a year and who still emails a relatively small circle of people, this may not hurt so much. But if you have come into contact with hundreds of people and companies over the years, a problem like this can lead you to lose the trust people have placed in you and a lot of money. Not to mention the value that the inaccessible data and emails have for you.

Email is the most critical service in part because it can typically be used for changing the passwords for a user's other online services, and sometimes even the domain owner. So by breaking into your email, an attacker can break in everywhere.

But I can reassure you a bit. Gmail is still the safest of all the commonly used free email services, and the risk that you will encounter problems like this is lower than for less well-secured competing services. All the more so if you respect the personal IT security principles I mentioned and set up two-phase login and access-restoration contact data in your Google account. But even then the risk is still not zero.

Your work computer, and above all your phone, are the weak points in your IT security; always think before, for instance, letting your children play on them or letting visitors use them. A child can easily erase half the data on your G Suite Drive or share data with anyone in your address book. A work computer doesn't belong in a child's hands – especially if you work with confidential information.

As an emergency safeguard, regular backups for your emails, contacts, and cloud data can also help. You can also have copies of messages automatically forwarded to a backup address. So you can reasonably reduce the risk, but for free accounts, some risk will always exist. Essentially this is because the Gmail.com domain, to which your messages are delivered, isn't controlled by you, but by Google.

If you know the risks, they are acceptable for you, and you respect the need to secure your account, then it's all fine. However, if you don't wish to run this risk and the Google G Suite cloud office (i.e. email + calendar + documents) suits you well overall, then there is also the option of switching to the paid G Suite with an email on your own domain. And as we will soon see, the monthly fees start at about the cost of a pot of good coffee.

⊚ SIMPLICITY AND WORK IN THE CLOUD, ON YOUR OWN DOMAIN

The paid version of G Suite is governed by different contractual rules, and the fundamentally important thing here is that email routing is set up on your domain, so you have it under your control. That means you can have an email address such as name@surname.com, where surname. com is your own domain, with emails merely being directed to the Google mail servers. If you later decide against using Google, you can easily reconfigure the domain to redirect incoming emails somewhere else. That way, unlike with the free Gmail, you remain more or less independent. Not to mention that an email like name@surname.com looks better than something like bobbyvlach78@gmail.com.

For your old, unused addresses, I recommend forwarding them to your main address. Beyond a few exceptions, it's more practical when a freelancer uses one stable address for all personal and work correspondence, because some messages fall in a gray zone between these two categories, and if you are writing the same person on different topics from different email addresses, it can appear confusing and unprofessional. Some people that I work with have used at least a dozen addresses over the last decade, and the result is chaos.

G Suite accounts offer more space for your data than free accounts do. Their business model is simple; you pay (as of this writing) $72 or €62 a year for one Basic user account (email address), and the use of all the other G Suite services, such as Calendar, Drive, etc. is also included in that price. Their *Business* accounts with nearly unlimited storage capacity cost $144 or €125 yearly.

All of a domain's accounts can also be managed centrally via an administration console, which comes in especially handy when founding new accounts for coworkers. Unlike with free accounts, these accounts and their data belong to you; you can manage them fully, and you also have more access-recovery options.

The paid G Suite also gives you access to standard technical support, or even support from your local reseller. As you can see, G Suite eliminates both of the main problems of free Gmail – the lack of support and being tied to a Gmail.com email address. You can also turn off ads, and you have more control over how the suite's apps function.

If security is important for you or you own a valuable domain, don't forget to secure that as well via a registrar. This is an ironic aspect of having your email address based on your own domain: Google itself secures Gmail.com; meanwhile with your own domain, you have to take care of it yourself and never underestimate the importance of this, because any loss of control over it would logically also threaten all the services connected with it.

For that reason I personally think that proper domain security should definitely be a part of professional email configuration when you are on your own domain. Double-check the correctness of the registrant (owner) data in the domain registry, and watch the security of the email address from which domain changes can be authorized. For ordinary, generic domains such as .COM .INFO, etc. you can also ask your registrar to set up what are called EPP status codes for the domain, which make it harder to delete or hijack. Certain national domains, meanwhile, enable even stronger protection.

G Suite is the result of Google's long efforts to combine all of its services into one whole that fits and works together well and is solidly secured. Microsoft is aiming for the same with its Office 365, as is Apple with its iCloud application suite.

I could write many words here about the chances of success for Microsoft's and Apple's cloud offices. Apple has one enormous advantage: it develops excellent computers and phones with its own operating system. And it has legions of true believers who won't hear an ill word about it. Microsoft, meanwhile, has much more experience with developing office applications. But it makes few computers, and its mobile system was a disaster.

Cloud platforms are usually more reliable the less you have to interconnect apps and systems from multiple companies. Doing so causes compatibility problems, apps are less functionally interconnected, and backups generally have to be handled separately as well. The simplicity, which should generally come first here, is suddenly gone.

Google has one more ace up its sleeve here for us freelancers: the wide use of G Suite for sharing documents, spreadsheets, and presentations in important fields such as marketing, education, internet services, and in small and medium sized businesses overall.

But this doesn't mean competing packages can be ignored. Microsoft Office 365 still dominates among large firms and corporations, where it's the de facto professional standard. Apple's iWork package, meanwhile, lives more in its own world, but this can even be an advantage if you are seeking a fully integrated work environment and all of your colleagues use Macs.

In any case, it would be wise to start out by trying a cloud environment from only one major player, be that Google, Apple, or Microsoft. Even if one may have much better options for certain applications, for most professionals this way is much simpler. Advanced users will cherry-pick the best apps no matter what; this dilemma only partially applies to them.

That's it for the differences among Google, Apple, and Microsoft; now back to G Suite. What are the overall advantages of working in this cloud service that make it so popular with freelancers?

Above all, you can access your data from anywhere, through any internet-connected device – a desktop computer, a laptop, a phone, a smart watch, a tablet, or some other thin client or interface that lets you access the internet.

Other advantages include document sharing via Google Drive, as well as team cooperation where you can all see the same document version. Google docs, spreadsheets, and slideshows, work in all browsers. No more emailing files one after another, managing different versions, etc.

The other applications in the package and their overall integration are also superb. Gmail seems to be the best email client today, and the same goes for the Calendar: you can share its layers within your teams, or even put it on the web without details to tell your clients when you are available. Google Contacts can be accessed in all their services and also on your phone, and they serve some freelancers so well that they use them as a minimalistic CRM to record and manage clients. Their excellent Maps also deserve mention, as well as Google Photos with its unlimited capacity, reasonable size compression, and support for keyword searches. And, lastly, G Suite Team Drives are turning out to be one of best new features for supporting teamwork and organizing data online for your projects.

Google guarantees 99.9% uptime and lets you verify it 24/7 at Google.com/appsstatus. Google data centers are spread out evenly around the world, so access is quick as well. And they take security seriously – individual data leaks are caused by careless users and not by holes in Google's security.

You may naturally have some worries about entrusting your data to the cloud. Nevertheless, consider whether it's safer on a computer with average (in)security that can die or be stolen, or in the very same cloud that American government institutions and the top European banks and insurers use for their own data. And they work with a lot more confidential information than your average freelancer.

In your Google account settings, go to the *Personal Info and Privacy* settings. This gives you control over the information about you that Google gathers besides the data you have entrusted to it. Personally, I have everything turned off here, even though it does slightly restrict the functioning of certain Google services. The sense of greater security is worth it.

Most G Suite applications for phones naturally also support work in an offline, unconnected mode. You can work with your calendar, mail, documents, and photos in the subway, on the train, or in a cottage with a bad signal. The Chrome browser also supports it. In short, work in the cloud doesn't have to require a nonstop high-speed connection.

However, besides the fact that G Suite is a paid package, it does have one other significant disadvantage. If you previously mainly worked offline in MS Office and used MS Outlook for your email and calendar, switching to the cloud requires a change in mindset and a much greater focus on security, as I have discussed above. Because your data isn't mainly with you, but in the cloud.

So this is the G Suite in a nutshell. I have described it in detail because it's the solution that freelancers use probably the most (along with free Gmail accounts). But I hope it is clear that my interest was more in illustrating how simple cloud work contrasts with the older paradigm where every application is offline and works with one physical PC.

I personally use G Suite and recommend it, but many freelancers are equally excited about Apple products, or prefer Microsoft just as their corporate clients do.

If you are conservative and don't want to change your existing habits and way of working with desktop applications, Dropbox is there as a halfway point between a traditional desktop and the cloud – it's very popular among freelancers for cloud file sharing and document cooperation, which is further boosted by the Dropbox Paper service.

You simply install Dropbox as an app, select the folders to have mirrored in the cloud, wait for synchronization to complete, and voilà, your data is on your computer and the cloud simultaneously. You can then easily share your cloud copy with teammates or with anyone, at the level of individual files or whole folders. Dropbox supports encryption, 2FA, access from different devices, and also simultaneous cooperation in the cloud.

But its core is simply mirroring folders from your disk to the cloud. And that is what makes it attractive for conservative users: it lets them enjoy the benefits of the cloud without having to deeply change how they work with their computer and data. And in fact, Google understands this need and thus offers the Drive File Stream app, which provides access to cloud data as a virtual drive on your computer. Dropbox (like Google Drive) can also be used for file sharing, as an alternative to sharing over less safe services such as WeTransfer.

But let's move on from the cloud now to some tips on other useful apps and services for freelancers. I'll leave out stars such as MS Office, Outlook, WhatsApp, and Skype, because I suspect you are advanced enough to know them, and if you aren't, such tips wouldn't be enough on their own – that is a matter for a computer literacy class.

◎ TOUCH TYPISTS TYPE FASTER

We all spend lots of time on our computers writing emails, documents, articles, social media posts, and more. But meanwhile peoples' typing speeds vary greatly, and even though speech recognition is improving, in many situations it simply can't be used. And even when it can, it's only practical for entering short notes and messages, not for work with your everyday documents. So touch typing (i.e. typing without looking at the keyboard) is and apparently will long remain one of the keys to boosting your work productivity.

A few years back, I was working with someone who was in charge of customer support. He spent most of his day writing emails, but he refused to learn to touch type, arguing that he was a fast typist. So we ran a test. When he was focused, he typed at about 30–40 words per minute (WPM), plus some time for correcting typos – which are more common for non-touch typists due to all the looking up and down.

Meanwhile for touch typists it's no problem to write twice as fast, 60–80 WPM, after just a few months' training. After a couple of years, you can even reach, say, 100–120 WPM, which is almost more than you need for capturing your ordinary train of thought. Meanwhile speed typists can even reach speeds of over 200 WPM, and the current world record is 256 WPM.

Writing a longer email for 10 minutes or for half an hour, now that is a difference. Especially when you write lots of them and also produce articles, documents, and other texts. It speeds you up immensely.

But there are two catches. Touch typing does take some time to learn, and for a few weeks you will be typing even slower than you did before. But above all, you have to learn it well, because otherwise you won't gain much. This is because the typing speeds of hunt-and-peck typists and under-taught touch typists are similar, and only with thorough training can you work your way up, 200% to 300% above hunt-and-peck speeds.

The choice of the right learning application is important, because it has to fit your language and keyboard layout. You can test your typing speed in your language at 10FastFingers.com. For learners in English-speaking countries, the tools used include Typesy, Typing.com, UltraKey, and Kaz Typing.

If I have got you saying that writing 100 words a minute would be great, how would you like 100 a second? This is actually possible too; you just need to apply a little trick.

There are certain texts that we all write over and over again: postal, web, and email addresses, phone numbers, replies to inquiries, payment instructions, etc. And meanwhile, you can insert simple templates or text blocks significantly faster using a small app that writes them whenever you type a simple text of your choice.

So for example you type *xsi*, and the app immediately adds a text signature and closing to your email. Or you write *xbp2*, and the template for your business proposal no. 2. is inserted. Or you write *xcon*, and your terms-and-conditions paragraph is inserted.

Perhaps the best-known is TextExpander, both for Windows and for Mac, where system keyboard settings can also be used for this purpose.

I also strongly recommend using an improved system clipboard with a copy and paste memory. AlfredApp and Flycut, for example, exist only for Mac, while Windows has Flashpaste and Ditto – using a shortcut key, you can easily call up this clipboard memory and paste the text that you currently need.

KEEPING YOUR NOTES ORGANIZED

Whether you're processing your notes with a GTD system or just collecting ideas into a notebook, sooner or later you will need to store your notes for permanent findability and usability. You need your own system or note archive where you can quickly find what you need for your current work task or project.

The Evernote app is enormously popular here, but many alternatives exist.

Minimalists often even use an ordinary to-do list for this purpose, and for hundreds of notes this is certainly enough. Microsoft has developed a note application named OneNote that is great, but unfortunately rather slow (as of 2019) when managing large collections that contain thousands of notes. Apple has the simpler Notes app. As for me, I'm among those who prefer having a note archive directly on Google Drive. I have every-thing in one place, and as a result I don't have to switch among my notes and my other documents. For convenience, I throw quick notes on my projects into my to-do app and sort the rest into project folders on my cloud disk.

The advantage of both Evernote and Google Drive is that they enable simple searches of your whole archive, including texts recognized in images and PDF scans, using OCR technology. That lets you find the information you need in seconds. You have thousands of notes, documents, photos, drawings, and files available in one click from your browser or phone. A well-organized note collection saves a lot of time, and thus ultimately increases your productivity.

HOW TO HAVE A GREAT MEMORY VIA YOUR TO-DO LIST

In my last chapter, on productivity, I discussed the matter of priorities, which in practice means some kind of task list. Your memory is limited and unreliable, and so it's better to write your tasks down. Some people rely on a paper diary, but the most common way is to write work tasks into a calendar or a special application: a to-do list.

But here personal-productivity enthusiasts' opinions differ regarding whether it's better to write priority tasks in a digital calendar (like Outlook or G Suite Calendar) or separately in a to-do list outside of your work calendar.

Fans of a systematic approach often give preference to separating calendar events that are tied to a particular time (calls, meetings, etc.) from tasks, which do need to be done, but with varying priorities and unfixed timing. This camp leans towards the opinion that the calendar is only there for time-based records, and that tasks should be managed separately, which makes the whole system clearer and increases the relative weight of calendar items. Unfinished tasks will always be simple to move, while a pre-arranged meeting is firmly fixed.

The proponents of simplicity, meanwhile, are of the opinion that it's more practical to keep everything in one place and not suffer the constant switching back and forth among apps. So they work on bending a calendar's possibilities to keep track of both timed and untimed items, and they say they are satisfied.

Both camps have some truth to them. The key factor is the amount of work – the number of tasks and projects that a given professional is working on at once. If the tasks are few and orders or projects come one after the other, then a calendar can be sufficient enough for task management. But when there is a large number of tasks and contexts among which a professional has to switch between, it becomes unbearable, or rather the calendar stops being readable.

Among the best-loved to-do list apps out there are Wunderlist, Todoist, Trello, and Google Keep for simple notes and lists. Apple fans, meanwhile, love their OmniFocus, Things, and 2Do. It's good if your to-do list lets you arrange tasks into projects, add labels (e.g. for errands, calls, and place-related tasks) and notifications, and work with an inbox where you can throw tasks or notes into a jumble and then sort and delete them during a regular review once or twice a week.

⊙ TRACKING TIME

Tracking tasks and checking them off is one thing. Measuring the time spent on them is another. This is useful for any invoicing of the time spent, or for having your own control mechanism for how much time you spent on which activity. Even if you are only invoicing by job or by unit of work, rather than by the amount of time worked, by measuring the time spent you will be able to calculate the price of your work per hour. Measuring will also reveal to you how much work time you actually spend on paid work and how much is spent on managing yourself or even lost to procrastination disguised as work. In the end, doing this will help you maintain your mental hygiene and structure your time better.

Pros generally measure their time using a specialized app that can also generate reports for clients. By far the most popular one among freelancers is Toggl, which works both on phones and in browsers and has a powerful free version. You can track time separately for individual clients or projects, and it also enables work in teams.

The alternatives here are in the dozens, including favorites like the Taptile Timetracking app, automated measurement on your phone or computer using the Timely app, and even gadgets like ZEI° from Timeular for easy switching between projects.

In practice, I see each freelancer running into different time measurement problems, connected to their profession, personality, and work style. Some forget to measure, others don't always have a phone or PC around, and others don't categorize well. My only recommendation is: *Keep it simple.* Overcomplicating this can be just as stressful as not measuring at all, and the line between splitting hairs and honest precision is quite thin.

If Toggl doesn't suit you, no problem. Other applications and solutions exist. For example, I measure my consulting time in Toggl, but I track it in a spreadsheet with a separate sheet for each client. Sending out a report then just means copying from one table into an email.

ⓥ INVOICING MADE SIMPLE

You have got everything measured, ready, and handed over, and you can bill. But how?

This is the eternal beginner's question. Some seek answers on the web, while others take advice from a mentor or accountant. Word and Excel are traditional solutions, because who wants to install accounting software just for invoicing?

It's OK to be creative. Some graphic artists' invoices are works of art. It's no wonder – the pretty layout is a kind of business card, and it gives a new taste to the invoicing cherry atop their order. It's a practical example of their great work.

But many people don't want to tune their invoices *quite* like that. So they turn a compromise: replacing those ugly tables using a specialized application that simplifies invoice issuing and tracking. These will save you time, and also from having doubts about the format of your invoices, and the result will look better than an ugly Excel sheet. Other possible advantages include advanced features like the pairing of incoming payments or an integrated online payment gateway.

Logically your invoicing application should work with your language and the legislation in the place where you do business. So ask your colleagues what application they use. Wave Financial, Harvest, FreshBooks, And Co, and even PayPal are some common choices in the US. Some of these also cover accounting or time tracking in addition to invoicing.

⟩ WHERE TO LOOK FOR ALTERNATIVES?

There are many more apps that I could recommend – like Audible for listening to unabridged audiobooks (my favorite app of all), Pocket or Instapaper for saving interesting reads for later, Should I Answer? for filtering out and automatically hanging up on spam calls, TripMode for saving data on the road and so forth.

I'll get to some of these in the remaining chapters, but my goal here has primarily been to emphasize the principles behind personal IT. After all, tips for apps these days age ten times faster than tips for books. Some may not even work in a year, or a new version might come out that is not as good or as user-friendly.

So it's great that there are community-maintained comparison tools for alternative applications such as alternativeTo; the Product Hunt social network for curious pioneers and seekers of new solutions; and platforms like Quora or Reddit.

The personal technology profiles on UsesThis.com are excellent as well. Here top professionals reveal their dream hardware, software, and configurations. These profiles can also be filtered by field, making them all the more relevant as a source of inspiration on how to set up your personal IT.

Browsing resources like these will let you break free of the limitations of the specific tips that I have presented. Although my recommendations are based on a large number of freelancers' experiences, seeking alternatives will help you expand your horizons and make your IT truly personal.

KEY IDEAS

1. IT is important because it influences your productivity, reliability, and team cooperation.

2. Most freelancers work on computers for most of the day, so even small improvements can have a large impact.

3. You should start by being clear on your priorities and the scope of your IT needs.

4. The key priorities are health, simplicity and security, whose importance is growing constantly.

5. Your goal is a fine-tuned, personal IT approach that supports you and doesn't increase your stress or workload.

6. If you are working with sensitive and confidential information, superb security is a duty.

7. Gmail and G Suite are used by many freelancers. But the free version isn't well suited for professional work.

8. Working in the cloud is not an obligation, but it makes your work a lot easier.

9. Touch typing is an extremely practical skill. It lets you write two or three times faster.

10. Note and task management, time tracking, and invoicing applications are also among the basics.

PRACTICES

✓ Treat health as a priority in your IT, especially if you sit at a computer all day. Consider your options to reduce CO_2 levels, buy a sit-stand desk, more ergonomic hardware, etc.

✓ Perform a basic IT security audit using the list of principles in this chapter. It will only take a few hours to prevent major security flaws and risks you may be facing right now.

✓ If you are using free Gmail (without Google's customer and technical support) and email is important for you, switch and migrate your mail to a reliable paid service like G Suite.

✓ Learn to work in a cloud, if you haven't done so. Select your own combo of apps: email, calendar, documents, notes, secure messaging, to-do, time tracking, invoicing etc.

✓ IT will definitely influence the future of your field. Make plans therefore to stay in touch with the future. Try new apps trusted by your peers, learn new skills, go to courses.

How do you team up and share work with the right people?

Have you ever noticed how much the choice of peers reveals about people? This absolutely applies to freelancers too: Who are their friends? Who do they work with? What sort of clients do they have? Who recommends them?

This social context is critical for a professional, and I have already talked about how freelancers themselves call it the main engine of their success. Social bonds help to form a good name, and the people you work with or choose for your team become a part of your professional identity.

So here I'll explore the questions of who to cooperate with and how to do it, so that it all works and supports your good name and your business. And I will also describe the two most powerful tools for team cooperation: project and process management.

HERMITS PAY FOR THEIR ISOLATION

Not so long ago, coworking spaces, online marketplaces, and communities designed to enable and ease freelancers' work simply didn't exist. Today, isolation is a personal choice.

Unless you are an exceptional professional or a contractor who landed a huge client, isolation will likely give you a smaller income. Social capital earns exceptional interest. Even if a professional isn't a star, social connections give their expertise greater value.

An unknown expert generally earns less than a comparably capable colleague who seeks out cooperation. You can be great at what you do, but if nobody hears about it, you will only succeed with difficulty.

High-quality professionals attract both attention and teammates. Most have an informal team of other freelancers and experts around them, with whom they work on gigs and projects, or whose projects they join.

This is a typical example of peer-to-peer network bonds: no central node exists, but we could find a number of major connecting points and a gravitational center with the best-connected professionals, who act as network nodes.

The most influential professionals tend to have informal communities around them, for which they represent a certain approach or values. Sometimes these are celebrities in a given field in the very best sense: tested professionals who most of their peers know and respect.

A newcomer to freelancing can feel lonely, but the longer they stay at it, the more they will perceive the web of relationships that extend out and form a sort of *spirit of the field*. Each of us plays some role or roles in it: we help, recommend, interconnect, verify and share information, and raise awareness. Some professionals do many things for others for free because they know it will somehow come back to them through this complex network.

This web is always talking. While it's certainly possible to stay outside of it, there also aren't many good reasons for doing so. This is because its rules are loose, letting everyone participate to the degree that is comfortable for them. As freelancers we are all in the same boat.

⟫ TUNING INTO YOUR NETWORK

Entering the web of freelance relationships has one more huge advantage: you will get warnings. Any number of small warnings. Against non-payers, against people who are incompetent, against problematic clients, against dishonest professionals, and against people who like to take more than give, and know how to hide it. In the end they will get their due, but you have to be wary in case they get to you first. Yes, some of this is gossip – but this can also be useful, if you know who to trust.

Problematic people don't advertise their flaws on Facebook. This is why we rely on our colleagues and communities to distinguish the fifty shades of trustworthiness and see who is pleasant to work with and who is better kept at a distance even if they offer to help a hundred times. The world of professionals definitely isn't clear-cut, and in your own interest, you need to learn to be able to tell who to work with and how. People have their light and dark sides; you should learn to profit from the light, while protecting yourself from the dark – if you can.

Unfortunately, some fields are fragmented into opinion clusters or opposing camps centered around influential personalities who hate each other. This is generally bad for the field, and for anyone involved. To be honest, if the personal level prevails and constructive debate no longer interests anyone, it's best to go your own way and not get involved.

Fortunately, cooperation and friendships among freelancers dominate in most fields, because we need each other. Still, there are many antagonistic relationships and rivalries out there. Professional communities are large and complex, so it's natural (yet unfortunate) that out of the countless possible connections and relations, not all are great; i.e. to work in any reasonable way within a community, you have to be a diplomat and truly like people.

I like how my friend Adam Zbiejczuk does it. He is a leading social-media expert whom many of my colleagues respect as an authority on the subject. Many freelancers occasionally bad-mouth their colleagues, and perhaps even rightly so from their standpoint. But Adam merely smiles wryly at a certain name or doubtingly raises his eyebrows. He expresses his opinion, but it can't be quoted in the sense that Adam said this-or-that about someone. He really does mostly say nice things about others. It's no surprise that after fifteen years in the field, he has a great reputation and a vast network of valuable contacts.

I think that this is one influence that gradually changes a freelancer. They suddenly start placing more weight on good relationships, their colleagues, and their community. And when they do need to strike a sterner note, they try to attack the problems, not people.

WHERE TO FIND PARTNERS AND WHAT TO LOOK FOR

By now it should be clear that finding partners and colleagues for your team is much easier if you engage in professional and freelance communities. If you are in contact with people, then you'll get several times more opportunities, information…in short, possibilities. And it's unimportant if you are an extrovert who is better-suited to in-person group meetings, or an introvert who prefers online communities or deeper face-to-face conversations.

As an extrovert and an optimist, I enjoy personal meetings quite a bit. I can find someone to be likable, then randomly be bumping into them in person or online for a few years until one day I realize what I would like to work on with that person. As soon as the need arises, I generally can think of two or three people I could approach.

Finding possible future partners is something I have been doing for years intuitively and naturally. I enjoy it, and it ultimately helps both me and them, because contacts like these often lead to unexpected connections with other people in my surroundings as well.

One good starting point is to never team up with people you don't really trust or with whom you would work poorly. Even if they are cheaper than the rest, any deep disagreements will eventually bubble to the top, and you will simply lose time that you could otherwise spend building a better team. Also, as freelancers these aren't your subordinates, but always just colleagues, so you have no leverage to force their actions if they get all bull-headed. You will have to strengthen your soft-management methods, because you have no authority for the hard cases.

Focus on a person's character and on permanent traits that don't change too much in adulthood, such as thoroughness, reliability, and honorable behavior, as well as their ability to learn, prevent conflicts, and take justified criticism positively.

And because these traits can sometimes be hard to observe, it's good to leave some time and the right distance to think about these people and how they have behaved or behave in critical situations. Because one thing is clear: crises will come. For me it's unacceptable to have someone on my team who jumps into a lifeboat at the first sign of a leak. Yet a person's character reveals itself over time and under pressure, not during a few conversations over coffee. This is why I stick to the old principle of *hire slow, fire fast*.

Sometimes it's great to work even with people who can't do much at the moment, but are visibly willing to learn. If you are looking for someone to help on your small team, that is definitely one alternative. A helper like this will be cheaper than an accomplished professional, you will be passing on your experience, and you will also strongly influence their professional growth.

It's just as important that you find someone who genuinely wants to learn, who is curious and also reasonably loyal, or else you will have to push your apprentice too hard, or they learn something and then leave. On the other hand, we aren't talking about employees here, but freelancers – they won't be cooperating with you full-time. If they can follow their dreams and work on their own projects, there is no need to stop working with you entirely.

So: you can put together a team from verified professionals and hardworking beginners whom you are teaching new things. Your invoicing will either be job-related or done at regular intervals, based on an agreement. I recommend supporting replaceability in roles and cooperation among members, because this strengthens your ability to take action when handling unusual problems. Personally, I organize a group call for my team every month, along with exceptional meetings when needed. The more independent your team members are, the better it will all work for you. Freelancers work poorly in chains.

But definitely clarify with your coworkers to what extent they may seek their own cooperation with the clients for whose orders you have invited them on as team members. Otherwise you'll one day be shocked to find that the beginner whom you invited onto the team for a tiny matter has been negotiating a much more demanding job with the client behind your back. Or that the client has been addressing them because they rightly felt that they belong to you and are therefore trustworthy. This can ultimately hurt you quite a bit, if the junior handles that order poorly or recommends other people who lack in quality. Even though agreements like this are practically impossible to enforce contractually, true professionals respect and uphold them. They know their good name is on the line.

And if you are truly well known within your field, you should keep in mind that a number of colleagues will either directly refer to their collaboration with you in their pitches, or a client could automatically assume that they are good because they worked with you.

⊙ WATCH OUT FOR PASSIVE AGGRESSIVE BEHAVIOR

Many people visibly have no place on a team. The unreliable, argumentative, lazy, unprincipled, untruthful, etc. You definitely understand this yourself, and I don't have to emphasize it.

However, there is one type that often flies under the radar, which can potentially cause a lot of damage or even destroy an entire team's morale. These are individuals with passive-aggressive behavior, and unfortunately many team leaders and project managers don't know how to spot them in time.

Passive-aggressive behavior at first manifests inconspicuously – through unwillingness, excuses, procrastination, delays, negativity, starting very long, unfruitful discussions, ignoring agreements, etc. The smarter aggressors even try to present their actions as beneficial. Here is an example:

We were looking for a video-production supplier for a client who has a number of other activities covered under one brand. We chose a cameraman who seemed to be a good fit, was cheap, and handled the technical aspects of the test filming well. We decided to invite him in to cooperate. I added a condition: a long phone call where I would explain to him how the videos fit into the brand's strategy. His answer floored me: He said that he understood the job well and saw no reason to talk about it for two hours. He wrote it politely, but he was essentially telling me to go to hell.

This is a textbook example of passive-aggressive behavior. Naturally, I could have accepted his unwillingness to review what I saw as an entirely essential layer of the assignment.

But that would have been an enormous mistake! I know from experience that this behavior never ends. In time we would encounter other problems with him, and one day he might put a knife in our back. So: NO. Because I want only the best for my clients and try to provide them with team members with whom it's a joy to cooperate, he received no further room. After his polite refusal, he received an equally polite answer: We thanked him, but would find someone else to work with. I didn't explain anything, but simply paid the invoice he issued, said thank you and goodbye.

Or another example that is a bit less clear:

We needed to replace a key member on a client project, and we found a person who had the prerequisites for the given work. He was forthcoming and the communication was pleasant right from the start, nothing was a problem, fantastic. I clearly explained to him several times at the start that the client was overloaded, I was managing the project, and that he should take all questions and proposals straight to me. We also assigned an evaluator, who had been with the project for over two years and who was to give him feedback for a clean, smooth transition. And as tends to be the case, some problems did appear. The evaluator told the new contractor that he should work on them directly with me, but he did not. He essentially ignored the assignment, deliberately bypassed me, and sent technical questions straight to the client. He acted pleasantly, helpfully...and completely in conflict with my instructions.

The outcome was the same as in the first example: We ended the cooperation immediately. We went over it with the client and agreed that this was no omission, but a deliberate violation of our agreement in an effort to bypass supervision and gain direct influence. And notice as well here how the mask of pleasantness and helpfulness was unimportant.

For inexperienced managers, passive-aggressive behavior can be unclear because of these conflicting expressions. Unfortunately market laws apply here. A bad manager will fail to spot such people and willingly add them to their team, then suffer with them for years. A good manager will see them right away and happily send them on their way, because they know what would follow and that it's much better to build a team without any saboteurs.

My experience from managing many projects is that it's best to cut such people off as soon as possible. Whenever I have let them work in a team unrestricted, it has had serious consequences over time. My managerial experience has taught me to watch for the signs of passive-aggressive behavior very carefully and to take steps to prevent it – that "laid-back dude" has to leave the team, or simply be put on the back burner where he can't do much harm. But it's really best if these people go fish somewhere else.

It may sound cruel, but this is business. A demanding client will get rid of me in just the same way, quickly and cleanly, if they are unsatisfied with my work or if they feel that I'm unable to handle a project. And because I don't have many *un*demanding clients, I handle problems before they arise.

The actions of passive-aggressive individuals are easier to recognize if they are working alongside willing, smoothly-working colleagues with whom it's a joy to cooperate. Joy from cooperation is something that passive-aggressive people will almost never provide.

Yes, finding replacements is hard, but there are lots of people out there, and the change will pay off in the end. Instead of suffering months or even years with someone who will just be undermining a team's efforts and playing in their own sandbox, I would rather spend a few days building new contacts.

Try to also think about what kind of cooperation you personally offer – do you show some passive-aggressive behavior? It may not be directly in your nature, but just a habit from your previous work, your family, etc. If so, you will have to fix this issue yourself, because for everyone else, it's far more convenient to simply not work with you.

FAIR TRADE

If you want to build up a strong team as a freelancer, you have to be fair in what you do and what you give. Fairness is largely subjective, or is based on the customs of the trade – you should know them. I can recall for example the very first case where I served as a mediator:

One acquaintance of mine hired a young graphic designer whom I had recommended. He ordered visuals that were to intended to become part of a larger order for a client and the designer supplied them as a subcontractor. But the client didn't pay, and my acquaintance also refused to pay the designer, reasoning that he himself hadn't been paid. Yet no such option had been agreed on in advance, the graphic designer had done his work and couldn't influence how the order would turn out. So it wouldn't be fair if he didn't get paid.

One of the unwritten rules of business states that *whoever takes the profits runs the risks*. My acquaintance had intended to profit from the order, and his poor management did not entitle him to not pay the designer. Since the designer was not sharing in the final profit, he also should not have shared in the risk of a failed order. This is fair, and also logical.

When I get an order from a client and sub-contract other professionals, I guarantee that they will get paid (unless otherwise agreed upon right from the start). They will get their usual rates in return for their properly done work. I bear the risk of failure, as well as the risk that if my client doesn't pay me and there is no advance payment to cover my costs, I will still have to pay for subcontracted work myself. On the other hand, if I handle an order well, my profit from the income minus the costs can be several times larger than the payments for subcontractors, even if they have worked just as hard. This too is fair, because I have added value. I have acquired the client (which is difficult), put my name out there on the market, and risked a loss. My profit comes from my business activity and the risks that I considered and decided to undertake. The client is satisfied; the subcontractors bear no risk but that of their own failure, and are thus rewarded at their usual rate; and I can create profit only if I prove myself to be a capable manager and professional. Because a key part of the work and the coordination of the order will doubtlessly depend on me.

A fair trade like this makes sense, and freelancers have no problem with it. Problems can arise if the middleman's added value is too small.

For example, agencies that acquire orders and merely pass them on to other professionals with a high margin or commission without adding extra value certainly have their place on the market, but if a freelancer acts like that, their colleagues can view it negatively, as a sort of freeloading. While I don't share this opinion, since doing business and closing deals isn't at all easy, I'm not in the position of the person whose work is being resold like this, am I?

I also understand the people who are bothered by this, and if your profession involves such an activity, I recommend explaining your exact benefit to the cooperating professionals.

Incidentally, reciprocal recommendations, or in some cases non-financial benefits and gifts, are much more common among freelancers than financial commissions. Even if you are used to commissions from the corporate world, you should know that among freelancers, this can be quite a controversial issue. Some even refuse commissions *a priori* as unethical, because they perceive them as a sort of bribe, a hidden extra fee for the customer, or even a threat to their own independence and loyalty towards the client who is paying for it all.

So it definitely isn't appropriate to demand or force commissions in any way. This is more a matter of a sensitive agreement and the free will of both parties. On the other hand, reciprocal recommendations between colleagues are common, or in some cases also gifts large or small. Some freelancers even offer a choice of several rewards for recommendations, which can even include the fruits of other freelancers' labor, in place of commissions. This is one of the best solutions – you are still rewarding people for recommendations, while you are also supporting your colleagues' work.

Paying commissions can make sense, however, if you are recommended over the long term by someone whom you can't otherwise reasonably reward, and you also want them to keep at it. However, all this must have the blessings of your accountant (how you pay) and lawyer (whether it's legal). But in any case, don't promise commissions in advance, and only pay a commission free of obligation, to people who you feel have truly earned it and who agree with this kind of reward.

The mention of commissions is in order here, so that you can know it's uncommon for a freelancer to demand a commission from you for an invitation into a large project. While not completely unimaginable, it's also not normal.

Sub-deliveries also have other limitations. It's not customary for a freelancer to resell their colleagues' work in any large volume. That is because by being the guarantor of a whole order, they are taking on significantly more liability and risks, and in some countries also more taxes and a greater administrative burden.

Once larger payments are involved, it's customary for the invited professionals to become direct suppliers and negotiate directly with the client. The professional who acquired the order and invited them, meanwhile, becomes a coordinator and mediator of fair agreements between them and the client. It's in the interest of this professional to satisfy both sides, but if they also manage the whole project as a project manager (PM), they have to mainly be loyal to the client, who is paying them for it, and clearly inform their colleagues of this. Project management can then be a quite important pricing factor on top of their expert work. This PM-expert then manages the order, defends the client's interests, and may never tolerate colleagues' actions that might harm those interests.

The simple rule for deciding between the two models (sub-deliveries under one roof vs. dividing an order into separate orders) is that if small sums are involved and it serves the client, sub-deliveries under one roof are better. The responsibility all lies with the person serving as the delivery's guarantor, and the client doesn't have to pay what might be a dozen small invoices, or waste time dealing with a dozen people they have never met.

The client doesn't have to care how many people have contributed to the gig. For them what is important is a high-quality, professional result, smooth progress, and a clearly defined author's license and liability, not the specific workflow. Large deliveries, meanwhile, are more frequently separated as independent parts. A combination of both approaches is common as well:

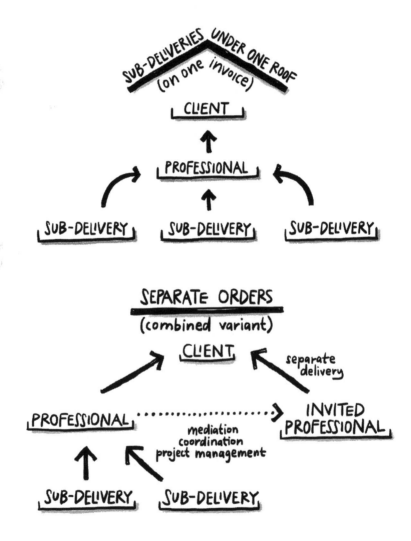

When an order is divided into separate deliveries, each direct supplier bears no small share of the risk. When a supplier fails, they harm mainly themselves, and so they have more room to negotiate about the price, conditions, etc. In short, it's a separate agreement within the overall order or project.

This model has countless variants that variously balance out or change the conditions for the parties involved. But it makes no sense to go into those details here, because common practice varies strongly among fields, and what is common in one place may be seen elsewhere as bizarre. And there are also differences among countries. In some, free-lancers might even found a single-purpose corporation for large joint orders. This limited-liability company then acts a legal entity contracted by the clients.

You might be asking: how does dividing up orders among multiple freelancers work in practice? The answer is: surprisingly well. Managing orders as projects is very flexible and lets one assemble a team from various freelancers while always respecting an order's needs. Problematic and unreliable professionals don't get invited twice, and with each new foul, they are more and more marginalized by the professional community into the role of loners who hunt small gigs from who knows where. The remaining professionals generally say yes to cooperation, seek colleagues on their level, and become more confident in order management and execution with every new experience.

For top freelancers the final quality of project-type orders is often strongly above the market average. Such long-term "adventuring parties" of well-coordinated freelancers work very effectively, reliably, and quickly, even as their composition evolves.

Thus the mechanism for cooperation among freelancers is largely reputation-based self-regulation. All of the actors have a huge interest in gaining the satisfaction of both the client and their colleagues – who will then be glad to invite them onto other future jobs.

One cooperation model that, on the other hand, works poorly in the long term is various freelancers' cooperatives under one brand. In practice I rarely see groups like this surviving for more than a few years. The reason lies mainly in members' differing growth rates and the fact that instead of a good name, they often build a pseudo-brand over which they don't have full control. And this strongly harms the team's most capable members, who usually realize over time that it's better to work under their own name. Limited cooperation under a shared brand is certainly fine, if you don't give up on building your own good name. But for larger, longer-term cooperation, it's better to transform the informal association into a company, where the partners will have clearly defined shares, rights, and responsibilities.

⊙ EVEN FREELANCERS CAN HAVE STRATEGIC PARTNERS

However, cooperation isn't just limited to other professionals or companies. Other partners can participate in orders indirectly, or can variously enhance your possibilities.

- The coworking space where you organize regular trainings can be a strategic partner.
- Projects with a large community can also be a partner.
- Friendly media or journalists whom you help as professionals can also be partners.
- So can the publisher of your book.
- Or the conference organizer who regularly invites you for cooperation.
- Or a non-profit that you aid and helps you fulfill your professional calling.
- Or a field association that supports a project of yours because it helps everyone.
- Or a university where you lecture, or your alma mater.

In short, any individual or institution with whose help you can achieve higher goals is a strategic partner. Most strategic partnerships grow slowly, with one party or the other speaking up now and then, and the trust crystallizing until it leads to cooperation.

When you see a first-rate professional launch their Big Project, there will suddenly be a growing chorus of voices to support it, aid it, spread the news, interpret it for other groups, defend it, and explain it. Precisely this is the result of a healthy partnership – when something is on the line, these loose relationships come to life and you will find support for the good cause left and right.

When you are seeking partnerships, don't aim for immediate results. This is the destructive growth-hacking approach that pushes businesses up with no real foundations. Good, stable businesses grow differently. They arise from a shared root system and become as strong as a tree with deep roots, thanks to which they can safely grow that much higher.

In ten years, your fundamental personality traits will probably be more or less the same as they are today. All that an adult can count on for sure in the future are the cards they have been dealt. Yet despite this they can achieve higher and higher goals, primarily thanks to the people – the colleagues and partners – they surround themselves with. Your professional growth isn't actually just yours; it comes from cooperation among many people who have in some way supported you.

MISTAKES ARE...FREE!

But back to your team of collaborators. Teammates are people; they make mistakes. Sometimes terrible, brutal mistakes that make you want to scream. But you can't work without mistakes.

You basically have two options. You can punish the person for their mistake, which can even mean ending your cooperation. Or you can be easy on people, and hard on mistakes.

Penalizing mistakes is problematic, because you are not in a superior position relative to your team. Two freelancers will have a hard time trumping each other. So you can't just command and direct. There is probably some contractual relationship between you that isn't entirely precisely broken down to cover all the situations that might arise.

Nevertheless, even if you do have some form of punishment for mistakes agreed upon in advance, for example via reduced payment, you have to go easy on that. Conscientious professionals most often make mistakes in areas where they are innovating or learning new things. If you penalize them for this, you are ultimately depriving yourself and your business of their creative and innovative potential. By punishing mistakes, you are pushing yourself into a blind alley with those who only do what you tell them and never try to do more.

So the other route is to be hard on the mistakes themselves. This is much tougher than cutting someone's payment. It actually means combining several different approaches into one workable whole – and I'll spend the rest of this chapter explaining these.

Above all it means selecting reliable, eager, *teachable* people who really seek to improve and to do things well. You can also cooperate with other kinds of people, but those will be harder to manage and will have to receive lower rewards and less responsibility – otherwise they just won't pay off. So let's say that you now have your informal team of eager and relatively reliable people – freelancers and others. But mistakes are still happening; it's unavoidable. So what do you do?

Above all you have to speak about them openly and fairly. You might see a serious mistake where your colleague does not. And it's crucial to talk about things exactly as you see them, because otherwise you will just increase the misunderstandings and differing perceptions of the same thing.

If you believe that a mistake is so serious and critical that it could threaten a whole project and anger the client, say exactly that. Use an appropriate level of tact, of course, choose the right moment, and try to mainly discuss facts (what happened), not people (who is at fault). But name the problem clearly.

Don't say "well and there is one more small thing" when you know perfectly well that it's no small thing. That is an approach you can save for meetings with the client. Internally you had better call problems by their real names, or else real misunderstandings await. A mistake is a mistake, and you can't call it a small thing just to protect someone's feelings.

What happens next is the key. Your counterpart might see things the same as you and admit the problem; then you can talk more deeply, draw conclusions to prevent it from happening again, and be done with it. But you also might see things differently. They understand your viewpoint, but they have a different opinion. You discuss and try to jointly arrive at why you see the matter so differently, and what is its cause.

Speaking like this about mistakes is beneficial, it clears the air, and it strengthens the mindset of striving for a superb, professional result. True professionals welcome such behavior, when they know that the goal isn't to punish them or blame them in front of the client, but to root out problems.

Anyone in the team can come with internal criticism; it's not just for the project manager. I personally have a reputation as a straight talker, but I expect and welcome the same from the colleagues with whom I cooperate. One even sent me, all on his own, a three-page analysis of a completed project with some reproaches on what I could improve in the future. Another told me with disarming sincerity: your laptop's keyboard is horribly dirty, and it doesn't leave a good impression at all. And a third told me straight up that the design changes I was promoting were obviously lacking expertise and that if I kept trying to decide everything myself without studying up, he would stop working with me. Wouldn't you just want to kill them? I certainly do sometimes, but above all I'm grateful.

These discussions are sometimes demanding and tiring, but they work. You get to the root of things. Or you learn that your views on a matter differ so much that no further cooperation makes sense, and you part ways on good terms. Or you realize that what you saw as the other person's mistake was actually your own. When it comes to an informal team for your own projects or orders, you will probably be managing or coordinating it yourself. And the mistake may have arisen mainly due to your own insufficient management. Your colleagues didn't receive a precise task definition, or key information wasn't transferred. The left hand didn't know what the right hand was doing.

So here we have arrived at the unpleasant truth that while individuals make mistakes, the root causes are often in poor project or order management. Mistakes arise in the space you leave open for them by neglecting management. It's like a piece of land that is part of your garden, but since you have neglected it, it is covered in weeds.

Insufficient management is an often-criticized sore point in cooperation with freelancers. Always watch who is actually managing a project and whether anyone is actually managing it at all. It may be the colleague who invited you in, it may be the client, or it may be no-one – this is an arrangement where, if any serious problems ever occur, fingers will start being pointed in circles. Even if the individual professionals are fantastic, the absence of management is a problem that can reduce the benefit for everyone involved. It's no wonder that after a few such experiences, some freelancers preventively avoid getting involved in insufficiently managed orders.

When you see a great example of cooperation among independent professionals somewhere, it's generally not a spontaneously managed project. And the more demanding the project, the greater the role of the coordinator, or of an actual project manager. Meanwhile for larger projects such as building a house or a professional website or, say, organizing a conference, professional management is simply a prerequisite for success.

If you want team cooperation to work well in both routine matters and difficult projects, it's not enough to just hunt mistakes like flies on a table. You need to approach things systematically and engage in management fairly strongly. And this has two basic levels.

⬥ PROCESSES VS. PROJECTS

If you're going to work deeply on managing or coordinating cooperation among a team, without question you must start distinguishing between processes and projects.

Projects are unique and one-off in nature. Their goal is to achieve a desired yet uncertain result while minimizing problems, as well as lost time and money. This might be an important order, or it might be a development project like building a website, moving an office, innovating on a product, etc. These are all steps into the unknown. So in the interest of reducing risks, we apply *project management* here, as a systematic approach for doing projects. A well-managed project ends with the desired results, on time, and at the set quality and price.

Processes, on the other hand, constantly repeat. Every day, week, month, quarter, or year: email handling, accounting, client support, blogs and social media posts, backups, warehouse inventory, etc. These are often dozens of repeating workflows that constitute the imaginary clockwork of our business. We find them being used by both freelancers and companies, whose overall business performance depends on their optimal operation. You can imagine vital processes of a business as activities supporting its health – just as your body has to maintain its blood circulation, breathing, eating, and sleep cycles in order to live and prosper. The failure of important business processes can cause a temporary breakdown.

Classifying projects and processes can be tricky. For example, for mediocre web designers creating a new website is a routine process, while for their more ambitious colleagues, every website amounts to a unique project. Also, don't be confused by the fact that adding and implementing new processes is itself a project.

Still, once you get used to the terminology of projects and processes, they will be easy to distinguish. Start out by simply placing new and large goals among projects, and repeating, routine workflows among processes. The approaches and strategies for managing projects and processes differ significantly, so I will go through them separately.

❯ PROJECT COMPETENCIES

Cooperation by independent professionals on large orders has been getting more project-oriented over time. So gigs are managed as projects, and all team members are expected to know roughly what this entails. This knowledge is one of the keys to large and important orders.

To start coordinating and managing projects professionally, you must largely lead by example. A project manager who doesn't meet deadlines and who is unreliable won't be respected by anyone. They must above all be able to do themselves what they ask of others. So in connection with freelance business, we have to speak of the two levels involved in fully professional project management:

The first, simpler level is *project competencies*, i.e. the set of skills that you need to smoothly cooperate on projects as professionals.

The second, more demanding level is *project management,* i.e. leading the order and the whole team on to an excellent, near to flawless result as possible.

My brother Mira Vlach, an independent trainer and project management consultant, describes a project-competent professional as having these basic traits:

"A capable, reliable, and tested expert without any blemishes on their reputation (unfair behavior, conflict escalation, etc.). Available and affordable: not constantly overloaded, and charging a market price that matches their skills and experience. They act as the glue, not the acid, in the team. They have unbreakable morale and don't run away at the first sign of problems. You don't have to hold their hand; when a task is done, they don't stand around, but take an interest in the project status, in what is next and if they can help. Ideally the professional not only takes an interest in follow-up steps, but also perceives the project scope, and how their own work fits into it, throughout their cooperation."

A person who only sees their corner of the work will tend towards self-centered behavior, which is also the best way to convince others to never invite you to a project again:

"Play in your own sandbox and stroke your professional ego. Perceive only the needs of your own subcontracted work and don't care about the project as a whole, even though you are complicating others' lives. Are exceptionally inflexible and unhelpful during any changes. Don't hesitate to argue with other team members. Forget about constructively led, polite discussion. Blow up at others so they are afraid to tell you anything," Mira recommends sarcastically, adding: "I think assertiveness and defending your position and interests are fine. The problem is that in a team full of overly assertive people, it can be a problem to do and arrange anything worthwhile."

Everyone's degree of self-centeredness is different, and even people who see themselves as team players have some. My experience with a group of friends while hiking in the Austrian Alps is illustrative. For most of them, it was relatively easy hike, and so they showed no consideration for the group members who did have difficulties. They ran ahead and ignored the basic rule that in difficult terrain, you need to have someone in view in the front and in the back. And so it happened that a friend who was one of the last in line took a wrong turn in confusing, rocky terrain with no trees or other landmarks. Nobody waited for her. I was walking further behind with another friend with an aching foot and if we hadn't seen her at the last moment as a red dot among the rocks, she would have continued wandering further into the hostile mountains. We would only have realized she was missing an hour before twilight at our final meeting point. While I don't want to condemn anyone for this kind of behavior, since then I have learned to seek among my collaborators something that I call an *expedition mentality* – the ability to show regard for a group's weakest members, offer help, prevent risks, and not let anyone wander off of the safe path.

A professional overflowing in project competencies has nerves of steel and can stay professional even in tense and stressful situations. Not only do they cooperate smoothly with the project manager, the client, and other team members, they also care about project management. They get what it involves and how they can benefit their project-managing colleague. They ask for cooperation and feedback, see risks, and notify others of possible problems in advance. They also have a mature personal productivity system so that they can keep deadlines, and have at least some idea of the apps typically used for managing freelancers' projects.

Don't worry; you don't have to run out and buy Microsoft Project and draw complex Gantt charts for your project's timing. Freelance project management is mostly supported by the applications I discussed in the previous chapter.

For managing smaller projects, freelancers make heavy use of shared calendars and documents (e.g. in G Suite) and to-do lists that let them share tasks within a project team. For freelancer project management itself, specialized yet still fairly undemanding web apps are used. Although Basecamp is the best-known, Asana is also very popular, as is the simpler Trello, as well as Slack, a modern platform designed for team communication.

Naturally you don't have to master all of these specialized apps, but it can be good to glance at one of them occasionally. And if you are using one on your team, it's good to spend some time exploring and mastering it.

◉ PROJECT MANAGEMENT

You can think of the difference between project competencies and project management like this: competencies make it easier for you to cooperate on a project, while management lets you plan and reliably lead projects even if you are managing several at once.

With full concentration, many people can handle one complex project well even without project management. Its main benefit comes when you are managing multiple projects at once, you have to switch focus, and without a systematic approach you could easily miss significant links or details. Remember, projects can affect each other in many ways, for example, when they share resources or budgets. When they do, an experienced project manager is also a negotiator, balancing the interests of various parties, putting out fires, or taming greedy suppliers.

Meanwhile your stance towards work, not your choice of tools, is what matters.

One example is Eva Hermans, a freelancer with an unbeatable humility to performance ratio who organizes nearly 400 events a year for the most demanding of clientele, mainly from Germany, the Netherlands, Denmark, and Sweden, communicating daily in these languages and as needed in English. She organizes customized events for companies such as Deutsche Bank, Bosch, KLM, Miele and SAP, from weekend trips for 15 people to large events for 150 or more. And now hold on: Eva uses neither a to-do app, nor a digital calendar, nor special software. And yet during the high season she may have five or more events running at once. She relies mainly on her great memory, her experience, her proven partners, and her team. However, for every event she does prepare by writing down what will happen when, contact info for key persons, and also alternative crisis scenarios for each phase. She leads the team members in place at the event based on the principle *"Only call Eva when things go from bad to worst."* She expects them to handle ordinary problems themselves.

The trend towards flexible methods that lean on simple principles and project software rather than certification and formalized approaches is clearly visible today even in large corporations. For example, I have a client who worked for 25 years at Procter & Gamble as a top project manager and led large global projects without any formal project certification. He definitely worked from project methodologies, but only to the extent that he and his employer considered necessary.

The same applies to freelancers who manage their orders as projects. A good freelance project manager is generally above all 1. an experienced professional, who 2. has excellent project competencies, 3. can use project management software, and 4. has a solid idea of what project management is about and has either read books on it or went through some training. The top project managers also 5. share their experience and know-how with their colleagues who manage projects of other types. They may even be members of an organization that joins PMs across all fields, organizes conferences for them, etc.

One prime example of an unconventional approach is the *Lean Startup* method described in the book of the same name by Eric Ries. In projects with many variables such as app development, cycles replace rigid planning. These cycles lead gradually from the rough mock-up to the final project and factor in the experience gained along the way.

The flexible approach is also supported by the fact that most freelancer teams are assembled by freelancers themselves. Members aren't designated to them from the outside. If they were, it would be a good reason to use standard project management methodologies. These hold up much better under unfavorable and unpredictable circumstances, such as an incompetent subcontractor sabotaging the project.

As I see it, the ability to enable cooperation among people who are unusable for others due to some limitation such as communication problems or poor reliability is among project management's greatest strengths. I take this into account in advance and adapt my management to it, and this lets me choose collaborators from among a much wider group of people, including amateurs who don't yet have the right work habits.

With top professionals, we often try to figure out the secret ingredient of their success. And often it's their ability to manage a project team and find collaborators for themselves, maybe even juniors who are exceptional in some way – loyal, responsible, smart, etc.

⊚ NEVER HEARD OF PROCESS MANAGEMENT? YOU'RE NOT ALONE...

When comparing processes and projects, I touched upon process management. Like everything, management has its fashion trends, and so while project management has been in fashion for years, process-management awareness is poor – especially among freelancers and small companies.

You may see projects and thousands of certified and self-taught PMs everywhere. The educational programs, institutions, certification, etc. all work superbly here. And there are dozens, if not hundreds, of apps, tools and project management methodologies. There are even whole project-oriented corporations, like IBM. Projects have swept the business world, and thanks to good awareness-building, freelancers and the public know about them too.

Processes (and process management), meanwhile, are relatively unknown territory guarded by ancient evils: monstrous process diagrams, ivory-tower methodologies, and software tools from the distant 20th century. And this is a problem, because mastering processes is fundamental for raising reliability and productivity in practically every field.

You *will* need processes. Many people believe that managing projects and processes takes only intuition and common sense, but this is false. Being systematic, just like being reliable, is definitely not part of human nature. Not at all. Process (and project) management is directly opposed to the intuitive approach. While the techniques or approaches inside it can certainly be intuitive, the system overall is not. Giving birth to it hurts and costs hours of boring grind. But it brings a few a-ha moments that slowly produce order and a system.

So what does a process look like? Complex company processes are generally non-linear; their diagrams branch and join. But I don't know any freelancers who complicate it that much. Most of us make do with linear processes, typically in the form of checklists, which describe a given workflow step by step.

⦿ THE POINT OF FREELANCE PROCESSES

Before I describe the foundations of *how* to deploy processes, I should also say *why*. What does it bring me as an entrepreneur? And why should you start thinking about process management?

Unifying know-how in a logical timeline is one clear benefit of linear, non-branched processes. If you do some complex workflow with over a dozen steps repeatedly, and you rely only on your memory in the process, you will often forget something. In his excellent book on creating professional checklists *The Checklist Manifesto,* Atul Gawande states that this even applies to highly expert activities such as surgery or controlling flight operations.

Unfortunately, we are only human. Even top experts make mistakes and overlook key steps in routine procedures. Thus it's better to rely on checklists that describe the given activity step by step and don't allow you to skip anything. Also, we gradually supplement our processes with steps that we initially forgot. So every process matures to greater fullness and perfection, until in time it truly contains all the relevant know-how.

The level of detail depends mainly on the nature of a given activity. Gawande emphasizes that a good checklist should be relatively brief, which is definitely true for a risky maneuver, such as emergency plane landings, but doesn't apply for all processes. You see, a checklist isn't the same as a process; it's only an aid that is often used in process management. Some processes can comprise even hundreds of steps.

Less stress and greater flexibility is an entirely unexpected benefit for most people. Many fight processes because they hate checklists and reports. Some even proclaim that they left the corporate world in order to *not* have to fill out any more spreadsheets. And I understand them. But when you are facing a heavy workload, there is nothing better than a precisely described and fine-tuned process. You don't have to remember everything that you need to do under stress; you proceed step by step through your process, and your brain can relax a bit. Having an underlying process still enables you to deviate, where it makes sense, and to be more flexible in rescheduling and giving estimates, as you have a clear list of steps that need to be finished. Processes thus reduce cognitive strain, and if they are set up reasonably and only for important things, you definitely aren't running the risk of getting spreadsheet poisoning.

Smooth operation and significant time and money savings, in tens of percent, come from the reduced mistakes in process repetitions and speeding up the well-described steps.

The ability to delegate and outsource activities – in short, if you map and describe a process well, you can delegate it to someone effectively. Delegating key routines without processes is a common business mistake. If you are delegating without keeping records or ongoing checks, you face the risk of serious omissions or mistakes, and you may also become dependent on your helper, who, if they leave, will take details and an established optimal workflow with them in their head.

So whenever I'm a *process owner*, I insist that even minor process improvements be recorded. If I later delegate the process to someone else, I can be sure that all the important steps have been described. We just have to go through them and train the novice. Many entrepreneurs have a huge problem with delegation precisely because they (often rightly) fear losing control. The magic of process management is precisely that you are delegating *without losing control*. You keep control because you own and design the process and can monitor its individual *instances* (the singular runs of a process) via records, reports, or third-party evaluations.

Data records for future analysis pile up just by recording every single process instance somewhere. This makes it possible for you to then examine process effectiveness and see trends, where there is room for improvement, etc. You may never use these records, but you can't know that in advance.

Having free hands for other adventures and business projects could ultimately be the main benefit of established processes. For me, they help to create a space where I can devote myself to new interests and development projects – like this book. I'm always sad when I see a successful professional who can't break their chains and who personally handles a daily agenda that they could, with processes, delegate in a controlled way to create time for more important work. These trapped entrepreneurs can spend up to four hours a day on routine activities that they really could delegate.

⬢ EMBRYONIC PROCESSES

One prerequisite for introducing processes is that you have a healthy business foundation and core. Processes are an excellent tool for tuning up your business, but they won't make a bad product a best-seller, nor will they fill up gaping holes in marketing or pricing. That is for a general overhaul, not for fine-tuning.

So let's assume that you have a healthy core. But which process do you start with? Or is it better to go straight ahead and deploy one system for everything?

Processifying your whole business in one go is a titanic task. And doing it randomly can be just as bad. So the usual jumping-off point is to recognize and list your repeating workflows. These are born on their own out of your routines or habits and help to keep your business running. In other words, you already have some processes in your business whether you realize it or not.

These latent, embryonic processes are rarely optimized. So you need to realize their existence, importance, complexity, and maturity. This list of main workflows then forms a rough foundation that you can gradually develop and perfect using process management.

What should be the first process you cover? Here are some options:

* *A non-trivial one.* Don't make your inbox check an independent process.

* *But no monster.* A check of a thousand-item warehouse would turn you off.

- *A linear one.* Without branching into sub-processes based on a diagram or some condition.

- *A frequent one.* Repeated daily, weekly, or monthly – so that improving it won't drag on.

- *An important, beneficial one.* It should help you in an area that somewhat troubles you.

- *A team or tandem one.* So that it's a good candidate for delegation.

In addition to these general traits, here are some specific processes you might develop: *Daily or weekly work reviews. A new client, from order to delivery and a paid invoice. Preparations for a presentation or training. Backing up critical data and organizing files. Filing your taxes. Monthly maintenance and office cleaning. Research and preparing new social media posts.*

These are generally activities you already do on your own. But only process management can handle their systematic improvement, interconnection, delegation, etc.

So that's that for the introduction – and, I hope, for your choice of first process. So let's experiment! Here is my 5-step process management crash course:

I. MAPPING THE PROCESS

Repeating a workflow doesn't have to mean doing it the same way every time. Sometimes you can't fully concentrate, your mind is elsewhere, and you skip steps. Other times, you completely forget you need to do it. The result is an irregular course with deviations. An un-tuned machine.

So first of all, map out the whole process as the series of steps or actions that lead to its successful completion. You can work here with a pencil and paper, as well as an Excel or Google spreadsheet. Every line represents one step on the path of the whole process. You can also use PowerPoint to draw a simple flow chart as a visual aid. Already in this phase, you record individual process instances (occurrences), generally by adding a new column, checking off completed tasks, and writing notes on them.

Here is an example of what a simplified new-order process at a small carpentry workshop with three initiated instances in the columns on the right might look like. In practice it would probably be twice as long, but even then it would take just one look to see each order's status and what are the next steps. If it's also an online spreadsheet in G Suite, it can be shared within a team and tasks can be divided up, or discussions can be had using comments in individual cells.

Client	Beltbox Ltd.	Austin family	Paul Douglas
Date of the inquiry	May 30th	May 27th	May 25th
Item(s) inquired about	conference table	double bed	large bookcase
Was it based on a recommendation?	no	yes (Paul Douglas)	no, found us on Google
Is this a trustworthy person with no red flags?	not really	yes	yes, well-known dentist
Contact call (date and optional note)	no reply yet	May 28th	May 25th
Could this be a premium client?		no	yes, definitely
Is there room for upselling?		no, they mostly want it cheap	yes, he also ordered a cabinet
Do I have the info I need for a calculation?		yes	yes
Price in offer		$950	$6,350
Offer sent on		May 28th	May 27th
Order status or other result		waiting for reply	paid, in production
Recommendation bonus?		P. Douglas gift	-
Notes	company website is broken, nobody answers the phone, waiting for a reply	they're not in a hurry	knows half the town, treat him well

II. PROCESS ANALYSIS

Your initial process map is rarely complete, especially if it has dozens of steps. So with each new process instance, you add in-between steps that were initially forgotten. But you should also slightly simplify them, because your process map isn't meant as a detailed record of its course down to the smallest, 1:1 details. It's meant more as a smart roadmap, so it should be clear, but not drowned in details.

The process analysis and monitoring phase will lead to fine-tuned documentation and a deeper understanding. Here you are trying to describe the ordinary, customary form of the process. This generally takes a few weeks. Smaller processes can be mapped after as few as three instances. Complex ones that involve the participation of more people need more time and questions. The result should be a realistic map of the process sequence and a record of several instances, including working notes.

Learn to describe individual steps so that anyone can understand them. If you create a cleaning process in your home coworking space for your colleagues, don't just write "flowers"; write precise instructions like "water the flowers with the water kept in the closet and then refill the container."

III. PROCESS OPTIMIZATION

You can often spot giant holes and reserves in the existing process already during its mapping and analysis. So through optimization you try to determine:

- *What should the process look like?*
- *What can you simplify?*
- *Where are the risks, and how can you prevent them?*
- *How often should the process take place?*
  - *Regularly every day, week, two weeks, month; the last day of the month, etc.*
  - *At most X days, weeks, months after the last instance (the flexible option)*
  - *As needed (the process is triggered by some event or condition)*

In this phase, you start playing with the process as a model. You think about where to speed it up, supplement it or otherwise adjust it. You either change the process gradually, or the original one proves itself so unsuitable that you redesign it from the ground up. One way or the other, it's an experiment that may or may not lead to an improvement. So be sure to carefully document and evaluate every process instance, as that is the only way to recognize objective improvements.

One example of an improvement might be optimizing a process for profitability by adding a premium variant to your calculation. That lets the client pick from at least two options. Wherever we have introduced this improvement to the order process, we have seen higher revenue and profits from high value clients. This is one small extra step in your process, and yet it can bring more revenue growth than, say, thinking hard about prices for a whole month. Meanwhile every small improvement is reflected in all future instances!

You can also tell that you are on the right track by the fact that the process isn't inflating, but instead becoming a simpler and cleaner set of critical points. After a few years of tuning it will be incomparably more efficient than it was in its initial, undocumented form.

IV. FIGHT BRAVELY

Process optimization may look peaceful and easy, just like the resulting report emailed by the person to whom you delegate the process. But habits take prisoners and in reality it's a war against bad habits and our natural resistance to change.

This is why it's best to start with one simple process, which you will also learn from. A mentor is also important. They can show you countless smart tricks and shortcuts that already exist. On the one hand these will sometimes be miraculously effective, but on the other hand you have to know how to use them sensitively.

Here is one example of such an improvement: by applying time-tested process management practices, such as the rule that one specific person should be accountable for a process instance. And that person is then held responsible if the work stands still or contains mistakes. If nobody is accountable for an instance, problems like these happen much more often.

Not everyone likes the introduction of processes. Some people hate spreadsheets and tables, some lack time or desire – and some are completely unwilling to let other people review their work. And some hold their tongues. So introducing complex processes in work teams is often a game of diplomacy. Everyone should be in agreement on the final process, which doesn't however mean that it won't get jammed up a few times. In that case you will need to keep restarting the process in improved forms until you have identified and overcome its major flaws.

V. TESTING THROUGH DELEGATION

You can recognize a well-implemented process by how it helps you and saves money and time. It runs smoothly with a regular interval and scope, as can be verified in its records.

But that doesn't yet mean that it's properly documented. The person performing a process may partly be working from their memory, and if so, the whole process lives and dies with them. The true quality test for process deployment is thus its delegation to a different person – after some training, naturally.

Especially where the embryonic process and the newly deployed one are performed by the same person, only delegation will show you the real holes in it. This leads to a re-strengthening of the process, which thus becomes a universal workflow enabling full replaceability within the team. This will then help you out during vacations, sick days, and unexpected departures.

Delegation would be a good end to our crash course. But since this book tries to go beyond the basics, I'm adding five extra areas for advanced process-makers.

VI. PROCESS EVALUATION

You can optionally also add an evaluation layer to your deployed process. That means that while one person performs the process and records its instances, another person evaluates their work and adds this evaluation to the record.

The point of evaluation is not to nitpick, but to provide feedback, leading to further process improvements. Over time, doing a process routinely leads one to miss minor flaws, which you try to catch through this type of evaluation.

The evaluator has the advantage of a bird's eye view and can be more objective and detached in their observations. If, for example, you are outsourcing your project's social media presence and you have introduced a process for it, you can then ask a different specialist to, say, go over published posts twice a month and suggest improvements.

VII. REPORTING

A correctly deployed and outsourced process can be automated to the point where all you get as its owner is an email report with an overview of its key points or statistics.

Mature processes can even run so smoothly that although you get a weekly (or monthly) report, you only have to intervene in the process a few times a year, if at all – perhaps when a report shows a major problem or the evaluator recommends changes.

Many people naturally have resistance to reporting, after having written long corporate reports that nobody read. But my response to this is always that a good report is brief, useful, and it's not a formality. It points out things that there is no column for in the process and that should not be missed. For my processes, I demand reports *and read them,* otherwise I would cut back on them. And I thank people for every dutifully prepared report; I don't take it as something automatic.

VIII. SUB-PROCESSES

Sub-processes are minor branches in the main process. They can be fixed, or can run after some condition is met. A process might for example state that if a new client is less transparent, you apply a stricter protocol to screen for non-payers and take a few extra steps to check them out a bit more thoroughly.

IX. THE META-PROCESS

Naturally things don't end with your first process. As you gradually add three or four more, the need will also arise to join them into some kind of continuous system or whole, which you can of course optimize as well.

If you are delegating multiple routine activities to an assistant via processes, think of the meta-process as a thorough system for naming, repeating, and reporting on them – for example: every Monday, the assistant sends out invoices and reminders; on Tuesdays and Thursdays, prompts due tasks, tie up loose ends and clean up Basecamp; on Wednesdays, they research news in the field, and every Friday, they send a summary. And you can probably also include outputs from processes you are involved in through your clients to this weekly overview.

I know that the meta-process looks suspicious. That is until one day you find that you need it. I have seen three different forms: 1. a fully automated report, 2. a summary table with an overview of all processes, or 3. a text summary for the outputs of processes in a report. In any case, it helps you keep a top-down view, especially when your processes have long been running well.

X. A PROCESS AUDIT

Things that run reliably long-term may still lag behind the rest of your business. I thus have to close by mentioning auditing processes and boosting their capacity.

The simple way to audit is to re-open the process, check it, fill in new steps, and re-optimize. You are fine-tuning the machine.

Every process is also designed for a certain load – a maximum number of simultaneous instances or the overall capacity of the person performing the process. If the burden rises, then during the audit, you strengthen the process design so that it meets the growing demands with a reasonable reserve.

And finally, the audit may also cause you to merge several standalone processes into one, if this makes preparations more efficient and brings you savings.

◉ PROCESS MANAGEMENT APPS

I have mentioned several times that shared G Suite spreadsheets can be used for process deployment, but in reality this is a makeshift approach. It has the clear disadvantage that it doesn't at all guide you towards good process practices; it's just an online spreadsheet.

It also has the clear disadvantage that every new collaborator has access over the shared spreadsheet to all historical process instances, which can be a bit risky if the records contain confidential data on your orders, clients, profits, etc. One other disadvantage of G Suite spreadsheets is that once they grow a bit, they can be slow to load and manage on a mobile.

My colleagues and I wanted to find a better app and tried many of them – unfortunately without success. The professional ones were all based on process diagrams that are too complex and unappealing for managing the processes of freelancers and small businesses. And the rest of them, which do let you design linear processes based on checklists to a limited extent, had problems with cost, speed, design, or user-management complexity. Certain to-do apps are a category of their own; they let you create templates for repeating tasks, but again it's done in a way that isn't enough for real process management, and especially for keeping records and subsequent analyses.

We were so frustrated by these results and the flaws in managing our own processes in G Suite that we decided to develop Procesoid – probably the world's simplest process-management app at present. It's aimed at the linear processes of freelancers and teams as well as larger organizations and non-manufacturing firms. However, Process Street is also a fine application, even though it's still fairly complex and expensive for beginners.

I personally can't imagine my business without process management. I use it for myself and for my clients, to improve and manage repeating activities, as well as for my own routine workflows. Whenever I start working on something that will be repeated, I automatically think about whether or not to make it a process right away, writing down each step. Most of the time I won't do it, because it means extra work that, for small tasks, will not pay off, but if the workflow is fairly complex and I plan to repeat it twenty times, it's a clear candidate for creating a process for my own needs. And after all, a good process manager trains all the time.

KEY IDEAS

1. The teammates we choose are our business card. And hermits pay for their isolation.

2. Successful professionals generally also play an important role in their profession's community and web of relationships.

3. Building your own team is a task that takes years. Character traits are fundamental.

4. Watch out for passive-aggressive behavior. It's hard to recognize and causes major damage.

5. Cooperation on gigs among freelancers has its unwritten rules and established norms.

6. Learn to give your colleagues good feedback and to name and examine problems.

7. Process and project management are the two most powerful tools for team cooperation.

8. Projects are unique. A project manager must themselves have project competencies.

9. Processes are repeated. They lie hidden in every business; management just reveals them.

10. Basic tools and flexible methods are generally enough for process and project management.

PRACTICES

✔ Who's who? Explore and map the vast network of freelancers in your field, as well as in your local area. Who are the prominent ones and why? Meet them, if you can.

✓ Get together with a few fellow freelancers to talk about how they manage their teams and projects. Your field (and country) has its customs that you need to know by heart.

✓ Try to boost your project competencies in your next gigs or team projects. Observe how they are managed, by whom, and try to be extra useful and helpful for others.

✓ Map and manage your first process in order to improve a specific workflow you do every day or week. Start with a simple checklist and then update it with each instance.

YOU'RE ONLY AS GOOD AS YOUR CLIENTS

How do you care for your clients and build a clientele?

In the last few chapters, I have mainly focused on our work habits and performance – from personal productivity to professional IT to team cooperation. But I have neglected the key thing: the wishes of our customers, the people paying for all this. So now I will bring you up to speed on that. This is the first of four chapters on working together with clients. I will start from the basics: what they want and how to care for them.

◉ YOUR CLIENT PORTFOLIO

It's not important if you call your customers clients, buyers, contractees, participants or something else entirely. What is important is that they pay for your work or its outputs.

In her *Freelancer's Bible*, Sara Horowitz rightly compares client composition to an investment portfolio. When you invest your money, it's not good to put it all in one stock, because that stock might crash. There is no investment that is so good as to be worth betting everything you own on it. That would be gambling, not an investment. So a wise investor splits their funds among different investment assets and assumes some won't work out. They rely on *most* of their investments yielding a positive return, but not all.

Horowitz draws our attention to the fact that the situation with a freelancer's clients is similar. A contractor's long-term dependence on income from a single client isn't healthy. It can work for a few years, but it inevitably also brings the risk of an income drop from up high down to…zero.

Dividing income among multiple clients was also one reason why freelancers did relatively well even during the 2008 financial crisis and the economic crisis that followed. Many of them confided in me that even though the markets, and some customers, panicked, they hardly felt the crisis when it came to their own income. (This was aided by the fact that although many companies had layoffs, they also started hiring more freelancers.)

Freelancers generally don't bet it all on one customer, and so they automatically diversify their income. There are rather few freelancers with just one to three clients a year (for instance in our survey it was only 15%) and far from all of these have long-term dependence on a single client. Even a project manager who handles just one large project a year as a contractor is fairly crisis-resistant, because they choose their projects in advance and give priority to the largest or most attractive ones. They are not dependent on a single client, and on the contrary they try to have a number of irons in the fire.

An eternal flame burns within any well-built portfolio. One thing ends, another starts. Important clients, the ones that really sustain you or define you as a professional, are your pillar. You're only as good as your clients, and whether you admit it or not, who they are says something fundamental about you. Major clients also carry no small financial value, which you can easily put into numbers by multiplying their average yearly spending on your services by five or ten years. The loss of such a client can really hurt financially.

The next segment in your client portfolio is made up of ordinary orders with a small or medium scope, the kind that some freelancers handle in the high double digits per year. This also includes minor consulting, collaborative work on colleagues' projects. This whole bundle of well-handled daily work, which – while it may not be the stuff of daydreams – demonstrably helps someone and helps us make a living. Most important clients are actually recruited from these everyday orders. As I have mentioned, many clients, especially the conservative, premium ones, prefer to first thoroughly test out and verify a new supplier before loosening the purse strings on their budget.

A portfolio will also contain side jobs and minor jobs, perhaps even outside your area of expertise. For beginning, still-unburdened freelancers, they often are a welcome source of income. This includes assistance for colleagues and work via agencies, online platforms like microstock photo banks or Airbnb, and online marketplaces like Freelancer.com or Upwork.

And last comes the segment of development projects – new services that you are testing on your friends and acquaintances, various experiments, start-ups with colleagues, Kickstarter crowdfunding projects, and even open training courses that you're organizing just to have more contact with people. Many freelancers work on some projects of their own, and although far from all of these are successful, they are often what gives birth to some future business success. However, development projects come with their own risks: missing out on opportunities and working with the wrong people. So I advise that you choose only teammates who won't harm your reputation, and if a project goes badly, that you know when to quit, so that you don't neglect your core business. Also, these projects should have some place in your career strategy.

◉ WHAT CLIENTS EXPECT

Steady, high-quality services is what every client automatically expects. A customer will see even a quality drop from excellent to above-average as negative, so always set your quality level to be sustainable. Superhuman binges followed by burnout and running at half speed are awful. Providing great client care is a long-distance run, as is doing business in general.

> Customers are much more likely to understand that as you grow professionally, your prices will rise along with your expertise and productivity, than to accept fluctuations or drops in the quality of your services.

Most customers will understand price hikes joined with productivity hikes and will adapt their assignments or split their orders into an expertise-based part (which they will give to you, just as you want) and the routine, which can even be handled by cheaper junior professionals. However, an expert can't provide an excellent solution one time and then an average one a year later. Professional business isn't like professional racing, where you tune up for the season's main races, and if you sometimes have a bad showing, it's OK.

Flexibility means meeting the client halfway and adapting your service or workflow to their wishes and needs within some reasonable limits. Nobody wants inflexible services, and the customer expects that we as professionals will show some empathy here. This is a huge problem in service design. Restrictively limited services are easier to design and market. Services with more flexible configuration are harder to create, but customers love them. You probably know it from your own experience. When you head in somewhere and restrictions scream at you that you shouldn't do this and can't do that, you as a customer feel awful. Convenient services, meanwhile, are smartly designed so as to minimize restrictions and make the customer feels favored and thus comfortable – and ultimately, willing to spend. So when you are designing and selling a service, always consider whether this or that restriction is really needed, and view things through the customer's eyes.

Problem-solving is part of business. Customers generally accept that problems may occur. But these problems must be solved to a customer's full satisfaction, while also keeping them informed of the progress along the way. The bigger the mistake, the more upset the client may be, and that complicates the whole situation. Here is how to work in these crises:

1. Above all keep calm and don't panic, no matter what.

2. Communicate and reassure the client of your determination to fix the problem.

3. Analyze the problem and its likely cause; don't act in haste.

4. Solve it resolutely and without delay.

5. Formulate conclusions and proposals for preventive measures and acquaint the client with them. The problem may not have been your fault, but you will explain that to the client more easily once it's *solved*.

An apology and compensation are something you should offer before they are asked for, because this may be your last chance to turn the customer experience around and turn mild disappointment (the problem was solved, but I may try someone else next time) into honest excitement (the problem was solved, I got an apology, and I even received the service almost for free, wow, I have to tell my friends).

My friend Barbora runs a small business named Sushiqueen that delivers exclusive sushi, and she is a great example here. When she happens to reach the customer late, she cares. For her it may be just one delivery out of many, but for the customer, it might be a wedding, a fiftieth birthday, or another life event that has been complicated by her delay. So in these cases she gives the client a whole plate of expensive sushi for free, with apologies. What is she silently saying? That if it were to happen often, she would quickly go broke. So through this gesture she clearly tells the client that she utterly appreciates their satisfaction, and also that she only makes this kind of mistake rarely, thus further stressing her professionalism. (Here we are, back at the fact that the client picks up on non-verbal signals much more than what you shout about yourself.)

⬎ WHAT CLIENTS DREAM OF

Meeting the basic expectations of clients may seem like a no-brainer, but everyday experience has repeatedly shown me it's not. Or more precisely that what we automatically demand as customers, we may not always provide as professionals. And meanwhile, that is just the beginning.

Over the years I have had the good fortune to cooperate with a number of demanding, premium clients. I will reveal to you the secret of how to care for these clients in a way they won't often experience with other free-lancers, so that they will likely fall in love with you. It's actually something that nearly every customer with whom you come into contact truly desires (whether they realize it or not).

Let me mention that the notes below concern ordinary 1:1 orders (you / client). For multi-sided N:1 (your team / client) or 1:N relation-ships (you and a group of customers, purchasers, course participants, etc.), you have to adapt this, perhaps via anchoring in the order process, but the principle remains the same. Above all, you have to stay aware that: *What matters in a client relationship is the overall experience, not just the purchased product or service.*

Many entrepreneurs make the enormous, and from the custom-er's standpoint unforgivable, mistake of focusing only on the quality of their product or core service. What the client experiences before, during, and afterwards is secondary for them. But this is a mistake.

The customer doesn't perceive the line between the order's fulfillment and customer service as sharply as we do. And when they do sense those borders, they are probably not at all where you would place them. This is natural, due to the difference between the layman and expert views.

One basic step towards excellent customer care is to be aware that from their point of view, it starts with the first contact and ends with the final thank-you or handshake – and servicing after that. This is the scope you need to think about and look at during your service-quality consider-ations. Expert qualities are the main ingredients, but they are not enough on their own to be saviors.

When you think about it all for a bit, you will certainly realize what the catch is. In short, you can't please every client, and some don't even deserve it. You know perfectly well that there are all sorts of people. Some are unpleasant, arrogant, they aggressively demand discounts basically for nothing, demand free work samples, etc. So how do you escape?

❯ AN INQUIRY DOESN'T MAKE SOMEONE A CLIENT

A newborn client relationship has two fundamentally different, strictly separated phases, even though the customer often sees them as one: 1. sales negotiations and 2. the actual course of the cooperation or order. And so watch out: during the negotiation phase, both of you are not in the same boat yet.

You can't be in the same boat with someone who is trying to talk you into a disadvantageous contract or manipulate you, or for whom you can clearly see that they need a therapist more than they need you. You can't be on the same boat with a person who would love to buy your services at a 90% discount.

I'm not talking here about the style of communication. That can even be very friendly and polite on both sides; it's unrelated. I'm talking about how under the pleasant words, two sets of interests clash: theirs and yours. And until you reach an agreement, you are each sailing freely on your own boat, and only negotiating about *possible* business cooperation. You will only be in the same boat from the moment when you reach that agreement and start to work on the agreed on order.

The consequence here is that it's in your foremost interest to verify and master the negotiation phase to keep from later bitterly regretting going into the deal. Regretting that you agreed to terrible conditions and now you are sailing with someone who is more like a free rider than a client. And yet they are acting like they are the captain.

I will get to sales-negotiation strategies in a later chapter. Right now I want you to understand that the difference between what I will call a *prospect* or *inquirer*, i.e. a potential client with whom you are negotiating, and a *client* for whom you basically live and breathe, may be unclear to them. But for you this difference is fundamental.

Not every negotiation ends with an order. And that's great! Through skillful negotiations, elementary personal branding, pricing, and other fine business mechanisms, you influence who will ultimately be your client, whom you will be caring for. In other words, you yourself decide on the makeup of your client portfolio. You choose your major clients. This isn't about who contacts you, but who you reach agreements with.

Every top professional uses a different strategy for creating an advantageous starting position in negotiations. Some rely on having a strong, dominant brand that evokes respect. Others play hard to get. Or they know how to bargain really well and have great pricing. Or they emphasize the order's individual benefit for their contact person within the inquiring company. Or they play tough, shock with brutal honesty, swear a bit every now and then, and then watch what it does to people.

But no matter what the negotiating strategy and starting position are, to provide superb client care in the actual course of the order, you have to be able to arrange conditions that you yourself perceive as a good foundation for fruitful and beneficial cooperation. Otherwise it won't work, you will be frustrated and dissatisfied, and you won't be able to provide excellent care and services to your customers.

The hardest part about all of this is that even in the initial negotiation phase, your communication and personal approach have to be first-rate. From the inquirer's standpoint, the order starts with the first contact, and even if you don't reach an agreement, they should have a good feeling from this communication, or better yet some tangible benefit: you gave them sound advice or pointed them in the right direction.

In practice I see how only a fraction of independent professionals grasp these basic principles and can, whether intuitively or in a controlled way, apply them so that everyone who comes into contact with them is basically excited. Even if no agreement is reached.

You see, you are selling the client both a service and a relationship. That is, you are selling the fact that you will be caring personally for the good of the client. And that is the secret to excellent client care.

HOW PROFESSIONALS CARE

I sometimes hear it said that there are no VIP clients, just standard good treatment for all. My reply is always that it's a nice theory, but in practice it can't work, unless you are an automaton and your clients mere numbers in a computer. It especially amuses me when a client of someone who has said this then complains: "He takes calls from you on the weekend, huh? I guess he respects *you*. I've been with him three times as long, and I'm lucky to reach him on weekdays from nine to five."

Naturally *in principle* all clients are equal, but in practice, we differentiate. When somebody has been a client of mine for several years, we get closer and friendlier. I will have a much better understanding of their personality, interests, relationships, preferred work and communication style, etc. In short, I will really get to know the person, in part because we have overcome many crises in their business dealings together.

I have truly had moments when a client has sobbed over the phone because she was crushed and humiliated by some situation. But these things can be overcome together, and each such small victory forms a bond and deeper level of empathy and understanding. For good clients with whom I have been in regular contact for years, I precisely know my limits, what gifts to bring for special occasions, what information and contacts will interest them during my efforts to expand their business horizons, etc. Sometimes I get it wrong, but that teaches me something too. After a few years, often just one sentence is enough to let me know what the client needs and how to help right now.

Over time, the value of such a relationship grows significantly on both sides. And because of just this, not all clients (or professionals) are really equal. With some of them, you can build a special relationship, which if damaged or lost can hurt like losing a friend.

Many professionals have the problem that they devote *less* attention to long-term, seemingly sure clients, giving them worse service than the new ones. Are you bothered when the mobile operator or bank that you have been with for a decade lures in new customers with much better conditions and prices than the ones you have? This is what I call discrimination against long-term clients. Cafes or pubs that take extra special care of their regular customers are an opposite example. Those customers are then happy to bring in their friends, hold celebrations there, etc.

Top professionals know how to form these good relationships and strengthen them more successfully than others, and that is indeed one reason why they are top professionals.

⬭ WHERE ARE MY LIMITS?

As I just mentioned, I know my limits in a close customer relationship. To reach that point, I have to know business customs above all else – both the general ones and those specific to a field. I have to deeply know business etiquette and the rules that every experienced professional knows, and yet they are mostly unwritten. Some are always true, others change.

Now you're probably thinking that this is something easily said… but for beginners, how is it done? They shouldn't despair. First, there are some universal foundations of social behavior that also apply in business. Second, there are mentors and colleagues out there with whom you can share experiences and ask what they feel is too much, and why.

It's best to patch holes here quickly. Not knowing business customs puts you at a disadvantage in negotiations, where the other party will quickly recognize a greenhorn who doesn't even know what a business proposal or estimate looks like or how to hold a meeting. Good to know!

But in addition to this general level, the personal level is important too. For me as a professional, it's fundamental to know my limits with a given client *individually*.

So I take an interest in the person. In their motivations, plans, dreams, hobbies, their joys in life. Sometimes I can share my own personal values for living or observations. But I never, never burden the client with my problems. Yes, it's self-censorship, but quite deliberate, because the customer is paying me to solve *their* problems, not for me to give them *mine*. So I don't complain. Most clients take no interest in our problems, even if they show us a hundred polite expressions of empathy, as a social obligation.

Humor can be another bond in a relationship, because if you share a sense of humor with someone, it's easier to be on the same wavelength and make light of even quite sad situations. But inappropriate humor can be off putting. So don't push too hard here, and carefully determine what kind of humor your counterpart enjoys, and what kinds they really don't. Some people can't take black humor or sarcasm, or have no sense of humor at all.

Lastly, we all like what is genuine – directness, sincerity, credibility, and fairness. Authenticity and real, direct behavior doesn't mean acting inappropriately; it's more about being who you are. Being genuine means my clients rightly feel that they really know me and can trust me.

ENGAGEMENT, LOYALTY, READINESS, AVAILABILITY

Many professionals lack a clear sense of engagement. They don't seem to enjoy or care about their work. But the client wants to see that you are giving the work your full attention and can keep things in context.

Demanding customers despise sloppiness, unpunctuality, unreliability, inflexibility, constant excuses, and problematic communication: *Why should I, for heaven's sake, have to chase them down?! I'm the paying customer; they should be hunting me! They don't deserve my money!*

Engagement problems are multi-dimensional. They are a thousand and one things, such as visible disinterest (multiple phone checks during a work meeting), repeated questions (that were answered at the last meeting and are on the record), or zero expression of positive emotions (it's just another job).

The customer should never get the feeling that you are trying to rush the order as fast as possible just so you can invoice and move on to the next one – even if that is how you feel. If you have a problem with orders that customers drag out and don't have a clear endpoint, then go and set some reasonable limits for the final touches and offer extra work or consultations for an added fee.

Engagement also means that you educate your client so that they better understand your work, your field, and other things that are a part of your profession. When I see that a client isn't doing some things effectively or correctly, I tactfully tell them my opinion and show them a better way, even if it's unrelated to what I was actually hired for.

My mission is to help my clients not just within a tightly defined corridor of an order, but also in the adjacent areas with which I come into contact. What I personally understand, I explain, and for the rest, I recommend appropriate trainers or consultants. My goal is an educated, knowledgeable customer who will improve and grow, in part thanks to me.

When I work for someone, I make it clear in many ways that they interest me and that I think about them. After all, it's true. It's not some kind of act, and I don't run checklists for this or that interest. When a Eureka moment comes, I just pick up my phone and call, and I try to get the client excited about my new vision.

When I run into an interesting article or website, I click the Send from Gmail icon in my browser, email the client, and include a short comment. If I feel that I could form a business connection between my client and someone, or I have a team-member tip, I do what I can so that both sides are able to see how this is a unique chance, and so that it works. So when I work for someone, I *give it my all.* I engage myself. And I'm loyal.

I can show loyalty for example when a hater attacks my client on social media and I stand up for them. Or when I engage in a conflict with a supplier in an attempt to resolve it, even when I don't have to.

Preparedness is another sign of good care. For every scheduled meeting or call I think out in advance what I'm going to talk about, and I prepare specific proposals so that the talks don't drag on and steal my client's time. I would rather lose my time than theirs, or better yet someone else's. I work with a few researchers to whom I can send tasks at any time:

Take a look at global trends in interior wallpaper production over the last five years. What materials, designs, motifs, etc. are used? And find me photos from the ten best wallpaper sales points, including a description of their specializations and unique traits. By Friday I need to know everything about contemporary wallpaper sales. Go, go, go!

Research isn't especially expensive, and in practice it takes just a few hours. Every year I conduct a number of such small or large surveys, paid for out of my own pocket, and it's not unusual for me to have in the end a better overview of current trends than my client, despite it being their field.

And research is just the start. I read a lot. When I work with a client as a consultant over the long term, I ask what books on or about their field they would recommend to deepen my understanding of the issue. I read two or three so that I can better help them or even review texts, prepare presentations, etc. And I ask questions. When I'm working for a company, I care about who works there and what they do. I don't rely on client documents; I instead try to form an independent opinion based on my own point of view.

My inspiration for devoting extra time to investigate things, even when I don't have to, came from physicist Richard Feynman, who thought about problems in precisely this way, and was never afraid to ask people, study, and build up his own independent professional opinion even in fields that were new to him. His way of thinking is perfectly illustrated in one of the best books I have read in my life, the humorous biography *Surely You're Joking, Mr. Feynman!* (It's no coincidence that our first-born son is named Richard.)

Engagement, loyalty, and also preparedness and familiarity are all expressions of *closeness* – I get closer to my customer by comprehending the problems they are handling and by trying to understand their field. And with closeness comes accessibility as well.

Frequent unavailability truly angers clients. Did you know that? Not always and not all of them, but often. There are plumbers who don't take calls even when they were due on-site hours before. Copywriters who promise to deliver something on-time, and when nothing arrives, you can't reach them for two days. And web designers who won't take calls when their site goes down and still don't call back after three missed calls. You try texts, email, Facebook…nothing. Their first reaction the next day: *What's the hurry?* The customer is angry, but they usually don't say it. They complain about such things to me, since I'm consulting on the project, and together we think about how to replace Mr. Unavailable.

Unavailability has become a sort of hipster fashion with a nod to *work-life balance* and all that. But the customer doesn't give a damn about my balanced workflow, if they have a problem and *can't reach me*. All it takes, meanwhile, is a basic agreement on how to contact me if urgently needed. When, for instance, I'm at a meeting or I'm working on a demanding task, I mute my phone, but check it later during breaks. And if I see an urgent message or missed call that can't wait, I respond immediately. This is a small sacrifice for greater client comfort or helping a member of the team get out of a jam.

Any fears you may have that it will break up your fine-tuned work style are unfounded, as long as you have a pinch of discipline for sticking to important issues only. Some days can be more hectic, to be sure, but those are perhaps precisely the days when you *should* be available. Freelancing isn't just about the expert work that you are being paid to do, but also about precisely this type of flexibility and cooperation.

Regarding availability, it is also wise to set up a healthy approach to checking and responding to your emails. These are generally not expected to be read and replied to at once, for sure, but as a dominant form of written team and business communication, you probably can't disregard them either. "Email is not household clutter and you're not Marie Kondo. Ping!" quips Adam Grant, the top global expert in work and organizational psychology, on the etiquette of (not) responding to emails in his blunt 2019 New York Times article *No, You Can't Ignore Email. It's Rude.*

If you are not an elite expert, who can afford an assistant to deal with emails (which is an option as well), a good compromise is to think first, how often and how fast do you want and have to respond to work-related emails. Naturally there are lots of emails that you do have to answer, but this does not at all apply to every message. I, for instance, usually check my mail only once a day after finishing major tasks, while also planning my work schedule for another day or two. There are also days, when I have to be available on email all day long due to finishing projects, or not at all, and I deal with them a day later. I certainly don't answer *all* emails, but only the important ones, and I also use an auto-reply to set reasonable expectations, as to which emails I may respond to and in what time frame.

Try to express your ideas briefly and clearly in emails and other work communication online. Short emails or messages on one specific topic are becoming sort of a standard (see the website Five.Sentenc.es). Being brief saves time and also increases the likelihood that your recipient will read and answer your message.

Being reachable for clients is obviously important, but it should be kept in balance with your interest to do focused expert work without unnecessary interruptions. After all, a freelancer is an entrepreneur and the master of their own time, not an errand boy.

A sensible foundation is to be reachable for clients during normal working hours. If that is not desirable or possible (e.g. for remote workers in distant time zones), you can either specify what are the best times to reach you, or make sure to react promptly to important messages through the communication channels that you yourself advertise either publicly or when dealing with clients. So double check your website, business cards, paper and email footers, as well as other presentations or profiles, to make sure it all fits. There are times when I get a business card with three different phone numbers and when I try to call them, no one answers, and I don't even get any return call. Surely I won't be trying them again!

Engagement, loyalty, readiness and availability are, however, only components that help to form the customer's impression and their whole experience.

THAT COMFY WEIGHTLESS EXPERIENCE

There is a customer-experience difference between ordinary and first-rate customer care. When I hire a professional who doesn't care about care, the best I can hope for is merely being satisfied. And that simply isn't enough for me to tell my contacts, networks and the whole world: "This person is great!"

The result of outstanding care is comfort – the truly great, extraordinary feeling of lightness. There can be some small missteps that give it all a human quality. We are people, not gods. Such care means that you are at the center of an exceptional professional's interest, they perceive your needs and peculiarities, and they fully adapt their services to this. And they also know when to slow down or let you stop for breath.

The client best cared for is the one who you ultimately make independent, to whom you give freedom that they can use at any time. They understand that you are helping them towards autonomy. Exceptional professionals thus leave excited and educated clients behind them who then come back like a boomerang with a new need for a big jump forward.

Your client care shouldn't lead towards an unhealthy addiction, where they feel that they can't easily drop you, because that creates negative subconscious emotions and fears.

Creating dependence was a favorite technique of old-school businesses and their salesmen, and whole company sales systems have been set up to make it as hard as possible for the customer to leave once they start using the company's products and related services. But then the client, with no speck of loyalty or empathy, escapes as soon as they see a chance to leave this unhealthy dependent relationship.

Service as an experience is a strong turn away from conventional service design, which more strongly stressed the actual service, as well as its contractual, organizational, and financial aspects – which is not to say that you can ignore these.

Think about what shapes the customer experience. What are the key moments, the surprises, or maybe the a-ha and wow moments? Does an order finish with a bang of excitement, or just fizzle out at the end? How does the customer actually see you?

Overcome your shyness and don't just ask the customer about their expectations and primary needs *before* the project. Be sure to also spend some time on questions *after* the cooperation ends. Wait for the right opportunity, then ask how they see your cooperation looking back, and if it met their expectations. You may learn some unexpected things. The key here is to really listen rather than getting defensive.

Improving your customer care will gradually help you to build a good name, reduce client fluctuations, and also deepen cooperation with important clients. In other words, it strengthens a stable business, which brings with it a much more predictable income and leaves a much better feeling in you and your customers. When something big turns out right for one of my important clients, I'm often as happy as they are. We have walked a long path together, and our efforts have brought results.

THE CUSTOMER IS RARELY AT FAULT

Sometimes my colleagues or consulting clients complain that a client is causing them trouble. They pay late, they think up more and more extra work, they call on weekends or evenings, they can't say what they dislike in a proposal, etc.

I have analyzed countless such situations with my clients, and in the vast majority of cases, we reached the conclusion that the mistake basically wasn't on the side of their customer. The mistake is generally in bad order management and poorly set limits for cooperation.

Do they pay late? Because you tolerate it, you don't have a fine-tuned order-management process, and the client has also been enabled to do so because of a terribly written contract or non-existent contractual conditions. While that isn't a moral excuse for making payments a month late, it *enables* them, and that is the fundamental thing.

Are they thinking up more and more extra work? Because the scope of the work and the optional extras weren't clearly defined. The customer may have a valid feeling that this or that detail *is supposed to be* a part of the delivery. They aren't the expert here and aren't telepathic, so it's no wonder that your views differ.

Are they bothering you on weekends or evenings? Because you let things go that far: you didn't set any reasonable limits on communication, or for example an extra fee for availability outside of working hours. However, you could also solve things by raising prices and transitioning to a more reasonable clientele.

Are they unable to say what they dislike about your proposed solutions? Because they are not experts and nobody has helped them to become more capable of ordering expert work. You can set up an order process that assumes such clients exist and adds (with a corresponding price hike) extra time to help them understand the creative process and to give feedback on the presented proposals, such as for websites and other creative work.

Every time you encounter these and similar problems with a customer, you can act reactively (resolve it) or proactively (change the order process so as to avoid the problem). After a few iterations, your immunity to such problems will be many times higher.

Professionals who repeatedly complain about their customers often resolve complaints only reactively, without taking any real steps for future prevention. Perhaps because their business has been unchanged for years, and they expect the same of those around them.

If I'm an expert in something, and not just a replaceable unit of workforce, cheaply hired by the customer to cover someone's downtime, I have a good position for setting limits and conditions on our cooperation. Why? Because the customer has turned to me as an expert and expects me to lead them to the goal with as few scrapes and bruises as possible.

An inquirer rarely understands your field so well that they are able to set an optimal order process themselves. And even if they do have some misconceptions, it's up to you and your expert authority to put them on the right track – yours. And with this I don't mean any sort of top-down leadership, but a cultivated, fact-based discussion, where your job is to win over the customer. As an expert, you have the upper hand in professional questions, just like a doctor visited by patients who each have a layman's notion of their own diagnosis.

But even if the client does have the upper hand, or they are firmly convinced they are right, you still have many means to proactively handle problem areas via an explicit contractual agreement, or in extreme cases, to exit the cooperation. Naturally there are also clients who turn out to be highly problematic despite every preventive measure. But these are much fewer in number than the situations that you as a professional can avoid.

◗ A FREELANCER CURATES THEIR OWN CLIENT PORTFOLIO

A client portfolio is an imaginary whole, with a customer trunk that gradually grows, puts down roots, and branches out. But many professionals don't realize that this client tree is their own creation. It comes from their work and the daily decisions they make.

For some, this tree is beautifully developed, symmetrical and healthy. For others, it's dwarfed or carelessly trimmed and is only barely alive. There are trees that grow up to the heights, in one direction, while others split in two or grow out to all sides. And they either bear fruit or don't.

I know that in any short or medium term it's hard to see what effect your client-portfolio decisions have. You will understand the importance of some choices only over time. But you definitely won't spoil anything if you occasionally divert your attention from the care of individual clients out to the tree as a whole.

How is your client portfolio built? Is it balanced enough? When you are tending to it, do you think about your past (former clients) and your future (creating contacts, running development projects, building expertise)? And what if another economic crisis comes? Will it survive?

Certain principles start to make sense when you shift your attention to this level. For example that of following up and making good use of each and every lead that anyone ever gives you in good faith. *Hey, call my friend, he's looking for someone just like you.* Or: *I'd like to connect you here with my friend who has a store that could sell what you make.* You know perfectly well that most such tips will come to nothing in the end, but there are two good reasons to not ignore them. Freelancers get the vast majority of their new clients directly through social bonds. But above all, you're doing right for the person who recommended you.

I personally follow up on every reasonable tip, if only to make my colleagues look better in their client's eyes, even if I myself gain nothing from it. I expect it might be wasted time, but I still put in some energy, so that in that limited time, I can help to puzzle through the problem they are trying to solve, and perhaps inadvertently highlighting the qualities of the professional who recommended me, reciprocally boosting their position.

In her *Freelancer's Bible*, Sara Horowitz gives a great recommendation: "Follow up all leads you're given. Yes, all. Not following up on someone's suggestion basically trashes their time and info – and the time you spent getting it. So follow up. Let them know you did. Thank them again."

If you work as an active force that not only builds individual contacts (a star structure) but also interconnects them, it increases the value of your client and collaborator portfolio. For example, when you go to start up a new service or project, thanks to these lateral connections, that information will more easily spread throughout the trunk of your network, without you having to work to awaken each individual contact.

All of this might seem banal, but if you devote yourself to this type of curating and recommending good people systematically for years, the cumulative effect is huge.

Refusing good orders is a similar example. Why shouldn't you refuse them? From the standpoint of individual orders, this advice is silly. But when you look at the matter in the broader context of all those customers who are satisfied with your work and love to recommend you, it suddenly does make sense. If more people reach the conclusion that you just don't have time and will refuse, they will simply stop recommending you in their *own* interest, so that you at least have time for them. Or worse yet, they may decide to keep you as their business secret, a limited resource not to be shared with others.

So among other things, having a well-tended client portfolio means that good work stays with you, as do healthy relationships with people to whom you might come back, and for whom you leave some reasonable spare capacity. Over the years you build up dozens or maybe hundreds of such relationships, and if you stick with your work, sooner or later you will reach a tipping point – a moment when you are ceasing to expand the client base yourself and when it's slowly starting to expand on its own and bring in further and further contacts like a snowball rolling down a hill. You will achieve a good name.

But in the opening and the closing phase, you can still influence which orders you will ultimately accept and which you will pass on to your colleagues or only act as a consultant on. The snowball effect doesn't mean that you will attend to all of these people personally and that you will be doing the same thing as you were twenty years before. Your business can grow and branch out, or you can start specializing; many things can change, but you can still gain from the good relationships that you founded years before.

⊗ YOUR CLIENT REGISTRY

Time plays a key role in building a client portfolio. Imagine you have been freelancing for ten or fifteen years. How well will you remember a client for whom you did something years ago and who suddenly contacts you again? What were you working on back then? And do you remember them at all?

My experience as a customer is that a typical professional remembers little to nothing after four or five years.

A good example is one tradesman from whom I need something once every few years – generally adjustments or repairs to a water pump or cleaning for my well. But every time I have to explain to him who I am and that we have a fairly long history together. Wouldn't it be that much better if he contacted me himself every couple of years to offer preventive maintenance? And also the cleaning of the well and taking water samples for an analysis? I would pay whatever he asked, and I would consider him a treasure. Not to mention that if I ever needed a new pump, he would easily convince me that it was time (that the old one really *is* worn out) and that I should leave the replacement to him, because I trust him and know he will choose better than me. But back to reality: instead of caring for his client tree, he is visibly struggling and, full of hope, advertises in a local paper that no one really reads. So many people are like that...

If you have been doing business for years and have served hundreds or even thousands of customers over that time, you should keep a registry of them. It's nothing complicated. Your registry just has to meet three conditions – recording 1. the customer's name, 2. their current contact details, and 3. the history of your business relationship.

For us freelancers, this is generally a registry kept in an Excel table, in a cloud Google spreadsheet, in Evernote, in Google contacts, or in a specialized CRM (*Customer Relationship Management*) application such as Insightly.

In a digital registry, one can very quickly find the record they need by name, email, phone number, or some keyword. So even if a client contacts me after eight years (and such reunions do happen), in twenty seconds, during our call, I can find their record and recollect what was the gig about.

One great advantage of a well-kept registry is that you can remind yourself to your customers regularly. With reasonable amount of periodicity and timing, of course. You can come with a targeted offer, or just organize some event for your clients, some lecture, or a summer garden party, appropriate for everyone's standing and needs.

Just watch out that your registry respects laws on personal data protection such as Europe's GDPR and other such regulations worldwide. Keeping a typical registry on a safe storage point is normally fine, but processing and storing sensitive data such as health or biometric data is something you will probably have to go over with a lawyer.

One other channel for keeping in touch with clients is a newsletter, if you find a way to get them to agree to subscribing. A valuable and professionally mature newsletter strongly increases the likelihood that recipients will come back to you perhaps years after their last cooperation because they still have you in their mind. (I'll offer practical tips on this later.)

Google Contacts has its advantage as a simple CRM in that it's also accessible from Gmail or mobile, and it lets you enter contact details, and file attachments can be stored on your Google Drive and added to contact cards as hyperlinks. With support for grouping they can work surprisingly well, and the advantage is that you have all of your contacts, including details, at hand at any time from your phone. So when a known number calls, you can open the contact card in your phone and look at your notes and details.

There is also a CRM extension to Gmail, called Streak, with a claim that says it all, *CRM in your inbox.* It's mostly useful for professionals who manage a large number of leads in different stages of negotiation and need to keep track of them.

But cloud contacts aren't necessarily better than a well-kept Excel table. What is essential is that you keep at least some type of client registry, and that it can be used to reconnect with clients you have lost contact with or allows you to quickly contact them when needed. Having such a list of people who you've helped can also be a source of great pride.

There are countless ways to use a customer registry, and you will surely discover many of them yourself. You can send your faithful customers small gifts, or perhaps even pay commissions to those who intensively recommend you. You can approach permanent customers with news and special offers; you can send out annual letters, New Years' greetings, or congratulations; you can send targeted offers or even build provision-based affiliate systems and loyalty programs based on information you have about your customers. Valuable information can be hidden in many places, even outside of your main registry.

For example, I recently worked with a manufacturing firm that was switching owners after twenty years. The previous owner was an older man who had never been wooed by the web; the company only had a landline and a fax and received most of its orders by phone or in person. The new owner modernized the company, but only in time did he appreciate the small parting gift from the old man – a carefully kept registry of all orders and customers from the founding of the firm onwards, in handwritten notebooks.

KEY IDEAS

1. Your client portfolio should be balanced and nicely developed. This is a great form of risk prevention.

2. Important clients come first. Every one of them has a huge value.

3. A client expects stable service quality and flexibility, as well as exemplary problem-solving.

4. But their real dream is perfect care with a view to their needs: A perfect relationship.

5. Customers will understand better when your quality grows and so does your price than when your quality fluctuates.

6. In the client's eyes, an order begins with the first contact and ends with their use of the fruits of your labor.

7. But remember, not every inquirer is a client. They only become one once you reach an agreement.

8. Care for VIP clients includes engagement, loyalty, careful preparation, and availability.

9. The customer is rarely at fault. Much more frequently the fault lies in bad order management.

10. Your long-term client care will only be as good as your client registry.

PRACTICE

✓ If you don't have a complete list or registry of your customers, start building it right away. Go through your past invoices and records, and keep it up-to-date from now on.

✓ Analyze the whole customer experience you provide from the first contact to the final handshake. Just write down the steps as a sort of process, and make improvements.

✓ Step up the quality of the overall service you provide to important clients. If you think of service as an experience, even small things like free extras make a huge difference.

✓ Define how, when and through which channels you will be available to clients so that they can reach you if needed. When you find the ideal setup, make it clear for everyone.

✓ Whenever you encounter a problem with a customer, fix it but also fix your general order management. Improving it as a process will make you immune to typical problems.

PRICING

How much should you ask for your work?

Pricing is the most undervalued and neglected skill in freelancing. This has its reasons. When a freelancer has a problem with reliability or personal productivity and is constantly missing deadlines, they generally recognize it quickly. But when they have badly set prices for two or three years and they are selling their services too cheaply, they generally don't have a clue.

It's a consequence of price asymmetry. When you advertise prices several times higher than your comparably well-known and capable peers, you will feel it for sure. Potential clients either won't accept the price and will search elsewhere, or they will ultimately be dissatisfied with the value they got for the price, because they expected much more.

But if you are too cheap, you won't get any negative signals of this kind. Clients will be excited about the advantageous cost to quality ratio and will drown you in work, and until the rising demand *forces* you to think about your prices, you have no real reason to wake up. But at the same time it's possible that at the given quality of service you could be charging two or three times as much and thus be earning several times more.

Underpricing by tens of percent is quite common among freelancers. The only good news is that if this also applies to you, then you may have prices that are too-low, but also room for doing better business. As Warren Buffett says, the single most important factor in evaluating a business is *pricing power*. "If you've got the power to raise prices without losing business to a competitor, you've got a very good business. And if you have to have a prayer session before raising the price by 10 percent, then you've got a terrible business."

Because I often help freelancers shape and set prices, I know firsthand what an enormously undervalued business area this is. It's no exception for a beginner who kept their prices at the level of say $30/hr. for years while they were growing professionally and gathering experience to suddenly have room price-wise to go to $60 or even $70/hr. without losing any significant clients. However, this doesn't have to mean that being in that situation is enviable.

Raising prices isn't pleasant, but at the end of the day it's more of a banal complication, which you will be able to handle once you focus on it. For more experienced freelancers, the bigger problem is their poor knowledge of various pricing methods. Instead of mastering three or four ways to price a gig, they often work with a single one, stretching it to its limits and beyond, leaving them in a bad negotiating position.

In practice this might show up when they have an order where it's immediately clear that the work won't go smoothly. If you bill it using the normal per-hour or per-task rate that you advertise online, that order won't pay off. If you have multiple methods up your sleeve, you can push negotiations towards pricing that is more advantageous for you and offers more possibilities – such as man-days, structured variant offers, or some form of paid initial analysis (and then you will see). But if a professional only works with an hourly rate, they would either reject such an offer, or wiggle one way or another to get out of accepting it. And that creates a bad impression, not to mention that with the right pricing, it could be quite a lucrative job after all.

PRICING DETERMINES PROFITS

Let's go back over the reasons to care about pricing and add a few more:

- Pricing can stimulate or suppress demand. Prices directly influence workload.

- A public price list works as an effective filter for inquiries and saves you unwanted negotiations.

- Your price is a testament to your level of expertise and thus predetermines customers' expectations.

- Knowledge of multiple pricing methods gives you an advantage in negotiating deals.

- Pro-active pricing helps you adequately set prices and increase your profits.

- Heavily neglected pricing can threaten your whole business and reputation.

That last point deserves two specific examples, because it's a frequent error:

A psychotherapist friend of mine set a low price when she first started doing business, and kept it low for the next four years even though the demand for her services had grown by several times. New potential customers call her often, even on weekends. Unfortunately, she is afraid to raise prices, so she keeps her price low despite the pressure from the demand for her services. When she is fully booked – and recently she has been fully booked quite often – she simply doesn't take calls or respond to messages. Through this she is starting to damage her reputation, and some people have stopped recommending her. They either consider her behavior unprofessional or have reached the conclusion that she isn't taking on clients anyway. Playing dead is no solution, and as a therapist, she herself knows this perfectly well. But we often act in irrational ways under pressure.

Here is a similar case: There was a handyman, just starting out, who I happened to discover did good work for peanuts. It was clear to me his prices were unsustainable, but as a customer I wasn't going to teach him pricing, was I? So we had him do tens of hours of work at this low price, and everything ran quite smoothly. Until one day he realized that he had set his prices terribly: in practice he should have been charging at least twice as much. But he apparently had a problem telling his customers, so he went out of business instead. He stopped taking calls, and we never heard from him again. Personally, I would have preferred if he had simply raised his prices, but that was his battle to fight, not ours.

These two everyday tragedies superbly illustrate both 1. ordinary professionals' resistance to working with and raising prices and 2. the fact that neglecting this key level of business can directly influence your reputation, stall a promisingly launched business in mid-air, and prevent profits. In short, a good price makes a good business, but we have to start with ourselves.

◉ OF PRICE AND MEN

As freelancers we are generally selling our time in some form, no matter what our prices are or how we set them. And this even applies to celebrities, for example when Robbie Williams asked £1.6 million to perform at the wedding of the daughter of a Russian oligarch, or Ian McKellen refused $1.5 million to marry off businessman Sean Parker while dressed as Gandalf. Or when the unbeatable boxer Floyd Mayweather Jr. left early retirement to rake in an estimated $300 million for a single fight with Conor McGregor and, through a technical KO, raised his number of wins without a defeat to an even 50.

Our price is tightly tied to our person and to the time that we have available for work.

And likewise various semi-passive sources of income such as the sales of e-books or images through a microstock site can ultimately be converted into hours of time invested. As a result, the sales price and volume will influence how well we convert this time into money.

In freelancing, your price is in no way an abstract factor. Price is something customers will associate directly to your person and will also compare with other information they have about you and your field. If all the indicators fit and don't contradict, then the higher your price, the more customers will see you as an authority, and the more they will listen to your recommendations and advice – and the more expertise they will expect.

Your price expresses how much you value your time and roughly the level of your expertise. Price is a key indicator customers base their final decision on, sometimes even in minutes. A price, however simple, tells them an awful lot.

When you go to a shop and see a no-name washer for $99, you don't have to be an expert in appliances to see that it probably isn't a first-rate product. It's not the only quality indicator, and it's not fully reliable, but we still all use such logic every day.

A price is a message. If you are working with your price correctly, it's boosting the image that you are also trying to build through your other marketing tools or channels.

Or think of it like this: If you keep the price that you had a few years ago when you were starting out, what does that say about you? That you are still the same beginner for eternity with no faith in yourself, who makes mistakes, and whose price reflects low quality and a lack of professionalism? Because that is how the customer sees it.

No. Your price can't lag behind your progress as a freelancer. If it does, you are probably ruining your first impression of doing professional, quality work, and robbing yourself of profit.

Your price has to be in full accord with your expertise, reputation, and available time; these all flow into each other. This means balancing pricing, professional growth, sales and marketing activity and your time management so that it all fits together. This is one reason why it's one of the toughest disciplines in business. Pricing is a professional decathlon.

And your price not only says a lot about you, but also indirectly decides your income. In advanced freelance economies, the incomes of comparably qualified colleagues with better or worse pricing can easily differ by tens, or even hundreds, of percentage points.

It's often a combination of high productivity and appropriate price. My friend who has a very high income as a freelance graphic designer describes his recipe for success like this: "I'm not an elite graphic designer. But I still earn several times more on average than comparable graphic designers working for agencies. I'm not expensive. I do graphics for acceptable prices, and create added value thanks to my high work efficiency. What a beginner might sweat over for half a day, I do in half an hour and get right the first time. And I do orders that mean something to me. It's the only way to keep loving my work."

While a beginning freelancer may be struggling to cover their cost of living, in general freelancers earn more than you might think. According to an MBO Partners report, *The State of Independence in America 2018*, every fifth American who does freelance work for over 15 hours a week has an income exceeding $100,000 a year, with this high-income group having grown for the seventh year in a row. According to MBO, the average income of full-time freelancers is $69,100 a year, which also exceeds the national average.

According to the *Freelancing in America 2018* survey, the proportion of high-income freelancers with revenues above $75,000 a year was 32%, and 4% of them had even reached an income level of $150,000 or more. Three quarters of full-time freelancers also said they were earning more than they previously were as employees, and a total of 77% of new freelancers surpassed their prior income level as an employee within a year.

When we consider the relatively low cost level given by the lack of capital demands in freelance business, it can be said that qualified freelancers aren't doing badly at all.

⊗ HOW HIGH CAN YOU GO?

If, for instance, you want to bring a certain top global expert on supply-chain management from the US to Europe for a two-day consultation, it will cost you $25,000, implying this person has a yearly income most likely exceeding a million dollars.

Or here is another example, an overview of the prices of paid PR posts by influencers on social networks, grouped by the average number of followers:

	YouTube	Instagram	Facebook	Twitter
7m+	$300,000	$150,000	$187,500	$60,000
3–7m	$187,500	$75,000	$93,750	$30,000
1–3m	$125,000	$50,000	$62,500	$20,000
500k–1m	$25,000	$10,000	$12,500	$4,000
100k–500k	$12,500	$5,000	$6,250	$2,000
50k–500k	$2,500	$1,000	$1,250	$400

(Source: CNBC & Captiv8, 2016; edited)

It doesn't matter whether you are doing business in America, in Europe, in Australia, or in Asia, if you are truly good, it's important for you to know the top price limit in your country, i.e. the highest market price for which your service is actually sold. But this generally isn't freely available information. So unless some more experienced colleague writes about it or there is a relevant survey, you will have to ask around. Or you can run your own survey. It will interest your colleagues as well and many will surely be happy to join in.

Things are tougher if you are a *de facto* market maker and already have the highest price on the local market or are just below the upper limit. Then all you can do is probe the top end by gradually raising prices and comparing with the prices of comparable services on the larger global market, where the most significant and expensive professionals are active.

Try to find data from more expensive markets than your own, local one. For example, in 2012, I corrected my European hourly rate based on the American survey named the *Freelance Industry Report*. It listed $100–150 an hour as the most common rate for freelance business consultants, with $150–200 as the second most common, and with a bit under 7% of consultants charging over $200 an hour (or even much more). Take a look at the following table and how the whole price scale looked for business consultants in comparison with graphic designers, and note how the differences in prices among fields, but also within them, can run into the hundreds of percent:

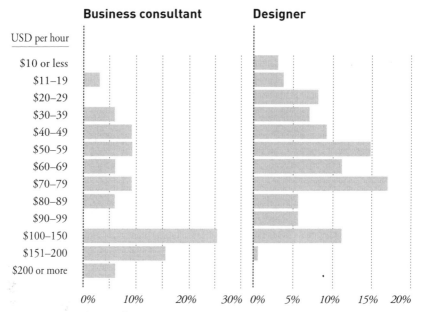

Source: 2012 Freelance Industry Report

A clear idea of what pricing looks like elsewhere in the world thus helped me to set a price that, while it may have been among the highest on the local market, was also easier to defend as common within the overall international context.

Many freelancers unfortunately wrongly believe that their earnings are determined mainly by expertise and reputation, and then wonder and envy when they learn that a similarly qualified (or worse yet, less-qualified) colleague earns several times more than them. The difference is understandably in pricing and in a thorough reevaluation of prices.

Where one freelancer works under bad contractual agreements and wastes time on gigs for friends for pennies, another gradually optimizes their price list or templates for business proposals and estimates and never does underpriced work or enters bad agreements. The latter earns more, because even minor pricing changes can bring dramatically higher profits.

Nevertheless it's good to not forget that comparing freelancers' immediate earnings can be tricky. A professional who invests into stability and income diversification can be doing better over time than a colleague with a high rate who is facing quickly growing competition.

⊘ BE INTIMATE WITH YOUR PRICE

Our price says so much about us that the worst thing we can do as entrepreneurs is to ignore the price and leave it untouched for years. By doing that, we are sending out a very bad signal and losing money.

An independent professional should have an intimate relationship with their price. They should care for it, touch it often, and watch if and how small price and pricing changes affect customer reactions. That is the only way to tell what is cheap or expensive, attractive or uninteresting.

A professional who works with their price constantly knows how elastic it is and how far they can go in terms of any increases or negotiation. They also know how their customers react to various types of prices, and set and offer them based on that in different situations – if they want to stimulate demand, or turn demand away, or aim at a certain length of cooperation, etc. All of this can be achieved easily when you are closely in touch with your price and pricing tools and don't treat them as something beneath an expert of your stature. Yes, it's about money. I recommend as a basic strategy to improve your sense for the connections between:

1. price and demand

2. price and workload

3. price and the message it sends to customers

I have already touched a few times on the relationship between price and demand. A higher price places a downward pressure on demand, or at least helps to turn away those who want cheap work without regard to quality. One of the wittiest remarks on pricing I have heard is:

❚ Raise prices until you no longer have inquiries from weirdos.

But raising prices doesn't always have to lead to a quick drop in orders. Sometimes it can surprisingly even do the opposite. If you used your previous price to address a small segment of undemanding clients and your low price was suspiciously cheap for a fairly large group of demanding ones, then a price hike can even bring increased demand. In practice, to suppress demand, you will have to take your price even higher.

Another anomaly that you can run into during a jump increase and a pricing shift into a higher customer segment is a temporary drop in demand. That happens when after raising prices, you are just too expensive for your original clientele and they stop inquiring, but the higher customer segment you are aiming at with your new price hasn't turned to you yet. This kind of drop in demand can even last several weeks or months. And because it's hard to distinguish from the situation where you really are too expensive, it's also another reason to prevent price jumps by making more frequent price corrections instead.

But essentially the principle of decreasing demand by raising prices does apply, and this is a basic pricing mechanism that you have to know and master like a yo-yo.

The tie between price and workload is seemingly the same, but not to the full extent. In business we all do a number of unpaid activities, and as I mentioned in the chapter on career strategies, it's very advantageous for you to leave a sufficient time reserve to be able to grab exceptional opportunities by the horns.

The vast majority of freelancers make the move to raise prices too late, when their workload is 100% or more – meaning that they are fairly bogged down by work stress. So they intuitively avoid raising prices all the more, because they want to avoid confronting client complaints. The result then is delaying a price increase for months or years, and an unfortunate state that is so chronic it can truly harm your health or reputation.

The top long-term workload after which you should start seriously thinking about a slight upward price correction is roughly 80%. This should be long-term workload, not seasonal swings that you know about from experience and that will surely disappear in a few weeks.

I know, it's easier said than done. Demand rarely rises as a constant, like when you step on the gas in a car and it smoothly accelerates. For most freelancers, increased demand comes in a series of bursts. You have a few tough busy weeks where you don't know what to do first, then things are briefly calm, but then comes another peak, and another, and so on. It definitely isn't good to wait until the occasional bursts meld into a constant overload where you are grinding out ten, twelve, or even fourteen hours a day, or even seven days a week including holidays, long past where you enjoy it.

Learn to correctly interpret the initial bursts and predict a little what is about to come. If it's not currently peak season and you still see that avalanche of new work rushing towards you, this is precisely the right moment to push your prices up a little or apply a different pricing model that will push demand back into acceptable limits.

It isn't simple, and you might not get it right at first, but who says pricing is simple? It's not, it's a bit like alchemy, and until you start tinkering with it and find the right level of intimacy, you will have a hard time using price to exert appropriate counterpressure to suppress demand.

Probably the main thing at first is to prevent 100% workloads and get used to adjusting your price when you are still fairly at ease, and not stressed out from being behind. Believe me, at that moment you will be able to manage it with much more peace and detachment.

The third aspect, finally, is the relationship between price and sending some sign to your customers about your level of expertise and overall professionalism. As I have mentioned, a higher price brings increased expectations and a much lower tolerance for mistakes, and luckily even beginners realize that.

What I might gladly forgive in a cheap web designer setting up someone's WordPress blog, I definitely wouldn't tolerate from their colleague at 20× the price, with whom I would nitpick over details and demand professional work with full service and show very little tolerance for any grave mistakes.

Sometimes as a customer I meet a professional who seems too cheap for their quality, and I may even hint at that. I see two kinds of reactions. They either raise prices, or say something along the lines that they still have flaws, know about them, and don't want raise any false expectations.

Having a price that is lower than the value your clients see is better from a reputational standpoint than overshooting and risking a worsened reputation due to unmet expectations. This is why so many professionals prefer the seeming safety of undershooting their prices. Still, rather than modesty, these say more about a lack of ambition and about trying to avoid the more demanding measures that come with having a higher price. And it's not even sustainable, because an advantageous price to quality ratio stimulates demand and recommendations for your services. Not to mention the lost profits.

So rather than lowering customer expectations through a low price, it's better to focus on professionalizing and above all asking for open feedback – thanking the client for cooperation and also asking if they were satisfied and if you can improve something. Through this you can gradually pair up service quality with rising prices.

A solid, regular client essentially has no need for a freelancer who has an unsustainably low price and either burns out and lowers their quality and reliability, or packs up their bags because they don't know how to ask for more. Customers want a level of service quality that is continuous and sustainable. In essence, reasonable pricing generally serves both the customer and the professional.

I sometimes see critical opinions saying that the freelance-services market will go on to become more and more precarious and commoditized, with freelancers as replaceable units. But I personally find it hard to imagine how that transformation could occur.

On the contrary, I see a need for customers to cooperate long-term with high-quality experts who grow together with their business. That is the dominant dynamic of this market. Even though there are definitely services where extremely low rates are paid for the work of very inexperienced freelancers, there is great market mobility, and anyone willing to grow can raise their expertise and prices fairly quickly.

RAISING PRICES ISN'T GREED

It's very important that you understand and consciously accept that for most freelancers, raising prices isn't primarily driven by a lust for money. Not at all. As I have mentioned, many resist it and only proceed to do so when it's already too late.

Increased prices are an indirect result of gaining in professionalism, expertise, productivity, quality, and reputation. You are working more effectively and doing much more in the same amount of time. You understand your field better and offer clients better solutions. And as a result, they then recommend you even more.

Every exceptional professional inevitably attracts customers who have been dissatisfied elsewhere and are seeking a better solution. Pricing is then the primary tool for keeping this demand under control over the long run.

It's ironic, but few freelancers raise prices primarily due to wanting more money. For the most part, we simply feel that we have made progress professionally and are getting more and more work and that raising prices is just the simplest, cleanest, and most effective solution.

People who consider raising prices to be somehow immoral generally sacrifice the most here. It keeps them too poor for better equipment, professional software, good assistants, decent insurance, a work-free vacation, etc., etc. That approach isn't *moral*, it's *shortsighted*.

But even if you raise prices to profit just because you feel you can, that isn't bad either. Your higher profit will turn into higher reserves and thus give you greater immunity to future problems. I optimize my own business for more profits, not so that I can buy expensive things, but so that I'm better prepared to face future risks.

There is also another major, but mostly neglected reason, why you should push for fair prices and better profits. As I have described in the previous chapter, solid freelancers are highly customer-oriented, providing excellent service to their clients and taking great care to satisfy their needs.

Some are so good at it, that they tend to forget their side of the deal. But it has two sides, really.

Your clients obviously want something *from* you and they feel comfortable telling you their needs. But there is something you want from *them* as well, right? That is why you should be able to discuss money, prices and your compensation openly with your customers. Pay attention to proper timing and form, but freely express what you want from the deal, if it is to happen, or even after it has been in progress for some time already and you want to renegotiate conditions. The goal is to have well-balanced business relationships, where the needs of both sides are satisfied and the terms are clear, fair and respected.

Greed is really the last thing I tend to see in freelancers, and nearly everyone who does honest work in the long term starts to change how they view money. Even professionals who earn large sums often live quite humbly, create reserves for bad times, and if needed reinvest their profits into promising business projects. And that is how it should be.

So raising prices is natural. If you start out freelancing with a low hourly rate, it's very unlikely that you can keep it on that level for years. As a professional you gain experience and grow, with your prices gradually drifting higher. So how does it all work in practice?

STEPS ARE BETTER THAN JUMPS

The main principle is to raise prices gradually, in small steps, and avoid price jumps whenever possible. With gradual increases, the risk that you will overshoot the mark is minimal. After each step, you can evaluate customers' reactions and the trends in demand and revenues, and easily see if the increase had any effect. For a large price jump, meanwhile, the risk of over- or undershooting the optimum price is high, and if pricing doesn't happen to be your expertise, you will often also need to consult with an expert.

Let's say you haven't raised prices for two years, and at your current price of $30/hr., your demand now unbearably exceeds your supply. You are working at 150% (12-hour days daily) and telling new clients that you won't have time for them for at least three months. That really isn't good! What would be a good new price so that the work rolls back at least a bit, you don't have to work from dawn till dusk, and you can serve a new client within a month? This is a tricky question, because there are too many factors at play, and no universal formula exists. You can raise your price to $45/hr. and find out that you overshot and the drop in demand is too great. Or you can discover that even this 50% price jump wasn't enough, and even though you've *just* managed to explain everything to your clients, you will soon have to raise your price even more, to say $60 or $70, to get the desired effect.

These are very unpleasant situations, but they are also common, and if you have ever done a jump in prices, you know what I mean. I have even seen the case of a very talented illustrator who had neglected pricing so badly that she booked clients a year in advance, which was already absolutely unbearable. As a result, even the 150% price jump that we proposed and successfully pushed through wasn't enough. Another jump came just a few months afterwards. You will probably be unsurprised that after this experience, she started working with her price and now gradually adapts it to demand.

Price jumps that miss even by a few tens of percent are hardly uncommon. A freelancer who has announced the price jump to clients with a justification, is suddenly in an unenviable situation: Having just presented solid, rational arguments, it looks rather dumb when it's suddenly shown that they weren't that solid after all. If they aren't a master of persuasion and communication, they may well feel the need to stick with their first proposal, and thus again stay at a price that has been set incorrectly.

The second argument against jump-like increases lies in the unpredictable reactions by clients, who are naturally sensitive towards such steps. This is beautifully illustrated by one story from my family:

I had a safe deposit box in a bank. Every December, an invoice for the box rental was delivered, I paid it, and that was that. For years...until one day an invoice came that was higher by 250%. Just like that, without explanation. Some genius had apparently decided that their clients were sheep and the increase would meet no real resistance. I got upset, I went to the bank the very next day, and cancelled the box and all other services. Never again! But the real point? A few weeks later, my parents, who had a box rented at the same branch but didn't react as quickly, got a letter of apology with an adjusted proposal. I obviously wasn't the only client who had walked into the bank steaming mad to cancel.

If the bank had only done their homework and tried to reasonably justify the increase while offering me as a long-term client some kind of temporary discount, so that I wouldn't have to immediately cancel and seek a replacement, they could have easily kept me as a client. Like most customers, I don't like to switch well functioning services, because it's extra work, and I don't have the time or any certainty I will find a comparable replacement. That is, if I get decent treatment, a reasonable justification, and some kind of compensation for my loyalty, I tend to stay in such a relationship unless I have some better, accessible alternative up my sleeve.

RAISING PRICES, STEP BY STEP

Constant, subtle balancing of pricing, your time, and demand is something that I call having an intimate relationship with your price. The more often you look at your price from different viewpoints and weigh it against your own possibilities and the market situation, the better you will balance all these factors and influences to fit squarely with your needs, and the less likely is the risk that you miss some fundamental connections.

We can divide gradual, step-based increases into two basic strategies based on the type of service sold. You have a certain advantage in pricing if you are a professional who sells a one-off service and thus aren't necessarily building a long-term relationship – wedding photography, inventing new company names, project-based house construction, laser eye surgery, etc. These are all services that the customer buys just once, and if you decide to raise prices, you don't have to worry so much about their reaction. (These professionals naturally also have an advantage with price jumps.)

Things are more complicated when there is some kind of long-term cooperation or with clients that come back regularly: long-term contract orders, managing a large project, psychotherapy, language teaching, writing commissioned articles, etc. Step-based increases are possible here as well, but you also have to pay more attention based on the field and order specific factors, including the unwritten rules of doing business in a given country.

If, for example, I reach an agreement with a freelancer that they will work on a medium-sized project for their hourly rate, I would be disappointed if they raised it mid-project. As a customer, I just wouldn't feel this was fair as I treat the price agreement as implicitly valid for the entire length of the project.

On the other hand, a programmer who has been working two or three years as a contractor on a larger project and wasn't bound to a fixed price by a contract can easily negotiate on raising their rate. Two or three years are an eternity in IT and a developer's evolution, and so a growth in market demand or their qualifications can be used as a strong argument in rate-increase negotiations.

A psychotherapist who accepts a client for some cycle of sessions is another case. They can theoretically raise prices, but such a step would be controversial, especially if the client is mentally ill. It simply wouldn't be ethical.

You definitely don't want clients to perceive your increase as blackmail. So it's better for your good name when you evaluate your ongoing cooperation projects and then bring the sensitive ones into your new pricing only after at least some milestone or conclusion.

The same can also apply in language teaching, where the student enters lessons with some idea about the price and it's good if that idea is respected for the whole semester or school year. Nothing is stopping the teacher from raising prices, but it's much more strategic to only do it from the next period onwards, and to think through the increase all the better.

While it's impractical to have different prices for different clients, this is an exception that proves the rule. Wherever some kind of time-limited, agreed cooperation is ongoing, it's generally unwise to raise prices before the end. It's fair, and thus also wise, even though it slightly complicates pricing as such.

If you stick to this basic limitation, step-based increases are intuitive and clear. Typically how I work is that I occasionally, or even regularly every month, think about my pricing and the current form of my prices. If I see them as adequate and fitting the given situation, I leave them unchanged.

But a few times a year I might make some corrections. I might raise prices by five, ten percent. Or I add a new point to my terms and conditions. Or I try some new pricing method that I feel may be suitable. It's not always a change for the better, but thanks to the constant work on my pricing, any missteps are fixed immediately. I gradually move towards an ever better pricing model, which I immediately measure against the reality of my business and test in daily situations.

By working with pricing in this way, I have several orders of magnitude more information and signals than a professional who doesn't touch their prices. The resulting prices are then a balanced synthesis of creative pricing and continuously evaluated feedback from inquirers, clients and colleagues.

Naturally, sometimes one of your long-term clients will protest the higher price, or it will turn off some new prospects. Things are also decided by how you generally present your prices and whether you perhaps also guarantee them for some long-term period. There is a difference between stepping up a price that customers generally see as flexible and floating, and stepping up a rate that you clearly advertise on the web as a price for this school year, and thus fixed by default.

In fact, an excessive emphasis on fixed prices can complicate any increases, and so it's generally better to not guarantee prices, unless it's a sensible contractual obligation. The market is dynamic, and you have to assume that as market factors change, your optimum price will shift too.

Don't guarantee a price to anyone for years in advance. If you can keep your price floating and raise it in small steps continuously, maybe even several times a year, don't be afraid to do so. It's better than jumping too high later on. The main principle is to work on pricing continuously and to raise prices when you are approaching a full workload, rather than when you no longer know what to do first. And you definitely will raise prices, because it reflects your professional development.

If you occasionally lose a client or inquiry due to a higher price, that isn't necessarily a bad thing. You are growing as an expert and also shifting your price towards more qualified work that not everyone requires and is willing to pay for. It's definitely better than burning out and ruining your health through overwork; or constantly rejecting new clients and thus gradually robbing yourself of sources for recommendations; or raising prices in giant jumps and praying that you have hit the bullseye; or complicating your pricing by charging each client differently.

INDIVIDUAL RATES: A DIFFERENT PRICE FOR EACH CLIENT?

Good, step-based increases and price tuning are certainly super, but what if it's too late for such carefully calibrated work? Let's be honest. Free-lancers are generally afraid of price jumps and will do anything to avoid them.

One typical result is the widespread yet debatable strategy of having different prices for different clients. In order words, existing clients get no price hikes, while new ones get them – sometimes large ones. According to our research, individual price increases are the most extensive form of increase, used by up to 40% of freelancers.

Let's not misunderstand here: I don't mean different prices for different types of work, but truly different prices for one and the same service for different clients, where the final price differs by tens, or even over one hundred percent.

An example: A professional works for clients whom they took on in 2008, for their original rate of $30/hr. or an only slightly increased rate, but they charge all their new ones twice or three times as much.

But why then is it debatable, when so many people do it?

Well, above all, clients can meet and find out that you are charging them significantly different prices for the same work. A new customer, who is typically giving you more work than your client from year one, is paying a significantly higher price. Is it fair? From your standpoint maybe yes, but they won't think so. It's a fairly explosive situation, which you will have trouble avoiding as your number of clients with different prices grows. Just assume that your clients will talk to each other about your work and the prices and conditions they get; it's human nature. And the one with the higher price will feel betrayed and harmed. Can you really blame them?

A while back I filmed an interview with a professional who mentioned that if he likes a project or client and wants to show support, he offers them a better price, even if they are a new client. That sounds fair, but once the interview was released, things exploded. Several long-term (and important) clients contacted him to ask, how they should understand this. Are they not likable enough, and so they have to suffer a higher price? In just a few days, the whole problem escalated so terribly that we had to simply take down the interview and re-film it. The professional ate his words and apologized, and things were solved.

This story illustrates how sensitive we are as customers to expressions of injustice and unfair behavior. And it's not important here whether the super-great price goes to the new client or the old one (which is definitely the better option). New clients will one day become old ones, and the problem of price discrimination will inevitably appear. Will you give them a discount then? I doubt it.

Even if your clients are unlikely to meet, because they are, say, based in various countries, I would still encourage you to think twice before charging a dramatically higher rate for what is basically the same work to only some of them – just because you think you can get away with it and they are well-known, successful, operating in a richer country or capital city, etc. Such a practice could create a strong incentive to discriminate against low-rate clients, possibly damaging a professional's reputation. In general, these gaps are much easier to bridge by advanced pricing, licensing, segmentation, or individual job rates, as described later in this chapter.

A harder question to ponder is whether it is worth offering a significantly lower rate to a well-known prospect, as a bet on extra publicity or adding a leading brand to your portfolio. There is no simple rule for this, as it also depends on your marketing strategy and how developed your business already is. If this is your dream brand and the gig seems great, sure you can throw in a little incentive, especially if you are competing with others for the job and there are more bids on it. But from the entrepreneurial side of things, there are other issues to consider. Firstly, to start off with a discounted price sets a bad precedent for the business relationship, and to make a solid profit this would push you towards more advanced pricing or deal-breaking. And secondly, well-known brands are often overrated and not all of them would make a good client. The best clients are those you would like to keep forever, right? So it might be better not to throw your profits away on companies who make big profits already, but rather chase after those stars you would be happy to keep forever, both as a great source of income and maturing professional relations that can open up new doors for you to an even higher class of clients.

But these are hardly the only problems with a price-splitting mania.

By keeping prices for current clients and raising them only for new ones, you aren't really solving the problem. You are just delaying it and probably also amplifying it, like when you cut off one head of a hydra and two grow back.

Once the difference becomes unbearable, you will need a price jump for your old clients as well. So instead of gradually raising one base rate, you will have to start perhaps even a dozen individual price re-negotiations. This kind of confrontation is unpleasant, and would delay the price increase all the more, until the problem reaches a chronic phase.

This is precisely where you get those burnt-out, unreliable professionals who are always late and always working hard. But by doing this they are making the problem even worse, because as a customer, I will have trouble accepting a price increase from someone whom I see as unreliable: *Why should I pay more for a service that is objectively getting worse?*

Remember, it's always better if you influence your demand in a controlled way by raising prices in steps, through skillful business negotiations, and perhaps by specializing and narrowing your services, than by having others do it for you when they reach the conclusion that you can't handle the workload. A professional has to be two or three steps ahead of demand, and has to be mentally fit.

This is another reason why when it comes to your pricing you should do all you can to avoid those hopeless situations. You should raise prices when you are in optimum mental and working condition, not when you are being dragged by events, crushed by unfinished work, and peppered with reminders from a growing number of upset clients.

Even if you were to charge, say, a dozen different prices to different clients for the same service and handle it, there is still the issue of the price increase itself. If you have one transparent rate for all of your clients, then raising rates by a step will be easy as 1-2-3. You will easily adjust one rate (with the exception of ongoing cooperation, where you are obligated to maintain the price for some time) and you're done. But with, say, six individual prices, you will have to repeatedly handle the question of how much to increase for whom, meaning more time and a greater risk of things getting out of hand.

PRICE JUMPS SHOULDN'T BE INTO A VOID

A price jump means a major price increase: 30%, 100%, or even more. The maximum that I have seen was around 300%, but that was truly an extreme case, where terminal risks loom at you left and right.

But even smaller jump-like increases always bear a risk of being badly aimed and needing to quickly change your price again, or not being able to convincingly defend your increase and losing long-term clients. That is a very stressful situation. But don't worry unnecessarily. If your increase makes sense and reflects your professional growth, you can manage even a daredevil price jump without doing any harm to your financial health or dealing with the loss of important clients. Your basic strategy has three pillars:

1. setting your new price correctly

2. justifying the increase reasonably

3. retention support for existing clients, so that they stay

For one-time sales of services, where no long-term cooperation is going on, it's still child's play. You simply raise your price and basically don't have to explain anything to anyone, except perhaps to people who have been recommending you for a long time. But that is an ideal situation that applies to few freelancers. Most of us have a fairly varied customer portfolio, from one-off orders and side jobs to major clients with constant revenue.

So the first pillar is to set your new price correctly. The more reference points and comparisons you have available, for example, the more rates from equally experienced colleagues, the lower the risk that you will completely miss the optimum range. But watch out; each professional is different, and if you feel you should raise prices, it doesn't matter whether a similarly experienced colleague charges less than you now. They may have hidden flaws, unknown to you. They may sometimes be unreliable or weak at negotiations, communication, or indeed, pricing. In short, not even a dozen indicators will let you hit the bullseye every time.

Because of all this, it's better to aim a bit lower, rather than higher, because going too high has a higher risk of angering or even losing clients. What is better is to aim a little lower and prepare to explain to your customers during your justification that your new price will change more often in the future, that is, that it won't stay unchanged for years like it has until now. That creates room for further price steps with no need for new lengthy explanations.

The second pillar is a reasonable justification. It shouldn't be long, but it should make sense and change minds. To go back to the example of the 250% price jump for a safe deposit box rental, I definitely would have accepted *any* reasonable justification; I didn't need a full-page letter personally signed by the bank director. (Though it would have been nice.)

The justification can be brief, but you shouldn't underestimate it. It's best to write down all the possible reasons that led you to the increase or have a direct influence on your price. Don't rush this; leave yourself a week or two so that you truly leave nothing important out. This also has a psychological effect – you will feel in your very bones how you should have raised prices long ago, and that you have many good reasons. For that matter, during your first increase, convincing yourself is often harder than convincing customers, who *know* they are underpaying.

What reasons can you give? High value, performance growth or the profits that you create for your customers. General growth in the demand for your services, or even on the market in general, and the corresponding growth in price levels for the field. Investments into education, equipment, or software that have helped you increase quality and productivity. A narrower specialization or other shift in what you do in practice. You can certainly think of many reasons, and far from all of them will look as good at second glance as they did at first, but write them down anyway.

Your factual justifications to clients for your increase will then only contain the most convincing arguments, worked naturally into your overall message. You really don't want clients to read a 20-point list of why you are raising prices with horror in their eyes. In your final justification, give just the two or three best.

The third, and last pillar, is retention support for existing clients, so they stay. Either for all of them, or at least for those who have been recently active or even just a selected few, important ones. The final call is yours, but in practice it's about accompanying your bad news (the increase) with good news – such as, *I appreciate our cooperation, and so I would like to enable you to prepay my services during a two-month transition period at the existing lower price.*

Retention benefits amount to a strong incentive for maintaining cooperation, because a client who truly cares about it will often gladly accept such an offer – they clearly see that this is a concession from you, and a good deal for them. They will appreciate that you have thought of their needs, and will also manage the newly purchased package of your time with an awareness of its greater value. They will think more about what work they give you and what they can entrust to someone who is cheaper. This lets them adjust their workflow, internally accept the higher price, and then continue in cooperation with you smoothly.

Continuation of cooperation after a well-managed increase is also supported by the fact that the costs for changing qualified suppliers are high. It takes time to test out various alternatives, and there is the risk that your successors will fail in your role – it's common. So no reasonable client will rush to end cooperation just because of an acceptably justified price increase, because they would have to rebuild your currently-working cooperation from the ground up.

Retention offers are an indispensable buffer. First, the customer sees that you value your cooperation and you are willing to do a lot to continue it, and they also see that you're not placing a knife to their throat – you are giving them a transition time when they can think in peace and adapt to the situation.

Your offer doesn't have to just be a discount against an announced price increase. Some kind of bonus for long-term customers can also be an alternative – but in practice, what works best for freelancers is either some kind of advance payment option (e.g. I'm raising prices next month, and until then you can order my services at my current price) or price maintenance (e.g. I'm raising prices starting today, but I will maintain the lower price for you until the end of next month).

Personally, I'm a fan of limited advance payment for services at the existing price, because it generally leads to a temporary jump in revenue, and thus the creation of a financial cushion if your price increase really does cause a major drop in demand. So pre-payment arrangements like this can also be advantageous for the professional who is raising prices, because it gives them extra time for any future price correction needed.

Even though they can bring surprisingly good revenue growth in the end, price jumps are risky. You're putting your trustworthiness and stability in the eyes of valued clients on the line. So give maximum attention to all three pillars: setting the new price as well as possible based on independent indicators, preparing supporting arguments, and creating retention offers that existing clients will reach for without hesitation and order immediately. And if you can't manage it yourself, invite someone to help, at least for a review.

A carefully formulated email is generally an appropriate medium for this kind of message. You can also personally call important clients a few days later and reassure them of your good intentions. It shouldn't be a tough call if you have prepared a good retention offer. This is more a call where you further strengthen the customer's conviction that you really do think of everything and that you value future cooperation, even though you need to raise your price.

By the way, you can also bargain for retention conditions of your own if you are in the position of a customer towards a colleague or long-term contractor and they didn't inform you well in advance. Your argument can be that you simply didn't take their increase into consideration for your calculations.

I have worked through tens of such price jumps with my clients – some for products, some for services. Naturally it was most demanding where the jump was 100% or even 200% and mismanagement would mean the irrevocable loss of a part of their core clientele. If pricing is truly left neglected for many years, these situations can arise, and then you really do need to consider every word. Meanwhile, raising by steps is no longer an alternative, because after such a long period of stagnation, a quick series of stepped up increases without explanations would likely cause panic among your customers rather than the understanding you are likely to get for a well-justified jump.

Let me stress that if you prepare well, everything tends to end well. An undervalued service is easy to see, and generally your customers see it as well. In all these years, I haven't seen a single case where a well-considered price jump has seriously harmed an entrepreneur if they had a reason for it. Instead, they suddenly have more time and money.

THERE IS NO SHAME IN PRICE DROPS

Since raising prices for freelancing is a side effect of professional growth, it's logically more common than lowering them. *Professional growth*, as a term, doesn't even have an opposite.

But it's not your growth itself that raises the price. It's primarily raised by the demand for professionals who have a needed expertise and experience. This demand can also be affected by market factors, and if it weakens, that leads to dropping prices.

Perhaps demand for the given expertise is continuously declining, or the whole profession (or trade) is gradually fading away and dying out. This is generally a slow process that drags on for years. If a professional is following the trends in their field even a little – and they should – they can generally change directions and react before the field's decline drives their own price down.

Competition, and thus supply in the field, can also grow, once again driving prices downwards.

Exceptionally, there can also be market collapses, such as the 2008 financial crisis. In my field, business consulting, the temporary drop in demand was so rapid that, after careful thought, I temporarily dropped my price by 70% to a "crisis level." I told my clients I wanted to help them navigate the crisis, and some credit me for that to this day.

And lastly, a small price drop can also be a part of ordinary pricing – or price correction, if you realize that you overdid it with your last step or jump upwards.

From the above it should be clear that the price and demand relationship works in both directions. And that although you will probably only go up, it's good to remember that it's sometimes right to go down. Lastly, I generally wouldn't recommend sticking to work where the market rates are falling year after year.

◉ WHAT'S A GOOD PRICE?

A good price is simple. A well-composed price offer lets the customer understand roughly how much the service will cost and what may most strongly influence the final price. But simple and brief aren't always the same thing. Even a detailed price list can be clearly structured and understandable; it just becomes a bit harder to compose and maintain.

A good price filters demand. It helps you aim at precisely the customers with whom you want to be working. And it turns away those who might be only seeking warm bodies dirt-cheap, or the opposite: expensive expert work you can't do (yet).

This ties in to the fairly frequent question of whether it's good to put your prices on the web. Sagan Morrow's article on the *Freelancers Union* blog gives these recommendations: "Include your prices. If your prices scare people away, that's probably a good thing, because it means they don't value your work at its true value. It's better to remove that extra step a potential client would have to take (in contacting you for your rates), because there is a very real possibility that someone won't bother to contact you to inquire. Make it as easy as possible for someone to hire you!"

My basic recommendation is simple: If you have high demand, and it's tough to respond to everyone, a public price list will help you to filter this demand down to relevant inquirers. A price list sent out on request could serve the same ends, but this is an extra step you would have to take every time, and sometimes also add a few sentences (or paragraphs) on the specific questions that inquirers have, plus extra phrases for politeness. You can't just write, *Here's your price list. Bye-bye!* Business correspondence has its rules. The more you are in demand, the better a public price list can serve you. It doesn't have to be complete; it's enough if it roughly sets inquirers' expectations, but still leaves room for price negotiations.

A good price is transparent. It's clear what it does and doesn't contain. It doesn't lead the customer off course, and it gives them the whole price picture. No hidden charges, no "essential extra work," nothing of the kind.

The lack of transparency with prices is often unintended. Friends of ours wanted to build a house and chose an architect who led them astray by only giving the price of the study. They placed their order believing it was the full project price. Only a few months later did they learn that the whole job would be significantly more expensive. The fault lay with the architect, who had presented them with an incomprehensible price offer. And it later became clear that it wasn't the only fault in his work. Take this as an extra lesson: a lack of clarity in a price offer can be a sign of deeper problems in an entire business.

A good price is attractive. It's attractive for the customer whom you want to acquire. This applies both for the price level itself and for its other attributes. Your pricing offer may be time-limited and motivate the inquirer towards making a quicker decision, etc.

A good price is personal. It matches where you are in your field, and your overall professional level. So when someone looks at you and your price, they feel like it all fits.

A good price is profitable. This may sound banal and obvious, but don't be misled. In reality there are many fields where the final price calculation is a fairly tough question. Among freelancers, this applies, for example, to handicrafts and small manufacturers with countless cost items, as well as to services with high levels of uncertainty or risks, like developing technological innovations.

So: a good price is simple, transparent, attractive to the customer, and profitable for you. It also filters demand as needed. And all this applies generally, no matter whether it's a simple hourly rate for a beginning freelancer, a more complex price list, or an individually composed price offer for a company client.

LIST PRICES VS. INDIVIDUAL PRICES

There are fundamental practical differences between a price customized individually for a client and a list price that is basically the same for everyone. An individually set job price means that you are taking the task or inquiry as the foundation for preparing your price offer. A list price amounts to the opposite approach. The price is given in advance – how much something costs and for what it covers.

Fixed list prices definitely have enormous advantages. They tend to have been really thought through and, thanks to this, they rarely have major pricing errors. Whereas with a customized price, a less experienced professional can go far too high or low – and they often do, especially if they work in an industry, where prices are not public by default.

You can present fixed prices publicly and advertise them; work with this type of pricing is much better for marketing. Meanwhile, publicly presenting customized prices can only be done very clumsily, for example via sample orders or case studies and their pricing. But from the customer's standpoint this isn't ideal, because they have to really stretch their imagination to see from that example what their own price would and should be. And where their imagination fails, misunderstandings prevail, because their estimations might be completely wrong.

Also, a good price list is the result of constant improvements and adjustments to make it fit the most common assignments. So it represents the entrepreneur's accumulated experience, in a way. Thus you can say that a price list tells a lot about a professional:

Show me your price list, and I'll tell you what kind of professional you are.

Last but not least there is the time aspect. Calculating an individual price well is work that demands close attention. A small mistake in your calculations can have far-reaching consequences, so you can't calculate such offers as just a formality. And that, sadly, means you will be slower to respond. My experience has been that with professionals who price orders individually, I will usually wait a few days to even a week or more for a price offer, while their list-price colleague will send it along within a day or immediately.

Meanwhile, ironically, when I'm cooperating long-term with someone who prices orders individually, I see myself that the individual calculations are similar in practice and could wonderfully be worked into a basic price list that would speed up sales significantly.

Individual calculations can mean lots of work and time, and thus bring the risk of wasting both. But they also have their definite advantages. The biggest one is that in theory, you are free to negotiate with, and accommodate, everyone. This applies both for certain fields and for advanced professionals who aren't working on projects that all fit one mold. Many freelancers *always* use individual prices for major projects, and this is supported by the fact that by now they truly know pricing. Preparing an offer takes them significantly less time.

It's no accident that nearly all advanced price formation methods include some form of individual pricing. This has its logic. Individual pricing is more demanding and definitely represents a greater risk for the beginner than for their more experienced colleagues who already have all the pricing methods mastered and know their many limitations and benefits.

So it's good practice to take the best of both worlds. Most experienced freelancers have some basic hourly rate or price list, which lets them set prices and handle ordinary orders quickly. But at the same time, they leave room for individual order pricing, either through job rates or by applying more flexible pricing methods based on the client's budget.

So now I will quickly go through the individual pricing methods, starting from the basic, widespread ones. And I will make a few digressions into related topics where appropriate.

HOURLY RATES
Difficulty: low

The good old hourly rate is the most common method for pricing freelance work. You will find it among both beginners and top professionals, among both workmen lifting heavy loads and experts working on heavy questions.

Hourly rates are exceptionally popular and widespread in part because they are relatively safe for both sides of a deal. The professional has the certainty that they will receive pay that reflects their time worked. The client, meanwhile, knows what they are paying for, and can set some kind of reasonable limits.

I recommend having, if at all possible, the same basic hourly rate for all clients; you will work with it more easily that way. However, a universal hourly rate won't work if you're afraid to move prices overall. So: one universal hourly rate yes, but only if it copies and anticipates demand.

But an hourly rate has disadvantages too. Although having a different rate for every client and order is a swamp I hope you won't fall into anymore, a universal hourly rate is also imperfect: it's inflexible and clumsy. It will inevitably sometimes get you into borderline cases where the client will see the work being billed as overpriced, or where you on the other hand will know that you are selling your know-how for a price far below its value. You can smooth out some edges here, but not all.

This typically applies to cases where your basic hourly rate is essentially being used for consulting purposes and it's not so much about the time spent, but rather the hard-earned know-how you are sharing. Then it makes sense to have two rates – for routine work, and for consulting – and distinguish them.

If you are billing by the hour, then you should definitely strive to ensure that as much as possible of your work for the client gets billed. Yes, including work-related calls and correspondence, including work meetings, necessary trips and errands, document analysis, and generating ideas. In short, all of the working time that you could have been spent doing something else.

That means measuring your time and keeping precise records, for instance through apps like Toggl. Here I could speculate on what is and isn't work, but in practice it's not really a problem to distinguish it, and you can certainly evaluate the few borderline cases. If your approach is honest and proper, your clients won't really protest your time sheets; don't worry.

Some freelancers include even minor 5-minute tasks in their billing, such as phone calls, quick assessments of presented ideas or proposals, sending files, handling Basecamp comments, etc. If there are many of these mini-tasks, it's good to apply some minimum task time, let's say 10 minutes, even when a task itself takes just six. Switching your focus and context is in itself demanding, and this restriction, if it's clearly presented in your price list, will lead both you and your client to group tasks into blocks.

A universal hourly rate also won't let you bend the price based on an order's difficulty. Naturally you can charge express fees, but meanwhile it's hard to justify a higher hourly rate by telling the customer that they are being too demanding, that their project is difficult, or that it isn't routine work and will take extra thought. Yes, you can negotiate about such things as an exception, but it's certainly not common. After all it's expected that the greater difficulty will simply be reflected in your greater amount of time needed to do the work.

The better solution might be to have two basic rates, depending on the difficulty of the work or the task performed. While it's not completely common, it's always better to present a higher hourly rate as a well-considered price-list alternative than to tell the customer indirectly that it's a higher price especially for them. Of course, if your price list has, say, five standard rates, that is confusing. Two, or at most three hourly rates including consulting, is the maximum acceptable amount.

If you take a stronger interest in pricing, you will soon learn that hourly rates are kind of an outcast. The headlines read: *Stop exchanging your time for money! Don't sell your time, sell your value!* Take them with a grain of salt, especially if you work in a field where the hourly rate (or day rate) is a widely accepted transaction standard.

The guru who recommends dropping hourly rates might be smart, but the market's smarter. Generally only what is effective will find and keep its place on the market. And if the hourly rate is freelancers' most common service-pricing method, that evidently has many market and personal reasons. It's hard to drop what works. And just try explaining the silliness of "selling time" to an elite consultant who charges a few thousand dollars per day – they will surely be amused.

JOB RATES
Difficulty: medium

A *job rate*, that is, an individualized project price, is another widespread pricing method, and roughly half of our surveyed freelancers utilize it. But often it's the rate type preferred by the customer, as they want to have costs under control, while the freelancer as a supplier internally calculates it through an hourly rate, with some reserve for finishing touches and some supplementary work.

In practice how this hidden-hourly-rate pricing works is that the freelancer studies the inquiry or assignment, and if they have experience with similar orders, they can estimate how much time that specific project will need. Let's say they estimate 3 weeks of work (15 days / 120 hours) and try to also "estimate" the client. Based on the assignment and the communication so far, they might, for example, conclude they are a detail-loving perfectionist who will require a large time buffer for extra work, and raise the time estimate by 2/3, to say 25 days. Then all that's left is to multiply this estimate by their internal hourly rate, and their job-rate pricing is done. While far from everyone does this, it really is common, because people do need a measuring stick, and a time estimate helps.

A side note here: Even from this simple example it's clear that the client often pays for the security of a fixed rate via a hidden surcharge, in the form of a massive time buffer for the supplier, and also with no way to know the overall time needed for the work, because with a job rate, it's just not customary to state it, and nothing entitles the client to ask. So job rates can also be quite disadvantageous for inexperienced buyers who don't know normal market prices. This is also confirmed by my consulting experience, where I regularly see clients who don't know what the normal prices are, are paying several times what is common for the work they ordered. So sometimes I arrange hybrid pricing for my clients, i.e. the order is billed by the hour (e.g. $50/hr.), but is also limited by a certain maximum price (e.g. $1,000). This gives the client the best of both worlds – the transparency of an hourly rate and the certainty that the work won't be overpriced.

And one more tip from my working experience: With individual pricing, when you are working with a new client, avoid round numbers, which just beg for price negotiations. When you send an offer for, say, $1,000, it's clear to everyone that you have a large margin and reserve. $1,060 is perhaps better than going down to $980, because that leaves you a larger reserve and room for negotiations.

Let me add a joke here that went viral on the web. It wonderfully illustrates the ironic, and often absurd, price differences among various professionals and between normal work and consulting, with its point taken to the extreme:

PRICE LIST
I design everything... $100
I design, you watch... $200
I design, you advise... $300
I design, you help... $500
You design, I help... $800
You design, I advise... $1,300
You design, I look... $2,100
You design everything... $3,400

⊗ AUTHOR'S FEES AND ROYALTIES
Difficulty: medium

From the client's standpoint, the financial rewards for an author's work, which is the result of your creative labor, are very similar to a typical job rate. But looks can be deceiving. The difference is in licensing. A client can pay dramatically different sums for one and the same piece of creative work depending on: whether it's licensed only for the EU, the US or for the whole world, whether the license is time-limited; whether they have the right to modify the work without the author's consent, etc.

Similarly, in the pricing of these licenses it's fundamental whether they are exclusive (the author can't license the work to anyone else) or non-exclusive (the author can license it to others), whether they are restricted to a certain specific use, whether the author is contractually passing some other rights on to the purchaser, etc.

If an authorial or copyrighted work is the result of your labor, that definitely affects pricing. There is a difference between drawing a cartoon character to serve in your local butcher shop's window, and producing that same character, or a slogan, as the pillar of a global campaign with a million-dollar ad budget. Depending on the scope of the license offered, you can demand radically different fees for one and the same work. If, that is, you know that licensing is important.

Your agreement may include secondary compensation in the form of *royalties*: a share for you, the author of the work, in the profits or sales of the work. These are typically contractually guaranteed for the authors of books or recordings, but they again have to be agreed on with the publisher in advance.

My basic recommendation for you as the author and price-setter is to above all know the local legislation on author's licenses, because not knowing this works against you.

◉ PRICE PER UNIT
Difficulty: low

Unit prices are the third common pricing method – and in some fields, they are absolutely dominant. You will probably pay a copywriter or translator per page, with no regard to how much time it will take them. A professional painter or wallpaperer will bill you by the square meter or foot. A mover will charge by the kilometer or mile and add a loading/unloading fee.

Unit prices suffer the same flaws as hourly rates in the sense that it's sometimes hard to adapt them to the difficulty of a specific order, or even to guess that difficulty correctly. When things are exceptionally unsure, for a less experienced professional it's better to divide up the order, bill the first part separately, and correct the remaining work based on how the first assignment went. While this means a complication for the customer, it's smaller than your complication if you learn that the translation you estimated as eight weeks of work will actually take you three times as long and that you can't take it back without looking like a desperate amateur in the eyes of the customer.

It's not perfect, of course. But on the other hand, if a certain pricing method dominates in your field (unit pricing in this case) and it's also normally used for this same work type in other countries, there must be a reason. This may be convention – just something customers are used to and automatically expect in pricing – or, when compared to other alternatives, the conventional pricing may have advantages that might be hidden at first sight and only revealed by experience.

Tradition and convention have their importance; they speed up ordering and help market participants to compare what might seem incomparable using other pricing methods. So you have to know customary pricing and master it, including field specialties such as travel fees, billing costs to the client, etc. Ask your more experienced colleagues or feel free to run your own small survey. And also remember your field's blogs, books, or podcasts, where you will sometimes also find minor tips and tricks to push you ahead.

◉ DAY RATE
Difficulty: low

Day rates are typically used for orders where tracking and billing by the hour would be too complicated. It's also a bit more flexible than hourly rate, because a man-day can represent five intensive hours of programming work, a standard eight-hour day, or even a sixteen-hour day-trip to meet the client. And the price range is just as broad.

For stars in a given field who are active on the international market, the rates for one man-day, or one appearance at a conference or company event, can range up to tens of thousands of dollars. Meanwhile for normal freelancing professionals like lecturers, consultants, or developers, a daily rate might be within the hundreds of dollars or euros. For developers and lecturers, a daily rate is more common than for those of us working as consultants. For lecturers this logically means one-day trainings, while for developers it's a day of work on a long-term project.

◉ PRODUCT PRICES
Difficulty: medium

A product price for your own physical products is another form of pricing that is a bit similar to unit pricing. A freelancer who makes such products must be able to precisely calculate the prices of all the inputs reflected in the product price, or things can end badly.

One baker I knew experienced just this. He founded a small bakery and was affordable and baked well; soon people were coming to him from all around town. He didn't worry about prices. His cakes were selling hot, so he bought ingredients to stock up, expanded his production, and took out a loan on a van for distribution. But not even the added revenue could repay these investments, and things got worse over time. In the end he lost the company, his new car, and his family's house that he had a mortgage on. Only later did he realize with horror that all along he had accidentally been selling his products at below cost.

You might be facepalming now, but it's not simple at all in baking to arrive at the right sales prices, and it definitely won't even help to set prices based on the competition, who might have entirely different costs. Ovens and machines are very expensive. Energy costs are handled in advance payments, but the bill for the remaining annual balance might be high as well. Flour is bought in advance all at once, other ingredients as fresh only. And some customers pay immediately while others get invoices – with varying terms. Now add wages, taxes, etc., seasonal sales swings, and you get a quite complex cash flow that would give headaches to someone with an MBA, let alone to an uneducated enthusiast who decided to bake the best bread around. Yes, he baked…his way to the bottom.

My basic recommendation is: already when developing your proto-types, record the time, money, or materials invested, and then supple-ment and refine this calculation. You can also factor in the wear and tear on machines, defect and claims rates, and costs for storage, shipping, marketing, etc.

Precise calculations are more important for products than for normal services. While freelancers can estimate and set prices based on time invested for services, in the production of physical products, you are also competing with the outputs of companies, often from abroad, and calcula-tions are tough. Even just the fact that inputs are bought once and then consumed for maybe a year (or can spoil, like food) is a brain-teaser for ordinary small producers. Now imagine they are gradually buying more with different prices and quality! They already need advanced knowledge about commodities and warehousing expertise.

If you can't afford to pay a consultant to help with your product pricing, then I recommend proceeding gradually, carefully recording all the relevant costs and consumption, and going through the base calculation before every production increase or expansion of your production facilities, to make sure that your margins are large enough even if not all of the products you make get sold.

PRICING BASED ON THE CLIENT BUDGET
Difficulty: medium

One rather atypical pricing method is the inverted model: compensation is based on the client's budget, and the order's scope or quality is adapted to that. In other words, the price is more or less given, and negotiations then concern what the client will get for it.

One graphic designer with whom I cooperate works this way often. He listens to what the client needs and how much money they have for it, and if it is within acceptable limits, he proposes quality and scope levels. The advantage of this approach is that he can work with both clients who have tiny logo budgets and those with budgets ten times larger.

The difference is that for the low-cost logo, he doesn't supply four, prioritized designs, but only one – weeks later, and with no graphics manual or other elements of a visual identity. This is a minimalist solution for a minimal price.

One clear advantage of this type of pricing is it has built-in segmentation. The professional can satisfy a wider range of clients than if they had a fixed price, but without losing their bonus from working with premium clients who have large budgets.

By the way, here is one other trick this designer uses when the customer has no clear idea of the price. He asks: *If this logo were a car, would you prefer a compact city car, a mid-range family car, or a limousine with all the extras?*

After all, asking for a Ferrari, shouting *Take my money!* and then only ordering a low-end Fiat with limited options is a bit suspicious, and it usually also has a reason, which you should care about to avoid problems. Recognizing premium clients correctly is an art. It probably makes little sense to go by what they *want* you to see.

Many people make a point of looking rich and successful, yet they are living on debt and could easily start drowning in it. And then there are many truly rich people who don't care about status symbols and look thoroughly humble and austere. There are many successful people, perhaps most of them, whom we don't know about because they don't show off their success. And there are even countries (as those in Scandinavia) where doing so is outright impolite.

The ability to recognize a premium client and to adapt the preparation phase of your order is mainly important when you work hard to individually adapt your offer to the customer and don't want to waste time on those who demand ten variants and then have their secretary say they are all too expensive. Or they play dead.

One pleasant advantage of pricing by client budget is the fact that premium clients are easier to recognize, because they will either explain their vision right away, or at least hint at, what they can handle. Even if the exact budget is unknown, an experienced professional can guess the core from the context. The freelancer can simply ask them: *How much did the project's preparation phase cost you? Who have you cooperated with so far and what, roughly, was the price? How does the assignment documentation look?*

Each answer is a tile in the mosaic, and for an experienced professional, a few hints are sometimes enough to estimate correctly how much the inquirer is capable of paying for the job. In time you can also tell what behavior matches what type of client. You can then tell the ones who act like they're something they're not when they walk in the door, even if their shoes and watches shine.

The disadvantage of billing based on client budget is the risk that if you are inexperienced, you can give the nod to a price that brings zero, or negative, profits. By having the initiative, the client can push the price and quality down. So I would mainly recommend this method to more experienced freelancers.

◉ FLAT RATE
Difficulty: medium

Another basic pricing method is the *flat rate*, typically for service subscriptions. This may be web services (a yearly fee for hosting or the use of an app), print or online media (yearly subscriptions), or various memberships. Professionals in law, accounting, IT, etc. also charge flat fees for providing ongoing support.

This is a fairly frequent form of pricing for services where the supplier is performing small one-off regular tasks long-term, and it would be complicated to send reports and invoices one by one. So they price them with a single monthly, quarterly, or yearly flat fee that every customer can use.

If they manage to set the flat fee profitably, the result is to strengthen their regular income stream and revenue stability. And to bring a considerable drop in administration. Flat rates give them unified pricing for a fairly wide range of situations while also leaving them the freedom to change their price or expand on their rate by selling extra supplementary services.

The varying amount of use of the given service as such can be a problem. When you have many flat rate customers, some will only draw on services worth a fraction of the fee. Others will completely forget the fee because they see it as a sort of insurance, and will only remember it when they really need you – and will then want a quick and professional response. Then there are the many customers who use the fee to a reasonable degree. And at the other end of the spectrum are those who milk it for all it's worth and only the limits that you have set just to be sure in the contract conditions (if you have them) will stop them.

Flat rate service sales represent an interesting form of aggregation of customers into a more predictable whole. You can then focus all the more on service design and on the customer experience as such. And that will be essential, because the risk of a flat rate is that customers will rightfully demand performance precisely when you don't want it, for instance, during the high season. This places increased demands on a professional's reliability and their management overall. Arranging that level of service provision is no small feat.

With a flat fee, the thing you might fear – the service-milkers – is really a far smaller challenge than handling seasonal or other swings. While a normal entrepreneur would see the milker as a troublemaker, flat fees force a systematic approach that takes them into account, sets fair conditions for all, and picks away less at the details.

Aggregating many customers under one flat rate is also a powerful pricing tool in the sense that you can go on and work with that fee further. Any increase, when leveraged through one flat rate for many customers, delivers a visible impact on revenue and profit. This is extremely effective compared to increasing a number of individually set prices.

Under a flat rate system, the loss of a customer represents a financial loss that is several times greater than one renewal fee. I thus recommend meeting each cancellation with work for retention. If the client wants to cancel their subscription, have arguments and benefits prepared that can help you keep them. Sometimes the cancellation is caused by temporary problems on their side that you can easily bridge. Simply fight to keep the client – at least during their first cancellation request, you just have to try. By having a well-designed retention process, you can halve your confirmed cancellations while also confirming for the client that you care.

⊙ PRICE PACKAGES
Difficulty: low

Price packages have many forms. In simple terms, this is either a standardized service offer or a customized service package for a predefined (and sometimes also discounted) price.

You can find the most common type of package, for example, in your local tanning salon or gym. One hour costs $20, but when you buy a package of 10 hours, you only pay $170. Or they sell you a family package of 40 hours, for the price of 30.

Packages built like this are used wherever hourly service payments are customary and the service provider wants to reduce fluctuation and increase client loyalty. For services like tennis or language lessons, or massage therapy, it's clear to the professional that regular visits are what will benefit the customer the most, and so they use a package to try to motivate and favor those who accept this form of service provision.

This is also one reason why the use of these packages tends to be time-limited. I don't see that as the best of practices, because even without such built-in pressure conditions, many customers won't use up the whole package, especially if it was a gift. From the client's standpoint, need-based access is definitely more convenient. It was enough that they paid in advance.

⊙ SERVICE AS A PRODUCT
Difficulty: medium

Sometimes a service is advertised in a pretty package that is so well-crafted that you can also compare it with a physical product:

It has a name. It has precise parameters. It has a simple price tag for the whole of the work. It has clearly set conditions and delivery terms. It has testimonials from customers who bought this service in the past. Or it even has its own website with an order form.

You can define a *service as a product* as a predetermined scope of services for one final price. Or better yet, as a service offered and sold as a product.

So for example a web designer can negotiate on orders separately and price them based on the client's requirements. Or after some time they can realize that they are most often serving a specific customer segment with quite predictable needs. And to speed up negotiations and also sales, they will present an offer they have standardized, for creating a basic website in a certain scope for a great price, let's say $1,290. That price can be lower than usual precisely due to the faster handling and standardized execution, which sufficiently covers the target group's typical needs.

It can also be an established one-day training for $200. Or an overall shop audit including mystery shopping (a test purchase) and a final report for $370. Or publishing a book on demand, from proofreading to producing hundreds of first-edition prints.

Independent professionals usually offer expert services whose technical details may be hard for a customer to understand. They thus need to devote all the more effort to preparing source materials and a sales strategy that can overcome this barrier. Offering services as a finished product can then be better than explaining basic terms to each inquirer separately.

For customers, a service as a product gains such sharp and tangible contours that they don't want to negotiate on scope as much (why would they, when it's all clearly described) and they are even willing to pay in advance (since they would pay the same way for a physical product in a shop).

So this sales type benefits from an established market custom: when buying a finished product, you pay in advance. Whereas for work where you can't be sure how the result will look, you will hesitate to pay more than a deposit in advance. So selling a service as a product and collecting the whole payment in advance is the result of being able to present your service as something finished that will be supplied on time, at the expected quality, and within the defined scope.

From the business standpoint, such repeated sales of ordinary services can be fantastic. No more complex negotiations and wrestling with conditions, customers will often willingly pay in advance, and sales are handled all the quicker to everyone's satisfaction.

The only catch is that product development always has a cost. Building a service as a product demands some persistence. It's nothing for speed demons: something you create and then debug over the weekend. In a weekend you might create a prototype, sure. But the path from a prototype to a mature service that excites clients and is being sold repeatedly and better over time is a winding one, full of puddles and fallen trees – like dissatisfied clients.

And it's also more marketing-intensive than just offering services as such, because besides pricing, you also have to know a bit about service design, branding, sales, financial planning, and order management, especially if it takes off and you have to handle lots of orders reliably. In practice this is a sales method that works for experienced professionals, but can be problematic for beginners.

Developing a service as a product leads an entrepreneur to be systematic, just like with a flat fee. Through repeated sales, you are aggregating orders into a unified workflow, and then a single demanding customer will preoccupy you less. They aren't a troublemaker; they are someone who can help you define the service even better and set clearer guidelines.

Incidentally, this is perhaps the main reason why I don't love sites like Clients From Hell that publish anonymous and – I must admit – often funny problematic client hate stories. Careful. It's all a question of mindset, and once I have accepted the idea that clients can be from Hell, I'll never create a better service for them with fairer conditions, but instead blame my bad problem-solving on the clients, hellish or not.

⊙ CUSTOMER SEGMENTATION
Difficulty: high

Now I'll move on to more demanding pricing approaches. Segmentation isn't so much a pricing method as it is a price-strategy foundation that, when set correctly, lets you create a better price list and have more satisfied clients, and thus better earnings too.

Imagine the whole set of customers who buy services or products in your field or could do so in the near future. This complete set is your market. A customer segment is a slice of this whole pie. It's a subset of customers with certain shared traits, needs, or habits.

Segmentation is simply slicing up the market pie into individual pieces, or segments, based on the criteria of your choice. This is a free-style discipline; slice however you want. But here is a frequent choice: segmentation by the estimated purchase power of your clients – from the ones who won't earn you a red cent to the super premium clients who expect the very highest quality and are ready to pay for it.

Some entrepreneurs go even further. They try to visualize a typical representative of the given segment and then imagine this idealized *persona* when they try to address that segment. Working with personas is a common and useful marketing tool, but let's skip past that for now.

What good is segmentation for freelancers, when most of them aim towards a price that matches their expertise, and thus only one market segment?

Well, imagine the following situation: A professional does good work at decent prices, and their prices and overall order management reflect this. It's not Top of the Pops, but customers are happy. Though what if sometimes, maybe twice a year, they meet a customer from a higher segment who would be willing to pay even five times as much for better services?

The sad truth is that normal freelancers can't fit this higher-class client in, and thus can only offer service at their normal price and quality. Through their inability to offer a service matching the client's class, they lose a lot of money.

Or the opposite: a professional with a high price who is always rejecting orders from lower segments or is hard-filtering them via prices. Perhaps they could offer the lower segment a less sophisticated service as a product? Or maybe acquire them in some other way by suggesting a workshop, writing a book, offering a consultation or another means for transferring concentrated know-how?

It may not be huge income, but by opening up a new segment, they can evoke a small miracle – some customers from the lower segment can drift higher, perhaps because their business has grown, they have greater demands and budgets, and they are naturally reaching out for a tested professional.

It sometimes makes sense to also address individuals who don't want to buy *anything* right now, yet are seeking information and care about the subject. You can provide information to this group via social networks or a newsletter, a free e-book or an educational website, or also reach them personally via lectures or appearances, or perhaps through the media. This low-threshold segment is then a recruiting ground for your future customers, and this, alongside education, is another reason why such free public services make sense.

Here is an example: a high-rate, experienced copywriter whose main target is the upper-middle segment, let's say companies and experienced professionals. For the lower-middle segment that can't, or wouldn't want to, pay her normal rate, she can start offering workshops, consultations, or some other form of coaching for better writing. If she wants to approach lower segments too, she can, for instance, sell an e-book or a short video course online. And meanwhile for those infrequent super-premium clients, she can have a basic proposal lined up for an all-inclusive service where she will spend a month on their project alone or ghostwrite an entire book.

So segmentation within freelance price formation means clearly defining with which customer groups you want to work and adapting your price list and offered services to that. If you're able to offer each group something reasonable, you won't miss leads and send away inquirers who were told to turn to *you*. You can also try upselling, that is, moving the customer into a higher segment, if you believe this would be interesting for them.

On the other hand, it's demanding to segment services so that it all makes sense and doesn't tend to turn people away. It generally takes years before a professional knows what precisely to offer which segment for complete, unbroken coverage. Customers aren't stupid, and if they see that your setup makes no sense and your "premium" service for richer clients is lipstick on a pig, it can hurt you badly.

I recommend not creating your segmentation all at once, but instead drafting it as a long-term goal or plan and then gradually testing what fits which segment in your field.

VARIANT PRICING
Difficulty: high

Variant pricing proposals are a comprehensive tool. With their aid, you can create a business proposal or estimate covering multiple segments at once, typically two or three. You have already encountered them for sure a number of times when ordering web based services, like Buffer.com for example. A freelancer's variant offer, meanwhile, might look like this:

	Budget	Pro	VIP
Web strategy concept	no	no	yes
Consulting included	no	2 hrs.	unlimited
Web graphic design	template	1 design	3 designs
Responsive version for mobile	no	yes	yes
WordPress CMS	yes	yes	yes
Preparing website texts	no	basic	yes
Social web links and graphics	no	basic	yes
Prioritized delivery	no	no	yes
Warranty/maintenance included	6 months	1 year	2 years
Basic Package Price	**$1,200**	**$3,500**	**$7,000**
Individual discount for whole package	none	5%	7%
Advance payment discount	5%	5%	5%
Your final price after discounts	**$1,140**	**$3,150**	**$6,160**

This offer contains three variants – the low-cost Budget, the standard Pro, and the premium VIP. These are, let's say, the hypothetical segments that it targets.

The left column lists the properties or elements of the service that the variants may or may not include. Or may include to a limited extent only, for example, the built-in warranty and maintenance levels are 6 months, 1 year or 2 years.

Every variant is precisely defined and has a clearly defined price. In other words, this is a service offered as a product, but in three gradated variants.

What do your individual variants represent? You have to give customers a meaningful answer. It largely depends on how precisely you have managed your segmentation and where exactly your current professional and quality peak is – that is the premium variant.

Your basic variant generally addresses the client's problem with a cheap, rough patch. Your premium option brings them the highest possible value. And in-between is the golden mean – in short, solid quality at a reasonable price.

A table can be a nice illustration here. A low-cost, functional table, a board and four legs IKEA-style that you assemble yourself using a guide, is the basic, cheap variant. A solid-wood table, made to be stable and lasting, is the middle variant. And one that is practically an artwork, a unique piece of furniture that immediately catches each visitor's eyes with an engraving or some inlay, is the premium variant. A table like that will dominate a whole interior and might be inherited by future generations.

Your variant offer should be simple enough for the average person to understand it. If it is fifty lines long, full of jargon, and has technical parameters with no deeper explanations, it won't work. Don't forget that it's primarily a sales tool, not a technical specification. Put that in an attachment.

The premium variant should ideally contain something extra, some unique traits sketched especially for that customer. Leave your standardized solutions for your low-cost and standard variants; you can go wild in your premium variant – the customer should see that you are bringing them the highest level of creativity and invention, while the lower variants represent solid, tried-and-true solutions. So when presenting your variant offer, you should emphasize and explain the exceptional things provided by your premium solution. If all you are doing in each variant is increasing parameters, that won't be enough of a convincing argument, or won't be enough for premium clients. When they are paying such a high sum, they want something exceptional.

When a variant offer like this is composed and presented properly, relatively few customers will choose the premium variant. Most people will reach for the middle one; the rest will try to save and choose the cheapest. The final ratio depends mainly on how skillfully you compose and sell the offer.

The prices match the levels of quality. The conventional scheme is 1:3:5, i.e. the standard variant is three times as expensive as the low-cost one, and the premium is five times as much. But this is no obligation, and you can actually set whatever ratio you want. In practice, freelancers who lack experience with this kind of segmentation often choose a conservative 1:2:3, because they have trouble differentiating the variants. It takes time.

If the middle variant doesn't have the strongest sales, then your offer is likely set up incorrectly (or it's a different type of variant offer where the middle variant just helps to sell the top, but let's skip that for now). If most sales are for the low-cost variant, then the higher two variants are overpriced or uninteresting. And if most are for the premium choice, you are likely aiming too low (or you are a sales genius, which is fine).

The psychology of variant offers typically pulls customers to the middle, so experienced sellers often play with the price ratio and push the standard price towards the premium one. They can move from, say, 1:3:5 on out to 1 to 4.5 to 5 ratio, while still selling the middle variant to nearly everyone. But that is an art.

Don't forget profits as well. Price ratio is one thing, but you also have to correctly calculate the margins. It's unthinkable for your premium variant to have the highest price and a huge added value, but also the lowest margin and negligible profit. If it includes a large degree of creativity and invention, that will inevitably have to be reflected in its profitability. Otherwise you would be better off just sticking with your standard quality. Don't sell your best work at a price below its value.

Let's move on to the last lines of the sample table. The reason for a discount for an advance payment should be clear. The individual discount for the whole package needs some explanation. It may mean a true individual benefit in our model variant offer. But at the same time, it's a reasonable safeguard against the situation where calculating and assembling an offer takes some time and an inquirer demands more and more adjustments. In that situation you can say: yes, I can prepare a new variant, but the individual discount applies only for standard-ized variants in their presented default configurations, a bit like when you bring a showroom car out of the dealership with a good discount, but have to accept its current configuration. For variant offers for large projects, such as complete construction project documentation, where every calculation for a new variant can even take several hours, such measures make sense.

The disadvantages of variant offers are similar as for other advanced freelance pricing tools – they aren't for everyone, and mastering them can often take years of practice. If you don't have a talent for sales like these, invite an experienced reviewer or consultant into the creation process. Also, don't underestimate the visual design and the text accompanying the offer on your website or in your email. One good habit is to send out the offer and then call the recipient on that day or the next day, answer questions, and clarify what is unclear, perhaps stressing the benefits of premium variant again. Engagement sells too.

HOURLY SUPER-PACKAGES
Difficulty: high

Although the hourly rate is the most widespread pricing method, it's also an inflexible tool that can't easily be adapted to an individual order's character if you don't want to drown in individually set rates. Individual hourly super-packages are one of the best innovations to the good old hourly rate. Your offer might look for example like this:

> **50 hours** with a 27% discount for $5,475
> (50 hrs. = $7,500 – 27% = $5,475 at $110/hr.)
>
> **30 hours** with an 18% for $3,690
> (30 hrs. = $4,500 – 18% = $3,690 at $123/hr.)
>
> *Note:* This offer applies to orders until March 31st, 2019 only. Package payment is billed and paid in advance. There are no time limits on package use.

So a customer who receives an offer like this can buy a large package of 30 or 50 hours with a good discount. Despite appearances, this synthesizes several discounts into one:

+ The *quantity discount* is clear.

+ The *advance-payment discount* might also be.

+ An *action discount* is there in the time-limited nature. You are pushing for action. Right now the price is this; next month it might be different.

And you aren't bound to offer the same conditions later. In half a year you might have more work and a lower discount.

+ A *seasonal discount* represents another time angle. You can offer a bigger discount at the start of the low season to motivate customers to order during this low period of yours. And meanwhile at the top of the high season, this discount will likely be low.

+ There is an *individual discount* in that the offer in non-transferable, for one client, right now, and one work type. So it's basically OK if different clients have different conditions, because this is a one-time offer that won't be repeated in this form. That means no more problems with *permanently* maintaining client-specific prices.

+ The *loyalty discount* reflects the length of your cooperation with that client.

In other words, an hourly package designed this way can integrate even, say, six discount factors in one short time window, which an inquiring customer may use, or not. The final package design, variant count, scope in hours, and discount levels are, of course, up to you alone. This is a fairly simple pricing model; its risks aren't in its complexity.

As you can see, the discounts are justified by various advantages, which we all perceive differently. For some of us, these benefits will justify a large 30% discount, while for others it will be 15%. And if it's even smaller – let's say, if you get no benefit from collecting a large amount of money off-season, from having a satisfied client who is happy about a good deal, or from preventing the risk of interruptions, cancellations, and non-payment in pay-as-you-go cooperation, then packages like this will be meaningless for you. This isn't a universal tool for everyone.

I personally use these packages for long-term client cooperation that lasts for years; my experience with them is superb. But I generally offer them after some initial phase is complete, to kick off long-term cooperation that is fragmented into hourly, and not daily, units.

The biggest risk of these packages lies in selling too many, causing a sort of overbooking – the client will flood you with requests for which you can't provide a reasonable response time, and quality will suffer. You can fight it by defining how many large projects, clients, or orders you can handle at once. And selling packages to match that level. Some people can handle two or three; a better-organized professional maybe five or six; it depends on the field. You can also estimate by using a spreadsheet to divide up your monthly available time among important clients with a reasonable reserve.

I price and offer my packages in part based on my current available capacity. If it's the low season and I'm in the mood for a big project, I push my package price downwards, while in the high season, I don't even offer it to new clients, precisely for fear of hitting top capacity.

When you're starting out with packages, sell just one. Start with one client and test it out – how long will it take them to use up the whole package, if it changes how you work, if they need ongoing reporting or they are OK with a final report, if they accept the conditions, etc.

One important thing: to offer any kind of discount for large packages, you have to have room to go down. These packages only work with a high enough hourly rate, or else they would push the price too low. So in practice it demands that you have a superbly set basic hourly rate, because this is pricing squared.

Well-handled hourly super-packages can benefit you by strongly raising revenues and boosting long-term cooperation with important clients, since they are naturally the main recipients of these packages. The packages are not publicly listed and are not part of your standard prices. They're a special, tailored deal that you offer to a specific customer. That is their strength.

⊗ PRE-SALES
Difficulty: high

Pre-sales is yet another tool that is excellent, yet demanding. You definitely know it from major cultural events, where tickets are cheaper a half-year in advance than a few months later. The sooner the ticket is purchased, the cheaper.

Pre-sales have several benefits for organizers – and for service providers. They have the money long in advance and can use that money to cover costs rather than having to find it elsewhere. And they can guess the overall interest and adapt the event preparations to that.

The danger of pre-sales lies in the fact that you are offering and selling something that doesn't yet exist, but you have to meet your obligations one way or another, even if sales fail. In practice this means working from the start not only with an optimistic outlook, but also having a pessimistic backup plan.

The risk of harm to your good name if you pre-sell something you can't later provide is significant. Everything has to be thought through, planned, and managed as a project; this is one reason why I consider this pricing method demanding.

This problem is partly addressed by crowdfunding portals such as Kickstarter, Indiegogo, or the British Crowdcube. Through these, a large number of people come together to realize an attractive dream. However, the sums paid in are returned if not enough money is collected. Creative work can also be funded long-term through a crowdfunding platform like Patreon.

⊘ SATISFACTION FEES AND SUCCESS FEES
Difficulty: high

I'll close with two demanding freelancer pricing methods: *satisfaction fees* and *success fees*.

With a *satisfaction fee*, a part of the professional's fee, or even all of it, is tied to how satisfied the client is with the result. This is primarily a subjective evaluation.

With a *success fee* meanwhile, the fee, or a part of it, is tied to meeting predefined performance criteria, and so this is an objectively-based assessment.

You certainly know *100% money-back guarantees* for dissatisfaction or bad results. This is perhaps the most common application of these principles, which you can sometimes also find among freelancers, for instance, when ordering training courses, e-books, or apps.

Experienced professionals lean towards these pricing methods when they have reached the point where selling the customer the value of their results is both more beneficial for them and safer for the customer than classic hourly or job rates. They work from the conviction that the client may not care how many hours they spend, as long as their result is high-quality. And that any pre-agreed job rate won't reflect the fact that their output may be good or bad.

The difficulty of both methods lies especially in the negotiations, which can be much more complicated than for conventional methods, especially if the method is new for the client. They are also demanding due to the risk of not achieving the expected results or client satisfaction, and thus of reduced payment – even down to zero.

The above-mentioned *100% money-back guarantee* is the most widespread, but it is far more useful for a service as a product than for ordinary orders and projects. The reason is simple: this is a service that you are optimizing and selling repeatedly in large amounts. So this guarantee is one of your marketing stimuli, and if the product is well-tuned, you will only be giving money back rarely, if ever.

A 100% satisfaction fee for a large order which you work on for half a year definitely isn't as easy as a 100% satisfaction guarantee for a workshop where 1 out 20 people might want their money back. For an ordinary order, a high satisfaction fee puts you at risk that if things go wrong and the client is hard-headed or has trouble paying, or turns out to be a non-payer, you're out of luck. This means not only will you not get paid, but all of the order's execution costs will be sunk.

So how can you set up a satisfaction fee so that it helps and doesn't hurt? One good practice is to define how large a part of your overall order compensation will be tied to client satisfaction and how that satisfaction fee will be divided among the project phases. Why would someone offer to do this? Perhaps because the order is truly large and the client is worried about its successful execution, and thus is trying to reflect their risks in reduced prices. In that case, you can propose a satisfaction fee as a compromise and tie perhaps one-third of your fee to satisfaction. So with full satisfaction, the client will pay for example $15,000, and if it's very low, theoretically only $10,000. I say theoretically, because satisfaction fees shouldn't be defined only in black and white, as either there, or not.

For both parties it's better to agree in advance, look at the individual order stages, and say that for instance 20% of the fee is related to the preparation phase, 60% for a flawless progress over the course of the order, and 20% for concluding and documenting the work. After each phase is completed, you can sit down and evaluate how things went. The final decision is up to the client and their satisfaction, but this system will lead them to rationally discuss how the work actually went.

Besides automatically giving you feedback, this fee distribution has the benefit that the client will tell you which order phase they personally find most important, and why. You can then focus on it all the more. Sometimes you will also be surprised that a part that seems unimportant for you is fundamental for the client. Even better, you know this in advance.

Setting a success fee can work along the same lines. With the important difference that if the assessment criteria are highly objective, theoretically your success fee can even be 100% of your fee. Nevertheless, it's good practice to support success fees with parameters that you have fully under control and that can't be distorted or questioned. A won court case or an increase in order-form conversions are two good examples. And in practice, of course, both models can blend into one satisfaction or performance model that includes both subjective and objective factors.

A success fee can be a fantastic form of payment if you save the client a few million and your agreement is that you'll get 5 cents on every dollar saved. But it's an open question whether the client will accept such an agreement, and if so, whether you will be able to monitor the results.

There are far fewer situations that meet both these conditions than those that don't; it requires experience and professional authority to promote this fee model and guide things to a successful conclusion. If you want to try it, it's better to start with just a part of your fee and try this method several times in practice before using it on a large order.

⊙ DEFINING PRICES

Our trip past strategy and basic and advanced freelance pricing methods has brought us back to the basic question of how to approach pricing if you are just starting or, say, kicking off a completely new project. How much should you initially ask for your work? And how?

As is probably clear from this whole chapter, the answer isn't simple and clear. Pricing isn't a one-time act, but a continuous process, in the course of which you are correcting errors and optimizing your offered prices. But some basic initial recommendations do exist.

For beginners, the variety of pricing methods is more an obstacle than a support. Fortunately there is a reliable and time-tested way to reduce the risks. This can be done by offering *introductory prices* for a new business or product. Customers accept an introductory price as something temporary. So if you learn in time that the price is too low, you can raise it without upsetting your clients.

Such temporary prices similarly help when starting long-term cooperation with a company or organization. The beginner often can't precisely estimate the difficulty of the work, and so they may at first agree to temporary prices while noting that in a few months, these may be corrected based on the real difficulty.

It's generally better to build a price from the bottom up, i.e. from a low introductory level to one where you clearly feel it suppressing demand and changing behaviors. If you don't fear the price-raising process, this is much surer approach than trying to set a high price correctly right away.

If you don't want to directly advertise a price as introductory, present it as a price until a certain date or for a certain time, say, *until December 31st*. Or you can advertise a price as a special offer and use a strike-through to denote what it would be without that offer.

In all of these ways you let your clients know that the price is temporary and may still change greatly. Through this, you make plenty of room for a one-time or repeated jump that you won't really have to justify to anyone.

An introductory price is in essence a temporary one, and you can work with it from there or even replace it with a completely different pricing.

Is there any point in offering prices with nines at the end, like $990 or $9.90? This still basically works. It's enough to check the prices of titans like Apple; they certainly know what they are doing. For special offers specifically this isn't inappropriate at all, but respect the context. In some places these prices are fine, in others not at all. Follow your nose.

So now you know how to make room for price corrections. But how do you do the initial pricing as such?

For a start it certainly won't hurt to calculate your minimum hourly rate. You simply add up all your monthly costs, then add in an appropriate monthly share of all yearly costs, also remembering costs you previously didn't have, such as the rent for an office or coworking space, web hosting, accounting services, work applications, and also taxes, etc. Divide the result by your realistic estimate of billable hours.

Your costs may for example come out, with a reserve, to $1,600 per month, and you estimate that you're billing at least 40 hours a month, so by simple division you conclude you definitely shouldn't charge less than $40 per hour.

It is better to estimate fewer billable hours, rather than more. Unless you are a one-client contractor, it's hard to have more than five billable hours a day even if clients are knocking down your door. For one thing, you can't stay fully concentrated all day, and for another, downtimes and unpaid business activities will also eat up time.

If you aren't throwing money around, the result of your calculation will likely be some relatively low minimum hourly rate. But that doesn't mean that you should actually charge such a low rate. That is only the price floor, that you can't (on average) go below if you don't want to sell your work at deeply below it's value. It's the lower limit of the zone with your optimum price.

The harder part is to set this zone's upper limit. Or more precisely: you will likely have to evaluate information from a variety of sources.

You can start by looking at job offers to see wages in the field. While it's not directly relevant for setting your price as a freelancer, it will give you an elementary idea of the level at which your expertise is priced in this or that region and how strongly experience affects pay levels. The number of positions announced also says something about the overall demand. This is a first small step towards knowing the market. But you should do more.

A market survey is also in order. Go through the websites of freelancers in your field. Do they advertise prices? And what is charged by those whose work and expertise are on par with yours? That doesn't mean you should immediately charge the same, but it offers you some sort of point of reference, let's say the upper half of the price range that you may be moving within in the future. A comparison table, describing who offers what and for how much, is a sufficient aid.

This kind of mini-survey is also useful because it shows the field's dominant pricing methods and other price nuances, terms and conditions, etc. It may be an hourly rate, an individual job rate, a unit or product price, a flat fee, etc. At first it will be good to stick to this foundation.

If you don't neglect this homework, you will reach some hypothesis on the range where your freelancing price should be. The lower limit is set by the minimum rate for bread and water, while the upper limit is set by normal prices for freelancers with comparable skill and many years of freelancing experience. And this spread may be very large, that is: it may be time to find a consultant.

During your mini-survey, someone may have caught your eye as very approachable, open, or communicative. That may just be an impression, but give it a try. Freelancers tend to be friendly and helpful, and if you show them respect, you have a chance. But option number 2 is to request consulting from them and prepare questions on what interests you. Experienced freelancers can guess your market value better than you yourself or some consultant outside the field. Get two or three such views, and you will have a fairly precise idea of your price range. And who knows, maybe some of these personal contacts will turn into cooperation. I wouldn't be surprised.

Your introductory price may naturally be far lower than the optimum you have arrived at, but it shouldn't be lower than the minimum you have calculated, because otherwise you are subsidizing your clients. But if your introductory price is set well, it serves as a demand generator and an indicator that you are just starting out and your work or professionalism may still have gaps.

DISCOUNT POLICY

This meditation on pricing wouldn't be complete without a mention of discounts. Individual countries' cultures play a large role here, and some customers ask for them directly. Instead of scolding them, it's better to try a smarter approach.

Your resistance to discount requests will be in direct proportion to your sales skills and alternatives. If you have lots of other work and guaranteed sales, you don't need to give discounts. You give them because you want to. I'll talk about building a stronger position for sales negotiations in the next chapter. But I will state the key discount principle here:

> Don't give discounts just because. Set a clear discount policy and maintain it, even for friends and acquaintances. It's important to have a system and to respect it.

Few freelancers are capable negotiators, and some customers are great at manipulating feelings – they complain of their sad fate and beg for a discount, only to say a month later that their *new* car is nothing but trouble, and their life is only pain and suffering.

It's better to fine-tune prices and discount options in advance with a cool-head and to remain within these limits if possible. It's not important whether you advertise discount options publicly or have them as internal rules. It's mainly important to have them.

If you want to offer better prices to friends, fine, but observe reasonably set limits and have thought out rules, so you don't later feel abused. And after all, your friends expect the same quality as other clients, so I see no reason for a far lower price. Many freelancers complain that friendly-priced deals are ruining their business, but usually they can blame themselves. Be principled, always measure with the same discount stick, and you'll do fine.

What could be included in such a discount policy? For example, a few percent when a larger order is paid in advance. Or you can offer a discount for schools or non-profits, as I do. Or a discount for clients who will accept a significantly delayed delivery and thus de facto fill in downtimes between other orders. The rule in these and similar examples is:

> A discount is a reward for desirable customer behavior.

I recommend that you explicitly advertise public discounts as *optional* or *possible*. This way there is still room to not grant the discount, for example, during the high season when you are hardly keeping up.

Don't blame people for requesting discounts. You can treat this as a negotiation game and let it make you a better negotiator. If someone asks for a better price, try to suggest that they loosen some requirement in return, and see what happens. Good negotiators train when they can.

1. Your pricing fundamentally affects final earnings or profits. It's a key skill.

2. A price says a great deal about a professional's level. A price is a message, a claim, and a carrier of information.

3. An independent professional should have an intimate relationship with their price.

4. Increased prices are an indirect result of increased professionalism, expertise, quality, and renown.

5. Increasing by steps is much better and safer than jumps with unsure results.

6. Having fundamentally different rates for different customers is a debatable, problematic practice.

7. A good price is simple, transparent, attractive, personal, profitable, and it filters demand.

8. A top professional should master several pricing methods, including advanced ones.

9. Hourly, individual, and unit prices and flat rate are the most common; it depends on the field.

10. No immediate discounts for anyone. Set a clear discount policy and stick to it.

PRACTICE

✓ Make your pricing more flexible in order to react to rising demand, your productivity and professional growth. At the same time, try to simplify and have as few rates as possible.

✓ If you fear raising your prices, start measuring how much time you actually spend working. And when you are really busy over the long-term, raise your rate accordingly.

✓ Expand your knowledge of pricing methods beyond the main one in your field. Choose 2-3 alternative methods described in this chapter and test them out with some future gigs.

✓ Have a discussion on how you and your colleagues or fellow freelancers present, structure and determine prices or price lists. Use their hints and hacks to improve yours.

BUSINESS NEGOTIATIONS

What are the best practices for negotiations?

Negotiation skills are key, for both freelancers and for everyone else. If you don't have them, you will keep on losing. But improving them is fairly easy and can be done according to proven methods free of the risks that you might fear.

As freelancers, we are special in that we handle all of our own business negotiations ourselves, and we can't just send someone off to take care of them for us – unlike companies with their full-time salesmen and negotiators. They have the time to hatch that golden egg at meetings all day if they want to. And yes, a freelancer can do that too, but then you have to include that hatching time into your price – and into your reserves in case the order doesn't work out. This isn't an effective strategy for most freelancers. So which way should you go? My basic recommendation is simple:

1. You have to get better at negotiations as such, because that is the only way to successfully face the various business practices and situations that will come up. Knowledge of common negotiation strategies, manipulation techniques, and customs is an indispensable foundation.

2. Start differentiating people with whom it makes sense to hold long negotiations (typically potential premium clients), while reducing the length of ordinary negotiations to a reasonable minimum, using your own negotiating funnel or process. There is a model example later in the chapter.

In short, get better at negotiating, yes, but also try to minimize demanding negotiations – guide inquirers towards an abbreviated process that is convenient for them and that will save tens to hundreds of hours of unpaid work for you.

HOW CAN YOU TELL IF YOU ARE A BAD NEGOTIATOR?

It's simple: if you can't usually reach satisfactory agreements in important negotiations, you are. Either the other side is often pushing you up against a wall (i.e. you're a *soft negotiator*). Or you're insisting on what you want so strongly that an agreement isn't reached, or you get your way, but only with some damage to your reputation (you're a *hard negotiator*).

Ironically, *soft negotiators* have a better chance to improve, as they can more easily see their handicap. I was a soft negotiator myself as a student. Subtype: enthusiast. I dove into work with such enthusiasm that I didn't care what it would bring me. And I often earned someone else a pretty penny, but not a penny for myself.

Meanwhile, *hard negotiators* often don't see their ignorance. Nobody is pushing them into bad deals, and sometimes they can even defend their position and rip someone off. Their problems are subtle, but serious: their negotiations tend to fail, their relationships and reputation decline, and when they are the ones in need, it's karma time. They will have ruined their good name.

Unprepared negotiators generally fall into one of these two groups, with far more of them being on the soft side of things. Along with these, there is also a third, minority group: people who seem to have been born for negotiations.

Born negotiators tend to be very successful within a certain style of negotiations that matches their inborn talent. My mother, for example, is excellent at one-on-one negotiations. But she is unsure outside of them, for instance, agreements via email or more lengthy talks are harder for her. She knows this and sticks to what she is good at. So born negotiators generally score in their areas, but lack finesse, knowledge, and the rich repertoires of their professional counterparts. The moment they go outside their talents, bad agreements crop up like weeds.

"Not reaching a satisfactory agreement" might sound vague. So here are a few examples of bad negotiations by freelancers. You might well see yourself in some of them:

- Orders are cancelled or don't work out even though you were close to an agreement.

- You have weak conversion rate for recommendations and order inquiries. You say or hear "no" too often.

- You accept conditions that are a threat: extremely tight deadlines, contractual fines, etc.

- You take orders for too little money, and you can feel how you failed at bargaining.

- Your orders often have needless problems because one side didn't clarify expectations.

- Problems often grow into conflicts due to your hardheadedness or poor communication.

- You are serving premium clients at standard prices and quality – a real missed opportunity.

These are completely common situations where poor negotiation skill is reflected in reduced profits. These don't always come from bad negotiations, but it's often the main cause.

Capable negotiators are truly rare. In our survey, only 14% of freelancers said that they consider themselves good negotiators who regularly achieve their goals. I'll assume that you want to join this 14%. So what do you do now?

THE CONSULTATIVE NEGOTIATOR

Above all, you should have an idea of how most experienced negotiators work. Right now I'm not thinking of people who start from a position of strength – no matter whether that means backing from a state institution, a billion-dollar business, or a SWAT team of snipers. They have advantages that you don't. They can strike hard bargains and get the upper hand with a show of force.

No, I mean negotiators like you and me who don't start at a clear advantage. We have to bargain for better conditions. So how do the successful ones negotiate?

Above all they try to avoid ineffective (soft or hard) tactics rooted in raw human nature, the laws of the jungle, and *might makes right*. Their approach is comprehensive: their emotions are controlled; they observe the subject of the negotiations with detachment and systematically; they explore the other side's interests and motivations; they seek common ground and build a mutually beneficial agreement on it, then subtly sweep a clear path to it.

A good negotiator behaves differently than you might expect. It's not a tough guy with a tough act. No, it's someone who can divide the actors from the plot via this key principle:

Soft on a person, hard on a problem.

That is, they are polite and calm towards the person with whom they are negotiating and building a relationship, but at the same time they don't retreat into bad positions when seeking the best solution.

They watch interests, not positions. They know that a starting position might not at all match the other party's long-term interests, whom they thus try to know and understand.

They understand people. They see them as partners and allies for an agreement, not obstacles, and want to take their motivations into account in the agreement too.

They know how to perceive and listen. They intuit quite a lot, because they don't just hear themselves. They hear the unspoken thoughts behind the words of others.

They prevent conflicts. They have empathy, show respect, and use polite speech. They don't say tough things with harsh words. They sensitively choose the most appropriate way to express themselves. They deliver emotions in precise batches, in part to shape the atmosphere. They don't lose their nerve.

They offer creative solutions. They score even when it seems things are stuck. They won't confront you with a fake "take it or leave it" dilemma, if a failed bluff could block negotiations.

They have superb preparations. They have thought up options for every round of negotiations and can pull them out of their sleeves as needed. They know precisely how far they can step back if they have to.

They lean on facts, not their impressions. They point to objective arguments and independent authorities. They refer to sources, surveys, and studies. And they know the market and the playing field.

They know business customs well. It's clear from first sight that they know how to play the game. They know how to communicate with the client, how a business proposal and a contract should look, etc.

They know the tactics, the usual opening moves, and end games. They can immediately recognize and avoid problematic situations. And when all goes well, they know how to make a run at the goal. They set the pace.

They reject foul play and manipulation. They can immediately counter these with a warning that they are ready to negotiate, but not here to fight. They demand fair play, but can outsmart the cheaters if needed.

They are patient. They know that sometimes negotiations can drag on, only to rise again after being at a dead end for months. They don't lose their patience for quick results.

They have strong allies. They use their contacts to get appraisals, build supporting arguments, and overcome objections and obstacles. They consult with people they trust during their preparations.

They accept the possibility of failure. They don't start out from the position of needing to agree. They *can* agree.

Together, these abilities make up the modern approach called *principled negotiation.* I actually prefer to call it *consultative negotiation,* as this emphasizes communication, but this is a side issue. The vast majority of consultative negotiators today work from the same foundation, which basically matches the traits above. A professional negotiator is a creative diplomat who keeps their cool in every situation. But how do you become one?

⊗ REDUCE THEIR HEAD START

So now you know it's not good to be too soft or hard, and how the pros work, and you just need to apply these principles in practice – or is there more? Sadly, it's not that simple.

Improving on your own through trial and error is tiring and time consuming. If you have no idea how to handle a particular problem, you can think about it for hours and still choose a solution that makes sense in theory, but is really a wrong turn into a dead end. A self-taught negotiator won't recognize these situations and will bear the consequences themselves.

It's better to reduce the head start others have, if possible, by educating yourself about negotiations. Read a few books for inspiration and let them guide you through their examples, stories, tactics, and approaches. Naturally, you can learn from other negotiators too.

Negotiations are perhaps the only part of the alphabet of business where it makes sense to take in as much as you can from *several* books. When you understand others' mistakes, you won't repeat them, and your negotiations will immediately be more successful. Principled negotiations are based on empirical research and the experience of negotiators from business and politics – and life.

For starters I would recommend that you study these two:

Getting to Yes is a timeless classic, a modern negotiators' bible. It's one of the cornerstones of principled negotiation and it's still among the core literature decades later.

The Art of Negotiating the Best Deal is an audiobook from the Great Courses series. In it, lecturer Seth Freeman gives the best introduction to negotiations I have ever heard. He goes over the most common strategies and situations, understandably and in detail, without oversimplifications.

And since you're shopping anyway, consider the titles below as well. The first four basically concern hard and soft manipulation. Familiarity with these methods is a prerequisite for self-defense; a negotiator has to know everything about them.

Influence: The Psychology of Persuasion is a bestseller on manipulation techniques. In it, Robert Cialdini details the darkest sales and pressure techniques, including effective ways to prevent and defend against them. A remarkable book with a remarkable story. The author infiltrated car dealers, door-to-door salesmen, cold-callers, and other direct-sales masters so he could uncover their tricks that take advantage of natural human weaknesses.

Pre-suasion is a newer, more scientific book by Cialdini that mainly focuses on factors that quietly predetermine the results of negotiations. It's advanced and useful reading.

How to Win Friends and Influence People is slightly controversial, but with 30 million copies sold, it's also one of the most influential non-fiction books of all time. In addition, it's solidly researched and written, full of stories, and still being sold, and it moves at a pace that a thriller would envy. On the other hand, I see in it a model for deception, insincerity, and faked interest within business practice. But it's hard to blame Dale Carnegie for not foreseeing his success, and the rise of far worse motivational pseudo-literature that followed. I think a good person can take a lot from this book even today, but I'm really recommending it so that you can tell when someone is trying to work you over by using it as a manual. Those compliments, gifts, flattery, favors, signs of good graces, and other tricks.

Never Split the Difference is a former FBI negotiator's book on negotiations. Chris Voss offers psychological battle tactics that will help you outwit your adversaries and get ahead in most ordinary negotiations without a scratch. It's full of street tricks, and as long as you ignore the author's pompous words about super-functional techniques, it will serve you well and expand your tactical repertoire.

Customs of the World is an audiobook on cultural intelligence and different cultures' unwritten rules by David Livermore, an American expert on intercultural communication. If you will be cooperating with partners abroad, this title will make it quite a bit easier for you and prevent ugly misunderstandings. Livermore covers the world's cultural and geographic regions with an impressive bird's-eye view. I also appreciated how he worked from Geert Hofstede's respected cultural dimensions theory, while supplementing it with other advice based on his research and his own experience in a hundred countries.

One last tip, for first aid. If you need to prepare for a key negotiation *right now* – you are under time pressure and have no chance to study – use Seth Freeman's I FORESAW IT emergency method (just google the name). It will lead you through all the preparations, increasing your chances of success.

Out of the many methods and strategies that you can encounter in the literature, I would now like to point out two that are especially beneficial for freelancers: BATNA and bargaining.

⟩ YOU'RE ONLY AS STRONG AS YOUR BATNA

Recently I met a craftsman who has such great products that even if he doubled his production, he would have trouble meeting the growing demand. Yet despite this, he spends lots of time on promotion and approaching new customers. When I asked him why, he answered me honestly: he wants to always be a step ahead so that he won't be forced to accept bad deals. A flock of other buyers is his solid alternative to a disagreement during tough bargaining on the price of a product he is offering – that's his BATNA.

BATNA is short for the *Best Alternative To a Negotiated Agreement*: it's what's left if you can't agree. A strong BATNA means that not reaching an agreement won't really hurt. You have other, and perhaps better possibilities. Whether or not you admit it openly, your negotiating position is strong, and you only compromise out of goodwill.

A weak BATNA, meanwhile, means that non-agreement is a disaster for you. You have no backup plans, so your position is fragile and prone to making concessions. *Needing* to agree, for example because a mortgage payment you can't cover is coming, is an awful negotiating position to be in.

For inexperienced negotiators, BATNA is a key support, because if you have strong alternatives, nobody can victimize you and talk you into a 50% discount. BATNA is so important that professional negotiators work to increase it in advance, and you should do the same, just like the craftsman mentioned. It changes the tone of the whole negotiation.

Here is how this strengthening might look: Imagine that your landlord says they are raising your rent by 65% on January 1st, and they want to meet so you can sign a new contract or they will terminate your existing one. If you don't like it – as I expect – then you can find a few alternatives before that meeting; you may discover that some of them are quite attractive. There is a big difference between coming to a meeting unprepared, as if to the slaughter, and being able to lay your cards down and say: *Look, I have at least two solid alternatives at the old price, and I don't see a reason to pay 2/3 more. What do you say?*

In common freelancing practice, a strong BATNA mainly means you don't *have to* reach an agreement – because you have plenty of other work, for even months in advance; because you have financial reserves; because you have no debts with high payments; because you are doing fine and you have such negotiations under control.

A freelancer will rarely build their BATNA just for one single meeting. That wouldn't be efficient. So, no. Your goal has to be an overall good, secure, and stable position, where you have no problem refusing any kind of bad agreement.

BATNA is a respected – but also criticized – concept among negotiators. Practice has shown that an excessive focus on BATNA leads ordinary negotiators to aim low. This is a justified objection. BATNA is a superb support, but it shouldn't be the cornerstone of your negotiations. It's merely insurance, a secured fallback position.

Unambitious negotiators will end up somewhere near their BATNA annoyingly often. And this is bad. In freelancing, you can compare this to situations where, on the one hand, you have lots of work and a solid financial and professional position, and yet you aren't doing anything systematic to get better prices and delivery terms. If each gig is just like the next, then realistically, they are all nearing your BATNA. So next time, try saying: *For this job, I'll try to do it differently and negotiate for a better price or terms.*

You should also watch out not to accidentally strengthen the other side's BATNA. This can easily happen if you reveal too much too fast during your negotiations.

Imagine that you are one of the few experts who understands some complicated problem. If a prospect doesn't have any other alternative to your service, their BATNA is pitifully low. They may well just *have to* strike a deal with you, since they need a solution. But if you voluntarily outline a solution yourself during negotiations, that could enormously boost their position. In the end, they could (and often will) solve the problem with the help of someone else, not you, or gain confidence from their improved position and squeeze you on the price.

Now, don't get me wrong. I don't believe that know-how should be covered up and never, ever revealed. This isn't the right approach either. But sometimes it's better to keep some aces up your sleeve and not hand them out to everyone who enters non-binding negotiations with you and who may be playing two or three more sides to gather information.

There are variations to the rule, for sure. For example, creatives are often expected to pitch their designs or ideas, and thus to invest their time, possibly giving the opposite side an upper hand in negotiations. There is no quick-fix for this, obviously, but one good strategy might be to establish themselves on their market (have a good name so the clients come to them) and boost their BATNA (have a solid income, reserves and workload), so that they won't be forced to play their best ideas in the first round. After all, an idea doesn't sell when there is doubt about its subsequent execution. As clients, we hire creatives for their track record and their reputation to deliver. That's why, for example, major publishers around the world bid on upcoming books by established authors. They simply don't expect a new Dan Brown or Stephen King to be a market flop. That enables star creators to sell their creative ideas even *before* they create them. Now, that may seem as extreme to beginning freelancers, but in general it is good to be moving in that direction one way or another, for example by billing for the time spent preparing their pitch.

So for demanding business negotiations, always take the BATNA of both sides into account and don't act in haste. And when you do decide to strengthen their position, for example because you want to help, then at least make it clear that it's being done as a favor.

⊘ BARGAINING

Recently we picked a kind of *Surname.com* domain for a client's multi-lingual website. Naturally, it had an owner. I estimated its market price as $1,000 to $3,000; our maximum price was $2,500, and our intended initial offer was $500 (a lower initial offer could have just turned the other party away immediately). We contacted the owner, who pleasantly surprised us by directly offering a sale price of $150, without first demanding even an initial offer!

This domain sale is a prime example of mismanaging *distributive bargaining*, where the loser's loss is distributed to the winner. It typically occurs during negotiations on salaries or an item's sale price, where no win-win solution can be brought in. It's a fairly simple transaction where price, indeed, is the decisive factor.

If at all possible, *don't be the first to state your price* during distributive bargaining or negotiations on complex assignments with complicated, non-catalog pricing. Nor should you give the other side any hints that could let them guess it. There is a half serious joke among negotiators that typically goes:

> Whoever speaks first, loses.

Your advantage here is that most people know little about bargaining, so they will either state their intended price, or tell you enough that you can more or less guess it. As for me, when somebody comes up wanting to buy something that belongs to me and that I truly value, I won't be the first to state a price. I want to hear it from them. And I won't give in. And I won't even give them any hints.

Bargaining is common, but ideally in gig negotiations, you shouldn't reach this phase. It's better to know the other side's idea and aim your offer right at the bullseye. Still, bargaining over a contractual price may happen all the same. What then?

Logically your BATNA plays an important role, but if you have taken my advice and gone in with higher ambitions, your BATNA is far below your goal. So what then?

The golden rule is to set both a target price and an exit price in advance. Your counterpart may be an experienced negotiator who has produced a climate and emotions designed to force you to accept a price that you would never agree to otherwise. So you should also always have an exit price, at which you are ready to leave the negotiating table.

During bargaining itself, you can use one of three approaches. From the standpoint of the selling party:

A. *Overshooting an offer to put your target price roughly in the middle.* For example, your neighbor comes up saying they're interested in your shed, which is on a separate parcel, and offers to hand you $30,000. You would like at least 40 from him, so you ask for 50, knowing that this puts your optimum right in the middle. And either your neighbor will accept it directly, or in a few steps you'll reach your optimum price of around $40,000.

B. *Overshooting the price with a maximum acceptable charge.* An example: You provide trademark registration, and you charge $700 per filing. But a prospect says, "I've seen this service for $350; what's your take on that?" You counter by explaining that they can buy a cheaper registration for $350 from a non-specialist, or a more expensive registration from a patent attorney who knows their trade and gets results. Based on your experience and knowledge of the local market, you see $700 as the maximum acceptable charge for the client, who can get a similar service at half the price.

C. *Overshooting the price based on an independent, objective source.* For example, you are offering a feature-packed MacBook for sale on Facebook to serious inquirers, and you are imagining a price of around $1,200. A friend offers you $1,000. You reply that this model is typically sold secondhand on the web for $1,200 to $1,400, and you prove it with links on eBay and a buy-and-sell site for Apple. And you either let him offer a price, or you directly ask for $1,300 with some extra accessories thrown in so that he doesn't have to make any extra purchases.

An appraisal can also be an objective source; so can market research, etc. Pointing to independent, objective sources is a strength of experienced negotiators. By doing so, you state simply that it's not just your opinion: it's the price perspective of a respected third party. But even a simple market survey can be a strong support.

Bargaining can have several steps and a variety of arguments on why and how far to reduce a price. Fight with your heart, but above all: *Never give a discount just because.* Always ask for some concession from the other side in return whenever possible. And when you do have to take a step back, then take only small and carefully measured steps.

People who want big discounts can, in return, agree to pay in advance in full, accept a corresponding reduction in quality, a significantly later delivery date (for instance, after the high season), or another adjustment to the contractual terms. During bargaining on the price of a car, your possibilities are few, but while bargaining on gigs, you as the supplier have plenty of aces to play when you are the one setting up your service's parameters.

⊙ FITNESS TRAINING FOR DIFFICULT NEGOTIATIONS

My longest negotiation dragged out for three years. We were buying some land next to our house. When I found the owner and convinced her to sell – after she had already turned me down twice – that was followed by bargaining based on two completely opposite appraisals, correcting a half-dozen errors in the land register, a forced purchase of the adjacent driveway, and countless contract versions, hyper-analyzed by the owner's lawyer down to the punctuation marks. Lovely! But in the end we were able to finalize the sale successfully, to both sides' satisfaction.

This story will always remind me of two basics: First, even something as small as a piece of land can be as big a deal as Brexit. And second, even negotiations in my daily life can push me significantly forward as a negotiator.

It's an inevitable conclusion. While in business, I can handle many situations preventively and systematically via a price list or precise contractual conditions, in my daily life, I hold countless small negotiations in a variety of situations, and they are a valuable opportunity to study human nature and pick up additional negotiation skills.

Training can include a wide range of approaches. Now I'll add a few of my favorite tips and tricks that I find especially beneficial for us freelancers.

Negotiate and train everywhere. The idea here isn't to be an annoying freak, but to communicate amicably and not be afraid of win-win agreements, even those that bend conventions. This is especially important where you would have good reason to complain – such as with defective goods or services. Where people would normally get mad, a negotiator seeks a calm, conflict-free solution.

Constantly improve your preparations. A refined template for business proposals and estimates can do a lot to ease the start of negotiations – it will likely let you convince prospects and handle ordinary inquiries faster, creating more space for your work itself.

Rehearse before important negotiations. Regardless of whether it's me or one of my clients, we act it out, potentially the whole meeting if necessary. No theoretical preparation can replace a live rehearsal with the emotions, changes in opinion, and mistakes that a tired negotiator will make.

Improve what works. When you read books on negotiation and manipulation, you might be surprised by the stories of negotiators who have spent long years using one and the same trick. They had their favorite weapon of influence that they have excelled at wielding to the point of being masters.

Get better at long-distance negotiations. And this doesn't just mean preparing a business proposal like I mentioned. It's useful to know how to write and to express yourself clearly, briefly, and convincingly. To compose accurate meeting minutes. And to smoothly use remote communication tools such as Skype, Hangouts, or G Suite. The future of negotiations is online.

Nothing has been agreed on until it has all been agreed on. It's unfortunate to make concessions and end negotiations only to have the other side come and say: "It all stands except for this point here: our boss wants it different." This is a classic trick; don't be fooled. A contract should only apply once you have agreed on everything; your initial agreement should let you re-open any point until then. Some freelancers hesitate to go back to points that already have preliminary agreements if the other party is pressing elsewhere. But this is business. If the other party is pushing, push too, and push with all you've got.

That's all for my general introduction to negotiations; now let's turn to how to negotiate orders as a freelancer. I'll start a bit negatively, with some widespread problems. I would like for you to know about them and watch out for them in your business practice.

SPEC WORK

This is when an inexperienced freelancer is manipulated into doing some work for free or with a vague vision of a reward, reciprocal service, or other work. Some examples:

- Submit your entry to the tender for our company's logo, and if you win, $1,500 is yours.

- Prepare for us a sample of your work for free, and our next order will be paid.

- We don't have room in our budget to pay you, but we can think up a way to barter for it.

- This one here will be for peanuts, but if you handle it, we'll give you a lot more work.

- If your work is good, we'll pay you. We'll talk about the price later.

- Come work for us for free, in return for experience and references.

- The director needs a photographer for his fiftieth birthday party. Then once you're there, you can talk about paid cooperation.

- We would love to order from you, but draft a proposal with a sample solution for us first.

When you put them all together like this, these propositions' absurdity is clear, but many desperate or naive freelancers still agree to them. They work hard, but don't get their reward. Instead they get complaints, excuses, and diversions.

This phenomenon is especially common in the creative professions, where one's work goes towards producing something seemingly simple, like an attractive slogan, a draft for a new logo, a design for a garden, or an elegant cut for an evening dress. I don't know how many times I have heard creatives sob that a customer shamelessly stole the main idea of their last design, didn't pay, and had the rest done elsewhere, badly, but on the cheap.

Fortunately, typical spec work has such clear contours that you can recognize it easily. There is simply someone out there trying to twist you into working for a reward that is either very uncertain, for nothing, or laughably small, and with further vague promises flying somewhere above it all. Or they offer you dubious benefits in return that you don't even want.

Pushing beginners into disadvantageous agreements is of course legal; these aren't non-payers. As an entrepreneur, you are the architect of your own happiness. There is an amusing diagram by Jessica Hische on ShouldIWorkForFree.com that shows how things might look.

However, even experienced freelancers can run into trouble when they run into a trained manipulator. I asked Adam Grant, a psychologist specializing in work relationships, how you can recognize this kind of person in time, and he gave this great advice:

"Smart takers don't admit that they're selfish – but they do believe other people are selfish. That's how they rationalize it: 'It's a dog-eat-dog, competitive world, and if I don't put myself first, no one else will.' When someone expresses interest in hiring you, instead of asking them about their values, try asking them what they think other people value. For example: 'How common do you think it is for freelancers to take advantage of employers?' The more convinced they are that freelancers are takers, the more cautious you might want to be."

Two rough, effective patches exist for spec work:

The first is clear – get better at negotiations, recognize these situations, and don't get cornered into humiliating agreements or something that puts you in shackles.

The second is more broadly applicable and isn't just for spec work – be aware of your work's value and set a strict limit for how much time you want to sacrifice to inquirers *for free*.

HOW MUCH TIME ARE YOU WILLING TO GIVE FOR FREE?

The time that you sacrifice to negotiating with a prospect or client can safely be defined as work. They may not see it that way, but it's time you could spend doing something else.

Yes, many people may think it's your *responsibility* to work on their problem and their complex assignment description and spend hours on emails and calls before they order your service. It's their right to think that after all. But believe me, it's reasonable to set some limits.

> Define in advance how much time you are willing to give inquirers or prospects for free during your initial negotiations and the prep work involved.

It's best to have a general rule from which you make occasional exceptions before specific negotiations, for example, if it's a recommended premium partner and you want to be exceptionally accommodating.

This limit can be publicly stated (e.g. the first hour of coaching for free), individual (e.g. you say right during your call: *yes, we can talk about it for half an hour, and then you'll write me to say if you're interested or not*), or internal (you don't say anything, but you personally know and lead negotiations accordingly).

I admire professionals who have no such borders and yet can still negotiate well, without wasting time or seeming arrogant. After all, it's hard to stop communication that has already been started at the moment when you conclude that things have gone too far. If you don't want to look totally stupid, you need first-class communication skills.

When we have surveyed freelancers on how much time they are willing to spend on inquirers for free, the answers were surprisingly varied. Roughly half of the answers were up to one hour, with the others ranging from hours to days – which is remarkable. I hope that those orders that cost days of free work are worth it.

> It's not so important whether it's an hour of unpaid work, or a day. The important thing is for it to be an amount of time you won't regret having spent if the order doesn't work out.

In other words, the really unwanted situations are those where the prospect either consciously or accidentally draws you into negotiations on an order that drag on, and you feel uncomfortable. They send many pages of emails and documents that you are supposed to study so you can understand the assignment and price your offer. They may be right, or wrong, but for now it doesn't matter. What mainly bothers you is that you have allowed yourself to be pulled onto thin ice.

But if you set some sort of limit, two small miracles will come:

First, you start steering inquirers and prospects towards a point where they either have to place an order or just accept that you will no longer be working on this for free. This guidance towards the goal can be completely unassuming, and the more you get used to these handcrafted, clearly delineated boundaries, the more natural and sensible it will feel.

And second, you will start to feel more confidence and comfort throughout this opening phase, because you are within your comfort zone, which you defined with a cool head as a fair play arena for your new order negotiations. You wouldn't feel bothered any more by their long and confusing emails, or prying questions, or long calls where you show part of your know-how as an example of what you intend for the assignment and what you would do if you got it. You will feel comfortable, and this self-assurance will strengthen your success in converting inquirers into customers.

A specific form of a limited work for free are various samples, formal tenders or competitions. Your rule for setting firm boundaries can be used here as well – with one small adjustment.

Focus on who, in fact, will be evaluating your sample, proposal, or application. You may make beautiful and functional modern websites, but if the contest is being judged by the director's secretary, and the main selection criteria are that they like blue and that in one of the proposals someone has a nice smile, then who cares? It's in your interest to make sure that it's not all fixed and determined in advance, maybe just to comply with a law, a grant program's conditions, or the company's internal rules. And that the choice is in the hands of competent people who understand what they're doing.

For creative proposals, you can negotiate a sketch fee – a small compensation for your proposal. Your time will then be rewarded in at least some way even if your proposal doesn't succeed, and if it does, the sketch fee will be subtracted from your compensation. But this approach can be applied elsewhere too, for example, as a paid initial analysis whose price will be subtracted from the overall project price if the client decides to order the next part based on its results.

In some fields, and especially in the corporate sphere, it's common for a supplier to perform a quick free flash analysis of the problem or task in advance, with the order and assignment coming only after this. But you don't have to stick to this convention, especially if you are overloaded and you want to clearly prioritize paid work. Your initial analysis can also be paid, if you can negotiate that successfully. On the other hand, if your analysis is free, that lets you easily shake off inquiries where you quickly conclude that you can't help the client (or don't want to work with them).

EXCLUSIVITY SHOULD BE EXPENSIVE

In the business world, exclusivity has many forms. If, for example, you are producing something, a wholesaler can ask for exclusivity for exports of your product to German-speaking countries. Or you draw commercial illustrations and have a style that is so distinctive that a food manufacturer that uses your illustrations on their packaging wants field exclusivity so that your illustrations shouldn't be on any other competing products. Or you develop software and the ordering party doesn't want you to work for their competitors.

What stance towards these requests or, more often, mere suggestions, should you take?

Exclusivity is never a given. And it's expensive. It should have an exclusive price.

You are giving up part of your independence, and maybe even future profits.

For creative works, you set exclusivity through your licenses. Licenses can be bent as needed, and you can, for example, say you won't license a work to anyone else in the food industry. But it's always a matter of a specific creative work or works. A license does not relate to future works by the creator, even ones similar in style.

Professionals who depend on one large client tend to have exclusivity, not as a contractual point, but as an internal obligation. They would almost beg their client for permission to do some work for someone else. Watch out. *Loyalty isn't exclusivity.*

Loyalty can exist; that is up to your good will. But exclusivity should be expensive.

WATCH OUT FOR HIGH CONTRACTUAL FINES AND OBLIGATIONS

High contractual fines for missed deadlines are uncommon for freelance jobs. What is more common, meanwhile, are fines for breaking NDAs, i.e. Non-disclosure Agreements.

In these, a freelancer agrees to pay a fine if they reveal or accidentally enable the leaking of confidential information. Some customers take NDAs deadly seriously; naturally, this above all applies to those that use confidential information every day, like banks, insurance companies, and corporations in general. But it may also apply to other fields, working with industry patents, copyrighted material, preliminary designs, etc.

Opinions on signing NDAs vary dramatically among freelancers. The ones who come from a corporate environment take them as a necessary evil and sign them. Meanwhile, those who have never been a part of big companies, who built up their businesses from nothing, often view fines suspiciously. Some of them even refuse such orders outright.

But remember, these agreements are often an inevitable consequence of the risks taken by a client who works with confidential data, for whose potential leaking they would bear responsibility. Within the EU, especially, there is a danger of large fines under the new GDPR directive. On the other hand, these contracts' templates are usually written for corporate suppliers, not freelancers with turnover orders of magnitude lower.

What is left if you want to neither refuse every order that is under an NDA, nor sign up, through an NDA, for a lifetime of debt-fueled poverty? Negotiation, that's what!

The foremost question is whether a given NDA is more a formality, or the result of a real risk that the client is bearing, for example, because they themselves guarantee secrecy and data protection.

Based on this, you either can negotiate an exception from their NDA rules, or think through to what extent you need to be acquainted with any confidential information. A graphic designer sketching out a few banners or a copywriter writing a press release can handle such orders with proper management even without a blood-signed NDA.

When an NDA condition is sensible, there is still the matter of the fine. If it's absurdly high, you can negotiate to lower it. It's all about reason and proportionality. Agreeing to a $50,000 contractual fine because of a job for a few hundred is completely disproportionate. As a freelancer, you can successfully argue that this makes no sense and arrange to either increase the job's pay or decrease the fine – for example to the level of your reserves.

Freelancers don't sign NDAs commonly or happily. Many already have their ways for getting those NDA requirements quietly removed from the agenda. One quite workable argument is, for instance, that a professional with a good name in their field quite simply can't afford any serious mistakes, because it would ruin their reputation.

Things are similar when it comes to the liability of a consultant or other professional for any damages their mistakes might cause to a customer. Unfortunately, here the situation is far murkier than it is for voluntarily signed appendices to a contract. The default levels of liability and consumer protection vary from country to country. Some countries are highly protective and defend the consumer without any option for contractual exemptions.

In fields like accounting, law, and construction, standard liability insurance exist; things are worse in other fields. However, liability for damages can be limited among entrepreneurs contractually as well, or a limit can be stated in the conditions that the customer accepts within their order, the contract, or an appendix to it. There are many paths, and I recommend you discuss the risks and their minimization with your lawyer.

◉ OPTIMIZE YOUR NEGOTIATIONS

On the one hand, you should be the best negotiator you can be, because this will be a fundamental support for you in make-or-break situations. But on the other hand, you can't laboriously negotiate with everyone, because you would lose lots of valuable time that you would rather spend on paid work. Unless you work exclusively on large orders where long negotiations are natural, it's useful for you to make your negotiations on ordinary orders faster and more efficient.

The dividing line between these two actually isn't as low as you might think. Even a building designer working on long projects spanning weeks and months can make significant gains when they switch from disorganized, intuition-based project negotiations to a sophisticated, gradually improved process where every step has its meaning and eliminate some inquirers while shifting others closer towards an order. So even a professional who only does large projects can gain from gradually optimizing their negotiations and managing them so as to save both sides' time.

And honestly, as a customer I actually expect this from top experts: I expect them to lead me through the job by the hand so I don't have to think too much.

And that brings us back around to process management. Negotiations for ordinary (and sometimes even extraordinary) orders are a repeating business process. A professional generally has some stable order-negotiation process in place that they basically stick to. But as things tend to be with these latent, spontaneously created processes, it's often highly inefficient – and doesn't even prevent problems or risks.

So your aim should be to reshape your process so that you don't waste time on needless meetings and negotiations, so that you only do business with whom you really want to, and so that you avoid all predictable problems.

The catch, however, is that there is no universal template for this, so you will have to engage all of your neurons to make it fit your particular business well. But I'll give one such model, so that I can talk about specific approaches and explain a few principles.

This is not a universal process, but it's roughly usable for freelancers who negotiate orders remotely and provide some kind of predefined outputs. If you're doing some other type of work, where you have to, for example, visit your customer several times before finalizing the order price, your process will vary, but one basic principle will still apply: your goal is to create an optimized funnel to avoid useless work and filter away clients you don't want to work with.

So this is our model process. As you can see, it has four, or ideally only three, phases, and I have some notes on each of them.

THE NEGOTIATION PROCESS

- INITIAL CALL
- EMAIL FOLLOW-UP
- MEETING IN PERSON
- THE ORDER

1. INITIAL CALL

Inquirers find us in many ways: they fill out an order form online, they email, they call, or you get a tip from a friend that you should call someone because of a possible job. And some people get work over online social media channels – typically Messenger or LinkedIn.

If an inquiry is extremely vague or if it seems batch-mailed, uninformed, or otherwise out of place, you can save yourself time right at the start by first pointing the inquirer towards the price list on your website or sending them a general proposal as an input filter.

This simple step often reveals that the inquiry was completely misplaced, based on incorrect information or assumptions, and so you would never hear from them again. And this is fine, because negotiations like these would bring no results. Personally, when I have doubts, I only briefly reply with a question on whether the inquirer has seen the prices and contractual conditions on my website, that I would link in the email as well. It's just a pre-prepared two-line answer, but it's a real time saver. Briefly researching the prospect online for a few minutes can save lots of time too.

If the inquiry seems to be legitimate or the inquirer confirms they are aware of what you offer, you can reply over the same channel, or better yet ask for a phone number (if it wasn't provided) and call directly; this will be a key point for the first phase of my model.

It's often the best way forward. A personal phone call will bring you many benefits and will aid you more powerfully the more you master this tool. Calling is a skill, and whether or not you realize it, it's something you can improve to an exceptional extent.

Once you get the hang of taking the lead during phone calls, you'll be able to find out everything you need to know about the inquirer and their assignment.

You can even call within an hour after getting the inquiry, and go over the basic points in a quick fifteen minutes. Nothing else can tell you so much so fast. And moreover, customers love quick responses. A lot more than getting email responses two days later.

If someone has addressed another dozen professionals besides you, you'll know it as soon as you ask why they picked you.

If it's someone with practically no expert level of understanding of what they are inquiring about, you'll know after a few questions about the assignment.

If it's someone with completely unrealistic price expectations, you may outline your pricing for them and perhaps point them to a cheaper option, or offer a low-cost alternative.

If, meanwhile, it's someone who could be a premium client (based on their style of communication, their social standing, and their outline of the project's history), you'll learn that more easily than over email.

If they are arrogant, passive-aggressive, or otherwise clearly problematic, you can tell that by their style of communication and how they state their positions.

Incidentally, an experienced negotiator can usually immediately recognize a typical soft or hard negotiator. A soft negotiator is eager to give way on the slightest hint to do so, while a hard one may dig in even though nothing is at stake yet, or refuse to answer certain questions, vaguely noting that they would rather go over them in person.

Your advantage here is that if you have hundreds or thousands of such calls behind you like I do, you will easily interpret all of these signs in real time. In just a few minutes, you will form a fairly realistic image of who you're dealing with.

If someone is odd and confused, you'll know it, because their answers won't make sense; they contradict themselves, etc.

Sometimes it's hard to reach these conclusions directly, and you have to just work with a hypothesis. One time, for example, a complete stranger texted me to ask about consulting, and immediately asked for a lot of it, which is unusual. The *weirdo* hypothesis was in order, but I accepted his style of communication and answered politely. After a few messages I was certain, and politely ended our communication.

But at other times, someone might write very strange emails because of a handicap or disability that won't at all affect your collaboration. For example, I have a friend who has dysgraphia, and works freelance, so her secretary has to proofread most of her messages, since they are full of mistakes. People who despise phone calls are a similar case; I naturally respect this and communicate with them as they wish – usually via email.

In any case, you can spot problematic people more easily over the phone than through email, and if it's someone you definitely don't want to cooperate with, it's fine to point them towards alternatives and politely end your communication. Yes, I recommended never turning down a good job as a rule, but these jobs won't be good ones. It's more of a looming problem hiding under the surface of calm water.

If you present yourself long-term as a professional, not an hourly worker, you are at an advantage in your initial call, in part because you almost surely know more about your profession than the prospect does.

They perceive you as an expert; which is probably part of why they contacted you, and it's why they will usually answer your questions. It's also a reason for not exceeding your own professional competency and pretending to understand something you don't. If you are open and you willingly answer their questions, you can expect them to answer yours.

I, for example, immediately just ask what their budget and available finances are, and I usually get a reply. I also want to know the prospect's experiences and expectations, and who worked on the job before me – in short, I go straight to points that are key for me and that I would have an ever-harder time reaching in later phases, where the other party has become more careful in preparation for pricing. This is a major advantage:

I'm negotiating on the order while they're still asleep.

Prospects tend to only start preparing for order negotiations long after their first contact. So when someone contacts you for the first time, they generally only have a vague idea about the given cooperation, and almost never have a framework strategy for order negotiations. When you push your negotiations through email, they have time to think and will start filtering what they tell you. But not during the initial, break-through call. I get the vast majority of the important information that I need for my later negotiations during those first ten or fifteen minutes on the phone. It's the best-spent time in the process of every order that I acquire.

If the prospect is fair and has an interest in sound cooperation, they don't need to worry. I work in a fair way too, and if I see sincere interest and a willingness to cooperate without awkward sore points that they try to avoid in our communication, the result is clean, mutually beneficial cooperation.

But if I see the inquirer behaving evasively or strangely or setting restrictions and having a pointlessly tough position in advance, then I immediately downgrade the negotiations into the difficult category, I restrict the amount of unpaid time I'll spend on that person, I openly estimate a higher price, and I tighten my other cooperation requirements as well. And if the negotiations then come to a standstill, I end up glad that I don't have to cooperate with them. If I have a shaky feeling about cooperation, I incline towards formal price-setting with more reserve, as would every experienced freelancer.

Why don't I reject this kind of person directly? Because even difficult negotiations can conceal a lucrative job, as I have seen many times. I won't condemn a whole company because of one person. My principle is to never overreact or get upset, even when I dislike someone's communica-tion. People vary. In these cases, I prefer to go for formal communication.

If, during a call, you offer your inquirer some useful insight into their assigned task and problems and they repay this openness in their replies, you might be surprised at what an intense twenty minutes it can be. This is a good amount of time, and if information is flowing freely in both direc-tions, you can tell each other quite a lot.

If you call at a good time (for example after a brief agreement), but your inquirer still doesn't want to talk, that is their choice. But you do have to keep your guard up, because there will be a reason. And this isn't even mentioning people who don't want to say anything at all over the phone. The ones that will drag you into a meeting, where they will turn out to be, for example, someone who wants a ton of work, within a week, ideally for free.

So to summarize, the goal of your initial call is to understand the assign-ment, try to get to know the person, and based on that, either: 1. politely end your communication and recommend an alternative, stating that the project is below your price range, outside your expertise, under-documented, the assignment doesn't make sense, you don't have enough time within the given timeframe, etc., or 2. reach the conclusion that yes, this cooperation would make sense, and push the negotiations into the next phase.

Think hard about whether it's necessary to meet the prospect in person, especially if they don't insist on it and the order doesn't require it. Today even major international projects worth tens or hundreds of thousands of dollars are arranged remotely, so there's no reason to travel to another city because of a logo for a few hundred. (Still, at the end of this chapter I will briefly touch on some tips for personal meetings.)

The first step in our model process works as a basic filter; the top part is for quickly narrowing the funnel of inquires. In this phase you exclude inquirers who can't afford your work, or who are asking for something that is outside of your area of expertise or comfort zone, goes against your ethics, or in too little time, or more generally there is friction in the initial communication and you see no reason to take a ride down a long, sandpaper slide.

There are many ways to say no, and in practice the soft ones win – recommending cheaper alternatives or less burdened colleagues known for taking all orders and finishing them chop-chop, or even objecting to the assignment as one that simply doesn't fit your style of working, is poorly defined or ethically unacceptable.

Some freelancers have their code of ethics posted publicly online as a sort of advance notice about who they won't work with (e.g. weapons manufacturers, major polluters, opaque business models, etc.). These are often complex issues, and we all must determine on our own who we are willing to work for and to what extent. You will probably find it acceptable to provide a controversial customer everyday services, say at a restaurant or shop, where you don't throw people out just because. But it's another matter to provide comprehensive services like a customized PR campaign to a client who is ethically questionable.

This is one more reason why an initial call helps: it offers information on the broader and ethical context beyond what is somewhere in an email or written inquiry.

I know calling is hard at first. You may sound artificial, awkward, etc. But at the start you can set what amount of calling you can handle and what you definitely want to ask about, and stick roughly to that. Start with short informational calls to get at least basic info, and in a few years you will be doing so well, you will be surprised at what you can learn from an ordinary, relaxed call.

And don't forget authenticity: be yourself and show sincere, real interest in the subject. Don't do it as a formality, as a checkmark on a to-do list, like a call-center worker. You are a professional who is calling to clarify the nature of some potential job, to ask about unclear points and to fine-tune your understanding of the job inquiry.

Whether the other party realizes it or not, negotiations start with the first contact. So if you focus on this part, you will repeatedly get the upper hand in negotiations without making an arrogant or inappropriate impression.

When designing your own process, naturally you can replace the initial call with something else and test what it does. Some people prefer a personal meetings (even with those high time demands), while others point all inquirers to a brief web form where they have them type in lots of basic info, including an indicative budget (quite impersonal, but all right, some people feel obliged to fill in everything dutifully). And even I, for that matter, don't call right away; I first screen the inquirer online and decide what comes next based on that. (I'll say more about this in the next chapter.)

2. EMAIL FOLLOW-UP

The second phase of this model process ties in smoothly to the first, where the two of you agreed (presumably by phone) that cooperation makes sense and that you should give it some clearer outlines. They either have a specific description of the inquiry written down that you can react to with a price offer, or they have nothing and are awaiting your proposed solution.

Here is where your pricing skills will shine.

Even if you are just working with a simple hourly rate, you will likely have to set some limits, or at least an estimate. Likewise, you will combine your offer with some contractual and payment conditions. All of this, and sometimes much more, is the subject of this phase.

Be careful here again. The assumption is: wasting time is bad. For example, repeatedly creating complex individual offers from the ground up based on a detailed study of an assignment or specification can be a huge waste of time.

If an assignment is complex, it's far better to split it up, charge a fee for the initial phase, and not spend a day or two studying incomprehensible documentation and cursing the idiot who wrote it. If the assignment is bad, then you can immediately fire off an offer for an initial, paid part of your cooperation in which you and the client rework it into a usable form.

An expert should know how to negotiate the redefinition of a task assignment so as to make their expert work even possible. You can call it a feasibility study, an initial analysis, an independent examination, or project preparation – whatever sounds appropriate and reasonable. Besides, this will also reduce the degree of uncertainty for the other party and breaking large orders up into phases is simply a good practice.

You don't want to waste time. So here's what can help you to save some:

- *Having a well-written price list for quick pricing*
- *Maintaining clear Terms and Conditions for clients to approve with their orders*
- *Having price packages and standardized services-as-products at clearly defined prices*
- *Having a comprehensive presentation of the offered service as a PDF or on your website*
- *Pre-prepared variant proposals and estimate templates for your main target groups*
- *Having templates for orders, calculations, contracts, and even certain types of emails*
- *Intimate knowledge of various pricing methods, enabling quick adaptation for orders*
- *A process checklist to remind you what to ask about and find out*

In short, any kind of systematic preparation that you can repeatedly use to shorten the length of negotiations and effectively take the initiative will help. Here, for example, is how the graphic designer Vita Valka describes his initial client communication. Vita travels with his family for a few months every year throughout the EU as a digital nomad and writes about it on GuruCamper.com. He usually negotiates and executes his orders remotely:

The initial communication and my questions for clients are key for creating designs that fit immediately. I tell my clients: I'm like a tailor sewing a suit. It has to fit perfectly. And above all, it has to boost the client's confidence, not my ego.

In my calibration phase, I essentially ask my client the same thing: what do they expect from the (re)design, what must I keep, what doesn't work, the state of the competition, what their favorite websites or styles are.

I only rarely meet up in person; Skype or Hangouts usually suffice. I greatly prefer when a client sees in advance the calculation, the work estimate, and a timeline, that they approve right away. This saves lots of time and awkward silences at meetings, where a client learns that I'm not just working for a room and breakfast.

A firm price list helps me price orders quickly. I always throw in a few questions with my preliminary pricing, as well as recommendations on how I would approach the project if I were the client. My price individualization after that fully depends on how well we click with each other, in other words, how effectively we can cooperate.

Invoicing is the finish line. That is perhaps the biggest and simultaneously simplest motivational tool of all time. Do everything to invoice it as soon as possible. I don't mean rushing an order, or invoicing before the client is satisfied with the results. On the contrary; a satisfied client is generally a client that comes back.

When you focus on invoicing as the finish line, you won't distract yourself with nonsense. You won't ask your client about what is clear in advance. You won't wait a long time for their statements. You'll organize the whole order so that the holy invoicing moment will come ASAP.

Here again, systematic preparation gives you a huge advantage. Few customers out there are especially well prepared. And even if they do have an inquiry or assignment prepared in advance, it's almost never equal in quality to your preparations. You, after all, can replicate your preparations, and thus improve them with every order, whereas a customer typically only prepares once. A few years of such improvement, and your preparations will be more thorough than any assignment description.

Your preparations are the cornerstone of your whole negotiations, and if you present a sensible proposal, then most likely, it is what will be discussed. And if you have two or three backup options or alternatives, your customers will love that.

On the other hand, if your customer comes to you with a carefully prepared assignment that they have had drafted at great cost, and you have nothing similarly intricate on your side, they will have the initiative. And that is a worse scenario: your negotiations will be less predictable and take more time.

But have no fear. Human nature and its love of comfort, as well as the heavy workload of successful people and premium clients, will always play into your hands. Professionals are simply expected to present sensible and effective solutions for a customer's problem.

In this phase, the quality of your preparations and price-setting and the first impression from your call will shine through. But so will the strength of your good name and character and the overall level of your presentation; they too will decide whether the inquirer will trust you and accept your proposals. If the balance is positive, you can close most of your deals in this phase, *without* personal meetings. And if the prospect does insist on a meeting, then it will often be because they are still unsure if you can handle the job. But we'll get to that later. So: what is the goal of this second phase in our process model?

> The goal is to push the inquiry towards becoming an order. Or, if for any reason that is not possible and the prospect insists on a meeting, then the goal is to at least resolve all of the fundamental problematic points, e.g. the price, rough deadline, and scope.

No matter what, the goal is to wrap up the negotiations' main points here and not meet for no reason, just to find that you and the prospect have conflicting ideas.

I also typically work remotely with professionals whom I have never seen in my life, but because they understand their work and do it well, it has never occurred to me to worry about it or pull them into meetings. If I trust that they are genuine experts, and I see that they have an order's progress under control, I have no problem with this.

Here again, this can't be viewed rigidly. There are definitely professions with a different process, where personal meetings may really be needed. Or you can make an occasional exception and meet up with someone either because they are nearby or because they are an interesting contact for other reasons. It's more about the principles for fine-tuning the negotiation process so that you waste less time on meetings and can invoice that much more.

This second phase, generally over email, but sometimes partly over the phone or a video call, represents the key phase of negotiations from the standpoint of the inquirer as well. Here is where you flesh out unclear points in the order and differing ideas about the price, including bargaining or discount demands. This is where contractual and payment conditions are agreed on. This is where people use tactics and speak carefully while seeking the best positions. The points you scored in advance when the other side wasn't yet taking things seriously can bring a rich harvest in this phase.

Among other things, that means that if the customer has high demands on quality, deadline, or terms, this is precisely where you should fully employ your pricing and negotiation skill, because there won't be room for them later.

For example, large companies often have strict invoicing and payment conditions; you can't just automatically expect to get what you want as you would with small clients. You will need some serious skill to get it at all.

Negotiations with corporate clients have several specifics too. These business negotiations can even drag on for months, and there are dozens of outdated and ineffective strategies for them. What usually works best for professional freelancers is that they either 1. engage in multiple such negotiations simultaneously, closing a deal on one of them once in a while, or 2. they test out a corporate client through a small paid assignment like a consultation or a team workshop, and if it doesn't lead anywhere quickly, they will just drop them.

The first of these strategies is active and also more demanding, because you have to be able to alter the speed of various negotiations on the fly in order to fit it all neatly into your schedule. Or you have to invest just a little time in each prospect to build a network of personal contacts and then, when a lead comes, gear up for a focused negotiation with rather quick results. The second strategy is reactive – if a corporate client comes to me, I try to immediately work out some small cooperation, and if even that drags on, I know what's up.

Regardless of whether it's a corporation or not, for demanding new clients, we should raise the price estimate to a level that matches the difficulty of the assignment and the deadline, which is being negotiated on as well of course. As professionals, we should be able to ask for higher compensation for our work and if the other party doesn't accept the proposal, we weren't the party that declined.

What often isn't mentioned is the effect that mastering negotiations has on personal productivity. An experienced negotiator will never have the situation where the customer is pushing them to their very limit or beyond it to where a deadline can't be met. A skilled negotiator creates fundamentally more room for setting an optimal deadline. Or even sets the pace for the entire negotiation so that the order arrives at the right time – not sooner and not later.

Where a beginner gets carried away by the situation and closes a deal when it suits them the least (because for instance another three or four such negotiations are also reaching their end), an experienced negotiator can juggle priorities so skillfully that their orders ultimately line up nicely with no excess work pressure.

This phase of the process is in any case your last chance to say no if, during detailed examination, you learn it's outside your expertise or beyond your abilities. A junior professional can be a skilled expert, but still not senior enough to work out, for example, a client's entire strategy.

If you have handled the preparations well and you can manage this phase, then you can reach an agreement quickly after resolving all the tough or fuzzy points through a few emails or follow-up calls. It's hardly an exception to work out a small order on the same day.

You definitely know that email isn't 100% reliable. Some emails get lost, land in spam, or get rejected by a mail server or antivirus filter. The solution is simple. I check my spam folder regularly, and when I'm starting to communicate with someone, I respond to their initial inquiry by email and then notify them via SMS or an instant messenger, so they can look at my email right away and reply – or eventually let me know if they didn't get it. The text will vary but will look roughly like this:

Hello Peter. I've just sent a reply to your inquiry. I'm looking forward to hearing back from you and to our potential collaboration. Robert Vlach

I also send such a message when the prospect has called me and promised an email with details, but none has arrived after several days. This way I prevent a situation, where their email has been lost somehow and the prospect thinks that the ball is in my court, while I think the same about them.

I always try to react in as flexible a way as possible to keep the ball on their side. My primary goal is to lead the prospect to a *conversion point* where they will either cross the Rubicon without pushing or reminders from my side, or will let the communication fade away.

For example: *Here is my price list and terms and conditions. If they are acceptable, let's discuss the rest.*

Or later: *Please find below an attached estimate based on our prior agreement. If you accept it, we can arrange the order right away and set a start date for our collaboration.*

I don't push, don't chase, and don't remind. That would only weaken my negotiating position for the rounds to come. At the conversion point I leave the initiative to the other side, and only those interested in cooperation will cross it on their own. From the psychological standpoint, it's a breakthrough moment.

Leaving the other party to make the decisive step on their own also serves me well with soft negotiators, who are easy to push around but later seek some last-minute escape from the deal. Giving them space to exert their free will in the end saves me time as well.

Email correspondence that drags on, fades, or runs into dead ends indicates either (the more common) 1. your lack of preparedness or inability to bring the communication to a clear and unequivocal conclusion, or (and I'm sure you would recognize this) 2. a potential trouble-maker. The latter being a customer who is always thinking things up, complaining, and in the end wants their money back. While you should, perhaps, have caught them in phase one, this here is your last chance to jump off of the speeding train. And you would do well to jump. People like this will abuse absolutely any crack in your terms and conditions or paragraph in the law to get what they want. And they like to make threats, so watch out.

On the other hand, born trouble-makers are rare, and if there are a lot of them around you, they are more likely not actually trouble-makers, but dissatisfied customers who simply have a problem with the quality of your services. Here you just apply Occam's Razor:

> It's much more likely that there is something wrong with your service than that you have happened to land in a nest of trouble-makers.

A professional who has never ending problems with clients is most often themselves the cause, even if they don't realize it. (And here again I'll note that I'm talking about ordinary freelancers on the free market, not perma-temps and dependent professionals whose only clients are work agencies.)

The ideal conclusion for this phase of the model process is a unanimous agreement that the proposal you have presented is acceptable in every way, and the subsequent order.

3. MEETING IN PERSON

Sometimes despite overall agreement, a prospect will still want to meet you in person and add a personal touch to the agreement – *before* placing the order.

You may work in a field where this is a necessity. And polite.

It may be a large order and the prospect may have certain doubts about whether you can handle it.

Or they are old-school, they don't trust technology, and they only want to close deals in person.

Or there is some other thing behind it all, and they want to discuss that thing personally.

Or they are simply used to it.

If you have already cleared up the major sticking points, then this meeting is mainly about confirmation, so treat it as such. You can even openly define it that way, and you will see if the other party sees it the same.

If things go well, you will meet up with the client at their firm, in a rented meeting room where you have privacy, or over a working lunch on neutral ground. You will go over the whole offer together, fine-tune the details, and shake hands in an hour.

If things don't go well, you have either run into someone with hidden interests, or have mismanaged the second phase of the negotiation process.

Perhaps the agreement wasn't at all as clearly defined as you previously thought, putting your negotiations on thin ice. In these situations, my advice is that you suspend negotiations, with the justification that you need to think over the offer – and then do just that. After all, you were expecting confirmation of the preliminary agreement, not reopening negotiations on already closed points. Keep in mind: *Nothing has been agreed upon until it has all been agreed upon.*

The other party's motivations may vary; it may be a misunderstanding, but it may be deliberate, and it may be intended to weaken your position – suspending negotiations is then the best escape route.

If the negotiations are suspended, you then have room to consult the problem with your allies, think over the whole matter, and return with a counter-offer, or just back out of it. The important thing is to mainly do it all with some thought, and not under pressure in a meeting room before two men in suits with stony expressions, where you are likely to stumble.

A professional is a strategist, and as a negotiator, they won't run into obvious traps. If you encounter suspicious signals during personal meetings or you have a vague feeling that something is very wrong, breathe deeply, think, and don't act in haste.

But again I want to emphasize that there won't be many meetings like this. The vast majority of customers are good people and aren't any kind of threat. Still, this is all the more reason to double check what you might have overlooked when you *do* have a bad feeling. It might be self-deception…or a real reason for caution. Every major conflict has some warning signs. For us as professionals the main thing here is to not be blinded by the potential profit, which can temporarily make us unable to assess normal human behavior.

Here are a few more tips.

You have, I hope, made a good first impression in advance, but this is a chance to make a second, personal one. That means clothing, behavior, appearance, and how much vitality radiates from you. It's not hard – at least, not for most people. But at the same time it's easy to underestimate all this and create a bad, shaky, unsure impression. Unfortunately this does happen, and the result is quite simply losing the order, mostly on the basis of some banal excuse or an indefinite suspension. Few people will disclose the real reason to your face, because it isn't socially acceptable.

Arrange your meeting times so they fit your working habits and biorhythms and ideally also other errands that you have near the meeting point. And come on time.

Do your homework. Don't be afraid to pleasantly surprise someone. You can do some extra preparation to reach deeper into the client's field, read a few articles, read some basic Wikipedia entries. Nobody is going to ask you about it, but the end result could be notes that you have processed and maybe even bring with you in print – perhaps even in a folder with the prospect's logo. Your preparation doesn't have to be formal; it can be original and great.

Consider a gift or a little something, that is, if it's not an institution or company where gifts are forbidden. It also depends on the given country's customs. It may be an excellent book that you have read, a bottle of wine, or another trifle that will please them and give them a better impression of you.

I know a bit about wine, and I remember one meeting where it played a role. I had an important meeting with one corporate sales manager who wasn't too obliging, and I had to go there personally to convince him. On the way out, I grabbed a bottle of wine from our stock at home. When I reached his office, I introduced myself, shook hands, and handed him the bottle as a gift; he placed it unthinkingly on the table, and we began to talk. Things went along stiffly, until his eyes caught the bottle I had given him. He stopped me in mid-sentence and said: *Hey, I know that wine! That's an excellent producer, and a great year too. Thank you very much! You know, I've been doing this work for eight years, and until now, nobody has brought me any wine worth mentioning.* We spent the rest of our hour in friendly conversation, and from there we reached agreement on everything.

The meeting place can be another support. Sometimes you will be the one suggesting it, which also applies to situations where you need to meet a long-term client. It's good to have several tested places and choose one that matches your intentions. And you will also appreciate knowing where to rent a meeting room, due to confidential subjects or a particular client demands. (Most coworking spaces offer these rooms.)

It will also impress someone when you take them to a restaurant that is superb, not overpriced, and offers great service. If you're unsure here, try Yelp, TripAdvisor, Foursquare, or Facebook and read through the place's positive and negative reviews so you aren't in for a nasty surprise.

4. THE ORDER

After my long descriptions of the funnel's previous three phases, you may be surprised at how quickly a well-greased process can reach a binding order. (My record is roughly two hours after getting a vague initial inquiry to having an advance payment deposited into my bank account.)

Actually, speed and flexibility are among the main benefits of this whole process. A quick response to the first inquiry, a sizing-up call shortly after that, and if it all fits, you can immediately email your proposal or estimate – which, of course, you have carefully considered and prepared long in advance. Even adding in a few emails on details and delays on one side or the other, you can still bring ordinary inquiries to a conclusion in the form of an order in a few days.

This also works in the other direction – if I can't bring an inquiry into an order within two weeks, it's generally not coming at all. The prospect will have either changed their mind or their priorities, or other obligations will have overwhelmed them, and things will cool down. (There are exceptions of course, especially with large companies, where I naturally expect slower negotiations.)

So if you have your order negotiation process set up so it leads directly towards the goal, without heading into difficult dead spots and blind alleys, that is definitely a plus – which clients will like too. Either they will accept your offer right in the second phase, or you will end up also meeting them personally, but the result is a closed deal.

Some freelancers will accept just a written order and advance payment, and some even just a confirmed order over email. Others sign written contracts, including a full project description. Purely electronic signatures on contracts in DocuSign or Adobe Sign are also on the rise. The specific order confirmation process will depend on customs in the field and in your country, the level of risk, and the method you have chosen for securing the payment of orders, which I'll discuss in greater detail in the next chapter.

Solid security for the entire business transaction is all the more important when you consider that with a fully optimized negotiation process, you usually won't meet the client in person at all. A unified process is also better, because repetition reduces risks by preventing more and more of them. And the risks are logically higher when every deal is different.

Your methods for securing and closing orders are thus becoming a firm element within your whole process, so it pays to consult on them with the same lawyer you will ask to enforce any unpaid debts. They can also advise you on other preparations, from proposals and offers to contractual terms.

KEY IDEAS

1. What makes a good negotiator? They reach satisfactory agreements in important negotiations.

2. Naturally soft, hard, or born negotiators are not that successful.

3. Negotiation is a key superskill, usable both in business and elsewhere.

4. Professional negotiators are creative diplomats: *Soft on a person, hard on a problem.*

5. It's important to educate yourself here. This is one of the few areas where study is essential.

6. A strong BATNA, i.e. having good alternatives, is key for freelancers.

7. Negotiations are powerful, but laboriously negotiating with everyone would waste time.

8. Most ordinary orders are best worked out quickly based on an optimized process.

9. An effective process eliminates unattractive inquiries and leads straight to a deal.

10. And if things go well, you will meet many prospects in person only after the deal has been made and the work has already begun.

✓ First, figure out what your natural style is in negotiations and your general success rate. Improve from there. Read *Getting to Yes* or listen to *The Art of Negotiating the Best Deal* to grasp the basics of negotiations.

✓ Second, work consciously on your general BATNA (your Best Alternative To a Negotiated Agreement), i.e. have a reserve, enough work for two or three months, low debt, etc. It will give you a strong edge against bad deals.

✓ Once you have solidified your BATNA position, be more ambitious when negotiating your next jobs. Aim higher and don't settle for business-as-usual deals only.

✓ Define how much time you are willing to give inquirers or prospects for free and stick to it. You can also set your own rules for spec work, NDAs, exclusivity requests and so on.

✓ Build your optimized negotiation process to close regular deals quickly with the clients you want. Update this process and improve your preparations after each deal.

GETTING PAID

Can you outsmart non-payers?

My series of chapters on clients, pricing, and negotiations would be incomplete if I skipped one special category of clients: those who have, or could have, trouble paying. I'm talking about non-payers, frauds, liars, and other problematic people.

Yes, I could have included this topic in the chapter on negotiations, but it's so important it deserves its own short separate chapter. Unpaid claims reduce your confidence and faith in people, but above all, they threaten your financial stability. In extreme cases, they can even have the most serious of consequences on your business, personal life, or family.

And I want you to make it through everything in freelancing, including a run-in with a sophisticated serial non-payer, so I would like for you to be prepared and not give them the chance they are yearning for.

The payment-security issue is not especially complex for freelancers, but it varies quite strongly in some respects from country to country. So I will describe the main strategy, while assuming you will adapt your own to match local conditions and customs.

⊘ HOW REAL IS THE RISK THAT YOU WILL ENCOUNTER NON-PAYERS?

The answer is pretty tricky. *The risk is real, but sneaky: it increases over time.*

You won't run into non-payers immediately. And this can create a false sense of security.

Different surveys among freelancers show different views of non-payers, because it strongly depends on how the question is formulated, among other things. In simple terms, it can be said that you won't meet non-payers around every corner, but the longer you are freelancing, the higher the risk is. For example in our survey, 70% of beginning freelancers had no uncollectible debts, while among those who had been in business for ten years or more, an equally large percentage did indeed have some.

The maturity of the local economy and the strength of the rule of law in a given country also affect the prevalence of non-payers. And it's likewise important whether you are doing gigs on your local market, within one jurisdiction, or on the global market, where the rule of law is generally weaker. If a customer from inner China doesn't pay you, that will definitely be a much harder debt to collect than if the dentist next door doesn't. So internationally it's much more common for freelancers to use online platforms like Freelancer.com as intermediaries to partially shield themselves from risk and secure their orders.

Even if there were precise statistics for non-payers, the real numbers and losses would likely be considerably higher. After all, a number of disputes with masked non-payers end in settlements. This typically involves various complainers, who shamelessly use a service or product and then turn around and use some imaginary, made up, or minor defect to demand completely disproportionate compensation, often under threats of revenge if you refuse to yield to their blackmailing.

Less-experienced professionals often prefer to accept the argument (no matter how nonsensical) and give in, agreeing to a partial payment or refund, purely out of fear for their reputation and the possible consequences. These non-paying troublemakers outnumber those that we would call non-payers without hesitation. And you would be surprised how many freelancers give in to their pressure. This is because they don't have a contractual defense, and so they often don't have any choice.

From the above it's clear that the risk of non-payers can seem at first to be small, but over the years it adds up, and if you underestimate it over the long term, it's quite likely that in time a non-payer will find you, too. They either won't pay, or will pressure you to step back from your justified demands for payment, and the result, one way or another, is a tangible financial loss.

Beginning freelancers' non-payers are also typically only minor exploiters who lure beginners into doing spec work for them. Meanwhile, a non-payer or fraudster who succeeds with more experienced professionals can sink their teeth more deeply – into flesh.

The worst non-payers are manipulators who take care to give a good first impression and can even spend months building trust and common ground, only to later abuse this advantage. You likely won't recognize these frauds up front, unless, that is, you scrutinized them well. Also, certain other people only become non-payers when they see that you have secured an order badly. They may be in such a bad situation that they decide to abuse the circumstances.

⊙ PROPER BUSINESS WITH LEGAL AWARENESS

Your defense against non-payers should be systematic. You shouldn't rely just on intuition; set up approaches and limits to avoid problems. It's significantly easier to stop non-payers beforehand than to deal with situations that you have caused through your own negligence and that often simply cannot end well.

The foundation for preventing non-payment problems is doing business properly with legal awareness.

A blackmailing non-payer who sees you are doing some things illegally can have the upper hand. Likewise, steer clear of customers and business partners with shady reputations and visibly problematic styles of communication. The risks from cooperating with these people and entities don't end with non-payment alone. They can also damage your reputation – and put you in the sights of the authorities. You can even become an accomplice to a crime simply through silence. While this problem isn't frequent, it's not entirely hypothetical. This applies to accountants, consultants, etc.

Legal awareness is no less important, because ignorance is not a legal defense, and even in good faith, you can break the law or fail to see the legal risks of your actions.

Recently, for example, I assessed the business plan of an excavator driver who wanted to buy his own excavator and quit his job to start freelancing, and yet hadn't considered the fact that as an entrepreneur, he would be taking on far more responsibility for any damages than he had ever had as an employee. He hadn't realized that so far, all of these risks had been covered by his employer, and so naturally he wasn't able to name or calculate them in his plan.

So legal awareness means knowing the legislation, norms, and regulations for business and for your field, as well as the types of contracts and conditions used, etc. And let's not fool ourselves here; this awareness is quite weak among beginning professionals, and sometimes experienced ones too. Often even creative professionals don't know what is written in the laws governing licenses for creative works – fairly important laws for their particular business.

If you lack a basic overview and you don't want to be eternally dependent on advice from consultants and lawyers, I recommend that you attend some training sessions on the basics of taxation, accounting, and law for entrepreneurs. These are generally given by other freelancers, local universities, or employment offices. You can also study these basics on your own – through websites or books on business in your country, or, for the US, through the Freelancers Union website.

I also recommend that you have a lawyer at a pre-arranged rate whom you can call or write when you have a legal question. And this is something you truly shouldn't put off. Almost every time I witness some business dispute, a lawyer consultation was something held out as the last option.

Get used to contacting a lawyer *immediately* after the first suspicion that there may be a problem with an order. Describe the situation and go over your subsequent steps together. If you have some prepaid hours, a ten-minute consultation will cost you many times less than what you will save in possible damages. Your client doesn't have to know; you just go over your worries with someone who understands the issue and then adjust your tactics or communication accordingly.

DON'T OVERLOOK WARNING SIGNS

Correctly interpreting the signs that a given order, or even a long-term client, might be a problem is thus another level in prevention. Whenever I talk to people who have had a problem with a non-payer, I'm surprised at how many negative signals they went past without acting.

What are some examples?

For example, a new customer refusing to make a standard upfront payment when the order represents significant time, materials, or financial costs.

Or it may be a long-term client that has suddenly started ignoring the due dates on invoices, pays them weeks or even a month or more after they are due, and meanwhile constantly adds on orders and thus owes even more. This is alarming behavior, which can point to a serious cash-flow problem. Many professionals fall into this trap instead of stopping, or at least suspending, their services and insisting that due dates be respected.

"Many years ago, my husband David and I were both freelancing for the same startup in San Francisco," recalls Melissa Joulwan, the author of the best-selling *Well Fed* cookbook series. "They paid a great hourly rate, had lots of ongoing projects and an in-house staff as well. Everything looked reliable...until it wasn't. They didn't pay us for about 3 months of work, then folded. When their employees went to the office to try to take PCs, desks, chairs, etc. as compensation, they found it empty. *Everything* had been leased and the company was just gone. Poof! That was a hard lesson to learn at 25, but it was valuable, too, in a terrible way."

Excuses about why an invoice wasn't paid on time can be very inventive and creative, but problems in business can't be resolved with a written note like in school. Often these can be downright lies, and I recommend ignoring them and insisting on the payment of the amounts due. In short, month-overdue bills are month-overdue bills.

Another reason to not ignore major payment delays is that as a freelancer, you are in a fairly disadvantageous position compared to larger companies.

When a large company gets into temporary problems with paying off their debt obligations, they usually prioritize the ones that are the biggest risk for them. So they pay the state. They pay their employees and managers. They pay major creditors who have legal weapons for collection. They pay important and close business partners. Small businesses and freelancers are often the last in line.

Since we as freelancers can hardly push with legal force, we have to rely on building good relationships with key company contacts (maybe the owner, a manager, or the head accountant), negotiating at the first sign of trouble, and if possible, also preventing such situations from happening thanks to a good overall set-up for cooperation.

Payment periods that are too long are also a problem. Because of this, in its *Late Payment Directive*, the EU recommends 60-day payment period as the normal upper limit. Not to mention that a reasonably short payment period is in the public interest, because small businesses can't afford to wait a long time for payment.

Here, some American freelancers are benefiting from the Freelance Isn't Free Act. Since May 2017, New York has become the first US city to protect freelancers from non-payers, at least on a city level. Among other things, it requires written contracts for orders over $800 and the payment of work on time in the full amount under the threat of fines of up to $25,000. It can't help in case of service quality or delivery disputes, but according to a 2019 Financial Times' article *How Freelancers Are Fighting for Their Pay*, the new legislation has proven to be quite effective, mentioning also other similar efforts elsewhere in the US and the UK.

If your customer runs into problems during an extra-long invoice payment period, then throughout it, they are making you share their business risks without a corresponding share in their future profits. This is immoral and despicable behavior. For some companies, this kind of dragged-out invoice payment is a welcome short-term zero-interest loan. So I personally would never accept a 60-day, let alone a 90-day payment period without a major increase in my payment for this work.

If a company doesn't have enough money for its operations, it should borrow from a bank (or create reserves), not from suppliers and freelancers.

Incidentally, if another freelancer or business wants to borrow from you, this is suspicious. Why not visit a bank? Probably because the bank wouldn't lend to them. Or because they are unsure they can pay it back. It's sad, but I have seen enough such cases for me to warn you against them.

On the other hand, warning signs should always be viewed within their broader context, so check for other signs that your hypothesis and your hunch of possible problems are correct. It definitely isn't right to condemn a regular customer just because they paid late a couple of times. This is more a matter for diplomatic solutions than for threats and denouncements. A responsible customer understands that late payments are a problem.

Various odd requirements when arranging an order, or later during it, are another signal that can, but may not, predict problems.

If, for example, a new customer immediately offers barter instead of payment despite your not needing or asking for their services, this is definitely unwanted. Barter can work well among friendly parties (though even then, it should usually be taxed as income under the law), but among distant remote partners, it can on the contrary be a cause for disputes.

In practice, barters tend to lack documentation and a contractual anchor, and the service received often doesn't meet expectations. Unlike with standard forms of unpaid debts, this is hard to file claims for. So a barter offer from a stranger is suspicious.

Sometimes the warning signs don't come until cooperation has already begun. Signs of dissatisfaction, passive-aggressive behavior, demanding pointless changes, and so on. If the order is badly secured and documented, possibly meaning that there are no records of assignment changes that were agreed to orally, often the whole thing can only be saved by preventively catching critical points.

You can continue as if nothing were wrong, while privately going over a crisis scenario with your lawyer, working to document missing changes, and tightening the screws on the order overall, so you are prepared for the confrontation that your intuition is telling you may come.

Other warning signs include frequent unavailability, bad task definitions, chaos in the client's company competencies when placing the order, ignoring key work emails, ambiguities around payment, and unprofessional or even vulgar communication.

Intuitive evaluation of warning signs is the most widespread way of preventing problems with non-payers: freelancers avoid cooperation with people who behave oddly or from whom they get bad vibes. Some warning signs are clear and evident, and you can act on them immediately. But that in itself isn't enough of a foundation for securing your orders and debts, especially for large orders from strangers.

◎ LACKING INFORMATION? TIME TO PROBE

A good prevention system reflects the difference between a new customer about whom you know nothing, and a completely trustworthy partner, who you have been working with for a decade. The form you choose for securing your order should correspond to how much reliable information you have on the prospect:

On the left end are prospects about whom you have no information. This may be someone who approached you out of the blue on the internet. It may be someone with a common name and no website. In those cases it's good to assume they may be a non-payer or problem customer, and adapt your payment handling accordingly.

Prospects who are 100% trustworthy in every respect lie at the other end. These are typically parties that you have known for years; you trust them and *know* they won't have financial problems. This might be a family member, a close friend, or a long-term colleague, in short, a solid partner, with no hidden flaws who is reliable and predictable. I know there are few such people, but we are talking about the ideal here; the reality is usually somewhere in-between.

For completely trustworthy partners, your measures can be few (a summary in email and invoicing afterwards) or even none (promise-based). This often applies to stable cooperation among freelancers. When you work on small assignments for a trustworthy colleague amounting to a few hundred dollars every month, you will likely switch to a stream-based system and send them an invoice once per month without any upfront payments. No security needed.

But is a close family member, a parent, or a sibling a 100% trust-worthy person? I can say without hesitation that in my family, they are. But it's not always that way. I have a client who employed her younger sister in her company and her shop. After four years, she found out thanks to her accountant that her sister had been stealing from her the whole time by faking cash receipts. She lost enough money that she could have bought two new cars with it.

As you can see, not everyone shows good judgment even about their loved ones, so some kind of control mechanism is in order – to prevent counting errors if nothing else.

The third element in the above sketch is a quick bit of research performed online and by asking colleagues, which can shift the level of trust in the right direction on the trustworthiness scale. These steps represent an absolutely indispensable part of your defense, and yet few freelancers use them and few sources mention them. For example, the official Best Practices for Getting Paid on the Freelancers Union website include these steps:

1. Get a contract

2. Get paid a portion up-front

3. Document change orders

4. Practice prompt preventative invoicing

5. Delegate it to the cloud (a service to track time, invoice, payments etc.)

6. Have a follow-up system

7. Send a formal collection notice

8. Seek out legal resources

9. Threaten small claims court

10. It's off to small claims court, you go!

I agree with all of this, and I also recommend the above, but thorough research should be done in the first place, even before getting the contract.

There are many options for what to research and how, and they vary strongly based on whether you have enough information about the prospect or at least some basic information besides their name and email. If not, then it's not rude to ask where they are from, what company they represent, or how they discovered you, etc. A solid prospect will not act anonymously, and meanwhile, if someone sends me an inquiry signed only with their first name, I answer with two sentences at most, wasting no time until I have more information about them. (You, meanwhile, should never send such inquiries to anyone; they show pure amateurism.)

If you have basic information on the prospect, you can examine them on many levels and form a rough, but at least partial picture, of what sort of person or company they are.

If you know the whole name and two or three more facts, like the company name, their place of residence, or their telephone number, you can google them quite easily. I'm mainly interested in general mentions, so I enter these queries and go through what comes up.

If the prospect has a website, then I go through it quickly, look at their references, service portfolio, prices, and other basic information. (Often the website domain is contained right in their email address.)

I also try looking up the prospect on Facebook, LinkedIn, and Twitter. I check their communication style, their friend list, and whether we have any shared contacts. If we do, I can ask these about their experiences. This sort of probing is common among freelancers, and likewise my colleagues frequently ask me about my own contacts, to check them out. Having a network of contacts pays off. You can draw from the wisdom and experience of your community.

Even if you fail in your search and the person doesn't have a website or a profile on any social network, this also says something. The absence of information is information too. The digital footprint that we all leave is so large today that if someone doesn't have one, you will want to find out why. I wouldn't be afraid in that situation to be a bit cheeky and directly ask for some links or info, stating that I'm having trouble finding any information and would like to take a look at what the person does and works on.

Which doesn't exclude the opposite problem, where a person with very trustworthy social profiles turns out to be a troublemaker or non-payer – and this is why I put all the more emphasis on making discreet questions to shared contacts. I don't work with just first impressions, and I sometimes I end up learning even some ugly things.

Another place where you can look is the entrepreneur's record in various business registers, both paid and public. These exist in many advanced economies and are easy to find, starting with the List of company registers Wikipedia entry. Besides basic data and a history of any changes, they can, for companies, also contain a collection of the documents that the law requires companies in the given country to publish, and the names of authorized representatives and managers who may represent the company in important matters. For large orders, it should interest you whether the person you are negotiating with is authorized to make any decisions at all. Sometimes it will save you unpleasant surprises and hours of negotiations with someone who lacks decision making authority.

The documents published in the register don't tend to be fully up to date, but if you understand financial reports even a little (or you learn to – perhaps with an accountant's help), you can form a pretty solid picture of the company's financial health.

In countries where publishing this information is not legally required, a paid product or open database often provides it. These aggregate information on business entities and the persons within them. Finding some other detailed information, a credit rating, or some kind of community evaluation of the company by users can also be advantageous.

For individuals, you can also look into registers for bankruptcies, executions, debtors, etc., if these are public in your country. If your contact is in one of these registers, then you should definitely watch out and consider whether to work with them at all – or under what conditions. They can turn out to be quite a problem.

The goal of this research is not to discriminate and reject all even slightly suspicious prospects. It's to evaluate risks in advance and adapt your order management and payment security to them. If the prospect had problems in the past that you can find and assess, you can raise your price, demand full upfront payment, pay far closer attention to the contractual conditions, etc. In short, your goal is to not be victimized by risks you can easily avoid, and not have the shorter end of the stick when the time comes to pull. And as is always the rule: when you have major doubts, go straight to a lawyer.

It may look complicated, but it's not. Once you've assembled the needed resources and links, the basic research won't take more than 10–15 minutes.

Here is a real example from my practice: A prospect, who had been recommended my services by a shared friend (a positive signal), called me seeking a critical review of her business plan. The communication was flawless, she didn't have the slightest problem with a higher price, and we agreed in 15 minutes that I would email her my estimate for approval. But some quick research then showed me that 1. she had declared personal bankruptcy that she had filed for herself (very strange), 2. our shared friend didn't know about it and didn't know her well, she had only turned to him to inquire about some other work, and 3. she was quite an aggressive anti-Uber activist in public. So I wrote her politely that in light of her bankruptcy I would be withdrawing from cooperation, and even though our initial call had been perfect, she now didn't even write back. She was a clever manipulator, but research that didn't even take me ten minutes including a call to my friend, stopped her dead in her tracks.

⬡ UPFRONT PAYMENT PROTECTS YOU

Intuition and research are fine as prevention, but they aren't enough for actually securing payments. They will only help you to push aside problematic people and be tougher where you have justified doubts about whether a prospect is solvent. They won't protect against problems that arise along the way. So how do you handle those?

There are two main methods for security, and a number of others that are used only rarely. The most commonly used and most recommended method mentioned in the literature and resources for freelancers is upfront payments. Rather than distrust, these represent a reasonable counterweight to risks on both sides and a means for reducing uncertainty. Even a solid client can run into problems during an order, and without upfront payment, you would be in trouble.

This is why upfront payments are a widely respected, established instrument that clearly shows both sides' willingness and to some extent covers costs, and thus also the possible risk of financial losses for the supplier. This is why it's common for craftsmen to request a large upfront payment for non-standard jobs, to cover all of the costs for materials. Because if a client won't accept the work produced or tries to deny they ever placed such an order, it could put the craftsman at risk of a substantial financial loss.

You can either collect one or more upfront payments followed by a balance payment, or collect a full, 100% upfront payment.

⬡ 100% UPFRONT PAYMENTS

Upfront payment in full is common for services sold as products (the use of software, participation in a course, turnkey websites, one-off audits, etc.), for discount offers as one of the conditions for the discount (hour packages, pre-sales, etc.), and naturally in the direct sales of products or personal services (beauty treatments, tutoring, consultations, etc.).

In short, you will find upfront payment wherever you are paying for a predefined result, wherever upfront payment is a condition for a discount or other benefit, and wherever an entrepreneur has repeated experiences with non-payers and cannot or does not want to bear that risk.

For example, some landlords have such bad experiences with dishonest tenants that they demand both payment at the start of each month and a strict contract and a deposit equal to several months' rent. This is actually a sort of upfront payment squared; one payment every month in advance, and the other is a returnable deposit.

If upfront payments are used in your field regularly and are among its customs, this is an advantage, and it practically eliminates the problems with non-payers. But even if it's not customary, and you feel this kind of insurance against risky orders is appropriate, you as the creator of your pricing and negotiation strategy have plenty of room to try it. I'm not saying it's easy or needed. You have to judge for yourself how much it would benefit you and whether your negotiation and sales position will be strong enough to push through an atypical model.

Such things always go through more easily if you have a strong BATNA and plenty of work, than if you are struggling on a saturated market. In dynamic fields, it goes better than in conservative ones with established customs.

It's not about irritating people with odd payment conditions; it's about building your offer so it's attractive and acceptable. It's not simple, and in practice it's about advanced pricing, service design and marketing.

There are even cases where an entire transaction is paid for upfront, but until some condition is fulfilled, the money lies with a trustworthy intermediary. Usually it's because the two parties are strangers and have few reasons to trust each other. It suffices that they trust the intermediary, who charges a small commission.

This can be a lawyer or notary, who keeps the payment in escrow until the whole transaction is complete according to predefined conditions (e.g. the sale of a house). Airbnb also acts as an escrow; it collects money for reservations as much as months in advance, but only sends it to the host a day after the stay begins.

In exceptional cases, you can also find that 100% upfront payment is the only way to secure an express order that comes at you out of nowhere. A typical example is translators who are approached by someone on the internet who needs a translation the very next day. Since there is a large risk of encountering a non-payer here (yes, it happens), the translator may demand a 100% express payment in advance.

You have multiple possibilities here. Beside depositing cash on your account at any branch of your bank (impractical), sending confirmation of a bank transfer (can be falsified), or express payment over Revolut or PayPal (with the risk of a later cancellation), established cryptocurrencies like Bitcoin or Litecoin are proving themselves to be a safe channel for quick cashless transactions as well (though not everyone can or wants to use them).

Full upfront express payment is a nice example of a situation where you have zero information on the prospect, and no time to investigate them, and you have to choose correspondingly strict order security to avoid the risk of financial loss.

UPFRONT PAYMENT WITH A BALANCE PAYMENT

A partial upfront payment (or payments) with a balance payment after the work is finished or delivered is an equally widespread method. It's most commonly used when the result of the work isn't sure in advance, and a cautious prospect or customer hesitates to pay up front. This applies to doubts about both the freelancer as such (if they are a beginner, unreliable or lack references) and the order (a large order or unique project).

The simplest scheme is an upfront payment plus a balance payment. But if it's long-term work, there can even be several upfront payments, for example on a certain day of each month or at set project milestones, for example a 30% first payment, a 15% second, a 15% third, and a 40% final balance payment.

The specific distribution is a subject for your order negotiations; there is no set rule. However, it's customary that for services, a down payment of up to about 30% is acceptable for everyone.

Dividing up the payments so that they fit both sides' cash flows is a matter of bargaining skills. You shouldn't be left high and dry, and the customer shouldn't have large one-off costs at bad times.

The basic upfront-plus-balance method is used commonly, but several payments plus a balance payment can be considered an advanced securing tool. What is important is that your contract or a placed order should then have perfect coverage of what happens if any exceptional situations arise during the order, followed by one or the other party terminating the contract. The typical basic rules are based in law, and you will find your bearings in them with the help of a lawyer. However, the law usually doesn't cover what happens when an order has multiple separate parts or stages, what portion of the money should be returned if there is a rightful complaint on one of them, etc.

So if it's an expensive half-year project and there are upfront payments, it definitely makes sense to work on this. After all, you want upfront payments to control your risks, but at the same time that means not ignoring the other risks and problems that arise in the gray zone of undefined conditions. So it's no wonder that a good contract with an external developer for a big project is expensive.

Focus as well on when precisely the delivered work is considered complete and properly handed over, and when it becomes the client's property. It's not the same thing. The actual handing over can be via installation at the customer's location or through the signing of a handover protocol, which among other things sets the start of the warranty period. But the transfer of the property can have the condition of a balance payment. Here again, this is a point that doesn't have to be addressed with 100% upfront payment, but it is very important. This is why many professionals and craftsmen state directly in their orders, invoices, and handover protocols that the finished work only becomes the property of the customer after the full payment has been made.

I know many beginners have a problem asking for upfront payment, but believe me, it's much easier once you focus on it systematically and tell yourself how precisely these payments will fit into your negotiation process. There is a world of difference between proposing upfront payment to the prospect as a topic for discussion and presenting it as a done deal – as "that's what I do, it's my normal, standard approach for all orders." And if you have a problem asking people for upfront payment in person, learn to formulate it in an email or write it directly in your price list.

Upfront payments can be problematic for corporate clients, with their rigid internal rules and long invoice terms. But ironically this is more a disadvantage for them, because an expert with a strong BATNA may politely reject such an inquiry from them or recommend that they hire a much more expensive agency that can cover the order and meet their demands. If it's a trustworthy top expert, the firm's answer is often that "there are ways" and that they just needed to ask. If you are in demand, have a rare skill, and have a corresponding price, that is a strong negotiating position from which many successful negotiations can be led.

❯ CONTRACTUAL SECURITY

Upfront payments are an established instrument for securing orders, but they demand some time and support in the negotiation phase. In short, for the customer to accept the payment conditions without large objections and move on.

I think that this is one reason why so many professionals don't use upfront payments or any other security method and just rely on intuition and luck, with a risk of potential loss. Yes, naturally this saves time – the one time when you have to think things through and introduce your system of upfront payments – and it might slightly shorten negotiations. There are even a number of fields where the usual order size or turnover between order and delivery is so small that thoroughly collecting upfront payments would just make business complicated and expensive.

But in many cases, this time saving is an illusion. First, you will see long-term growth in the risk of meeting a non-payer, as well as in the amount of time spent on monitoring and reminders of late payments, or arguing with would-be non-payers. Invoicing applications can partially monitor due dates for you, but they will never remove all your cares.

If you have great customers with excellent payment history, not just anyone off the street, then tracking down late payments and struggling with complainers likely won't apply to you, and straightforward invoicing without upfront payments will make sense. But if troubles from poorly secured orders are among your risks, then it's better to do something about them, because over time, small mistakes and risks can grow into real problems.

Negotiations with complainers are easy if you have a fine-tuned negotiation process, you insist on upfront payments, and you have a precisely formulated contract or terms and conditions that seal up various cracks that a quickly closed deal wouldn't address.

But the same person can cause you major trouble if you don't demand any upfront payment and if a permissive or even oral agreement and a lack of written records enable them to not accept the work, not pay, or insist on a reduced price for calculated reasons.

Thus you should have the whole order properly documented and covered from all sides so that you can effectively collect what you are owed. Beside upfront payments it's the second most common, and often the last, form of defense.

The nuances of the process and any court case are so complex in most countries that you should prepare your contractual security for payments (especially large ones) in cooperation with a lawyer who superbly understands the issue and will recommend a precise approach customized to your risks and business.

The basic process is fairly simple. Above all you need to have the order documented, that is, records such as a contract or a confirmed order, a written record of any changes to the job assignment definition, confirmation of deliveries, a delivery note or handover protocol, and a properly issued invoice with a subsequent reminder. The optimal amount of documentation varies among countries, fields, and orders; define it with your lawyer.

Services like RocketLawyer or Freelance Contract Creator (for the US, on the Freelancers Union website) can be a cheaper alternative when you are creating generic contracts, but they have obvious disadvantages compared to customized contractual security.

If a customer doesn't pay on time and ignores your politely formulated requests and reminders, then it's time for collection itself, which, however, will already be handled by your lawyer.

Over the years I have met a number of freelancers and entrepreneurs who use the contractual method for security, and together with a lawyer, it works fairly reliably – if, that is, it's still at all possible to collect anything from the debtor. In other words, it's still up to you to check out the people you do business with in advance. You can't take anything from the bankrupt.

The time involved in gathering the necessary documentation is no smaller than that for arranging and managing upfront payments. But the two techniques can complement each other, and it's even possible that you will only be claiming an unpaid balance payment this way.

A SAFE APPROACH AS A SAFETY ROPE

Payment security is always about a combination of several methods. These create a sort of safety rope that runs parallel to the negotiations and the whole order, all the way to the top. Except that while every order is different, this security is more of a system, an established and fine-tuned method that reacts and works reliably the moment the main rope tightens or snaps.

The mentioned approaches for preventing non-payment and for order security should thus be a part of your order negotiation process, to reduce your risks to an acceptable level. Every professional uses a slightly different method for preventing problematic jobs, but what matters is whether it works overall. There aren't that many non-payers and problem people in the world, and so even a small, focused effort is enough to minimize their chances.

Some freelancers only take orders they are comfortable with or that speak to them personally. Others have a strict ethical code and only work for well-established companies with easily searchable histories. And others still are covered because they can turn off their (online) services at any time and the contract allows it, giving them the upper hand.

This too shows that there are many effective kinds of security, and that some come from a professional's unique position relative to the market or customer.

I won't deny that I sometimes see some quite original security or collection methods:

- *"On Christmas, I remember my non-payers; I send them a letter by post, and they are all happy to pay (they understand it will be best for them)."*

- *"I evaluate the client's financial situation based on information they themselves provide in a form."*

- *"I used a debt collection agency."*

It's worth mentioning that debt collectors, outside of the mentioned lawyer services, are rarely used by freelancers; the same goes for debt brokering or insurance. The main reason is that both collectors and insurance have their costs, and ordinary freelancers' orders are too small for specialized firms in this segment to be attractive.

There are many order security methods, but not all are reliable, and some take time to prove unreliable. I have met many freelancers who considered their intuitively slapped-together security bulletproof until it failed or until (ideally) we both looked under the shiny hood. My approach may seem too conservative, but it has one undeniable advantage: After 20 years of freelancing, I have no uncollected claims.

KEY IDEAS

1. The risk of non-payers is real, and sneaky, because it significantly grows over time.

2. Few people who have been freelancing for over 10 years have no unpaid claims.

3. But overall, payment habits tend to be better than it might seem from the horror stories.

4. The foundation for prevention is doing business properly with legal awareness. And having a lawyer.

5. Don't overlook warning signs: an unwillingness to make an upfront payment, late invoice payments, etc.

6. Find out more about new prospects and set your level of security based on that.

7. The most reliable security method is upfront payments – especially 100% payments.

8. Orders should be properly documented for use in collection and in case of any dispute.

9. The option of last resort is to collect the owed amount with help from a lawyer.

10. Debt security is always about a smart combination of several security methods.

PRACTICE

✓ Collect links and resources in order to research new prospects and inquirers online. Use social media networks too, to check up on them by discreetly asking shared contacts.

✓ From there, start improving your own fine-tuned defense against non-payers and various other trouble-makers. If at all possible, shift to collecting more upfront payments.

✓ If you are a beginner and hesitant to ask clients to pay upfront, make upfront payments an integral part of your overall negotiation process, add them to general proposals, etc.

✓ If you can't collect sufficient upfront payments, get a good lawyer and design a flawless system to document your orders in order to be able to claim your debts effectively.

WEBSITES, BLOGS, AND SOCIAL MEDIA

How can you fully harness the internet's potential?

The web and social media aren't among the topics where it's easy to find general consensus, or best practices that all freelancers agree on. So as an author, I faced the question of how to write about such things that visibly divide freelancers, both in terms of their opinions and their existing technical knowledge:

- For some, their smartphone never leaves their hand, while others try to use phones, and all other internet devices, as little as possible.

- While some of them base their strategy and their professional website on their own domain, others mix social media, online video, and publishing platforms, without needing to build their own website.

- While some emphasize an impressive look for their website and the use of the latest technologies, others bet on valuable content and the conviction that it will find its audience.

- While some invest enormous amounts into their website and actively promoting it, others only have it as a web business card, and find their customers in other ways and places.

- While some fiercely resist using new technologies and everything connected to the web, others work in this field as professionals and have mastered tools like MailChimp or Google Ads.

So who knows the truth, and is there any? Practice is definitely not uniform, and each of the mentioned approaches has its own grain of truth. And these aren't just empty words to please the techno-dinosaurs out there.

Take social media networks for example. Among the professionals who use them for self-promotion and work, there is broad agreement that they are important – even fundamental. Case closed, right?

But then you go and read Adam Alter's book *Irresistible* about "the rise of addictive technology and the business of keeping us hooked" or *Digital Minimalism* by Cal Newport, a fiery preacher against the overuse of social media networks and of every technology that fragments our attention, emotional stability, and ability to concentrate on important work. And perhaps you will change your mind.

The conflict of opinions between techno-optimists and their conservative opposition is as old as technology itself. So how have I solved this conflict within this chapter?

Mainly by offering explanations, examples, and arguments for and against, and fittingly soft recommendations. I know from consultations on many online strategies that there is no 'one to rule them all.' I'm also working from the available surveys here, which all tend to agree that although websites, online platforms, and social media networks are not the main source of new clients on their own – recommendations, contacts and social links are – they are a pillar of freelance marketing that helps to maintain those very contacts.

And I agree with the conservatives that the quality of your web content is what counts. *Content is king*, which ironically matches the progressive opinion that social media are at least as important today as a personal website.

THE BASIC GOAL IS SIMPLE: BE FINDABLE

A freelancer who isn't findable is often less trustworthy, and can hardly present themselves as an established professional. After all, the latter leave clearly traceable digital footprints.

An unfindable professional also faces an increased risk of being a victim of online shaming and slander – if any slander occurs, it can suddenly start getting top ranks in searches for your name. If better sources are lacking, search engines will gladly show criticism as relevant content. All of the sudden, you are being humiliated publicly.

There is also a fundamental difference between the situation where googling your name shows random web mentions of your namesakes that you can't influence and the one where it shows up-to-date resources that you somehow have under control: your website, your personal blog, previews of your photos, personal profiles on social media, articles, interviews, lectures, videos, various member profiles, maybe even a Wikipedia entry – in short, all the content that Google considers relevant and useful.

Just try going to an anonymous browser tab and checking your name, or your name and profession if you have lots of namesakes, and you can see for yourself how much these (anonymous and non-personalized) results match what you do and offer as a freelancer. And is it even you, or are you simply impossible to find? Now for a change try googling professionals or colleagues who excel as freelancers in your field. Do you see a difference?

From the above it should be clear that if you want to serve a large market and lots of clients as a freelancer, being findable should be one of the pillars of your web strategy. Your future clients, business partners, and colleagues will be searching for you; count on it. Make it easier for them.

In practice that means having your own website, or at least a one-page web presentation. And using social media, with a recognizable photo, your full name, and your area of expertise, which makes your profile distinguishable from many namesakes.

SOCIAL MEDIA AND HOW TO WORK WITH IT

This isn't just about Facebook, Instagram, LinkedIn, Twitter, and other social media networks. YouTube, blogs, podcasts, and community websites where information flows back and forth belong here too. In these places, listeners, readers, and fans share their experiences and create their own content.

No matter what your field or how introverted you are, I definitely recommend being on and using social media. For us independent professionals these platforms are far more than just a marketing tool; above all they are a source of new contacts and news, with our colleagues' comments. Networks help to strengthen relationships and bring together professional and freelance communities.

If you are just starting out in freelancing and looking for a way to inform the world, these networks are again the right place to begin. They already provide an enormous audience for your content, and you don't have to laboriously build it from scratch like with a website. And also, the core audience is people you know personally. Social media can be used intuitively and for free, although it can sometimes make sense to use ads or paid versions. What is perhaps more important is that you will get feedback.

Likes, claps, ratings, comments, and shares are a huge benefit, because even beginning creators get a public response to every post. You can thus gradually start to create better content for your audience, and it's all the same if that means your personal opinion about a professional article, a series of new photos, an illustration for a client, a video, or a short story written as a Facebook post – you will see the public response immediately.

Austin Kleon develops this idea of collecting feedback in his book *Show Your Work!* (To get an idea, take a look at #showyourwork on Twitter, Instagram, or Facebook). I asked Austin about whether freelancers should push their clients to agree with sharing the work's progress and results. He replied: "This seems to me so contingent on the business model of the client and the freelancer that no overall rule could be given. But overall, I think it's within the freelancer's interests to share with clients how positive showing your work can be to growing your audience and customer base."

I also asked Austin if there is a good rule of thumb how to choose the best social media network for showing one's work: "I would always suggest, first, that you invest in your website. Buy a domain, start a blog, and post work there with regular frequency. Include a signup for a mailing list. Then, look to social media sites that 1) you want to spend time on 2) the people you're trying to reach spend their time on. But always see social media as fleeting hangouts, never substitutes for a personal site and mailing list."

So let's take a closer look at these fleeting hangouts.

◉ FACEBOOK IS THE HUB: EVERYONE IS THERE

Of all the networks, Facebook is used for marketing purposes the most by freelancers. In fact, most freelancers are there. In my training courses, we usually take a group photo, and whoever I then find on Facebook, I tag. For the few I can't find, often it is just because they use a nickname or have strict privacy settings.

So the clear advantage of Facebook is that for most adults, it's the #1 network. It's where they will have their profile, friends, colleagues, family, and even acquaintances that they haven't seen in a few years. And this is a huge advantage for maintaining weak social bonds, because on Facebook, you will also find people who have changed their email addresses, phone numbers, cities, or states ages ago.

The foundation is a well-rounded, complete personal profile with your full name, a recognizable photo, and information on what you are currently doing. Also make sure in your settings to enable the safer *two-factor authentication* and choose a brief *Username* that will then work as a shortcut for your profile (i.e. facebook.com/username). The most common is either some combination of your name and surname or of your name and profession, your professional nickname, or the name of your domain. Also, consider what usernames you are using on other networks to stay consistent.

You can also creatively use your profile's cover photo – for inspiration, google "*facebook cover photo creative marketing ideas.*" Tasteful profile graphics can present your business or values, as well as current samples of your work, along with your website or other contacts. This is your personal advertising space, and it's the first statement a visitor to your profile will see. You can use the Canva online editor to quickly edit your photos and graphics, or a cheap Photoshop alternative like PaintShop Pro.

If you want to also use Facebook to connect with colleagues and occasionally promote your freelancing, I recommend checking your *Privacy* settings and opening your profile to the world. Be sure to enable public follows of your profile too (Settings > Public Posts). Then other users will be able to subscribe to and follow your posts without having to become one of your Facebook friends. It's a great setting for us freelancers.

Don't worry; you will still be able to restrict the reach of individual posts to just your friends. Still, I don't recommend changing the reach for every post, because there is a far better way to avoid bothering friends with your work, or clients and colleagues with pictures of babies and family reunions.

The simplest is to just write about work in a fun (humorous, revealing, or educational) way for friends, and write in moderation about your private life with the knowledge that an open profile is not a family album. If you are writing for two entirely different groups of people and find your own style and way to join them, it will make you a better author.

The work vs. private life divide can also easily be avoided by spontaneous writing about whatever fulfills and amuses you, in *any* part of your life. Ultimately this approach will catch the interest of the rest of us as your audience. It's surprisingly easy to achieve this, by not posting updates that you feel forced to write – in marketing posts especially, a forced effort is painfully easy to see.

The optimum post frequency is a few per week or month, but this is definitely not a fixed rule. Even if you bang out three posts a day, if they are truly interesting (as shown by the responses you get), this is fine. Your profile is truly yours alone, and nobody is being forced to follow it. On the other hand, the quality of your posts' contents heavily affect their reach. People's walls will mainly show things that get a response, and the rest will fall away fast.

Your posts will never be seen by all of your friends and fans. Facebook's algorithm decides what will be shown to whom on their wall. So your real reach will be far smaller (but for successful posts, also larger) than your number of friends and followers. This approach bothers many people, but as the number of friends in your network grows to include many you haven't seen in years, it helps to make Facebook a better service. You probably don't need to see what your old elementary-school acquaintances are posting.

More advanced uses of Facebook for freelancers are connected to Facebook pages and ads. And partially to groups as well.

Groups can be useful for connecting people with shared interests, and can be *public*, *closed* (with hidden posts), or *secret* (invitation-only). If you find a group in your field, you can ask questions there and seek advice, or help others and improve your karma.

Facebook pages are a special kind of profile. They resemble personal profiles, but their identity can be tied to a brand or other purpose, or even to your name as a professional. So you can have a personal profile on Facebook for private use and a page for work. Why do this? Perhaps because you really share a *lot* of work content, and it's becoming unbearable for your friends and acquaintances. Or because you want to support your posts' reach with paid advertising, which is only really possible for posts on a dedicated page.

Facebook ads let you considerably increase your pages' reach, to address thousands, tens of thousands, or hundreds of thousands of users, who will see them right on their wall or elsewhere. (To activate ads, go to facebook.com/ads.) The ad cost isn't high, and you can aim for not just your page's fans, but also their friends or the general public based on age, location, and interests. You can also target visitors of your website (if you place the corresponding code there) or users in a provided list of email addresses – perhaps your clients or newsletter subscribers.

You can also use a small trick in the page's promoted posts. Click open the list of people who have liked a post and click on the buttons for inviting those users to like your page as well, and thus subscribe to your content. That way you can profit from promotion twice.

The disadvantage of Facebook pages is that you have to build up their traffic from zero, and that their posts generally have a smaller reach than those on personal profiles. You will have to either accept the smaller reach, or reach for your wallet. And ads are where Facebook makes its money.

⬭ INSTAGRAM IS FOR BEAUTY AND FUN

Instagram is a Facebook-owned network, and its active-user count is growing – as of 2019, it has roughly as many users as Twitter, Snapchat, and LinkedIn combined. Its *Instagram Stories* let you share photos and videos temporarily, for one day. Beside these, there is also the vertical Instagram TV (IGTV), traditional sharing of short videos, beautified photos, and pictures, in short, endless, highly consumable content.

Beauty is something that always works on Instagram, and this is why stars love it, as well as everyone else who makes or seeks out beauty. Do you create beautiful furniture? Delicious meals? Are you a pro illustrator? Photographer? Barber or tattoo artist? Instagram will probably excite you, and your content can shine on it, just like you yourself, if you understand presentation and communication, or if you have a razor-sharp wit, which is an especially big draw for videos.

Instagram is special in that it's mainly managed through a mobile app, in which you can also use pictures you have edited on a computer (e.g. via cloud storage). Instagram's mobile focus gives it a big advantage over other networks, because it cuts deeper into our lives, but it's also a threat if you lack self-control. Out of all the social networks, Instagram has the users who are the least satisfied with how much time they spend there, which reflects the addictiveness – and a certain shallowness – of this site. In short, people go to Instagram to procrastinate. They may stay there longer in part because you can't link to external websites from posts.

Consider switching to a *Business Profile* in *Settings*, as it will enable you to access extra features as well as *Instagram Insights* with basic performance metrics. You can also easily expand your publishing to Facebook. I recommend enabling that, as well as going on to fine-tune those Facebook post texts, especially if your Instagram is @name and #tag-heavy. However, you can also share *Stories* on Facebook; their short lives and immediacy make them like a reality show for your life and work. Thanks to the interaction with your viewers, you can use them as an excellent tool for feedback, and also for community building.

So, can Instagram help your business? That probably depends on how appealing and impressive at a glance the results of your work are, or how well you can write or speak about them. If you make fashionable purses or play the clarinet, you can reap a sizeable harvest on Instagram, but even if you design water turbines, you can still invite your fans to places they would never see otherwise.

⊙ LINKEDIN INSTEAD OF A RESUME AND CV

LinkedIn is catching up to Facebook in freelance marketing, but people use it in a different way. This is a professional network, one that isn't used for free-time sharing with friends; people don't spend as much time there, and they keep their profiles more as a sort of CV.

For us freelancers, LinkedIn is also a bit foreign in that it's primarily designed for employers and employees. While that doesn't keep us from using it, this orientation is visible in many of its functions, and, as you can imagine, IT freelancers get a lot more headhunting requests here than inquiries from customers.

The dominant focus on employer-employee relationships leads some freelancers to reject LinkedIn as something unnecessary, unlike those who often work in the corporate sector. Some independent contractors even use a LinkedIn profile as their personal webpage.

This right here will probably be the main factor if you are considering whether or not to be on LinkedIn. If companies are your main target group, or you are thinking about going more international, then I strongly recommend being on LinkedIn simply because maintaining a profile doesn't cost much time, and the possible benefit is more than zero.

This is because LinkedIn excels in two features that are practical for us freelancers. The first is a profile style that resembles a resume. Traditional CVs and resumes seem to truly be on the way out. A LinkedIn profile is also the modern standard for summary bio information, because other users can endorse the skills you have define in your profile. This may not always be objective, but a large number of endorsements still says something. Another practical option is also to translate a profile into other languages and have it shown to other users primarily in their language. In other words, LinkedIn can be your multilingual web presentation. You can also set a short URL for your profile (e.g. linkedin.com/in/name.surname).

The other killer feature concerns written recommendations. Other users can write them for you, and you can then just approve them and make them public.

Advanced LinkedIn usage includes activities that are similar to what you see on Facebook. You can publish short posts or articles with a considerable reach beyond your own network, and even set up a company page. LinkedIn also offers paid subscriptions, but these don't add much value – at least not for freelancers.

LinkedIn groups, meanwhile, are more useful. Anyone can create and manage a group (Work > Groups > My groups > Create group), and if it takes off, it can be a very lively place for discussion in your field, or a consulting center for beginners. English-language groups serve as nodes for connecting experts regardless of their location. Try seeking out a few groups and judge for yourself how much they can professionally benefit you. For beginners, this can be one of the best places on the internet to seek advice.

One weakness of LinkedIn, meanwhile, is its annoying email notifications. These sometimes keep coming even if you turn them off. One sarcastic tweet describes it well:

> Unsubscribe from LinkedIn
> Delete email account
> Sell house, live in woods
> Find bottle in river
> Has note inside
> It's from LinkedIn

TWITTER SHARPENS WITS

Twitter is a very special network, one that many don't appreciate, even though it's clearly among the big four in freelance networking. As a microblogging platform, it restricts post length to 280 characters plus some pictures. That is a challenge on the one hand, because being understandable (let alone funny) in such a compact format is demanding. But it's also ideal for people who don't have a lot of time to write but still have something to say.

That may also be why nearly everyone who means something in the world is on Twitter. You can be in direct contact here with global personalities and experts, whose work you as experts draw on and follow. Even ones you would never find on Facebook are often active on Twitter.

I, for example, follow an author on Twitter after I have read one of their books. That way I stay in touch with the work of writers I admire and I can go over the content they share and comment on it or share their tweets. (Some people are even *too* active; in that case I use *Turn off Retweets* in their profile, and if that doesn't help, I move on to *Mute*.)

Here are some people who regularly tweet about work and freelancing: the psychologist @AdamMGrant, the @FreelancersU founder @Sara_Horowitz, the author @DanielPink, the @GTDguy David Allen, and Basecamp founders @JasonFried and @DHH. From among organizations, I would recommend the great @TheEconomist and the data sifters at @McKinsey_MGI, @Accenture, @Deloitte and @PwC.

Part of the secret to Twitter is learning how to write briefly and with style. A good tweet is a sort of anecdote or aphorism, which are very demanding literary forms. This is why Twitter is heaven for wordsmiths. It's one big catch-phrase party. Dry statements will be ignored, unless you are a celebrity that the world can't ignore. You can definitely share content from your field, but you should tailor it to the format. Even the basics of astronomy and cosmology can be fit into tweets, as wonderfully documented in the book *Tweeting the Universe*. There is also a special feature to create *threads* of several connected tweets, if necessary.

And you can network too. If you are sharing someone's book, an article, or tweeting about other people, mention them with their @username. That increases the chance that they will see the mention, and if it's interesting and positive, they might even retweet it – often to thousands of their fans. Mentions lead to interactions, and, if not done clearly for personal gain, they will quickly draw you deeper into the Twitterverse. (Don't however, start a tweet with a @username, because that makes it a *Reply* with limited reach.)

Twitter also lets you retweet your own tweets with some optional commentary, but do this carefully, to avoid seeming self-centered. You will appreciate this feature for well-written tweets with a low response, or extending the reach of successful ones.

ONLINE PORTFOLIOS: NOT JUST FOR CREATIVES

So that's that for the four main networks, but it's nowhere near the end of our excursion into the world of social media. A creative professional should have some sort of online portfolio. If you take pictures, make illustrations, produce any kind of graphics, record videos or audio, you need an online showcase with selected work samples to show potential customers what you actually do.

But work samples definitely aren't just for creatives. For example, if you help clients with online communication, your own website and social media presence will definitely be viewed as such a showcase. For developers, the code repository and sharing service GitHub can be just as useful, and so on.

Unsurprisingly, many creatives choose Facebook or Instagram as the place for presenting highlights from their portfolio. While these services aren't made for that, they are both extremely popular, and if you want to address the general public, it makes sense. Instagram above all is 100% visually oriented, and you will find world-renowned creators on it. Even major brands sometimes go right there to hunt for new talents or visual themes.

Services specialized in presenting and evaluating portfolios, such as Dribbble and Behance, are also very popular. If you have above-average skills, they can help you land new gigs.

Your portfolio should only include work you fully stand behind – the best of your best. Perhaps the biggest mistake in online portfolios is presenting average work alongside a few outstanding exceptions.

WWWORDS: BLOGGING YESTERDAY AND TODAY

Blogging is in a far different place than it once was. Brief written forms and commenting has poured over into social media (especially Facebook and Twitter), and video and audio are here too as alternatives. And there is far more online content than just a few years ago.

As a result, blogging isn't as cool as it was at its peak – but it's still not on the way out. Many freelancers have stopped blogging and mainly work through social media platforms, while others are trying other formats. But new successful blogs are still being started, and if Mark Twain or Oscar Wilde were alive today, I'm sure their blogs would be smash hits.

Why isn't writing on Facebook or LinkedIn enough, when both of them allow long texts? The main reason is their orientation towards fresh content, and thus their short content shelf-life. Even the very best content falls off people's news feeds in days or at most weeks. But a blog article can get hits from search engines and other sources for years.

Blogging will also bring you closer to readers and clients. Compared to self-presentation websites and brief social posts, it better shows the depth and mode of your thinking, as well as your problem-solving approach. Upon reading your blog, a customer will roughly know what to expect, and if you are an authority in the field for them, they will often adapt to your work style. Blogging thus significantly strengthens your negotiating position for orders.

First-rate writing over time can put you in the position of being an opinion maker or pioneer who helps to shape expert discourse – i.e. what people talk about. It presents you as an expert with an opinion, experience, etc. Writing forces you to be better and more precise in formulating your thoughts than your non-publishing colleagues are. No author wants to be a fool or a disappointment for their readers, and so they strive to write and think the best they can.

A person can hardly verify the quality of their arguments, and thus their professional opinions, if they aren't regularly confronted with opposing arguments from colleagues, or if the confrontations only ever take place in their head, with them as the winner every time.

Generally on your own blog, you have lots of control over its look, typography, and surrounding content. Every article has a permanent URL address, and while Facebook posts have one too, it's not as easy to find. Also, part of your social media profile will always be hidden to Google due to privacy settings, making it unfindable. Just try for yourself to reach some long Facebook post that you wrote four or five years back, and you'll see. On an ordinary blog, it would be easy.

Blogging strategies have changed overall. While it once was common for an expert to spend years blogging before reaching a wider audience, today social media networks let you succeed with a blog much faster, sometimes even overnight. It no longer makes sense to write for years for a hundred readers and believe in miracles. If you blog regularly for six months or a year and it's not getting a response, you will hardly see a reason to continue.

Nevertheless, if you want to publish articles with value that lasts beyond, say, a few days or weeks, I definitely recommend putting them on your blog. By combining social media and blogs, you get the best of both worlds. With short posts, you will reach your audience on social media, while putting your long articles on your blog, where they can get long-term readerships from a much broader circle: searchers.

The Medium.com blogging platform has achieved significant popularity; it's simple and free. It's also wonderfully optimized for reading and has a large community of readers that shares its content. The most successful platform worldwide is WordPress.com, which is available both as a free content management system for your website or blog on your own domain (more on this later) and as a blogging platform – for five dollars or euros a month and up with your own domain, or for free on a subdomain like Name.WordPress.com.

Google's Blogger.com can also be used; it's free for blogging on your own domain. You can also significantly improve the default look with a purchased or downloaded template.

Today, blogging is so freestyle that you can approach it spontaneously (via one-off articles) or strategically by clarifying your target readership in advance, choosing a unique topic, and thinking through article topics up to several months ahead.

But if you have an important topic that you want to describe as one whole, then go for a book or e-book rather than a blog. By the time you would cover that topic in a series of blog posts, the first articles would be partly outdated, meaning that you might have to start all over again in just a few years. A book will age as well, it's true, but it's also a much better-integrated whole, and it's up-to-date when published.

FREELANCERS' VLOGS AND YOUTUBE POWER

YouTube is a social network with a prominent place and an enormous audience. And it's given rise to YouTubers – people, mostly younger, who film personal and informal videos about their lives, hobbies, gaming, etc. The most successful of them have audiences easily comparable with conventional media and television. It's a brave new world.

And there are also other platforms for publishing videos and video blogs, or vlogs (also called *videocasts*). Video professionals love Vimeo thanks to its advanced features, including restrictions on which website a video can be embedded. Facebook is pushing into video hard as well, as is Instagram with its IGTV.

Can vlogging be attractive for us freelancers too? Yes, but there are a few catches.

Above all, we aren't teenage YouTubers; we are professionals with differing needs and far less desire to share our private lives in detail with the world. Vlogging professionals most often go for interviews, short educational or awareness-raising videos, YouTube Live streams for Q & A sessions and events, or a combination of formats. Some only shoot their videos with a single camera (usually a still camera, a phone, or a web camera), but fully professional productions are no exception. Here I would like to mention the phenomenal Marie Forleo and her Marie TV business channel, which works with edits, scenes, and animated graphics just like a TV channel would.

However, outsourcing the technical aspect is cheap. There are many freelance cameramen and photographers specialized in video production today. But when inquiring, be sure to ask for the price per day of filming, and also for post-production work: editing and exporting the video. If you are prepared, you can truly film a lot in a single day – maybe even fifteen short videos.

Selecting the right platform is a key choice. YouTube's advantage is that it can deliver attractive content to an enormous number of viewers without your having to promote it over the web or other networks. While that applies to Vimeo and Facebook too, it's less broadly true.

Facebook view counts look promising at first, but when you look at how many people viewed your video with the sound turned on, you will cry at the numbers. It might be one fifth, one tenth, or even less of the overall view count, and not even subtitles will save you. Facebook walls are places of high-competition, and videos' lives there are particularly short.

YouTube, meanwhile, can maintain viewership for good videos for a long time, sometimes even years. The graph below shows the views of one educational video on the YouTube channel of one of my clients between 2013 and 2018. Note how the viewership basically stayed stable even without promotion and peaked roughly three years after the video was published:

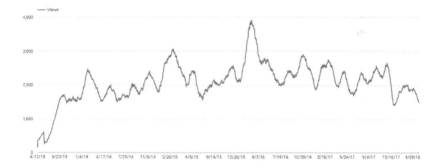

Short videos, roughly three to ten minutes, catch on well on YouTube, as people can play them, for instance, during work breaks. More and shorter videos is generally a better strategy than fewer and longer ones, in part because you can't really predict which video will succeed.

In recent years, I have contributed to a number of vlogs as a consultant or producer, and yet I'm still surprised at which videos ultimately get the most views. YouTube has a smart algorithm that can recognize and promote catchy content surprisingly well. So a new channel will often only catch fire after a longer period of time, and then it's no exception for its viewership to suddenly double.

Even if you aren't emphasizing your vlog's commercial effect, if its content is beneficial in terms of presenting your expertise and raising awareness, and if you are pleasant to watch, you might be nicely surprised at how many opportunities it brings. This is because video can enormously communicate both content and non-verbal context – how you look, what you are like, your body language, how you communicate; in short, what kind of person you are.

You should keep this in mind, especially if you are actively working on your personal branding. Your look in your videos significantly shapes your public image, and so it pays to devote extra attention to arranging the scene, and perhaps calling in a makeup artist or presentation-skills consultant if you start out nervous and insecure.

Non-commercial vlogs created with good intentions by a trustworthy, likable person often have a greater commercial effect than ones created to sell. They address a far broader audience and sometimes also bring viewers more value than a commercial video would.

But I still wouldn't reject outright the idea of selling videos somewhere on the web. You can produce them at your own cost and sell them on your website. There is also Udemy, whose team will help or advise you with production, distribution, and sales on commission. Just watch out for segmenting: don't make your video sales compete with your own courses. The two products – live and video courses – should be clearly distinguished and supplement each other.

PODCASTS: WHERE TO PLACE THEM?

With some exceptions, podcasts (audio blogs) have smaller audiences than YouTube stars, but this isn't a reason to disregard them within this overview.

If you know how to talk – or better yet, lead discussions – and you have topics in your field that you enjoy talking about and that could enrich your audience, a podcast may be an appropriate format for you. They can best be compared to a variable-length radio show – while some podcasts are only ten or twenty minutes in total, others can run up to three hours.

Length can be a plus, because people can listen to podcasts on their phones anywhere. Podcasts can accompany them on the road and out to every place where they can't watch videos. One nice bonus is that unlike videos, they don't tend to have distracting ads.

Many beginning podcasters would like to distribute on iTunes or Spotify, only find to their surprise that the actual sound files have to be stored elsewhere. Many podcasts use SoundCloud, which is a paid service (the ideal Pro Unlimited subscription costs €99 or $144 a year) and has a permanent user community. While it's not as big a hit as YouTube, it works well, and your podcasts can then be embedded, or downloaded over iTunes, Spotify, RSS, or podcast listening apps – including one from SoundCloud itself.

Other popular podcast hosting services include Libsyn, Podbean and Mixcloud.

Podcast production is less technically demanding, and also cheaper than the options for video. Essentially all you need is a reliable digital audio recorder like the Zoom H4N, and you can get started. Freeware like Audacity may be sufficient for editing your recording.

BE A GOOD GATEKEEPER

How much time should you spend on social media? What should you share, and how?

I'll say it simply: *Be a good gatekeeper.*

Every top professional on the net is expected not to spread nonsense, hoaxes, fake news, conspiracy theories, and lies. In fact, they should dispel these. Keep a close eye on what you share from your field, because it speaks about your knowledge and overall level of professionalism.

A professional on social media is a sort of gatekeeper who measures things strictly and only lets in the information that they find correct. And I don't just mean active sharing, but also everything that you like or comment on – it's there for other people to see

There will always be people around you who don't understand your field, or even grasp its basic principles or context. If they perceive you as an expert, that means that they will form a layman's opinion of your field through your posts and comments. And if you yourself spread disinformation (unfounded, untrue, incomplete, or otherwise inaccurate news), you are fooling the public and ultimately hurting yourself and your field.

Whenever something major happens in a field that I don't really understand, but that interests me, I go to the social media profiles of established experts whom I follow, because I want their viewpoints. I read the articles they share, and through them I reach my own conclusions.

So if you are acting as a professional on social media, a part of your mission will be to interpret and translate complex information for your friends and fans, because for them, at least, you are an expert on a given field. Social media networks strengthen your status as an expert, but also gently force you to speak more understandably about your work.

A true professional never violates the intellectual property rights of others, spreads lies, or acts aggressively; in short, they use social networks with the awareness that their clients and colleagues are there. They don't put themselves in a bad light. Social networks are a public space. And that means it's reasonable to behave as you would on the street, in a restaurant, or at a conference.

Your social media profile is definitely yours, and you can block anyone out of it, especially if they are vulgar and are insulting you or other people. But if your profiles are open, it's reasonable to behave by default so that you yourself don't give cause for conflicts.

All of this is a solid foundation you can start from – helping the public and people – and here it's not important whether that will be through slightly sarcastic notes on events, or by sharing articles from your field along with your own explanatory notes. In any case, what people care about isn't the actual sharing, but your opinion on the matter.

So it's best to not share articles on Facebook with meaningless comments like "Check out this interesting article" or "That went well," because for others, this means you have nothing to say. Also, not everyone wants to click on something that takes them out of Facebook. Your post should make sense on its own, although a preview of the article or link should of course come with it. Try this simple test:

> A social-network "passer-by" should be able to conclude from three random posts or comments you have made on your field that you understand it well.

Very brief or shallow posts don't look good, even if the link you share is superb. With one exception: For experts who are known as authorities in their field, the reason for sharing is obvious, and doesn't need to be repeated over and over again. Likewise there is no point in forcing yourself to make pretentious sounding expert statements on your shared content to ensure that everyone knows just how much of an expert you are. A professional posts to benefit people, and they take pleasure from doing so.

Don't just go to social networks to "do that marketing stuff." When you get to know freelancers with social media success and crowds of followers, you will find they deeply resonate with their media. They'll say: *I love Twitter! Instagram is awesome! I'm an FB addict, but what can I do…* It's not just a cold marketing calculation. They love and have grown together with their medium and audience.

⊙ KEEP YOUR ATTENTION FOCUSED

Growing together with your favorite social media network means setting your own tempo and heading there to post how *you* like. Its developers want you to go there nonstop, but that is them, not you. Actually, research suggests that some people have real issues with "internet addiction", which is a general scientific term used to describe all kinds of problematic online behavior including mobile and social media use, with the highest prevalence of 11% in the Middle East and lowest of 2,6% in Northern and Western Europe, according to the 2014 meta-analysis *Internet addiction prevalence and quality of (real) life*.

It makes sense therefore to prevent any behavioral addiction by setting reasonable boundaries where you feel like you need them. If your profession allows it, I recommend to start by turning off email and mobile notifications, so they won't fragment your attention. And also note how often you are clicking notifications on a particular social media site. Do you really need to do it each time that red number flashes at you?

I follow the comments under active posts, if I have the time and mood for it, but I rarely check notifications – usually only once or twice a month. This gives me a broader perspective on what is going on within my network, and although I usually go through everything, only two or three reactions will pique my interest.

If you have a real problem with jumping off to check social media (or other procrastination websites) even without notifications, and it's breaking your concentration, there are other ways to increase your self-control. In one click. This is enabled by blocking apps like Anti-Social, SelfControl, RescueTime, Freedom.to, or the Forest app based on the gamification of growing virtual (and even real) trees. Their shared goal is to limit the amount of time wasted roaming the web or on your mobile. There is only one way forward – to work!

By the way, if your smartphone is distracting you on its own, you can start monitoring and limiting its use with the Digital Wellbeing app for Android, and the Moment or Screen Time for iOS. You can also restrict its use only to calls, messaging and leisure activities such as listening to music and audiobooks. I have, for instance, permanently disabled the Gmail and Chrome apps, along with all social networks. I have intentionally kept only Google's Calendar, Keep and Drive apps so that I can work with my notes and documents. Go ahead and try to mix yourself your own app cocktail and see the wonders it can bring to your focus.

But what do you do when you also have to go to Facebook for work and your news feed is full of tempting posts by friends, immediately distracting you from your tasks? Don't blame yourself, Facebook was *made* to do that. For Chrome, the solution is called Kill News Feed, and it will simply hide your wall. And there are also alternatives for other browsers.

You can also add a Demetricator extension for Facebook or Twitter to your browser, which makes the metrics disappear on these sites, such as the number of likes and comments, so you will click less impulsively on them.

Opinions vary on whether you should also take a further step back from social media and plan and publish your posts automatically at selected times using tools like Buffer, Hootsuite, Sprout Social, or the official TweetDeck for Twitter and the post scheduling feature for Facebook pages.

Planners really start to be useful when you are managing multiple pages, but for simple personal use, you can make do with a network's normal interface in a browser or their app. In fact, it's better when you sometimes write something spontaneously even if you are blocking certain social media sites during other parts of the day due to deep work.

If you go to publish something personally, you can immediately comment on your friends' reactions and add content, reshare, fix mistakes a friend has pointed out, etc. Having a personal presence on networks also supports the good practice of distinguishing between the various networks and feeding each a slightly different or modified content. When a beginner posts on every network at once from a planner, meanwhile, it can look like carpet bombing. Doing the work yourself the old fashioned way will give you a better feel for the job.

Some freelancers also use the services of a researcher who finds and suggests attractive content to share on networks based on predefined criteria. A researcher can be a student or a friend; they feed you outputs in the form of links with notes in a planner or a shared spreadsheet. You then pick what is interesting from among these or add links of your own. Naturally you can also do your own research and use a spreadsheet to plan when you will publish it.

Link shorteners are a practical form of help on social networks. These are simply web applications that let you shorten long URLs, for example like this:

https://www.upwork.com/i/freelancing-in-america/2018/
→ http://bit.ly/18Fia

This is especially useful on networks where very long links look bad, and also in print. The best-known shortener is Bit.ly, which lets you choose your own text for your short link – and also collects click statistics; just add a plus to the link: http://bit.ly/18Fia+

⊘ SHUT THE DOOR ON TROLLS

If your social media usage (and dosage) is reasonable, then all of the mentioned disadvantages tend to be rather small, but there is one more that can send your social utopia up in flames: trolls and haters.

"They're turning the web into a cesspool of aggression and violence," warns the August 2016 cover article *How Trolls Are Ruining the Internet* in Time magazine. "It would be smarter to be cautious, because the Internet's personality has changed," writes the author, Joel Stein, and adds an example – if you are struggling with upload speeds, the web will eagerly help you, but if you let it slip that you are struggling with depression it will make you want to kill yourself. "Psychologists call this the online disinhibition effect, in which factors like anonymity, invisibility, a lack of authority and not communicating in real time strip away the mores society spent millennia building. And it's seeping from our smartphones into every aspect of our lives," writes Stein.

The voice of the mob was always coarse, but today it shouts through the megaphone of social media right in front of you. Many people truly behave on the net differently than they do in public. They lose their inhibitions.

Virtual mobbing and cyberbullying are large problems that society might remain unable to handle well for years to come. Furthermore, many professionals react in a hypersensitive way to criticism, and if they interpret something as an attack on their person, they only get all the more ideological and closed off within their own fan club. But confrontations of opinions are the foundation of useful public discussion, and can't be avoided when you are sharing your opinions.

In social media and online discussions, *trolls* are troublemakers who seek out conflict, and the more attention you feed them, the worse things get. Their relatives, the *haters,* are basically negative users who may or may not have some objective reason for their vitriol. Unlike with trolls, you can find common ground with them, though it can come with an incredible cost in nerves and stress. It's no wonder, since dozens of people are enjoying your heated exchange. I sometimes hear the opinion that haters are actually motivated positively, that their goal is to improve something. And while that may well be true at times, in practice it can be hard to tell the difference. Especially when you aren't sure who's who.

Fortunately, we are not defenseless against trolls: Above all, neither duty nor politeness requires us to reply to anything on social media networks – let alone immediately. (Just try to comment on some celebrity's post and see if they write an equally long answer.)

Don't respond at all to vulgar, aggressive, manipulative, or lying trolls. Don't hesitate to block them and report them. If a post is openly threatening, racist, or otherwise over the line, consider taking a screenshot for a possible crime report. Some countries take hate speech and threats on networks quite seriously, and it sometimes even leads to jail time. And this goes beyond just social media. For example, I know of one case where a freelancer ended up in jail overnight because of a threat emailed to a non-paying client, who immediately reported him to the police.

When it comes to haters, again you need to consider: who do you want to reply to, and how promptly? I recommend only coming back to active posts when *you* want to, not through constant clicking of notifications, which will easily pull you into flame wars. To ensure debates instead of flames, you need proper, pointed communication, and you yourself should take criticism without flaming. Let things cool down, and if you have a bad feeling from a discussion, don't get stuck in it. One long comment or note is more than enough.

You should also try to protect other participants. Being a good gatekeeper means that you are also a discussion moderator and that you shut the door on trolls that appear in your posts' comments. No-one else has as much power to act as you do.

Trolls and haters are few; the vast majority of professionals on the net behave properly. If you have the opposite feeling, I would take that more as reason to think about whether the content you are sharing is OK. The feedback that you get from social media goes beyond just likes, smiles, and praise encouraging your further work. It may be justified criticism too.

❯ HAVING A WEBSITE AND UNDERSTANDING HOW SEARCH ENGINES WORK

Now let's look at websites and their importance for a freelancer's online presence. Social media networks have changed their role, but a website is still very important.

If freelancing is your main source of income, you should have a web presence that understandably says what you do, what you offer, what your advantages are, and how to reach you. This is a reasonable minimum of information that you can fit on even the smallest website.

But your website can also contain customer references and testimonials, some samples of your portfolio of work, or a blog including article comments. And you can also offer documents for download, or sign-ups for your courses, and that will likely be too much for one page.

But no matter whether it's a one-page presentation or a large site, it's your business card. If your name is highlighted there, then it will likely also represent you in search engine results – often more than your social media profiles will.

You can have this web presence fully under control and use it to convert visitors from search engines and elsewhere into prospects, and then customers. So it's no wonder that for many freelancers, websites are a flagship personal marketing tool.

Before we go over the individual possibilities, from the cheapest to the most expensive, you should have an idea of how search engines work and what in fact leads them to your website.

Google was the first search engine to start ranking the quality of links leading to a page. If they are important and authoritative, this is a sign of quality. Google built its success upon this algorithm, because it could sort search results better than any previous engine.

Because the basic methods for evaluating and ranking pages in search engines were well-known, a whole new profession called *Search Engine Optimization* (SEO) arose. In accordance with best practices and recommendations, it tries to adapt websites so that they contain valuable content that is understandable for these engines and attractive for people.

But SEO also has its dark side. So called black hat SEO violates these recommendations and tries to actively abuse well known, or merely imagined, weaknesses in engines to gain an advantage over other pages in search results. Search engines heavily penalize this kind of manipulation, which should be a reminder for all website owners about why not to cooperate with an SEO expert who offers and carries out this kind of strategy.

Good SEO actually *helps* search engines, but the goal in any case is to improve rankings. However, this gets harder and harder as engines get smarter with each new generation. There are hundreds of signals by now that each engines' AI uses to assess a page's quality, and for a long time now, ranking hasn't merely been a simple calculation. And as Google's intelligence grows, it gets harder to convince it to dance on command.

So the importance of content quality is growing, because the logical expectation is that Google is trying to evaluate a page's quality similarly to a reasonably thinking person.

Search engine improvements also increase the importance of paid ads in search results. These are ads that are shown above the organic search results, and the advertiser only pays when a user clicks on such an ad. Thus the name PPC, *pay per click*. Google operates its own system, Ads (formerly AdWords), which can target all kinds of phrases.

PPC ads will be attractive for you when you have started to offer something on your website and you want to bring it higher traffic than ordinary search results would give. In that case you will definitely appreciate that you can optimize your website for incoming visitors (via a *landing page*) and also test different ad wordings. Such campaigns can also be timed for your low season to stimulate demand.

Google Ads is no simple system; the interface is quite complex compared to, for instance, Facebook Ads. One option is to hire a PPC expert to set up and manage your ads; they will also advise you on your landing pages. The other option is to roll up your sleeves, start your self-study, and manage your own campaigns. But you can expect ads for high-traffic words, especially in English, to cost considerable money.

One benefit of a standalone website is that you can measure traffic in detail over Google Analytics after placing a tracking code in the body of the page, or via passive statistics like AWStats on your server. Google Search Console is also quite practical; once you have activated it, you can use it to follow your website's Google search performance, favorite keywords, etc.

⊚ CHOOSING A SUITABLE DOMAIN FOR EMAIL AND THE WEB

Opinions differ on whether a domain is important, and how much so.

One camp states that it's unimportant, and that if it's at least a little memorable and original and you have good site content, people and search engines will find you.

The other camp views a domain as a part of your personal brand and marketing that you use everywhere, from business cards to email. A nice domain like Galbraith.com and the email robert@galbraith.com looks better than the domain Bob-Galbraith.info and the email bobby@bob-galbraith.info. It's a matter of image. (These are examples; please don't write to Bobby.)

I myself am somewhere in between. I do agree that when you put superb content on a weak domain name, it will hardly matter, because content is king after all. But I also agree that a nice domain makes an impression and has value. If I imagine a domain as a piece of land: I can certainly build a nice house on a bad piece of land, but should I?

So what are the main principles? For freelancers it's generally better if the domain name is made of their name or their core business, i.e. the basic elements of a good name. www.YourOccupation.com is just as good as www.YourName.com. Avoid domains with a hyphen (like Your-Occupation.com), as these have been abandoned and are now only being registered as aliases for main domains.

Freelancers who work locally will often benefit from a national domain (FR, ES, CH, CO.UK, etc.). It will likely be more memorable for local customers.

But if your key clientele is abroad and you are serving a large international market, then I would go for the most prestigious domain COM – or EU, if you're within the European Union and you want to stress that in your domain name.

These are the general principles, but there are exceptions, such as when you manage to join part of your name or profession with the domain name and it looks good (for example, I have the domain Vla.ch and the email robert@vla.ch). Likewise I wouldn't be afraid to use endings like BLOG or TV for blogs, vlogs, etc.

Choosing a domain is far more complex if you are creating a brand. There I recommend consulting with a specialist before your final choice and making sure that the name you have chosen can be a trademark and doesn't conflict with any older rights, because in later disputes you could be forced to cease the use of any problematic brand name.

DOMAIN PURCHASES: PROVE YOUR NEGOTIATING SKILLS

But where can you get a domain when your name and profession have long since been taken for both COM and other decent endings?

One alternative is to think harder about alternative names for your profession, or specific area of specialization. The other is to buy an existing domain from an owner who isn't using it, especially if you have prepared a reasonable budget for your website.

Prices are lower for national domains than for pretty and unused COM domains, which can even cost you several thousand dollars. Many are held by speculators who are willing to sell them, but at the highest possible price.

Start out by researching and listing worthwhile domains. You can go right away and register the available ones for a year, even if they are not the very best, so nobody else takes them before you.

You should be checking the availability of domains only at a trustworthy service that doesn't log your queries. It may be a national domain registrar, Whois.eu for European domains, or Whois.ICANN.org for international ones. Or you can make your search through your own domain registrar; there are plenty of trustworthy ones.

Always register domains to yourself – not to your web designer, your partner, a colleague, or a family member. A domain belongs to whoever is recorded in the domain registry as its bearer.

Listing suitable domains and registering free ones is also a good strategy because alternatives strengthen your BATNA in any price negotiations.

When adding COM or another generic domain to your list, check to see if it isn't perhaps already being offered for sale. Try the Sedo.com domain marketplace as well. It lists an enormous number of domains for immediate purchase or negotiation (in the form of haggling) and it also offers an assisted purchase service that will provide you, as the buyer, with a certain anonymity. Your payment can be placed in a Sedo escrow account where the funds are held until the transfer is complete. That way, even a purchase of a domain name from a speculator from who knows where is entirely safe.

So you have got a list of domains you are interested in, and they are visibly unused – what now? You can start with the most desirable domain on the list and think of how much you are willing to pay for it. If you find the owner's email in the Whois record, on the domain itself, or you are lucky enough to find the owner's contact info elsewhere, send a short message asking if they would sell. Don't tell them your price right away. If they answer obligingly, try directly asking for how much. If their price is acceptable, you can shake hands immediately, and if not, you can negotiate. If the difference in your pricing views isn't huge, you will likely reach an agreement.

If a domain owner doesn't want to state their price and insists that you offer one, or shows no interest, then there is no choice but to send an offer and hope that it hooks the owner enough to reply. It's not easy to hit the mark on an initial offer. It depends on the bits of information you have about the owner. If I have a feeling that the owner is wealthy and is also successful in business, then a low offer makes no sense. But apart from this, especially if the domain has been gathering dust for a long time – which you can often check on Archive.org – I would start with a low bid at first.

To give a general example, if my client and I have a secret maximum price of around $3,000, we make our initial offer around $500 and leads things on from there. If the other side's demand is anywhere up to four or five thousand, we might then get it for under our maximum. If it's higher, I let them know that I'm considering other alternatives (I sometimes do this in my first email if I want to lower expectations), and to keep things from dragging out, I directly suggest a final offer somewhere around our maximum, say $2,800, so I have some space left if needed to add some more if they are hesitating. Either the other side will budge, or we won't reach an agreement, and we will continue with the next candidate on our list.

The transaction itself can work in either of two ways. If it's an expensive domain, it can work in a complicated way via a middleman like Sedo. Or it's a relatively cheap domain and the two parties trust each other. Then we handle things simply, over email, with a 50% upfront payment, followed by a balance payment after the domain's successful transfer to a new owner.

1. A ONE-PAGE SITE AS YOUR BUSINESS CARD

Great, you have a domain, but what will you do with it? There are basically three options for how a freelancer's site can look, and naturally they all have their pros and cons:

1. A small one-page website (as a business card, a presentation, and a signpost in one)

2. A content website or professional blog

3. A turnkey professional website (also includes web apps and digital products)

Let's start with the first and most common option. One-page sites (sometimes called microsites) are more and more popular among freelancers due to their superb price to benefit ratio. They are an embodiment of the principle that it's better to reduce a website's scope than its quality. A small, but pretty, and above all superbly written one-page website that adapts for display on a PC, phone, or tablet will present you better than a complicated but amateurishly created website.

The one-page site of craftsman BrandonGore.com – you can find lots of other examples on OnePageLove.com in the *Inspiration / Personal* category.

Meanwhile, single-page presentations hosted, for example, on Carrd ($19 a year with a custom domain name) and About.me ($8 a month with a custom domain), are even simpler. They are built on powerful photos and brief texts supplemented with links to your other profiles or pages. If you have a truly great photo and you want it to shine and to speak for you more than words, then this is an instant web business card for you. (Services like Squarespace or Wix, for publishing small sites with a choice of attractive layouts, are also equally visually oriented.)

So it's definitely possible to break free of technical troubles by creating a simple web page that works like a business card. You can cleverly add interactive elements to a page that can considerably increase a one-page website's variability and possibilities. This may be a newsletter signup, your news or updates, a Facebook box, an e-book download, clickable testimonials or frequently asked questions, an overview of your next upcoming course or lecture dates, an embedded Google Calendar for showing your availability, an embedded Google Map with notes or a click-through to a Facebook photo gallery.

YouTube videos or Google Slides with any number of pictures or slides can also be embedded on your page. Hello portfolio! Some of the mentioned components can be custom-made, while others, like embedded Google elements, are completely standardized and available to all.

And if you want to change something on your website occasionally, you don't have to run to a content management system. The minimalist Adminer Editor lets you, for example, change course dates or add news or customer references, including photos, once it's been set up by your web developer.

Creating a simple webpage isn't in itself simple. If you don't have enough technical skill, ask a colleague who understands the web and can help you out as a webmaster or will even build the site. Or simply ask colleagues whose small sites you like who helped them.

And if you don't make your living by writing, I definitely recommend hiring a web copywriter to help you create superb texts for your presentation. Words are just as important as looks, and very few people know how to sell their work in writing in a way that is both effective and tasteful.

For your single-page site, you can either buy a cheap ready-made template (for WordPress, these are sold as Themes right on their site, and also on others, especially at ThemeForest or TemplateMonster), or have a customized graphic design created, which is far more expensive, but can give a higher class of results.

The approach from there highly varies based on this. With a purchased template, you will usually be fitting your text to the template, whereas with a customized design, it tends to be the opposite:

1. The *concept* is the foundation. Describe what kind of website this will be, on what domain, and what its contents and goals will be.

2. Start the *text* with your name and profession and a brief description of what you do.

3. The *graphic layout* is created based on the finished text, which is an advantage. Entrust it to a pro who understands usability and mobile-friendly responsive web design.

4. *Template coding* converts the graphic design into the form that will ultimately be shown in a browser with your finalized texts. This is typically done by an HTML/CSS coder.

5. *Site launch* mainly means deploying a template on a site, along with any management on the backend, inserting external components, etc. Basically, technical work.

2. YOU CAN BUILD CONTENT SITES GRADUALLY

If you want to save while still focusing on quality, a content site might the option for you.

In short, you can go to WordPress.com or have the WordPress system installed on your domain, fill in basic information, choose one of the graphical templates offered, and immediately start writing. All for a minimal cost.

If you write well about interesting things, visitors will forgive poor graphic design. As I have mentioned before, users mainly care about worthwhile content. It's not about looks, but about you and your knowledge, style, and story.

I have covered blogging enough in connection with social media, but blogs are only a part of content sites. Your web content doesn't have to be timelined like on a blog. It can be divided into sections and subpages, for instance an introduction to some topic. Although this kind of content gets old as well, you can continuously update it.

These content sites have the advantage that authors don't need to constantly feed new content into them. They can build them gradually, as they see fit, and traffic will grow gradually too. But even if you only have a few thousand visitors a month, these aren't bad numbers for a topic-oriented website.

WordPress is definitely the king of content management systems (CMS) today, and if you don't understand building websites well, it's the only system I would ever recommend for site-content management and creation. Today, WordPress has become the industry standard, making it easy to find an expert who will install it and customize it to your needs. And if you are dissatisfied with the expert's service, you will just as easily find someone else who can take over its administration.

Still, pay careful attention to the settings for security and automatic-updates, because WordPress is a frequent target of successful attacks on older versions. If you have more sites than usual, consider automated monitoring like ManageWP.com as well.

If you are technically capable and a static website is enough for you, static site generators such as Jekyll can be a safe alternative to WordPress. In these, you write your site in the simple Markdown markup language, uploading each new version to your web server. This kind of site is faster and stays safe even if you don't touch it for several years.

In any case, WordPress can cover all your everyday needs for web publishing, no matter whether that means blogging, or producing a categorized content web. It supports adding images and videos, creating private drafts, and collaboration between multiple users. So you can, for example, have a proofreader that goes over all your texts for you. And you can also add numerous functions to WordPress via free or commercial plugins.

Take, for example, email newsletters. MailChimp is what is most often used here; it's great, and it's free for up to 2,000 subscribers and 12,000 emails a month. But if you want to send a monthly newsletter and you have, say, 15,000 subscribers, you will pay MailChimp a good $150 a month, which is $1,800 a year – quite a lot. Then you will definitely appreciate how you can add a free plugin to WordPress for managing and sending newsletters, such as TheNewsletterPlugin.com, which won't be as fine-tuned as MailChimp, but will easily be enough for an ordinary newsletter. TinyLetter, meanwhile, is a free alternative offered by MailChimp itself.

Email newsletters are still important even in our social network age, because with these, the content that a social media reader misses will reliably land in their inbox. The optimal newsletter frequencies are either monthly or as enough news arrives, e.g. every few months.

⊗ THE SPECIFICS OF WRITING FOR THE WEB

So if content sites are so great, why aren't they used by everyone? There are two answers.

1. Their overall time demands are large, so the low financial costs are counterbalanced by the high time cost.

2. The competition is large, and far from everyone has enough to write about.

It's also a question of style; websites demand a different style than books or magazines. Web copy tends to be shorter, reflecting the trend towards shorter posts on social media. But longer texts, often referred to as *longreads,* are alive and well too.

Your social-media experience will make it easy for you to write short texts. And there is no point in forcing out longer ones; most authors simply find their way to those when the need arises.

But there are a few principles here that reflect the web's specifics as a medium, and which you should know. It's extremely important to have an attractive title and lead paragraph, and perhaps a title image to represent your article on social media as a preview. Sticking to the recommended 1,200 × 628 or smaller 600 × 314 Facebook picture format is a good idea. You can then use Facebook Open Graph Object Debugger, Twitter Card validator or LinkedIn Post Inspector to see if your preview is generated on the network correctly and is as attractive as you hoped it would be.

Far from all of your visitors will be arriving at your page because of you. They might often be seeking specific information or advice and going through search engine results. So it's practical to put what is important at the top and only then work your way down to the details. A visitor who is seeking something – and this can even be a returning visitor – will tend to scan a typical text rather than reading it. They often look for "anchor" points or keywords.

The use of typographical means for highlighting passages and key information, from bold text to block quotes, bullet points, tables or infographics, corresponds to this. All these show information in a visually attractive and digestible form. The infographics can also be shared separately on social media, if they are not too large.

Unless you are severely grammar-challenged, the main thing is to write and write until you have your own style. And also to read what others write, because having idols can help an author to try new approaches and grow.

3. PROFESSIONAL TURNKEY WEBSITES: EXPENSIVE INDEED

The third option, if you can't handle building your website yourself, is to have a turnkey site created by a pro.

A first-rate site that someone designs, builds, and codes directly for your needs is, however, truly expensive. Modern websites are an ever more expensive product.

If you want a site that looks great and shows you in the very best light, one that is easy to find, always up to date, and connected with your social media networks, and one that does precisely what you expect it to do (present, inform, or sell), it's very likely that the overall costs for consultations, creation, and the follow-up marketing will run into the thousands of dollars or euros.

Although a website like this is the best solution with the least compromises, it's mostly for those with deep pockets. It's not just about what a visitor will see in their browser. A website is a comprehensive project, an integrated whole that may include a marketing concept, a personal-brand clarification, original photos, and professionally written text that is far better than what you yourself could write.

And I'm not just talking about ordinary presentation websites. You may decide to set up your own e-shop, or even to develop your own web service along with a mobile app. And these are all tasks whose complexity goes far beyond ordinary site-building.

Purchasing a website that is this expensive might make sense for an established professional with a high income and stable business. But for an ordinary freelancer, it really is a high cost. And that isn't the only catch. There are major risks here that arise from the fact that even an expensive website can fail. The money you invest is not, in short, any guarantee that things will work. The site may have a bad concept or serious technical flaws, or you yourself could fail and, despite having resolved to fill the site with news and articles, leave it lying empty.

These are not hypothetical risks; these are problems that web consultants encounter every day. Also, there are few first-rate creators who know precisely how to build up a professional website of an independent professional including the associated marketing strategies, and they are expensive. But I'm not writing this book to scare you with everything that could fail, so what comes next?

If you can afford this kind of a project, and all of this chapter's previous alternatives are too unambitious for you, then I would recommend that you start by becoming an informed customer, turning to a web consultant for technical oversight, and choosing the right supplier.

Becoming an informed customer is a reasonable first step, especially for large projects such as various web apps, digital products, or other original projects. If you find a consultant who will educate you, then this is all the better. But you can also feel free to do some practical reading about site-building principles – the classic *Don't Make Me Think, Revisited* by Steve Krug (the #1 book in its genre on Amazon) is one popular example, as is Jakob Nielsen's highly regarded blog (to see its archive go to Alertbox.com).

My reason for suggesting to separate the supplier and consultant roles is exactly the same as you see in house construction, where you will likely want an independent supervisor to protect your investment. However, people have been building houses forever, so even laymen can tell if something is seriously wrong. When a website, however, is badly designed and constructed, the customer can easily be fooled when they see a pretty facade.

The problems only appear over time. The website isn't findable, it has terrible traffic, it doesn't sell, it's disorganized, it's badly structured, it crashes and shows error messages, it doesn't bring in orders, it makes a bad impression, or it is sometimes attacked by viruses or hackers. For example, one company I cooperate with had the bank account numbers on their site changed by hackers. And the punchline? Their web developer considers himself a security expert.

So your initial website-related goal should be to not get fooled by the first trickster you meet. Don't toss a website job to someone just because your friend knows them and says they're OK. Do the maximum to ensure that you choose a qualified professional the very first time. But even if you educate yourself a little and you suspect what site-building involves, it still won't be enough for you to supervise the project yourself.

The person who directs and supervises the project has to have an overview of both the current state of web technologies and design, and the sales, content, and marketing strategies that will support your site's success.

I know it's tempting to skip all this and go straight for a supplier who you feel is high-quality. But while you can always finish a house even if problems appear, a screwed up web project basically amounts to *throwing away your investment*. You are simply spending an enormous sum on something that will never pay off, and any potential replacement will likely have to be built from the ground up. And there is also the question of how many quality suppliers like this you can afford to burn through before finding the right one.

Your search for both your consultant and your supplier can be a lengthy process. They should definitely be independent of each other, and you will likely want to speak with multiple people to get an idea of how they work. Every consultant has a different approach. Some of them just help with preparing contracts and project documentation, and then check and critique results. Others are more involved and will also help you to manage the project and educate yourself for your entry into the world of digital marketing – they will make it easier for you to gain the needed skills, point you towards web copywriting courses, show you every corner of social media, etc. So you need to clarify in advance whether you are just seeking a consultant, or an all-in-one project manager and coach.

You will likely also go over your choice of supplier with your consultant. But always ask for and check out references. Which professionals or companies are currently using their websites, and how do they look? Don't be afraid to call their former clients and ask if they are satisfied with the result.

Also ask your colleagues to give you a recommendation for a web designer and ask how their website has helped them.

A web designer is an important strategic partner for you. For freelancers, I would recommend giving preference to individuals or well-coordinated groups of several freelancers. Independent web professionals have top-rate price to benefit ratios. Subcontractors like these are often even hired by renowned agencies, which are still then responsible for managing all the underlying aspects of orders for large clients.

Your consultant's task is also to let you know how large a contractual guarantee you need with this or that contractor. In practice I have seen lots of websites that were built solely on oral agreements, because an experienced web designer guaranteed them with their good name, as well as other websites, where it took several weeks just to finalize the contract. In any case, I recommend having a contract or a carefully prepared order and a detailed written assignment.

You will also need your consultant when accepting the finished work. Feel free to ask them in advance and have them show you their checklist or the foundations they use for checking a finished website. Actual acceptance should only take place after any defects found have been fixed. But your cooperation doesn't end there.

Naturally you should analyze a site's traffic and its sales and other metrics if you want to be sure that your investment into it doesn't go wasted. Professional sites go through continual development, new content keeps getting tested out, and something is always being improved, updated, and fine-tuned. Be sure to also measure a site's speed and stability to see if it doesn't have downtime you don't know about. Paid services such as Pingdom are used for this.

Does all this seem really complicated? I can assure you that it's far more so in reality. Creating a pro website is expensive and time-consuming. Its risks come mainly from the fact that low-quality contractors often don't know that they don't know, and still consider their sites to be first-rate.

Just to be clear, I'm not talking about ordinary web designers, who *do* know what they don't know, and who want to grow, even though this is a broad and demanding field that is rushing ahead at light speed. I'm talking about the masses of web-based dabblers who cut and paste one order after another and spit out dozens of websites that often feel like clones. They sometimes even shamelessly copy other websites or content from them and don't even care.

But let them be for now, because we still have much more important work to do. Before shelling out your hard-earned money for expensive website building, read the next chapter and see the options offered to you by freelance marketing. And you may go on and agree with me that there are less demanding roads forward than the creation of a large professional website.

KEY IDEAS

1. Opinions vary widely regarding the need to use social media and to have a website.

2. You should above all appear in searches, because colleagues and customers *will* be searching for you.

3. An unfindable professional is much less trustworthy. And moreover, they raise suspicion.

4. Social media is also useful for freelancers as the glue for the community of a given field.

5. The most important social media are the big five of Facebook, Instagram, LinkedIn, YouTube and Twitter.

6. Creatives should have an online portfolio with samples of their work and show off their best.

7. Blogging is useful for texts with lasting value; even quality content will fade away quickly on social media.

8. Video blogs and podcasts are more challenging to produce, but popular.

9. Most professionals can get by with a well-made one-page website on their own domain.

10. Content sites are one alternative for writers; while professional turnkey websites are there for those with money to burn.

PRACTICE

✓ Look yourself up on Google, Facebook, LinkedIn, etc. Are you findable? What does your digital footprint look like? And do you appear to be reliable and professional?

✓ Start showing your best work online, if you haven't been doing so yet. Schedule regular posts on your website, portfolio sites, or social media, and stick to it.

✓ Go over all your social media profiles and tweak them. Update your picture, bio, contact info, links and security settings, using two-factor authentication where possible. Do this every year or so.

✓ Think of planning your social media posts in advance by using a simple spreadsheet, while also taking better care of your digital well-being. Protect your focus by default.

✓ If you have a website already, or are just about to build one, pay extra attention to the quality of the text. This is something you may always improve, even on an existing site.

FREELANCE MARKETING

Which kinds of self-promotion should you choose?

Freelance marketing looks and works in a completely different way than marketing for companies. It's only minimally based on advertising, while having a very close link to the key strategies that I have already covered:

- A good name is the best advertisement on its own, and it doesn't cost a penny.

- Making your expertise clear (and keeping it consistent) is the foundation of self-presentation.

- Clients themselves seek out and are willing to pay for expertise, quality, and productivity.

- 100% reliability is so rare that if you achieve it, you will never be short of work.

- Finding a true professional calling will bring you visibility even if most of your work for clients is invisible.

- Pricing and a fine-tuned negotiation process influence your work's quality and quantity.

- Various social bonds are the most important source of new orders for freelancers.

- An online portfolio is a creative professional's marketing minimum.

- And the web can be a strong resource as well, especially if you blog or share know-how.

Should I continue? I will. This summary is needed nevertheless, because ignoring slow and reliable success strategies would be like raising a sail when your boat is leaking.

Many professionals make the mistake of investing into visibility and advertisement without building up their name, expertise, productivity, and reliability. Without ever going deeper into pricing, building good relations throughout their field, or sharing anything. And if a professional can't offer their permanent clients attentive, high-quality services without serious flaws, one really has to wonder if taking on new clients through expensive ads is worth it. They won't escape their problems anyway.

In this chapter I'll cover freelance marketing in more depth, but I don't want to make it seem like it brings salvation. It's certainly *important*, because a professional should be able to present and sell themselves. But if you don't do good (and ever-better) work and you ignore your professional foundations, the metaphorical boat that is your business won't bear new passengers, or it will tilt alarmingly to one side.

For a professional, good marketing is like a sail stretched just enough to give them the right direction and speed. It shouldn't endanger their safety, stability, or mobility. So here I'll say a bit more about how to achieve this, and what to use to make such a sail.

◉ SELF-PRAISE STINKS

When a marketer is promoting a product, it's a relationship between the person and the goods. These are two separate entities, each with their own existence. But when as a freelancer you are just promoting yourself, you are both the person and the goods. If you overdo it, you can easily lose all sense of proportion of what is acceptable and decent for other people.

Inappropriate personal marketing, self-centeredness, and self-praise can turn a professional into a self-caricature, convinced of half-truths about themselves that they repeat and spread nonstop.

When you claim that you are the best, it never creates a good impression. You might convince some people, but you will drive more people to laughter or disgust. This is why I assert that your marketing should be built on conservative, proven, and safe procedures.

Why conservative? Why proven? Why safe?

Because you only have one good name. And if you ruin it with some sad affair, you can't erase all that with a wave of your hand and start all over again. No. It will drag along with you for years.

When a marketer comes up with a new product campaign that is embarrassing, unethical, or simply a spectacular failure, it's a disaster. But while a product can be taken off the market, rebranded or redone, there is nowhere you can crawl away and hide to – and definitely not for years at a time. So it's best to approach your own marketing as if you don't get second chances, because in many ways you actually don't.

If you're not a professional marketer determined to become a pioneer of dead ends while trying out your own marketing snake-oils, this means precisely those three words:

Conservative. Proven. Safe.

That doesn't mean that you can't be creative; quite the opposite. But it does mean steering clear of every dubious approach. I have already mentioned many of them, but these also include multi-level marketing and pyramid schemes; manipulation and high-pressure sales techniques; vulgar marketing; the use of fake university degrees, plagiarism, or leeching off of others' brands; violating intellectual property rights; or abusing testimonials that someone provided in good faith to promote an entirely different service.

If someone rents an auditorium at Harvard to organize a lecture and later boasts on their website or resume they were lecturing at Harvard, this is precisely the kind of unethical marketing I'm talking about. Despite this, there are sources that recommend similar forms of insanity.

Please avoid such scams at all costs. Instead, aim to be *so good they can't ignore you* – so good that Harvard just might invite you to lecture there.

TO SELL IS HUMAN (AGAIN)

And then there is the opposite extreme. The fear of selling yourself or being seen as a sell out. A self-presentation phobia. False modesty. A strong resistance to even naming your strengths and successes. Simply, an inability to state clearly and matter-of-factly what you are really good at.

You see, we – your peers and customers – want and need to know. Please give us at least a tiny sign.

I do have an understanding for this kind of restraint, but at the same time I must say that modern sales works entirely differently, and it *doesn't* have much in common with the snake-oil I mentioned. Daniel Pink's book *To Sell Is Human* clears the skeletons out of the closet of sales skills. In it, he explains why business and sales have changed more in recent decades than in the entire last century.

Pink declares: *We're all in sales now.* He proclaims that the old hard-sell techniques are working less and less, because customers are less isolated. So in our new world, the best sales numbers go not to those who best know how to shake down a single customer who is cut off from information, but to those who have the greatest influence on the customer's opinion and their social surroundings.

A hard sell to people who will be dissatisfied and will instantly tell everyone via social networks, user ratings, or consumer sites is becoming less and less advantageous.

Another bias that Pink overturns is the conviction that sales is only for businesspeople and salesmen. He argues that today, every single professional must know how to *sell* their ideas or proposals, because it's easier for clients to get to information. Likewise doctors and leading experts who previously relied on the weight of their authority alone today must expect to face critical thinking and probing questions from emancipated laypeople.

Pressure-based sales and marketing methods are taking a back seat to softer ones that strengthen your *influence* and set up a favorable *business context* in which your work will fare well. Running a blog for your field is a good example: future customers will work in part from information that comes from you.

Thus in the 21st century, effective sales is returning to the foundations on which superb craftsmen and experts have built their businesses since the dawn of time – their reputation, trustworthiness, and ability to convince others that they are good at what they do.

PERSONAL MARKETING

My first advice for you as marketers of your own freelance selves is to forget the rules from books and articles written about marketing for companies. Really. You can make do without a marketing plan, and often even without ads and campaigns.

As freelancers we differ from companies in many ways described throughout this book and it is also pretty easy to fully load up a freelancer with work, especially if they are starting out and still cheap. That is precisely why our personal marketing has to prefer quality (better gigs, prices, and clients) over quantity, because our personal capacity is definitely limited.

No matter what ingredients you will be putting into your marketing mix, always rely on the foundations that I've mentioned in the opening of this chapter. If you have the feeling that this or that method goes against them, avoid it.

There are many things you can do to strengthen your good name and influence, and by far most of them can be done in ways that won't leave you feeling like you are over-promoting yourself. This feeling, by the way, will be your best advisor; don't try to suppress it. You can apply one recommendation in a hundred ways, and even though I'm convinced that all the methods below are inherently relatively harmless and beneficial, *everything* can be abused.

Moderation and a general orientation outwards, towards people, rather than inwards, towards your own sense of self-importance and qualities, is thus putting you on the right track. Sure, every potential customer is interested in what you are doing and what you are good at. But you don't have to tell the world directly that you are the best. In short, don't overdo it and don't forget that a top professional is marked mainly by their work and reputation. This is rather reminiscent of Margaret Thatcher's principle:

"Power is like being a lady…if you have to tell people you are, you aren't."
If you have to tell people you are top-notch, you aren't.

TELL YOUR FRIENDS AND PEOPLE AROUND YOU

Let's start once again from simple foundations. Let's assume that you are already clear on your area of expertise and core business, and have fine-tuned an elevator pitch that can be summed up nicely in one sentence. What now? How do you get this message out to people?

When your friends and acquaintances and your current and future peers know that you are freelancing and what you do, that can bring you quite a few gigs in the beginning. It's also possible some of them will support and recommend you, because they like you and want to help you.

You are always at an advantage with this group of people, because they already know you as a person, and you don't need to work hard to gain their trust. It's enough for them to know and need what you do and the rest goes smoothly.

How can you inform them? Inform your close friends personally, of course. They are certain to care. You can also engage a broader circle of acquaintances over social media networks and email, ideally in a custom-ized manner taking into account what a given person might need.

Sending a one-off message that you are starting to freelance to, perhaps, a broader circle of contacts is certainly fine, but when it comes to sending out emails, stick to the basic principle of one is enough.

Don't expect that your announcement emails will generate any great response. Your recipients will more likely remember what you are doing now, and at some time in the future they may turn to you or recommend you to someone. Especially when you occasionally mention your work on social networks or at other social occasions, as you should.

⊗ NETWORKING AND COMMUNITY INVOLVEMENT

Visit meetups and get involved in your professional and freelance communities. It's good practice to build up relationships with your freelancing colleagues right from the start – to share experiences and information; to help and support each other; to match experts with clients; to cooperate on projects; and to teach each other new skills.

Professional meetings, topic conferences, lectures, and coworking events, as well as membership in professional and entrepreneurial organizations, all create a wellspring from which you can draw and grow, learn to recognize people better, and compare your opinions with those of others.

Networking isn't about sales, but rather it's about building relationships. It also includes building up individual contacts, which is completely common among freelancers. If you are starting out, write to colleagues whose work you admire and meet up with them from time to time. You can show them your work, praise theirs, and if you click with each other, they may in time even involve you on their own initiative in their own projects.

Whenever you choose any kind of membership, group, or community to join in on, always consider if you can help them in some way. There tend to be far fewer active members than those who are just along for the ride, and often it's the best way to work your way into the community, and a good one even for introverts, because not all involvement means frequent contact with people.

You might say it's a bit like university studies. There are students who coast through school and meet their study requirements, but nothing more. And then there are those who get actively involved in student affairs, participate in group projects, and travel a good part of the world via exchange programs. For these people, university is a breakthrough life experience and a pillar of professional relationships.

Ask your colleagues what communities they are involved in. Or take a look directly. The best ones primarily promote their members rather than themselves.

Membership in your local chamber of commerce can be beneficial as well. Some regional chambers organize high-quality events and have lots of contacts for specialized consultants. But otherwise, freelancers tend to deliberately ignore large institutions that provide business-support, because they themselves know that these associations work on problems somewhat different from those of freelancers and small businesses.

⊘ WRITTEN RECOMMENDATIONS

Freelancers use testimonials from their clients and colleagues often and with pleasure. Testimonials are the embodiment of the marketing principle that goes: *let others speak for you.*

This isn't at all a new phenomenon. As far back as Roman times, letters of safe passage and later letters of recommendations through which a trustworthy third party vouched for someone were in use. Even today we can occasionally see recommendations in the form of letters, but in practice a briefer, more modern form dominates. A modern testimonial is typically a single paragraph of praise.

Its text should neither be too short nor too long. It should not be too general, or worse yet misleading. It should be clear what sort of cooperation the recommendation concerns, and what it's based on, i.e. above all that it was real and close cooperation.

A recommendation once received can be further edited and shortened, if the author agrees with it and it doesn't distort the message.

What I don't recommend though is to write testimonials yourself on behalf of your customers. This is a bad practice which is usually the result of one's repeated pressure on a client to *finally* write a recommendation. Even though this lets you squeeze a recommendation out of someone who might never have written one for you on their own, it won't be authentic. And what if someone calls that person in two years to ask about its details? Will they stand behind the recommendation, or will they let it slip that they didn't write it themselves?

The same applies to you if you write a recommendation for someone else. It's a serious matter.

A great testimonial is more than just a text; it also clearly states its author's full name, job position, and some kind of contact (ideally a website, phone number, or email). Forget about those recommendations signed with unclear initials such as "Jane M." or "Peter Smith, London" without any additional details; testimonials like these are untrustworthy and will tend to make you look like a peddler of some miracle product for losing weight. (Services of a confidential nature are an exception.)

A testimonial with a contact for its author is not only one you can trust more, but also serves a practical importance. Some potential customers may want to verify a few of positive things said about you, and they may pick out the ones where the work described is similar to their own assignment.

Another advantage of testimonials is that they are universal. You can place them on the web, in presentations, in invitations, and even in business proposals. Not everyone loves to use testimonials, but this is natural; no format will please everyone. But they are definitely better than just a list of logos for the companies you have worked for – even if they're just referring to a summer job you had as a student painting fences. Testimonials are more specific, and if they are from respected persons, they'll definitely open doors for you.

How can you ask for recommendations, and how can you get them? Always ask for the recommendation after you have successfully completed the assigned job and are certain that you have done first-rate work and that your client is satisfied, or even enthusiastic. Ideally you will want to write an email, thank them for their cooperation, and ask for a brief recommendation that you can use for further presentations of your services. You can even direct them to enter their recommendation via your Facebook page, LinkedIn profile, or an online service like Trustpilot, but only if you are pretty sure this would be easier for them, otherwise it's better to stick with an email.

Quite often clients are satisfied and yet they still don't write anything for you, either because they are busy, or because they simply don't like to write in general. Some people can take up to a half an hour to write one paragraph of text. In that case it makes sense to enhance your request with a small added benefit or gift.

I had a client who was a massage therapist and complained that even though she had dozens of satisfied, faithful clients, she had only gotten two or three recommendations for her new website. This radically changed once she offered, at my advice, her regular clients one hour of massage for free if they took the time to write a recommendation. Soon she had received praise from over half of them.

RECOMMENDING COLLEAGUES

It's common for freelancers to recommend each other, but this is most frequent among one's closest colleagues. And often this is more handing clients around and filling free capacity within an informal team of cooperating freelancers than truly recommending what is best for the client.

Recommending a large number of professionals is rather rare, because many freelancers lack contacts or don't grasp why they should be doing so. I'll tell you a secret. Actively recommending high-quality colleagues is one of the strongest marketing tools you can harness. All it takes is knowledge of who is truly good and contacts acquired by networking and deepening your insight into what is happening in and around your field.

Selflessly recommending others leads to reciprocation from them as well, but it also has a number of other surprising effects. It helps your whole field, because it spreads awareness of who is great at what, lessens misunderstandings, and gets more orders pointed at the right people.

Out of all the hundreds of freelancers that I know, only a handful actively recommend others, and it's no accident that absolutely everyone knows them. They themselves are among the most recommended of all, and yet they are doing it selflessly. I would recommend you take the same approach.

Recommendations can be dealt with both impulsively and systematically. Some freelancers include a list right on their website naming their most trusted colleagues who could either step in to partly serve in their place, or who complement their own expertise and supplement them wonderfully. Others wait to give recommendations until an order's development demands it.

I keep a list, for example, of a few hundred tried-and-true people whom I can recommend as top experts in their field or professional niche. I register their names, key competencies (as you can see, once again the core of business and expertise as distinguishing characteristics of a professional), up-to-date contacts, a link to their site or LinkedIn, and sometimes a brief bio as well. Then when a colleague, client, conference organizer, or journalist comes to me seeking tips for capable people, I can hand-pick and send a dozen carefully chosen contacts almost instantly.

YOU NEED A PORTRAIT PHOTO – THE BEST ONE POSSIBLE

For a freelancer, a photo is a bit like a logo for a company. You can get by without a logo, but without a photo? Not so much. Your photo represents you and says who you are and how you see yourself, it's a clear output of a certain amount of self-styling, and it's an expression of how you want others to see you.

Your photo will appear in countless places – on your website, in Google search results, in social-network profiles, and in other web presentations. And it will be demanded by everyone from publishers to journalists to the organizers of events where you are speaking or giving a presentation.

Your photo is a window into your soul for the rest of us. Visually oriented people often choose whom they approach based on photos and how pleasant people look. And the opposite applies as well: "When I put a photo on my website that shows how I look, people whom I find pleasant start contacting me," remarks Jan Tippman, a senior graphic designer.

So pay special attention both to your choice of portrait photo and to self-censoring the pictures you release over the web and social media networks or in which other people are tagging you. If you have been tagged in some really unflattering photos, the kind where perhaps a cousin has dug up an old family photo album and thrown the best ones on Facebook, that tagging can be removed.

Definitely avoid using all those cheap instant headshots, cropped images of you grinning from ear to ear on some mountain hike, or amateur photos taken with a flash at home where you're leaning up against a wall with a shiny forehead and a shadow behind you sharply tracing the outline of your head.

That being said, a freelancer's portrait doesn't at all have to be formal. It can definitely be a photo that shows you outdoors, in your workspace at home, or with some items that characterize you. But you should be photographed by someone who knows what they are doing and will produce a quality, well-composed picture of you at a high resolution.

There are countless professional portrait photographers out there. They usually offer reasonably priced packages that include taking and editing a certain number of photos. Their prices don't tend to be high unless they are truly renowned. Finding a photographer, meanwhile, is easy. Find a profile photo you like for another freelancer, and then just praise it and ask who took it and roughly how much it cost. (Or try googling *headshots* in your city and then choose a photographer based on the portfolios.)

It pays to take multiple pieces of clothing to your shoot and invite a stylist or a makeup artist. You may find that one outfit doesn't look good in photos at all, while another suits you surprisingly well, and you'll suddenly see that it's *it*. If you are preparing to set up your own website, decide how dominant the photo will be and how it should blend with the page's layout. And get some photos taken with a white background so they can be cropped cleanly, which you can also try to do on Remove.bg.

Avoid over-styled photos. Your photo shouldn't be too different from how you look and act normally – unless you are an artistic soul and being provocative with your photo entertains you and others. Then even something crazy is fine, as long as your clients understand that it's an exaggeration.

How can you choose the right photo from among the dozens that come out of even a single short shoot? Ideally by making a preliminary selection and then trying to associate every photo with an emotion, based on the nuances in your expressions, your posture, and overall impression. Your result will then be something like five retouched photos that you can go on and use for a variety of purposes.

BUSINESS CARDS AND DEGREES? OPTIONAL.

In general, business cards are not required for a freelancer – especially one who is easy to find on the web. And you definitely shouldn't be measuring yourself through them like the managers in *American Psycho*, where Christian Bale murders one of his colleagues for having a more luxurious card.

Cards have become optional in most fields, but there are exceptions. For example in many parts of Asia, business cards are not only obligatory, but you are also expected to closely examine the card you are given by someone (presumably) above your standing and make some nice comment about it – as part of the initial small talk.

If you have a website, there is no need to pack your card with information. Your name and your profession or core business, website, email, and phone number, and maybe your Twitter or Instagram handle are a fine foundation.

Minimalism is definitely in, as well as an original style for your cards – especially for creative professionals, it can show off their creative genius and their approach towards design. You can also add a QR code with all your data, so tech geeks can scan your card using a mobile app, instead of having to hand-enter your contact info.

A design for a nice-looking card is inexpensive, and just about every graphic designer can produce one. Don't be cheap or cut corners with the print quality though, since this creates a needlessly bad first impression. And if you are a stickler for originality, try something like Moo.com, which will also send you a sample pack for free.

The use of academic degrees is loosely connected with these cards. Many professionals wonder if they should state their degree(s), and if so, where. The basic rule is simple:

If you have a good university education in the same field as your business or a related one, and stating degrees is also typical for your field (law, architecture, medicine, etc.), it's generally better to state your degree within business and written communication, because it strengthens your trustworthiness relative to competitors without a (full) education, who are pushing in from all sides. You can state your degree on your cards, in your email signature, in printed materials, in your brief bio, on your website, etc.

Are there times when you shouldn't state your degree? If it's not from a good school. If you are writing personally or informally. On social networks. In fields where it's not customary (marketing, media, photography, etc.). In general, wherever the degree isn't needed to show your expertise. You definitely need to go with your sense of style here, but whenever you're unsure, just leave it out.

I recommend that you don't state a lower degree at all, and if you do, then only if it is tightly connected with your services. The same applies to the foreign degrees or certifications that professionals sometimes place after their names; see for example this catch from LinkedIn: *John Doe, CISA, CISM, CGEIT, PMP, ITIL*. One key certificate after the name, sure, but five?

⊗ YOUR EMAIL FOOTER ISN'T JUST A SIGNATURE

Thanks to social media networks and messaging, we all send fewer personal emails than we used to, but our work-email counts are likely rising. We send out tens (if not hundreds) every week to many recipients, who naturally read them as well.

So you can use your emails' footer, which is typically placed into every message automatically as a signature, as a space for sharing both what you do and what's new. Such a news footer might look something like this:

--

John Galt
Independent Recruiter & Headhunter
www.johngalt.nyc ~ whois@johngalt.nyc ~ (212) 212-2121

Read the revised edition of The Wealth of Nations: johngalt.nyc/won

If you do try to fit any sort of news or marketing message into your email footer, keep it as simple and as typographically clean as possible. In an overstuffed footer full of graphical elements, a message like this will be completely overlooked, and your recipients will go banner-blind.

But you can also play with a footer in other ways. If you make your living through writing, you can add here a recent phrase you have crafted well. And if you put your best on social media networks, you can promote your profiles instead of your news.

You also should know that when you add a link to a YouTube video or a Google doc to a footer, Gmail shows a clickable preview of it directly underneath the email.

CAREER STATISTICS, PERSONAL BIOS AND MILESTONES

Nobody cares where you went to high school or that you worked a year with some ancient technology 15 years ago. So more and more often, important biographical facts get compressed into just key statistics or highlights of career successes and milestones.

The statistics are fairly simple – you can simply meticulously collect some time-lapse data and present the most interesting ones on your website or presentation: How many people you have trained over the years. How many projects and orders you have behind you. How many people downloaded your e-book or app. In short, any objective indicators of your professional level and experience.

For example, Tim Ferriss lists these metrics right in the header of the website for his popular podcast The Tim Ferriss Show: *200+ million episodes downloaded, 6,000+ 5-star reviews, 3× annual "best of" iTunes.*

Naturally, clients do care about our career histories. We just need to avoid outdated structured CVs and resumes. People mainly want to know what makes us different, the pillars of our expertise, the stairs a professional climbed to greatness and success.

If people understand your story and mission, it powerfully increases your chances for acquiring orders and for harmonious cooperation. This is no small thing. Only a fraction of freelancers know how to tell the story of their business in a way that is unobtrusive, convincing, and gripping.

This *professional story* inevitably supports a good name, because when other people talk about your work, they're not just talking about raw facts and statistics: They are telling stories! And if you can't tell your own story yourself, what are the chances others can retell it for you?

Your overview of career successes and milestones is sort of a "best of" selection for people that are meeting you for the first time. Unlike a CV, it's not an unbroken full overview. You can skip years and pick out just the best highlights, ideally from the present backwards.

If you are a top expert, you can spice up your overview with a publishing and media history. You then have a sense of completeness that is close to a classic CV, but in a style that remains informal and simple.

Your brief career bio is even shorter. It's generally a single bio paragraph written formally in the third person, which you can use for brief presentations, when you are giving interviews for the media, lecturing at conferences, etc. Attach your photo, and you will have a brief author or speaker profile. Here is an example of a well composed bio used to present the books and work of Austin Kleon, who also keeps an extended version on his website:

> AUSTIN KLEON is a writer who draws. His books, *Steal Like an Artist*, *Show Your Work!*, and *Steal Like an Artist Journal* have over a million copies in print. His work has been featured on NPR's *Morning Edition*, PBS *NewsHour*, and in the *New York Times* and the *Wall Street Journal*; he also speaks frequently about creativity in the digital age for organizations such as Pixar, Google, SXSW, TEDx, and *The Economist*. He lives in Austin, Texas, with his wife and children, and online at austinkleon.com.

Professionals in demand tend to have a bio like this ready at hand. It's a sort of formal foundation that a recipient will either use as-is, or shorten, or supplement and adjust as needed.

Both your bio and the summary of your professional milestones are easy to create and hardly ever need maintenance; they're typically updated once a year, when reviewing what went well and what you stand behind. But it's important, that your bio, milestones, as well as all your other outputs tell the same story and accent the same expertise or core business.

◉ THE SINS AND PITFALLS OF PERSONAL BRANDING

The recommendations I've gone over in this chapter so far belong to the simple, basic ones. But when we look out farther ahead, things get harder – in terms of finances, time, brains, or knowledge. A freelancer will have to weigh the decision about whether or not to leap into the items below.

The issues of websites, blogging, and social networks that I went over in the last chapter are perfect examples of rather-demanding marketing. Your professional mission and the things that make you stand out – your ability to raise awareness and educate the public, the originality of your ideas, and the benefits you bring to your field – are also good examples.

Each topic below could be given its own lengthy chapter. While I won't be going into them so deeply, I would at least like you to have an idea of what they involve, so you can better decide where to invest your energy, money and time. But even this shouldn't be seen as a full list. After all, new forms of smart freelance marketing are constantly being born.

First of all, let's return to a topic that tempts many freelancers: personal branding, i.e. a marketing attempt to influence other people's image of you.

As I mentioned in the chapter on a good name, in some sense it is reasonable to work on your personal brand, and I'll get to the practical details in a bit. But you should also know that this is a slightly stale and outdated approach, due to how it tries to stuff complex human beings into predefined boxes. To review the reasons why many professionals are abandoning artificial brands and letting their work speak for them instead, see Jessica Holland's article *The Case Against Personal Brands,* written for BBC Business. One person whom she cites in it is the successful author and Facebook COO Sheryl Sandberg:

"You don't have a brand…Crest has a brand. Perrier has a brand. People are not that simple. When we are packaged, we're ineffective and inauthentic… Don't package yourself."

This names and pinpoints the whole problem. The *brand totality* approach is based on the conviction that a personal brand encompasses everything. It's practical to some degree, when you are working on *someone's* brand, because it leads you to realize that you really can't leave out *anything* that is in conflict with a newly installed brand. You can imagine this *totality* as a bubble that surrounds a freelancer from all sides. In that case it has to be a pretty damn tough bubble, one that will never pop or burst. Someone is always there to make sure it doesn't. And yes, all this really is done…when you are building the brand of a pop star or global celebrity. And it's enormously expensive.

But you are an expert above all, and you can have a stellar reputation without any kind of branding. And your reputation is worth more than an artificial brand, no matter how *total.*

Yet personal branding is useful all the same.

If you're able to distinguish between your personal brand and your real reputation, if you appreciate the difficulty, and if you don't overdo it, it will help you stand out, establish better expectations, get more interesting jobs, and influence others' perceptions a tiny bit more.

Still, personal branding is a *skill*. It's not a natural ability, but a very difficult marketing challenge, because a brand-builder can't make serious mistakes. Remember, you have only one reputation.

The biggest sins in badly done personal brands include self-centeredness bordering on narcissism, which mainly plagues those professionals who build their brand themselves and pull the strings until they are completely tangled up in them. They spend so long shouting *me, Me, ME* that they only hear their own echo and miss the world around them.

Overhyping and kitsch are some other common problems, as is amateurism, where your brand is being built by someone who doesn't know a thing about it. And actually, *most* personal brands are like this.

⊘ YOUR BRAND WON'T BE BUILT IN A DAY

It may seem that if you avoid mistakes when building your personal brand and if you don't mistake your reputation for your brand, you've won. But branding isn't just a battle that can be won. It's more an endless campaign that you can never abandon.

A good personal brand needs to be maintained and renewed; it's not a one-off act.

So once you have created your comprehensive personal brand, you've set a high bar. There is no way back. You have to constantly refine it to keep it relevant and current, or else it will fade and become outdated. Even the very best photo loses its touch of originality and shows its age, just like the person within the frame. Even a logo needs an update every once in a while, as do websites; blogs need entries, offices need repainting…

There are far more professionals who have kicked off their personal brand with a lovely website, blog, lectures, and lots of activities, only to give up in a few years, than veterans with decades on the market who see their brand still strengthening. While the first group, exhausted, have abandoned big plans, the second group has stuck to a few tools. Creating a nice personal brand is hard, but it's far harder to maintain and expand it for years.

For your brand to have an effect on others in some way, it logically has to connect with them somehow, which is done over various media and in different places. These are a brand's *touchpoints*, and there can truly be a lot of them. Here is a far from complete list of touchpoints for a personal brand:

A precisely defined expertise, specialization, and core business. A professional story. An elevator pitch. A representative photo. A well-set price matched with your expertise and professional status. A web presentation. An online portfolio. A professional blog. A video blog or podcast. Social media networks. A LinkedIn CV. Testimonials. Important contacts. Clothing and appearance. A logo and visual style. Business cards, flyers, etc. Media PR and cooperation. Your entry on Wikipedia (it's your problem if it contains mistakes). Training, lecturing, and publishing activities. A nice-looking office or shop. Professional activities within your field. Various memberships. Networking. Your public opinions...

Naturally you understand that keeping all this current and cohesive demands an abundance of time. This might be a solvable problem for a high-income established expert. However, if you are building your brand yourself and are short on resources and long on work, you have to ration your strength intelligently, because a swift initial sprint won't win the branding marathon. Exceptional personal brands are built to last. And the initial strategy for them comes out of this.

THE FOUNDATION OF PERSONAL BRANDING: BE CONSISTENT

On an elementary level you can think of a personal brand as a precise harmonization of your professional activities so that their individual elements don't clash and instead work together to create a meaningful, coherent whole.

Look into where and how you present yourself and whether one of your touchpoints isn't perhaps telling a completely different story. To start, you can just google your name and be aware of what each page, photo, or video says about you.

Taken this way, personal branding means that you don't add, but instead rather correct the outputs and activities you already have, potentially including your prices as well. Here and there you adjust, remove, or correct something; it's a fairly easy process. The result is a sort of foundation for a modest, conflict-free, and positive brand:

Modest in that you're not adding anything, just tightly joining what you have done so far. *Conflict-free* in that the brand's elements don't clash or compete: you remove or suppress those that do. *Positive*, because you are just trying to communicate the same thing in all directions better and more clearly.

On this elementary level, personal branding will help nearly every freelancer. It doesn't include any special marketing activities; it's just a cleaning-up and unifying of what you are already doing, and you don't need any experts for it. It's taking a deeper level of consideration about how understandable and consistent you are for other people.

But be sure to get used to the fact that no matter how unified your personal brand is, different people will still perceive it very differently. Although unification will prevent major misunderstandings and mistakes, don't suffer under the illusion that you can define your own image so precisely that everyone sees it the same way. This will save you many disappointments. Your brand should essentially help people to understand you better – not dictate to them how they should perceive you and what opinion they should have about you.

⊛ ADVANCED PERSONAL BRANDS: A RESHAPED WHOLE

Professional personal branding goes much farther. It involves reshaping the whole and adding or removing elements in order to create a new and better result. I won't go into the details, because that would take a whole chapter, but I will advise one thing: *Unless you're a born marketer, hire somebody else who already does personal brands well.*

And by this I don't mean people who create shallow psychobabble videos or e-books about how we *all* have a personal brand, or *all* are brands. I mean professionals who truly work on personal brands, have mastered this subject in great depth, and have a proven track record of already helping a number of successful professionals towards an appealing brand. One hour with such a person can mean more for you than weeks of your own thoughts, because their trained eye may quickly grasp your professional strengths and weaknesses.

Where can you find such a consultant? This is a great question, because personal branding is a fairly invisible profession due to its nature. The creators of great personal brands don't actively promote their work; they tend to rely on word-of-mouth. After all, high-profile clients care about having their brand look natural and authentic, and so they likely won't want to declare loudly to the world that it's an altered or entirely artificial self-styling.

Nevertheless, brand-builders' clients are still the guide for finding a good one. Ask professionals whose public presentation feels convincing and trustworthy for you, like a whole that has been fully worked out and thought through on all sides. Experience says that either they are talented and self-taught brand-builders, or there's another smart brand-maker working behind the scenes. Either way, you have hit on someone who is able to advise you.

A brand manager who only works on company brands will be worthless for you. Company brands are done completely differently and differ in their strategy and tools. To be honest, this kind of consultant can do more harm than good if they are inexperienced in personal branding.

A qualified consultant will give you strategy and feedback for your ideas, but most of the heavy lifting will probably be on you. Yet your cooperation can lead to a personal brand that is professional, maintained, and unforced.

Professional because it gives that impression and because professionals are involved in making it. *Maintained* because you haven't bitten off more than you can chew, and so it has continuity and doesn't feel outdated. *Unforced* because it feels natural, like perfect makeup. It emphasizes only your true merits.

Every consultant works with personal brands differently. With some of them the brand will feel so natural, you can hardly tell it was built. Others have a more obvious, distinguishable signature. Some creators work with *brand archetypes*, while others reject them and stylize personal brands based on their own opinions and principles. Some allow their clients to exercise total freedom to complete their brands, while others advise what they should or shouldn't say or do within the brand they're building.

Advanced personal branding is a decathlon, and so you can find yourself running and jumping through things that corporate branding ignores, like open courses, intellectual marketing, and dressing in style. Naturally, you can use each of these demanding approaches separately as well – and I'll be spending the rest of the chapter on them.

CLOTHING AND APPEARANCE

Personal styling applies mainly to those professionals who regularly visit companies, give lectures or trainings, or appear in the media, and need more than one good outfit.

Nice clothing and an overall vigorous, good appearance can definitely have an influence on whether you can justify a higher price or negotiate better conditions. Or whether you will get an order at all, because certain clients care a lot about appearance and behavior.

You'll need a slightly different appearance for every field. One and the same outfit will have a different effect for a lawyer, a craftsman, or an IT guy. Still, unless you are completely blind, it's not that hard to intuitively grasp the basic principles.

Top professionals who have to dress well for a variety of social events either have a sense of fashion and would be fully capable of managing this alone, or have a partner with a better eye. Or they have hired a stylist who cultivates their wardrobe, eliminates bad items, proposes a suitable personal style, advises them on keeping up with clothing and footwear trends, and helps them with purchases.

The purchase of a dozen new items of clothing can be cut down to just two or three hours at a pleasant pace, because a stylist's steps are sure. They know your preferences and measurements and have an eye for nice-looking, high-quality items at reasonable prices.

The result will generally be better and faster than if you had sought and tried on items yourself. Some stylists even know backstreet boutiques, or for major shopping sprees they will take you somewhere with a larger selection or the same clothing at lower prices.

A stylist can also tell you discreetly that you should use a (different) deodorant or perfume, or that a clothing item, hairstyle, beard, pair of glasses, etc. doesn't suit you. In short they can tell you things that are usually not socially acceptable to tell even one's friends or colleagues.

Experienced stylists can sometimes also serve as makeup artists, and they have great contacts for barbers, hair salons, cosmeticians, nutrition consultants, and other specialists.

When seeking a stylist, I recommend that you look both at the price and at whom they tend to serve: are these mainly people from fields like yours? And while I hate to say it, I have to discriminate here a little bit – stylists from big cities tend to charge higher rates, but also often have a better awareness of current fashion trends and access to shops.

Once again, make use of references. Top professionals who frequently appear in public either style their clothing themselves (maybe with help from their partner) or get help from professionals. There is nothing simpler than to praise their wardrobe and ask if they could give you a contact for their stylist. Even if it turns out they don't have one, you will have at least made their day a little brighter.

⊙ YOUR LOGO AND VISUAL STYLE

The need for a logo and a unified visual style can arise gradually as new visual outputs for a freelancer pile up – their website, business cards, presentations for lectures, letterheads, roll up banner stand ads for training courses, social media network graphics, etc.

If they design each element separately and use a mixture of fonts and colors, or do this work completely on their own with no prior experience, the result can look fairly disorganized, even off-putting.

A better solution is to hire a graphic designer and have them design a unified visual style that will contain everything needed. This style can include a logo, but it doesn't have to. The same applies to a photo portrait, colors, preferred fonts, graphic elements, or icons.

You'll find it easier and cheaper to arrive at unified visuals if the same designer is behind both your visual style and the graphic layout of your website. The alternative, meanwhile, is for one designer to design the visual style along with a graphics manual, and for the web designer to adhere to it, or for the web designer to produce a nice site, from which a universal visual style is deduced later. The first route is formally correct, the second is more common, but both of them can lead to good results.

It's smart to ask your colleagues about prices. For example I have one client who paid several thousand dollars for her logo, business cards, and letterhead. Is that a lot, or is it a little? Well, some other designer would provide a result in similar level of quality for less than a quarter of the price and with a much more detailed graphics manual.

Quality should be foremost, but reasonable prices and costs are also important considerations. A number of freelance graphic designers specialize in creating visual identities, and if you speak to them about this, they'll surely propose a price adapted to a freelancer's possibilities.

What I don't recommend is to use crowdsourcing services or ready-made designs for important graphics such as a personal logo and visual style. The price may seem attractive, but unfortunately independent reviews of these services show a disturbingly high number of stolen ideas, uncredited use of stock images, and other sins. If you want an original visual style and logo, speak to a specific designer, not a nameless crowd.

LOCATION, LOCATION, LOCATION

There is a difference between having a headquarters or place of business in a big city vs. a small town in the middle of nowhere. I'm not trying to say that a professional from Nowheresville can't be first-rate. But they're far away.

If they can't do all their work remotely and they want to work with premium city clients, they will have to head into the city sometimes, or set up an office or virtual headquarters, for example at some coworking space, where they can come for meetings and events.

The hubs of the freelance economy are often clustered around major cities. For example, a survey by the British association IPSE named *Exploring the UK Freelance Workforce in 2016* states that a full 43% of British freelancers are situated in southeastern England. Half of these live in Greater London, with their numbers having grown by 59% since 2008. And this isn't only true for Great Britain.

So for a freelancer from the countryside, one of the smartest and most beneficial marketing steps could be to occasionally head into a large city for work and face to face meetings.

When people talk about market positioning, they generally don't mean physical locations. But we freelancers are once again a small exception. If you live and work somewhere long-term, you meet the people there and create new contacts, and naturally it has an influence on your business. For jet-set professionals who are in a different city practically every day it doesn't really matter if they are from Nowheresville, but for their colleagues who have settled-down in the countryside, it's definitely something to think about.

COMMUNITY BUILDING

You can get involved and be active in a community, or you can also create one. It's definitely difficult and it's not for everyone, but you don't have to be alone. You can get together with other freelancers and divide up the work. This can be a local group of freelancers who regularly meet or hold meetups, or a professional community built around interesting methods, technologies, approaches, etc.

Building a community is an uplifting experience. As a (co)founder, you will learn a lot about human nature and might make more contacts than other people do over their whole lives. The wealth of stimuli and opportunities are also an advantage. Possible disadvantages lie in mismanaged relations with certain people and the possibility of burnout over time, if you don't find a successor or someone who can cover for you soon enough.

A community is a living organism, and as such it has its own character and phases of development. You will be expanding it, connecting it, cultivating it, informing, educating, and maybe even protecting it from the spread of nonsense and parasites, which swarm quite a bit around every functional community. The beautiful part is that there is nothing binding you; you don't have to complain about inflexible statutes and inability to change. You're starting from square one and you can bring as many people along as you can support.

PARTICIPATING IN BUSINESS CONTESTS

Looking back at what helped me the most to grow my own business, winning the Czech Self-Employed Person of the Year contest is definitely a top contender. But gold vs. silver doesn't matter here. What matters is the spotlight and how many people are suddenly interested in what you have to say and whether you can use this opportunity for something good.

I decided to use it to better promote the work of freelancers. For me, this was a pathway to the media and the start of my cooperation with many great journalists and editors; it pushed me forward in how I perceived my mission.

Similar contests surely exist in your country or region as well, and registration is usually free. So all that's left to ask is: *Why not give it a try?*

You can certainly find plenty of good reasons to compete, but the financial and other rewards for the winners generally aren't among them; these are mostly symbolic. Don't expect an instant jump in income either. The real rewards in such a contest is prestige. And think about it – you can enter for free. Just fill out the registration form, and you either will or won't join the finalists. This is about the worst that can happen.

Even just filling out the form will force you to think about your business from an unusual perspective. It will lead you to consider whether you stand out on the market and have anything that others don't. And you will also learn to tell your whole business story better. Before I stopped entering these contests and started helping others to do so, I signed up several years in a row and rewrote my submission each time. To make my story clearer and more comprehensive.

And you may have an exceptional story too – but not be able to write it well. The solution's easy. Join up with a copywriter and play with it.

PUBLIC SPEAKING AND PUBLISHING ACTIVITIES

There are still a few marketing topics related to spreading your ideas left to touch upon.

If you are publishing or lecturing at conferences and other professional events, be original and try to not constantly repeat yourself – in the online era of publicly available videos, detailed reports on attendees' blogs, and the 24/7 flow of information on social networks, it doesn't make sense.

Naturally it's *possible* to merely change your lectures only slightly depending on the circumstances and audience, but it's always good to say something new. That way even if someone is seeing you for the tenth time, they will look forward to your speech (or contribution) and take something from it. Just like journalists, public speakers and lecturers also have their own key topics, but that doesn't mean they should repeat themselves. We follow genuine personalities because they always entertain and surprise us with something new. They broaden our vision of the world.

The exception are the professional speakers or lecturers who earn their living by giving lectures or courses, presenting the same, or nearly the same, information to different audiences. A professional perfects their delivery and the topics they elaborate on; they can easily do five or six events a week. But even they want to shine all the brighter by adding something new at a big conference or other important occasion, where a number of people who have heard them many times might be in attendance.

If you have time to prepare and want to work on your public speaking skills, there are plenty of opportunities. Most organizers of repeating events are always on the lookout for new topics and faces.

If this is tempting for you, prepare two or three attractive topics in your field, including a brief summary, and try approaching the organizers of small events or the operators of local coworking centers who hold lectures and meetups. It's better to make your beginner's mistakes in front of a smaller audience rather than imploding on a big stage. Public speaking is a pastime that should fill you with excitement and energy. And when it excites you, it will likely excite your listeners too.

It's similar with publishing: good authors for topics are precious commodities, especially on the internet. Editors could truly tell you tales about finding and subsequently shepherding expert writers to meet their deadlines. The pay isn't great (or there's none), and not every author is reliable enough to deliver the promised articles on time. So if you've got an attractive topic and want to try out a few articles, it generally isn't hard to arrange some cooperation. But you can also publish on your blog beside this, or arrange a guest post on another author's blog.

Don't strive to have just any presentation at a prestigious event or an article on a well-known online media outlet. Strive to have an exceptional presentation or article there. You won't wow the world with an average performance.

For high-quality content, the size of a medium plays an ever smaller role, because on social networks, good content spreads on its own. A paid campaign on Facebook Ads can sometimes help as well. Promoting attractive content isn't expensive; in these cases a paid campaign can reach a low cost per click, and you can greatly expand the reach of your content for tens to a few hundreds of dollars.

The internet eases distribution, but it can't replace an experienced publisher or organizer. These serve as content gatekeepers, mentors, and curators. If you have a chance to cooperate with someone like this, it's generally better than self-publishing or self-producing. You can especially see this in non-fiction professional literature, where a publisher has the lion's share in determining the final product.

MEDIA COOPERATION

From publishing and public speaking activities, it's typically only a small step to media cooperation. You can find leading professionals in the media often. Cooperation of this kind is advantageous for both sides. Newspeople need independent authorities and experts for interviews or as quotable sources. And for freelancers, meanwhile, having a media presence confirms their expertise.

From this it follows that it's best to wait to begin your media cooperation until you are sure of your expertise and your core business. Because the moment the public has a fixed idea of you as something or other via the media, it will be hard to convince them that this proved to be a dead end and that you are already doing something else. And for people in the media as well, experts with a comprehensive professional history and a verifiable record of longstanding involvement in their field are more trustworthy.

It generally doesn't make any sense to nag journalists and editors. Here again, follow the principle once is enough. If you have an exceptional business story, topic, idea, or anything interesting at all, you won't have to wait until they sensationally discover you themselves. Approaching a journalist or editor who works on similar topics isn't impolite or imposing – quite the opposite. But you need to use common sense.

Many media professionals are grateful for a good tip. Many of them won't answer your messages, but if your proposal does interest someone, you've won. Don't hold it against the ones who don't react. They receive countless such proposals and press releases, and it's beyond their power to reply to all of them, especially if they do field work and face tight editorial deadlines. The media's reality runs faster than yours.

There is also a huge difference between suggesting a topic with a broad appeal, and sending journalists uninteresting content – de facto advertisements for you and your services. Here we are back to the problem of being too intrusive, stubborn and lacking good taste, which are among the sins in personal branding.

Don't try to force newspeople to write about how you are unique and number one. Try to look at it objectively: Have you pulled off something exceptional? Have you been the first in your country or the world to achieve something? Have you participated in a project with remarkable results? Maybe you've just done field research and have fresh data? Has something important happened in your field that the public should know about? This is an angle that journalists and editors in the media will like more than your heavy-handed self-recommendations.

The actual act of approaching people in the media basically amounts to ordinary polite communication. Most active members of an editorial team have either an editorial email address, a personal website (all the better if they are freelance), and often a findable Twitter or Facebook account as well. Choose the channel that seems the most appropriate for reaching out, and briefly write what is on your mind. This also implies you are reachable for further, or future comments and will be able to respond quickly, when needed.

However, if pushing topics personally upon the media isn't for you and you are fairly unsure if you can manage it yourself, there are still two alternatives. There are media PR classes out there, and then there is the option of cooperation with a PR consultant. For the less experienced, the latter it probably better at first than banging on closed gates, but comes with the risk of reaching out to the wrong person. So choose wisely.

I would say that established PR consultants are a safer and better bet, while I won't deny that even their junior colleagues (often journalism graduates) can have excellent ideas and get results as well.

So pay attention, not only to the terms of cooperation, but also who they have already represented, what the outputs looked like, and how they work. Don't accept general, evasive, or vague answers. Your PR consultant represents you for the media, so they should be reliable professionals with strong communication skills and a code of ethics. They can help you to express your message or story better and will use their contacts, strategies, and intimate knowledge of the media landscape to try to get you to specific editors or journalists.

PR services are not all that expensive, and some PR consultants will even agree to let you only pay for media outputs that actually get published – a sort of success fee. In the end everyone is satisfied – the editor, who has a relevant topic corresponding to their long-term focus, the PR consultant, who has made it happen, and of course you, because major media outlets have huge reach. For quality experts two or three major media outputs are generally enough for newspeople to start approaching you themselves when they are working on topics close to you.

The Nobel-winning physicist Richard Feynman, who was enormously popular with both the public and his students, once declared that he doesn't have bad experiences with media professionals, because his goal is to help them understand his field better. Not to help himself. I would recommend you take the same approach.

Media people usually don't understand a given topic in the same depth as you, an expert. So you can help both them and the public to understand it better, while also busting widespread myths and misconceptions. An admirable activity, and one that will bring more good than article quotes that stink of an effort to deliver self-promotion rather than information. An ordinary reader might not smell it, but your colleagues will, and so will anyone who understands the media.

Your media relationship isn't reciprocal, it's not 1:1, like other work and life relationships. It's an entirely counterintuitive 1:N relationship, where N might be thousands, maybe even millions of readers, listeners, or viewers. Be aware of this ratio – one article on a high-traffic site or one TV interview can impress more people than you will meet in person throughout your whole life! This relationship is so unimaginable and ungraspable for us that we have a tendency to view the media through the lens of ordinary relationships and, as a result, demand favors from newspeople. My advice is, don't do this.

Naturally you can agree with the author of an article or news report to have them, for example, include a link to your site, but I definitely wouldn't recommend insisting on it or making it a condition for cooperation. In the end, it's not the author who decides on the article's final appearance, but the editor or the editor-in-chief, and they don't care who promised what. Their job is to give their readers or viewers excellent content.

My experience is more that when I help some journalists, they themselves eventually find some way to thank me for my time in a way that is acceptable to their editors. But this isn't why I do it. My goal is to raise awareness, not do self-promotion. That then also brings a much better relationship with editors and reporters, many of whom have become my friends. We've even thought up some larger projects together. One other important rule applies here:

Don't publicly pretend to be an expert on topics outside your area of expertise.

That doesn't mean you can't publicly speak on things that affect you, for instance as a citizen. But avoid speaking as an expert to the media on things that are truly outside your professional knowledge, no matter how much the editors might think they are close and related topics. These types of media mishaps can harm an expert. Even if a layperson generally can't tell, experts in your field definitely can, and they may not soon forget it. It might end up making you one big joke among your colleagues.

The final authority on what lies entirely within your circle of competence isn't an editor; it's you. So if a request does cross the line here, just apologize, justify your reasons, refuse, and recommend a colleague. That makes it all the more likely that you will get a more targeted request later, and that you won't be seen as a talking head lecturing the public on A through Z.

⊘ PUBLIC COURSES

You might be saying: What is this doing in a chapter on marketing? Let me explain.

Activities that educate or train others are among the most powerful tools in freelance marketing, and it doesn't matter that the marketing effect is indirect via the recommendations of satisfied participants in the training or any subsequent business with them. It's hardly an exception for these secondary orders to bring in revenues several times larger than the sales for the course, even though these can be significant too.

For freelancers, it has never been easier to start giving courses than it is today, when coworking centers are trying to shape event programs for their members and fans. These communities' friendly atmosphere create exceptionally positive conditions for freelancers who want to educate others. They can explain the basics of their profession while also deepening their knowledge or working on all of the related skills – from rhetoric to event management, and these then lead them to organize more sophisticated courses.

A professional trainer or lecturer can devote an enormous amount of time to preparing their courses or other educational products such as e-books and e-learning videos. Their portfolio can also include a half-dozen readymade topics that they repeatedly sell to companies or via open public courses. But this route isn't viable for most other freelancers.

An expert lecturer who holds courses several times a week is quite different from a lecturing expert who holds them a few times a year. The latter tends to be far more involved in projects and a range of jobs, and lecturing is just one of them. They can spend far less time on it than a professional lecturer, for whom education is their main way of making a living in one way or another.

But there is one approach that lets even a busy expert organize first-rate courses at the level of professional lecturers: the product approach.

A course is a product. The question remains, is it a good, average, or bad product?

Creating a training course that leaves a deep impression on participants, gives them the needed knowledge or skills, and shakes their world is truly hard. It must be well developed and perfected in terms of teaching, content, production, and even maintenance, so that it still remains up-to-date after several years. It's an experience that has to be fine-tuned to perfection. And you won't manage that on the first go.

A course designed as a product has its distinct place on the market, just like an iPhone or a Volkswagen Golf. People buy it year after year and recommend it to each other. Because of this it has a place on the web, with a description, upcoming dates, and references. It's not a one-off act, but a repeating event, with a network of graduates built up around it.

The financial side of things is not unimportant here. Preparing an all-day or two-day professional course, including slides and other supplementary information for participants, can take weeks or even months. Then add in the hardly-small production costs, including managing the whole event on-site, and the risk that this new and unknown course will have empty seats. You might very well discover in the end that a one-time course like this simply doesn't pay off.

It may seem like a good compromise to hold such courses under the wings of some professional training agency that arranges the venue, people, marketing…everything. But then it's mainly their product, not yours. Some agencies offer dozens of different courses, and the trainer's role is secondary. But in any case you'll have to then find a partner that suits you in every way and will do good work, for a hefty fee charged on top of your own.

And years spent training under an agency means losing a lot of money. An ordinary trainer will only get a fraction of the profits from a day spent training. Top lecturers and presenters with carefully built up names make fairly good money, but it takes years to work up to that level.

Just try counting and comparing the typical pay for an agency lecturer (say for a few hundred dollars a day) with the profits from your own training course where you pay a bit for rent, refreshments, or help, and the rest goes to you. You will probably reach the conclusion that a few years of holding courses under an agency will rob you of a pile of money, and this is also the reason why top freelancers mostly organize their courses themselves. In short, it's a business too good to leave the profits to others.

Look up a dozen established courses organized by top freelancers around you, and you might find a number of things they have in common. If they are courses they run directly, sales will generally be direct, i.e. not done through an intermediary. And the course will either have an independent microsite, or a separate section on their main personal website with a description and a permanent URL address that can be linked to, which will almost certainly still be there in a year with at least one upcoming date.

But before you determinedly jump into preparing your own course, you should know that creating a training course as a product is very time-demanding, and it would be a mistake to ignore the time economy of the whole affair. When I sometimes help other freelancers to kick off their courses, I realize that especially for the ones who have family and limited time, this is a key issue.

So I would like to present you with a simple methodology for developing an independent course and launching it with limited risks and costs. You can bend it based on your own situation or needs; my main interest is to illustrate how step-by-step preparation with verification works at every level:

1. *The course topic.* It has to correspond to your expertise and be enjoyable in the long term.

2. *A one-page course summary:* Name, length, target group. Does it all make sense?

3. *The course outline* should be detailed. Ask one of your colleagues for feedback on it.

4. *The narrative test* consists of briefly describing the course to someone in an hour or so. Does it work for them?

5. *Announcing the plan* to organize the course on your website, social media networks, etc. Are enough people interested?

6. *A pilot course* that you give to a small group of colleagues and friends for the purpose of gathering feedback. What can you improve upon?

7. *An invitation only premiere* with a discount for people who gave you their email address after your announcement.

8. *Opening up registration* and making further improvements of each individual session.

Each phase represents a project milestone and insurance against dead ends. In each of the phases, you can show your preparation to someone and get feedback. If you are aware of the warning signals in time, you won't end up creating an expensive website and beautiful slides, spending half a year on preparation, to then find out that there isn't enough interest in your wonderful new course. You will discover any problems long before you spend your money and sacrifice time to preparations.

The same principles can be applied to online courses, that are even more expensive to produce and sell, as they require some advanced skills in video production and digital marketing. Not to mention full-fledged e-learning programs that also enable the lecturer to communicate with the participants. I have already touched on this topic in the previous chapter with advice about YouTube, so let me just add here that online courses can be both a steady source of income, and a powerful marketing tool to extend your good name to audiences around the world.

In any case, you will benefit from breaking up the costly production process into smaller steps, such as those described above, with a reality check closing out each one of them.

◉ INTELLECTUAL MARKETING

Public speaking and publishing activities, media cooperation, educating others and organizing courses…all this relates the formulating of your opinions and spreading your ideas. The next level after all this can lie in what I call, in brief, *intellectual marketing*, i.e. indirectly increasing the visibility of a professional by getting involved in professional public debate.

The term intellectual has a number of definitions, but here we are interested in the *public intellectual* – an educated person or professional who speaks on public issues. They actively choose topics and get engaged in public discussion, through which they help to shape its character and influence public opinion.

Almost every field has areas that overlaps into public life and into topics we all share. So it's no exception for leading experts to get involved in this public debate and formulate their opinions so that they express a professional standpoint on some broad problem:

An investor can give statements on how pension funds are managed and administered. A web designer can criticize an overpriced and unusable website of the state administration. A nutrition expert can advocate for changes in school lunches. A gamification expert can comment on how games like

Pokemon Go influence public spaces. A security analyst can comment on a case of identity theft.

I hardly have to add that practically no top experts do these things just to be seen; they do them as a part of advanced work in their field and as a civic duty. Despite this, the marketing effect is significant, and for this reason only, I call this intellectual marketing. It isn't exceptional that precisely such a fearless appearance in a heated public or political debate elevates an expert to a premier league of professionals in the eyes of the public.

And deservedly so, in a way, because public debates tend to be far more polarized and tense than professional ones. An expert who steps into it will often have to face insults, attacks from opponents, haters and anonymous trolls, which definitely isn't pleasant. But we as a society profit from the ongoing public debate. An honest interest in public affairs is valued highly, and this is why professionals in most developed countries will spice up their resumes with charity and non-profit activities.

But becoming a subject of public interest does have its risks. The arguments you bring into public discussion are a part of the historical record, making you, the intellectual, a historical and public figure. Through this you take on a certain kind of social responsibility, and you can be confronted with your current stances even after many years.

If this path is tempting for you, you should, above all else, have an idea of where public debate is ongoing, and among whom. This generally isn't debate under your Facebook posts – even though that is also a possibility if a few influencers join in on it, the public is enjoying it, and the bets on the winner are rising. There are no strict boundaries here, and quite often a debate will gel around influential media outlets, reporters, intellectuals, or experts, who repeatedly bring new topics into it or react to other people's comments from their own standpoint. So getting involved can actually be fairly easy.

The map of the resulting space for public debate can be complex. It may include Twitter, blogs on major news sites, important TV programs for debating current affairs, popular talk shows, influential independent opinion-based magazines, or even alternative media outlets, commercial or publicly funded media, and a number of other places where you can express yourself freely on a broad range of societal topics.

The same principle applies here as for media cooperation: stick to your expertise and your circle of competencies, and don't head off on a wild ride through subjects you don't really understand. You will usually serve yourself and the public best when you respect your limits, even though I'm sure it's not as fun as speaking with gusto on a wide spectrum of subjects that have no close connection to your main field. Being a universal intellectual is a rather hazardous sport.

MARKETING PLANS AND AD CAMPAIGNS

Ironically, marketing plans, which play such a strong role within corporate marketing (alongside the branding and marketing strategies), are a fairly marginal topic for freelancers. Only a small portion of freelancers create marketing plans and run classic ad campaigns, with a few exceptions I've already mentioned, such as PPC ads on the web.

It's due to our differing priorities. We freelancers have so many tools that are only indirectly or distantly related to conventional marketing and advertising that composing marketing budgets and planning them over time lacks any meaning.

If a good name, reliability, a clarified core business, quality, and professionalism lie at the top of marketing priorities, and if we additionally have a lot of other low-cost and highly effective options for promoting our businesses, this basically eliminates the need for conventional marketing for us. But I don't mean to say through this that it has *no* meaning. It's meaningful, and professionals who are growing and expanding will inevitably work their way to it in time. Although even then they will try to produce advertisements that are unobtrusive, unaggressive, and fully under their control.

KEY IDEAS

1. Freelancers' marketing looks and works completely differently from company marketing. Often without advertising.

2. The foundation lies mainly in reputation, a clear core business, expertise, quality, and reliability.

3. Social bonds, from weak to strong, are the dominant source of order leads for most freelancers.

4. Our marketing is based on conservative, proven, and safe approaches.

5. We each only have one good name. This is why we prioritize methods that we understand.

6. A freelancer doesn't so much need a logo as they do a great headshot. It will be everywhere.

7. Stating your degree is a matter of your field's unwritten rules. Sometimes appropriate, sometimes not.

8. Instead of a resume, use career statistics, a professional bio and milestones, and sometimes LinkedIn.

9. Personal branding is optional, and it's an absolute ultra-marathon.

10. There is a lot more out there if you are ambitious: styling, contests, media, intellectual marketing, and more.

PRACTICE

✓ Ask selected clients and colleagues for testimonials that you can use to promote your work and services. Do it also after each major successful gig or project.

✓ Get systematic in mapping outstanding freelance professionals in and around your field and consider recommending others more. Hopefully you will meet many of them too.

✓ Have your current portrait photo evaluated by people that understand its purpose and context. And if it is not good enough, have a new one taken by a pro.

✓ Consider compiling a personal bio and career milestones, that could be used on your website and wherever you will be presenting your work to a new audience.

✓ Personal branding check-up! If you have already tweaked your online profiles (as suggested in the last chapter), try now to fine-tune all the remaining touchpoints as well.

PERSONAL FINANCES
AND RISK PREVENTION

How can you prepare for the worst?

Doing business brings a number of risks as well as opportunities to make a profit. And the risks are hardly small. Otherwise nearly everyone would be running their own business, which clearly isn't the case.

The large risks come from uncertainty and swings in incomes and expenses. Other risks are the result of the different legal standing and increased liabilities of entrepreneurs relative to employees. And then there are the risks that are unknown. These come from exceptional events that can derail us entirely.

But professionals are not victims. A freelancer is an entrepreneur and an active player in the game, who can bend chance to their own benefit. They can meet opportunities halfway, while identifying, suppressing, and avoiding risks one by one.

However, risk will never be reduced to zero. No matter how much effort you invest in strengthening your security or trying to transfer risks to a third party, for instance through a contract or insurance, there will always be a not so small residual risk. And for precisely this reason, it makes sense to work with risks systematically even if you can deftly handle the risks that are well-known. There will still be more residual risks than you would prefer.

Your first line of defense against risks lies in things I have already gone over: the legality of your business, as well as your good name, quality, reliability, honesty, etc. But many risks are related to money, which is either itself the cause of the problem, or forms a cushion to swiftly resolve it. So here I'll shine a light on both *risks* and *finances*.

ACCEPT FAILURE AS A POSSIBILITY

Hundreds of business plans have passed through my hands, and one trait shared by most of them is that they are overly optimistic. This is good on the one hand, because if it weren't for bold entrepreneurial visions, we would all be robbed of innovations and the products of those who manage to succeed.

But if a plan only assumes quick and stable growth, or if it doesn't assume the possibility of failure, confrontation with reality is often crushing. Many businesses fail despite their founders' efforts (according to SBA.gov, roughly half within 5 years), and it often isn't even their fault. It may just be bad luck, or it may be bad timing, because some markets are so highly competitive that even a promising project can fail, and often will.

It's somewhat natural to downplay future risks. But many personality traits are natural – including aggression and laziness – so don't use your nature to excuse excessive risk tolerance. Still, I place the greatest blame on the salesmen of success with advice like *hold on and you'll succeed.* Determination is doubtlessly useful, but it's no guarantee of success. It's merely a prerequisite. And sometimes it's more reasonable to close up shop and try again later and in a better way.

Old hands are smarter than that, not to mention investors, who have already heard countless fairy tales. They know from experience that things rarely go as smoothly, as people believe they might, even with fantastic ideas. This is sometimes jokingly called a *spreadsheet business,* where all the factors in the tables grow beautifully for ten years to come. But the real world tends to be full of wrong turns and rough patches. Success is typically the product of enormous amounts of concentration, professionalism, luck, and last-minute redemptive decisions.

So an experienced entrepreneur plans for both success and failure. They assume that not every idea or plan will work out: out of ten projects perhaps five will work, but *not* all of them. They know how to tame the optimism that comes from their enthusiasm for something new – they have both optimistic and pessimistic scenarios, to deliberately admit the chance of failure.

Now, we all have an optimistic scenario. But we should all also have a pessimistic one, for what will happen when business is slow or just isn't happening. And what does that look like? How big will the losses be? And will it be possible to close down the failing business without angering your customers?

The third, realistic scenario is in-between – neither a spectacular overnight success nor a clear failure. In fact, it quite strongly fits the business stories of successful entrepreneurs (the real ones, not the ones who shout about their successes): lots of work, problem-solving, dead ends, and daily administration, but occasionally something working out, and that then appearing like an instant success. Many have gone through personal crises, burnout, and tough conflicts, which they had to resolve and overcome along the way, even if they don't mention it publicly. Their greatness lies in how they have been able to make it through these periods, how hard work is not a problem for them, and how they have learned to fully enjoy the climaxes and reap the rewards of their work.

How you will evaluate the different scenarios is also connected with your mindset, which will change over time. Daniel Gladis, a successful European investor and the founder of the EU-based Vltava Fund, offers an excellent guideline here. He never makes important decisions when he is 1. hungry, 2. underslept, 3. feeling any frustration or discomfort, or 4. under time pressure. Through this, he significantly reduces the risk of completely misreading a situation.

◉ HOW TO LOOK ON THE BRIGHT SIDE OF BAD SITUATIONS?

Where there's a will, there's a way. When your risk prevention works well and you eliminate problems before they happen, the result is a positive feeling. We probably all have a fundamental need for security and aversion to risks, large or small. But while a dash of risk may be the spice of life, only a fool would want it by the fistful.

Mapping risks and preventing them can thus be something rather pleasant.

Take some time to list all of the risks that you know could threaten your business and well-being. It might be a few dozen.

Next, rank them. Put the most damaging and probable at the top. While at the bottom place the least damaging and lowest probability ones.

Next, think about the list's top items and what steps you could take to reduce or eliminate these risks. Write down all the measures that occur to you and also state the approximate time and financial requirements for each measure.

Gradual risk prevention means that whenever you have the time, you simply tackle one risk after the other. You will likely start with those that are serious, but also the cheapest to prevent. Then you can move on to those that are equally serious, but a bit more expensive to prevent, etc. Your progress might not be so fast due to your other duties, but in a few months you will have a much better situation, and it will greatly affect how you feel about your business.

Risk mapping also requires a willingness to admit your own deficiencies. For example, a professional who tends to bend under pressure can draft some bulletproof terms and conditions and internal rules of negotiation for them to stick to under every circumstance.

It's not rocket science; it just takes time. A few examples of typical risks and how to prevent them:

- *Repeated non-payment problems → securing debts and taking upfront payments*
- *Break-ins and equipment theft → security doors and windows, an alarm with a security service, and insurance*
- *Income and expense fluctuations → stabilizing your client portfolio, financial self-management, and reserves*
- *Loss of a key colleague → introducing processes; duplicating roles and knowledge within your team*
- *Discrepancies in documents and invoices → finding a better accountant and running an audit*
- *Leaking of sensitive documents → shredding, PC security, and encrypting your phone and disk*
- *Data loss → regular backups in multiple secure locations*
- *Car breakdown → keeping a tune-up and maintenance schedule, insurance, and a roadside assistance service*
- *Equipment breakdown → servicing support, regular maintenance or repairs, financial reserves*
- *Risks due to your own high investment in the project → a second investor or crowdfunding*
- *Security for your family in the case of an accident or death → a high-quality, high-limit life-insurance policy*
- *Repeated health problems → changes in lifestyle, supplementary illness and disability insurance*
- *Debt spirals → living within your means and gradually reducing your debt, consulting with experts*

Business is always harder when you are in debt. Loans are often a sort of bet on a better future, one where you will easily be able to pay for what you can't afford now. Yet the future can also be different and worse than the picture you're painting for yourself (or someone else is painting for you). If you can handle your debt even in the pessimistic scenario, then why not – but never borrow large sums while imagining the best scenario.

Your health is fundamental. As freelancers, we are extra-vulnerable during illnesses and accidents due to our irreplaceability. If you are sick often, staying reliable for clients will be a difficult challenge – not to mention dealing with the loss of income.

So as freelancers we have an increased motivation to care about our long-term health and to have reasonable security during any long-term illness or disability. The fact that freelancers are active until an advanced age in advanced economies is partly due to their reasonable regimens and active lifestyles, along with access to good general health care and preventive medicine. A bad health regimen has a cumulative effect and will be more likely an issue for people over 60 than for people in their thirties.

Having quality health, injury, and life insurance, with no shortsighted compromises, should be a given for every established freelancer. Insurers let you configure your insurance coverage quite reasonably to cover what you need, from your family to the health risks related to your profession.

Your list can be much longer, but that shouldn't worry you; in any case it's best to eliminate risks gradually, one by one. As you can see, sometimes you can stop even large risks with fairly cheap, undemanding measures. Fire prevention is usually much cheaper than firefighting.

Your prevention will stop the risks you know about, and you have a financial reserve for the rest. This reserve thus serves to balance out income and expense fluctuations, and also as your universal insurance against catastrophes large and small, like a wrecked car, the loss of your work computer, or temporary disability along with income loss. Problems like these are easier to solve if you have money set aside for a rainy day and can reach for it immediately when needed.

FINANCIAL SELF-MANAGEMENT

Prevention is only the first half of the solution; financial self-management and having a reserve are the second.

As I mentioned in the chapter on the advantages and disadvantages of freelancing, the most frequently mentioned disadvantage of freelancing lies in its financial instability, and this is tightly connected with risks. Bad financial management combined with low reserves produces a kind of manic-depressive experience: *One month is a boom, the next month a bust.* And like every roller-coaster, it gets tiring fast. Financial instability brings stress and fears and makes you feel more insecure.

If your reserves are insufficient and your costs exceed your income, your rainy day funds will quickly be exhausted, and then you will be either in debt, desperately seeking some quick income, or forced to go out of business if your dive into the red goes too deep. Many freelancers have minor financial reserves, but not enough to save them from major problems. And also, having a reserve alone is not enough.

According to the *Freelancing in America 2017* survey, only 41% of the freelancers surveyed understand their finances, which is nearly one third less than for employees. Quite an alarming state of affairs. Three out of five American freelancers don't understand their own financial situation, and in my experience, things won't be much better in other countries. Can a professional – an entrepreneur – afford to not understand their finances? And what does that actually say about their resistance to risk?

"Before I made the decision to quit my full-time job in 2011, my husband David and I agreed that we would make a real budget (for the first time in our lives…oops) and stick to it, so that we would actually *know* whether or not we could sustain ourselves with freelancing," recalls Melissa Joulwan, author of the *Well Fed* cookbook series. "It was just a simple 2-hour meeting, but it changed our lives," she says about how important their decision proved to be.

It's convenient to ignore finances during an economic boom, because there is no shortage of work. So hard financial discipline tends to mainly pay off during such career transitions, or personal problems, illnesses, dry spells, and downswings. I would like to spend the rest of this chapter showing you how to acquire the necessary self-discipline, so that you can *enjoy* it instead of getting turned away by unnecessary complexity.

I have divided up financial self-management into five stages that naturally tie into each other. You can introduce them one by one, or all at once – which I don't recommend, but I know from experience that it does work as well. And you may want to add other approaches yourself. I certainly won't protest.

The five stages listed below have increasing degrees of difficulty. You can think of them like the scale from elementary education, which everyone should have, all the way up to your degree in finance that goes far beyond the needs of ordinary freelancers.

1. MONTHLY REVENUES
Time demands: 10 minutes a month

A precise record of your monthly revenues is a part of your time-lapse overviews and statistics that will help you monitor the governing dynamics and trends in your business. Thus besides revenue, you can also record other indicators such as website traffic, the number of new orders, and hours worked – but this is a side matter for now.

In any case, you can make do with a simple spreadsheet. Every month, enter your monthly income, either based on invoices issued or payments actually received, which is likely the better option. And the longer you keep these records, the more they will be able to tell you. That will make it easy to get an objective measure of business performance aside from your feelings.

If, for example, you have the feeling that this month and last month were seriously weak and something might be wrong, you can compare them with one year (and two years) ago. Then you might find out that it's only a seasonal swing that repeats every year and that you are actually doing better this year. But next time you could prepare better for the low season – proactively arrange more work, shift some clients to this period through clever pricing and negotiations, or use your free capacity for one of your own development projects.

You can easily turn your revenue spreadsheet into a bar chart, like the top one in the example below:

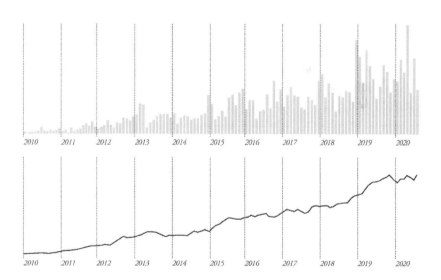

The monthly values in the chart are just illustrative, but their variability shows fairly well how things work in reality. It's no exception for one month to dip to a fraction of the one before, or to jump to double the revenue. This is a common fluctuation of income, caused among other things by overlapping and concurrent orders.

From glancing at such a chart, you can surely read the general trend, but for the year-to-year values (for example just for March in each year) you have to look into the original spreadsheet. To follow the general, stabilized trend line on a month-by-month basis, it's better to compose a moving-sum chart from the same values. The bottom chart shows a 12-month moving sum.

This isn't anything complicated. Simply add up twelve consecutive months, e.g. January 2010 through December 2010. On the next row, move over by a month, so you're adding up February 2010 through January 2011, etc. The result is a smoothed line that clearly shows a long-term trend.

Why precisely twelve months? This isn't a necessity. Feel free to add up 18 or 24 months instead – and the longer the selection, the less monthly swings will impact it. Nonetheless, for freelancers, twelve months is a reasonable length, because seasonality usually follows a regular yearly pattern.

Looking at the bottom graph, the long-term trend is so visible that based on it you could even try to predict your income two years in advance. Only roughly, of course, but it can be useful when you are making strategic decisions with a long-term impact, such as whether or not to take on a mortgage or when approximately a transformation of your status from self-employed to a limited company could pay off. The predictive use of carefully kept records is a nice bonus.

If your workload is stable or growing, your business should bring more revenue, and that should be clearly visible on the trend line. If your income has stagnated for years, then something is definitely wrong, and if you don't know what the cause is, make sure to go over your records with someone experienced.

Why should a business grow? Because in many ways you're growing too. Your reputation and productivity are growing, and you're getting better at negotiations, pricing, and many other aspects as well.

There are legitimate reasons for drops and downturns as well, like market crises, parental leave, serious illnesses, or simply slowing down as you age – but you know all this, and you'll know why the dip or stagnation is happening. It's not a mystery, because you know how to interpret the graph.

Monitoring revenue reveals quite a bit about your business, but as you can see, it does nothing to control costs, which generally involve many more items than income does. And out-of-control, unplanned high costs are precisely what can rock or even tip the boat of a freelancer's financial stability.

The next step, therefore, is to gain control over the largest one-off costs, such as yearly tax payments, purchases of expensive items, and other exceptional expenses. And here a simple financial overview, and a financial reserve, will help you the most.

2. A FINANCIAL OVERVIEW AND RESERVE
Time demands: 10 minutes a week (or 2 to 5 minutes a day)

The financial overview I'll be talking about here represents a simple financial tool for freelancers that distantly resembles a balance sheet, because it also has two sides, which can be (but don't have to be) in balance. But that is the only resemblance. An overview like this has no firm rules and serves only for your internal needs and records. You will likely keep it private, and you can bend it to your needs. So it's not a formal report or document.

Personal adaptation can be significant, because for most freelancers, personal and business finances are interconnected. Not that we don't have separate personal and business bank accounts – we usually do. But certain costs cover both business and personal or family needs, and so they are hard to break down. And when your business expenses are high, you tighten up at home, and vice-versa.

So in your financial overview, you can join these two levels into one logical whole. Or you can keep an overview for your business only and record and plan your family finances separately, along with your partner. This heavily depends on you and your situation.

Just remember that no matter how you are shifting money around within your financial overview, the actual movements on your accounts should be legal, and for tax auditing purposes, your business income should be recorded separately. If you aren't sure how freely you can use a given set of funds, go over it with your accountant or tax advisor.

You can imagine your financial overview as a table with two sides – one with assets (available money or funds) and one with liabilities tied to these assets.

We all easily and intuitively understand *assets*. They are essentially a complete listing of available balances that you have in cash or on various accounts that are also liquid, in the sense that you can use them freely and quickly. Avoid including non-liquid assets, from various savings accounts, to fixed-term deposits, to money shared with your partner. Nothing that you can't work with freely in the short term belongs here.

Your *liabilities* list a variety of items that your assets are tied up in. It's a bit as if you took a calculator and sliced up the pie of your assets into different pieces – "this is for bills I have to pay, this is for my vacation in a couple of months, this I'm stowing away for my quarterly social security and health insurance payments, here's something for a new car, and what's left is my financial reserve."

Your *reserve* can either be floating, with both sides of the sheet in balance, or set manually – the result of subtracting your liabilities from your assets, including your set reserve, is then a positive or negative status for your finances: your imaginary current balance.

Most people list assets and liabilities one under the other in an Excel spreadsheet to make it easier to add or subtract lines. Here's an example of how this can look, followed immediately by my comments on it:

Cash	$350
Business account	$17,000
Personal account #1	$10,400
Personal account #2	$15,000
Total assets	**$42,750**
Apartment rent (for 3 months)	$2,800
Family purchases (for 3 months)	$1,500
Set aside for annual coworking membership fee	$1,200
Current credit card debt	$1,100
Saving up for new car (+300 a month)	$3,300
Saving up for tax and insurance balance payments	$12,100
Financial reserve	$20,000
Total liabilities	**$42,000**
Current balance	**$750**

Count the remainder separately, or leave a floating reserve ▶ (points to Financial reserve / Total liabilities / Current balance)

What does this model overview tell us? That we have a total of $42,750 in cash and on our accounts on the assets side. Not bad, we're rich, let's go shopping! Well, maybe not quite. Our liabilities side tells us we're setting aside a total of $22,000 for various purposes. And we also have $20,000 set aside as a reserve that we don't want to touch at all if possible. So we only have the current balance remainder of $750 as the difference between our assets and liabilities, to throw around (or more as pocket money).

Our balance is positive, indicating solid financial health. A high negative current balance would mean that we have cut too deep into our financial reserve and it's high time to restore the balance – to start watching expenses and perhaps postpone purchases or investments.

Among the main benefits of this kind of financial overview is that when a planned major expense arrives, like tax payments or a down payment for a new car, you write the amount off of both your assets and your liabilities, and your current balance is unchanged.

You actually won't feel the planned expense at all, just like you don't feel the bumps and holes on a road in a jeep with good shocks. In other words, a financial overview will turn a roller-coaster ride into a sightseeing trip over rolling terrain, without unpleasant surprises.

Likewise, whenever you encounter an exceptional expense and decide to write it off of your reserve, you reduce your assets and the amount of reserve in your liabilities, and your current balance again remains unchanged.

Now I also want to take close up look at certain items and add a few practical tips to this.

Note how this freelancer manages personal and work money together and likewise the financial reserve isn't on a specific account, but represents a liability relative to *total assets*. If they are all comparably liquid and your accountant doesn't have any legal objections, it doesn't matter. This model is more flexible than creating a reserve in a special account, which is a method that is quite popular among freelancers. But both approaches are compatible.

While your assets give basically precise, current numbers, your liabilities are a colorful heap of funds that you as a freelancer set aside for a variety of short-term or long-term purposes. Here I show fixed sums for an apartment and a coworking fee. But also current credit-card debt – which this freelancer obviously has to watch closely and update in their spreadsheet.

It's entirely up to you how large the payments will be that you want to reserve within your liabilities. When you're starting out in business, you might want to even set aside money for minor expenses. Gradually, as your cash flow improves, smaller payments will be included in your ordinary expenses and won't be recorded any more.

This overview also includes large liabilities towards the state, and a freelancer will evidently be setting aside money for these periodically, let's say $1,100 a month. These expenses can truly be very high, and an entrepreneur has to be ready for them. So you should know what your expected yearly income will be, which you can partly estimate based on carefully kept monthly records.

Your accountant can easily calculate your approximate taxes and other mandatory payments based on your estimate of yearly income and expenses. You can then gradually set this money aside month-by-month year-round as a liability, just like in my example financial overview. And you will know that you're not allowed to spend this money. This may seem overly cautious, but believe me, you need it. In a few years, your model might be so precise that a year before the time for tax and other mandatory payments, you'll have a rough idea of how high they will be.

My liabilities also show a pile of money set aside for a new car, which grows by $300 every month. You can increase your reserves for any other large future expense in a similar way. Once it arrives, you'll hand over the money and remove that amount, and your financial overview will stay in perfect balance.

Last, but not least, in our liabilities here is the financial reserve, which can essentially be calculated in two ways:

1. You can increase the reserve manually, e.g. by $1,000 a month, or by 10% of your payments received. Then even if you start without reserves, in two years you'll be sitting on a nice financial cushion.

2. Or you can calculate a reserve automatically so that both sides of the sheet stay in balance. (In this case, there will be no *current balance*.)

Which method is better? If your reserve is sufficiently high, say enough to cover your costs for six, or better yet twelve months, I would recommend the second method. Even though it will make your reserve jump up and down by being calculated on the fly, it will still be probably large enough for you not to be bothered too much. You will still be able to adjust your spending behavior in time, or to re-plan your expenses when it starts to drop more than you would prefer.

The first method, where there is a firmly set reserve and alongside it you calculate a positive or negative current balance, is better for freelancers with a small reserve who have to react quickly to any excessive spending. If your financial health is poor, your current balance will fall into the red (a bite out of your reserve), and this stressor will scream at you until you do something about it.

Yes, it's definitely more stressful, but at the same time highly effective for strengthening your financial fitness and self-discipline. This is rough yet needed training to tame your volatile finances, and it will train you better than anything else. Imagine the situation: you have twenty thousand dollars in assets, but if your result is negative, you won't see that twenty thousand. You'll see a negative current balance, and that will guide your behavior. Without a financial overview, it's terribly easy to throw money around and cause yourself many times more stress when you discover you can't even cover taxes, let alone your comfortable lifestyle.

Business goes completely differently with large reserves. You then don't worry so much about monthly swings, you feel more at ease, you don't feel the urge to take on every awful job, and you can think more strategically. Feelings are important in freelancing, and this is one of the most reliable ways to avoid the bad ones and to strengthen your overall sense of enjoyment in life and business. That feeling will then radiate from you. Clients stay away from stressed-out people, because they themselves want to avoid risks.

So let's summarize the main advantages of having a personal financial overview. No matter whether you use it in this form or prioritize some other method of tracking reserves and saving up for big expenses, it will bring you a number of benefits:

- Keeping an overview won't take you more than a few minutes per day or week. Whenever you update it, it will show you how you are doing financially – what your overall financial health is.

- An overview of your assets and liabilities keeps you from throwing money around. Even when you have money, you won't spend it, because thanks to your overview, you are reserving it for internal and external liabilities.

- The liabilities in your overview let you gradually set aside money for major investments or expenses. Setting money aside protects you from impulse purchases that you would regret later.

- In your overview you can also record your financial reserve, which gradually grows and forms a buffer against every kind of trouble a life in business will throw at you. Let it try!

- Last, but not least, a financial overview set up like this is exceptionally conservative, because it takes into account both ongoing and future expenses, but at the same time doesn't count on future income.

So in practice the overview tells you what would happen if a new crisis were to come tomorrow and your business would dry up from one month to the next. If your financial situation is stable and your reserves are high, you will make it through and will be able to meet all your important obligations, despite the drop in income.

Constructing your finances this conservatively makes sense, because you surely want to be around a decade from now, and that is time enough for crises to arrive – and they will devastate anyone who had a few good years, got lazy, and stopped thinking that bad years can come. They can and will.

A financial overview like this is also conservative in that it doesn't account for any major debts. Naturally, you can have some money set aside in your liabilities for a few debt payments, but you will hardly be counting one there in full. For work with a major debt, a more sophisticated financial plan – which appears later in this chapter – works better than this kind of simple overview.

This overview also has one other disadvantage. It always only shows the current state along with a reserve and planned expenses. But it won't tell you where you are spending unnecessarily or how much you are actually making, that is, the net of your income minus your expenses. This is why we have to focus on your cash flow.

3. WATCHING YOUR CASH FLOW
Time demands: 0 to 5 minutes a day

A professional should know where they are losing money, and be able to reduce or eliminate these losses. Sometimes it's hard, but it's not like you're cutting off your little finger, trust me.

The hardest part is to figure out where you are bleeding finances. While recording your income and composing a financial overview in Excel or Google Sheets is easy to do, watching and analyzing expenses is a challenge even if you are systematic.

Most freelancers don't issue more than ten to twenty invoices per month. Expenses are a more complicated story.

If your business is at least a bit complicated, you have dozens of expenses large or small every month. And then there are personal expenses on top of that. Credit card payments, receipts for shopping, snacks and treats, restaurants, books, gifts, sports, accommodations, transportation, insurance, bank charges, etc. If you count in your household and family expenses for your children or spouse, that can make for hundreds of expense items. Month after month.

Intuition fails when you are evaluating a cash flow this complicated. It's no wonder that we all tend to have a distorted idea of how much we are really spending on what. Without a record, it's practically impossible to get the whole picture. And to tell the truth, businessmen and salesmen count on this a bit. One purchase here, one over there, it's easy for people to lose track. And meanwhile, a hundred wasted every month makes twelve hundred a year, which is hardly a small amount. And this is just expense tracking – but you also have to actually *earn* that extra twelve hundred somewhere!

Not to mention what happens when you place income and expenses side by side and discover how much you're really making, i.e. your real cash flow. Even a professional with above-average income can then reach the unflattering conclusion that they're spending so much on expenses and useless junk that their net income after subtracting expenses is negligible. Or that their net income is smaller than of someone with half or their revenue but with much better control over their liabilities and expenses. (A positive cash flow for a given period means that the income was larger than the expenses. A negative cash flow means that expenses dominated and the professional had to dig into their reserves.)

But not everyone needs such a register of expenses. Many people have heeded the call of minimalism or are frugal by nature and save wherever they can. They don't throw money away and stick to Ben Franklin's principle that *a penny saved is a penny earned* – if you have a mindset like this, stick to it even when you are making more, and one day you will truly be rich.

Meanwhile the rest of us, who aren't so oriented towards minimalism and frugality, do need to watch expenses. You can typically tell this by how one fine day you sit and ask yourself: *Where the hell did that money go?!* And you realize you don't have a good answer. This is precisely when it makes the most sense to start tracking and keeping count.

I know you may already be having nightmares about all the receipts and bank and credit card statements you would have to go through every month just to get any reasonable results. You hate paperwork, right? Don't worry, I hate it too. Fortunately, there are apps that can track your cash flow for you.

While something like Goodbudget works with a virtual envelope method, which is fine for managing family expenses or for professionals with regular income and expenses resembling employees, Toshl is an example of a typical cash flow app. You can enter your income and expense items one by one in your own categories, and the result is the net difference. This is all done simply, without complicated counting, and with support for regular payments (which you then don't have to enter repeatedly) and foreign currencies.

There are plenty of alternatives on the market; just to name a few, there is MoneyWiz, Spendee, iFinance, and BudgetBakers' Wallet. Certain apps support automated importing of bank statements, which can save a lot of data entry. And there are also smart accounts, or cards such as Revolut that analyze expenses for you automatically so that it's enough to just pay for everything with their card. It's a good solution because it costs you zero extra time.

I for one have used Toshl long-term to monitor my spending in restaurants and cafes, because I know this is my weakness. And because I wrote the last third of this book over the course of 5 weeks in a single cafe in Las Palmas de Gran Canaria, I could easily read from it that I had spent €250 during that time on coffee and snacks.

By the way, I recommend you also watch any currency exchange rates for your payments. If you leave currency conversion to your bank at the moment of payment, they can charge excessive fees or give bad rates – or today's rate can be bad overall. If you frequently pay in foreign currency, it's better to have a multi-currency account and buy foreign currency in advance, when it's cheap. The advantage is that when you then withdraw cash or pay in foreign currency, the money will be taken directly from the balance of the given currency account, with no further charges. That is, if your bank is on the level. For cheap conversions or transfers, you can also use services like Revolut or TransferWise, which specialize in low-cost transfers.

Similarly you can cut other costs one by one if they have gotten out of control and if the careful record in your cash flow app reveals them. You may soon start saving in other ways too.

One thing that works for me is postponing purchases by merely writing down purchase tips in my to-do and letting them ripen for a few weeks (some people opt for a shared family wishlist). If you have a tendency towards impulse purchases, postponing will save you tons of money. Also, there are consumer sites and magazines out there specialized in recommending products with the best price to quality ratios, and they test most of what they rate. In the EU they're mostly national non-profits, while the US has the paid website ConsumerReports.org.

On its own, using a cash flow app doesn't take much time. Even if you enter all your income and expenses manually, you won't spend more than five minutes a day, and typically just two or three. Just a few months of data collection and you will start learning lots of interesting things about your finances. And especially where you are spending noticeably more than you had thought. Once you find out, where the black holes are, it is fairly easy to do something about it to prevent waste.

If just reading this you are terrified by the thought of having to enter data in some kind of app for the rest of your life, fear not. Either you will find some completely work-free solution like paying with a smart card, or it will be enough to monitor your cash flow for a few months before you discover where you are spending needlessly, change your habits, and you're done. A few years later you can go back to measuring and correct your behavior once again.

Thus the benefit of monitoring your cash flow is that you will know your net income, as well as the structure of your expenses, their exact amounts in categories of your choice, and their evolution. That makes it easier to verify whether and how your change in behavior or habits is really making any difference. And you'll almost certainly soon plug the worst leaks.

What does this mean for you? Likely only that you will have considerably more money due to optimizing your cash flow. And that means less stress and fewer worries and fears. And more protection from risks waiting just behind the door. Or the horizon.

4. A FINANCIAL PLAN
Time demands: 5 to 15 minutes a week

Monthly revenues, a financial overview, and perhaps watching cash flow are sufficiently broad to cover financial self-management for most free-lancers. But you may want to know more than just your past and present. You may want to look into your future.

Why? Perhaps because you would like to take out a mortgage and you want to be sure that if financial problems gather on the horizon, you will know about them in time. That means planning. Having a financial plan, in any understandable form.

Here again, by financial plan, I don't mean a formal tool for corporate financial management – but only a slightly advanced spreadsheet into which you write both your current status and an outlook for the next several months to years. The result will give you a more precise idea of whether you are close to wrecking your ship in the shallows, or heading towards the smooth blue ocean and have hopeful vistas ahead of you.

To compose your plan, you will need the outputs of the three levels above:

Through your monthly income records, you will create pessimistic, realistic, and optimistic projections for your future income. Through your financial overview, you will know the current status of your assets and liabilities and your planned future expenses, so you will be able to enter them in the right months in your plan. And your expense and cash flow records will let you simulate typical monthly expenses in individual categories for the upcoming few months and add in any other periodic expenses.

If you don't want to create a whole financial plan from scratch, you can play with my template, which I'll explain below.

I'll start with the expenses, below the bold line across the middle, which are the easiest to fill in. The great advantage of a financial plan is that after adding and filling in a particular row, you instantly see the new cost item's long-term impact on the financial results of your business.

Some costs are not fixed, but differ each month, or only appear occasionally. But there's an easy solution. If they are mainly dependent on your work volume, estimate them, for instance, with a revenue-based formula. And if they jump around, such as with your phone bill, simply plan for some kind of long-term average, and enter in the precise numbers at the end of each month. The plan isn't rigid at all; with a two- or three-month outlook, it typically contains manually entered estimates.

Minor costs are trickier. It can be the final straw that breaks the camel's back…coffee, clothes, lunches, books, all the tiny impulse buys that end up slicing a pretty large piece out of the monthly income pie. They usually can't each be effectively planned, let alone tracked on separate rows. It's good practice to not do so and to aggregate these minor expenses into one or a few rows using what you know from tracking expenses. It's enough to know that you spend on average say $400 a month on minor expenses and then enter this number in the spreadsheet as an estimate for future months. When the time comes, you can add the precise figures.

Incomes (the part above the bold line) are naturally far more difficult to estimate than expenses. But it's not impossible, and the solution is to work smartly with development scenarios – realistic, pessimistic, and optimistic. When you're starting out, it will be very imprecise, but that will change once you have a few months of business behind you. And if you have already been tracking monthly revenues for a few years, a one or two-year outlook can have more weight. Sometimes you can even make it more precise by dividing the last few months by the same months a year ago, and use that as the real-growth coefficient to estimate the realistic scenario for the months to come. Your real numbers will typically fluctuate between the pessimistic and optimistic estimates.

Unfortunately no one can tell you precisely how to calculate the individual scenarios, because that depends on your work, your growth,

Personal Financial Plan / template by Robert Vlach	typical amount	Mar 2019	Apr 2019	May 2019	Jun 2019	Jul 2019	Aug 2019	Sep 2019	Oct 2019	Nov 2019	Dec 2019	Jan 2020	Feb 2020	Mar 2020	Apr 2020	May 2020
total costs (sum of all items below the bold black line)		$3,678	$10,643	$3,745	$4,145	$4,025	$3,745	$3,395	$3,645	$4,169	$3,395	$3,595	$3,745	$3,815	$15,845	$3,745
monthly business revenues																
pessimistic (an estimate, or the weakest revenue in the previous 12 months)		$3,700	$3,700	$3,700	$3,700	$3,700	$4,500	$4,500	$4,500	$4,500	$4,500	$4,500	$4,500	$4,000	$4,000	$4,000
realistic (real, or an estimate, or the same month last year +20%)	$5,513	$5,000	$5,000	$5,000	$4,600	$4,300	$6,000	$7,600	$6,000	$5,500	$8,500	$5,000	$5,200	$7,000	$9,100	$6,000
optimistic (an estimate, or the same month last year +50%)	$7,582	$7,000	$7,000	$7,000	$6,500	$5,800	$7,000	$9,500	$8,500	$7,000	$10,800	$7,000	$6,700	$8,000	$11,000	$8,000
monthly cash flow (the given scenario minus expenses)																
pessimistic				-$45	-$445	-$325	$755	$1,105	$855	$331	$1,105	$905	$755	$185	-$11,845	$255
realistic	$1,835			$1,256	$455	$275	$1,256	$4,205	$2,355	$1,331	$5,105	$1,405	$1,455	$3,185	-$6,745	$2,255
optimistic	$3,061			$3,256	$2,355	$1,775	$3,255	$6,105	$4,865	$2,831	$7,405	$3,405	$2,955	$4,185	-$4,845	$4,255
cumulative cash flow (for the given future scenario)																
pessimistic				-$45	-$490	-$815	-$60	$1,045	$1,900	$2,231	$3,336	$4,241	$4,996	$5,181	-$6,664	-$6,409
realistic				$1,256	$1,710	$1,985	$3,240	$7,445	$9,800	$11,131	$16,236	$17,641	$19,096	$22,281	$15,536	$17,791
optimistic				$3,256	$5,610	$7,385	$10,640	$16,745	$21,600	$24,431	$31,836	$35,241	$38,196	$42,361	$37,536	$41,791
exceptional revenues (non-business)																
profits from sales of investment assets (stocks, cryptocurrencies, etc.)	$6,600	$6,600														
minor sales, received gifts, etc.	$790	$790														
real monthly cash flow		$9,225	-$3,061	$1,255	$455	$275	$1,256	$4,205	$2,355	$1,331	$5,105	$1,405	$1,455	$3,185	-$6,745	$2,255
real cumulative cash flow		$9,225	$6,164	$7,419	$7,874	$8,148	$9,404	$13,609	$15,964	$17,295	$22,400	$23,805	$25,260	$28,445	$21,700	$23,955
realistic estimate of financial reserve from the current month forwards		$80,000	$80,000	$80,000	$80,465	$80,730	$81,985	$86,190	$88,545	$89,876	$94,981	$96,386	$97,841	$101,026	$94,281	$95,536
fixed business expenses (examples)																
health insurance	$411	$411	$411	$411	$411	$411	$411	$411	$411	$411	$411	$411	$411	$411	$411	$411
coworking membership	$150	$150	$150	$150	$150	$150	$150	$150	$150	$150	$150	$150	$150	$150	$150	$150
car payments	$260	$260	$260	$260	$260	$260	$260	$260	$260	$260	$260	$260	$260	$260	$260	$260
phone	$37	$37	$37	$37	$37	$37	$37	$37	$37	$37	$37	$37	$37	$37	$37	$37
invoicing software	$15	$15	$15	$15	$15	$15	$15	$15	$15	$15	$15	$15	$15	$15	$15	$15
variable business expenses (examples)																
office helper	$500	$478	$512	$500	$500	$500	$500	$500	$500	$500	$500	$500	$500	$500	$500	$500
virtual secretary	$390	$285	$313	$290	$290	$290	$290	$290	$290	$290	$290	$290	$290	$290	$290	$290
Facebook promo posts	$400	$470	$295	$470	$470	$470	$470	$470	$470	$470	$470	$470	$470	$470	$470	$470
other periodic business costs (month number, examples)																
1-4-7-10: accounting services	$150		$150			$150			$150			$150			$150	
2-5-8-11: classroom rental	$350			$350			$350			$350			$350			$350
3: insurance against business risks	$420	$420												$420		
4: taxes	$480															
7: web hosting	$480					$480										
10: yearly G Suite license	$100								$100			$50				
11: annual web maintenance	$424									$424						
personal and other variable monthly costs (examples)																
mortgage	$380	$380	$380	$380	$380	$380	$380	$380	$380	$380	$380	$380	$380	$380	$380	$380
electricity	$190	$190	$190	$190	$190	$190	$190	$190	$190	$190	$190	$190	$190	$190	$190	$190
life and accident insurance	$192	$192	$192	$192	$192	$192	$192	$192	$192	$192	$192	$192	$192	$192	$192	$192
minor expenses (groceries, restaurants, cafes, gas, clothing, books, etc.)	$390	$390	$461	$500	$500	$500	$500	$500	$500	$500	$500	$500	$500	$500	$500	$500
one-off expenses			$7,277		$750										$12,300	

You can copy or download this template at **FreelanceWay.eu/plan** (through the File menu) cycles and seasons in your sector, your success in personal marketing, etc. My template shows one possible solution. I calculate the pessimistic scenario for a given month as the lowest monthly revenue in the previous 12 months. So the full course of the pessimistic scenario is unlikely, yet possible under extreme conditions. I have already described how to produce the realistic scenario above. The optimistic scenario is based on higher than usual year-to-year growth. (In the template I count on, for example, 50% growth compared to the same month in the previous year.)

When you look at the rows for monthly cash flow, you see that they are simply the income numbers from the pessimistic, realistic, and optimistic scenarios after subtracting the given month's expenses. The monthly cash flow regularly jumps up and down due to exceptional monthly expenses or income swings, which most freelancers know very well from their own businesses as an ugly feeling of financial instability and insecurity. If this cash flow number is negative, you are biting into your reserve – which should in any case be designed so that it can handle swings this large or even larger.

The cumulative cash flow simply represents the sum of your monthly cash flows since the start of the financial plan, or from the current month into the future (depending on your template's design). This is an important numeric series that tells you how your financial health may develop based on this-or-that scenario. The pessimistic variant tends to be depressing, because it's an extreme one that is all the more unlikely to happen because you can preventively cut away expenses, too, if your income drops – and since you have a grip on your expenses, you can predict the effects of cuts more easily than if you were to tighten your belt intuitively and in the wrong places. The realistic scenario will likely have more to say about your future.

An estimate of your financial reserves' development from the present month forwards, by progressively adding the positive or negative cash flow from the realistic scenario, is useful too. (However, you can also count your reserves' development separately based on the pessimistic scenario; it's up to you.) In any case this is another key indicator, telling when a dangerous drop in reserves is looming, so you can handle it in advance. However, your outlook might also be rosy, with reserves that are growing constantly. You can then gradually put them into investments.

It's probably clear from my template that to compose a financial plan, you need to know quite a lot about your income and expenses. And predictions about income are typically surer when you have a few years of business behind you. And on the cost side, meanwhile, it's simpler to record regular monthly costs than to remember all the expenses that come, say, once a year. After filling it all out and playing around with it for a month or two, your financial plan should really make sense, and you'll turn to it on your own for not-just-intuitive trend estimates. After a year at the most, you should be certain that it contains everything important.

For most freelancers with a complex cash flow, it will take a few hours at most to compose a plan. Doing so will show you things that you would never realize through simple intuition, and also alert you to critical months – often a year in advance. The plan takes little time to maintain. In my case, at most a half-hour during my monthly work review process. I track my rough estimates in gray-colored cells, and once I know the precise numbers, I enter those and remove the gray. If you have been able to successfully aggregate your minor expenses, the whole update really will only take a short while.

You can think of the plan in short as a complex financial overview projected as an outlook into the future, i.e. with an added time dimension.

The plan can also have a completely different shape than mine; it's up to you and your creativity. Financial planning apps exist as well, but they always have limitations, given by the budgeting philosophies of their developers. In the corporate world they make more sense. For free-lancers I find it more sensible to plan based on your own needs, which such a plan will also highlight for you, and only then seek a suitable application.

Many freelancers never even arrive at using a financial plan: they don't have a reason to. But if they have a family, high liabilities, or a mortgage, and they don't want their business to threaten their family's happiness, a financial plan frees them from financial headaches.

5. INVESTMENTS

If you do well financially for a few years, perhaps partially thanks to the financial self-management tools described here, you will almost certainly start posing a more pleasant question to yourself: where should I put my money?

Naturally you can (and actually have to) invest into your business – get a better website, increase your qualifications, pay for ads, improve your premises, update your hardware, or try new things. But at the same time it's not sensible to invest it all in this way without any side investments.

This topic goes beyond the scope of this book, but I have to advise one thing:

Take an interest in investing and reasonably managing your money sooner, rather than later. When I look back at my business, likely the biggest mistake I made was that I only looked into investments relatively late, in my 30s.

Frugal management of your unused funds and investing them is an advanced matter that a person has to spend time learning, just like business or a demanding skill. Don't put it off, because it starts out slow and has many pitfalls.

But what is wise investment? In short it's investing in a way that you understand sufficiently and that protects and if possible multiplies your money. Some people understand property or land; others art or coins; some have a grasp of investment products on the market; others prioritize stocks.

The important thing is that it isn't done in blind faith, because then you're risking losses due to unknown risks. It's better to invest into areas you do understand and merely deepen your knowledge over the years than to pour money into something you don't understand.

My profession is business consulting, and so stocks, assessing companies, and evaluating the qualities of their management are all familiar to me. I pick the stocks I invest in based on that knowledge, and I'm satisfied with the results. I don't understand real estate, gold coins, or sports betting, nor do I understand art enough to buy paintings. Stocks also have the plus of being the long-term highest-paying class of assets.

For me, investing mainly means educating myself. Over time I have worked my way towards value-based investing, which is close to my business mentality. For beginners I would recommend, for example, the audio book *The Art of Investing* from Great Courses; for advanced investors, Benjamin Graham's works or the collected annual letters of Warren Buffett, *Berkshire Hathaway Letters to Shareholders* (sold on Kindle for $4). If you read it thoroughly, I wouldn't be surprised if you bought a bunch of Berkshire's BRK.B stocks as well, just as I did.

I see the great advantage of good stocks in both their long-term growth and their high liquidity: you can sell them at any time with the push of a button. In the context of this chapter, this mainly means that in my own financial overview, I keep part of my assets in liquid stocks, and these then form an appropriate part of my overall reserve. In short, keeping too large of a reserve in cash makes less sense to me than working with a part of it in the form of an investment portfolio.

Nevertheless, a good investment may mean something completely different for you than for me, and it may take you a while before you determine what it should be – for some people it's founding new projects or startups to be sold later, for others it's peer-to-peer loans over online platforms such as Lending Club. And I would be the last to tell you which way to turn here. But I would insist that you start as soon as possible, even with just a small investment, because you will tend to have a long initial period of mistakes and bad investments even if you study intensively. And you should.

Being a layman investor is disadvantageous in part because it means greater dependence on the advice of brokers or investment consultants. Even when they are honest, their profits come primarily from commissions and fees, and thus from their clients' active trading. But a large trading volume will decimate your profits.

A good solution can be an investment fund that manages investors' money with minimal fees for management and transaction costs. One very advantageous option in this regard would be the so-called *index funds* publicly traded as ETFs, where for instance the Vanguard S & P 500 (VOO) or the Total Stock Market (VTI) currently have expense ratios of only 0.04% while having mid-term yields of 6 to 10% p.a. You can buy them with low fees via an online broker (such as the solid Interactive Brokers service in the US or DeGiro in the EU). Nevertheless, not even this will rid you off the need to understand what you are buying, from whom, and the risks of such an investment.

Strive to be a qualified investor no matter where you are investing. The long-term yield from the capital you have saved up can be truly large, but only if you hold out and if you minimize transaction costs or fees, because those are earnings for others, not you.

KEY IDEAS

1. Besides the risks you know about, many are also unknown or hard to predict.

2. So you need to minimize known risks and face the rest by strengthening your resistance.

3. The first line of defense lies in the traits of successful business, which are already well-known to us.

4. You can avoid problems most easily (and cheaply) through prevention and financial self-management.

5. Map out the known risks and work on them systematically one after the other, starting from the worst.

6. Risks that can't be tackled head on, can be solved through insurance and having a strong reserve.

7. Freelancers' financial self-management is often weak. The biggest problem is the fluctuations of income and expenses.

8. The minimum here is to track revenues, have a financial overview with a reserve and an optimized cash flow.

9. If you are working with debt or a mortgage, or feeding a family, consider financial planning.

10. Take an interest in the investment of your leftover money sooner rather than later. Learning how to do so well takes years.

PRACTICE

✓ Map your risks and order the list with the most probable and damaging ones on top. Then start tackling them one by one, following the advice in this chapter.

✓ Since you will be recording monthly revenues, consider tracking other numbers as well: new orders, course participants, website traffic, new followers, etc.

✓ Visualize the data you have collected using simple graphs in a spreadsheet in order to see how your business is growing and changing over time.

✓ Make the maintenance of your financial overview part of your daily or weekly work review. Then try out two or three ways to monitor your cash flow as well.

✓ If the financial plan presented in this chapter scares you, trust me and just play with a copy of my plan available at FreelanceWay.eu/plan – in no time, you'll plan like a pro!

THE FREELANCE WAY

Where are the limits of professional growth?

Autonomy and creative freedom aren't free. A professional has to work their way towards them honestly.

When I started out freelancing, as a contracted web developer, I enjoyed my work to such a crazy extent that I often worked seven days a week. It was my entire world.

At the time, in the late 1990s, I worked in Catalonia, in the north of Spain. And even though it was hard sometimes and I returned home exhausted, I also had an unusual degree of freedom, because nobody else in the firm knew the tech-side of things. I had discovered a mentally demanding activity that was better than work. It was pure joy. Living in Barcelona at the turn of the millennium and heading out with the gang to bars where Picasso, Dali, or Hemingway had drunk decades earlier was a dream come true.

And I might have stayed, if it weren't for the inevitable burnout that turned my priorities upside down. Even though I had successfully completed my big web project, I was completely drained at the end of it. At just a few years past twenty, I had already gotten so tired of programming and the web that I couldn't go on.

Burnout is final. No matter if you're 25 or 50, you just can't go on. It manifests differently in everyone – for me, I lost every scrap of motivation, vigor, and enthusiasm. Every day I had to force myself to work, and it quickly showed in my results. I lost my creativity and the will to push our project towards new milestones. Most of all, my strongest desire was to hit the road again.

In the end I decided for a radical cure. After so much time in front of a computer, I wanted to do something with my hands. I had some money saved up, and my expenses were low, and since I was interested in wine and its culture, I cold-emailed several wineries to tell them I'd like to change jobs for a while and ask if they needed some help. One wine school in a town about an hour north of Vienna wrote back that they would gladly employ me for minimum wage, accommodations, and food. And I jumped at it!

It was wonderful work. We all got up at 5 a.m. and worked all day in the vineyards and the cellar; we helped with production, bottling, and delivery. And sometimes with tasting too. It was the exact opposite of what I had been doing before. Carefree manual labor, mostly outdoors in the country. We all got off at three; I had practically the whole afternoon to myself.

In the summer I rode my motorcycle through the countryside or went to read a book on the town square. Whole days went by with nothing happening there or anywhere else in town. Weeks went by, one after another without any changes.

I also did night shifts, feeding the heater with firewood to keep the greenhouse warm enough for the just-grafted seedlings in the stratification boxes. Before the harvest, meanwhile, I had to scare the birds away from the ripening grapes. I lay there in wait in a trailer on the vineyard, and when a flock of starlings flew in, a few firecrackers would scare them off. And in between, I read books or thought about things of all kinds. My workmates were great as well, and we soon became inseparable friends. One of them is now a professional cook in Switzerland, while another has become a tree doctor.

I spent one whole season there. Besides teaching me truly a lot about wine, it also unbelievably cleared my head. I realized that if I wanted to live free, in terms of work and finances, and do what I want to long-term, as a freelancer, I would have to work completely differently. That year in the vineyard led me to a fundamental career breakthrough.

I decided to return to work on web projects, but never again in a way that would be killing me. I stopped being an enthusiastic, overworked beginner and swore to work like a professional. My goal was to change virtually everything, except the profession. That is: to negotiate conditions completely differently and change my work style too.

If it hadn't been for that year-long pause and working in nature, I would never have made such a radical leap. But out there among the vines I realized that under the circumstances, I had nothing to lose. I enjoy everything I do, and I knew I would find my way. That gave me the courage to head out in a new direction.

This book is my attempt to distill a thousand stories into one. Through it we have looked at the freelance way from the first steps to running a fully professional business. And though we have taken some side trips into topics or problems that only affect certain freelancers or professions, we have also avoided many others…just like on real journeys.

But actually, what is this journey? That is a key question, and before you set off on yours, I would like to go over it in this last chapter.

For many of my recommendations, you may have thought: *there are other ways.* And there are! Or you may know experienced professionals whose methods directly clash with my tips and warnings. Also entirely possible. Freelancing is an open journey, and there are thousands of paths.

But there is also one more serious reason why some professionals' approaches to business vary so dramatically, and that is how far a distance they have traveled. That distance isn't measured in years or the money earned, but more in overall advancement and influence. I'll try to explain it using the visual metaphor below – a spiral for a freelancer's career growth:

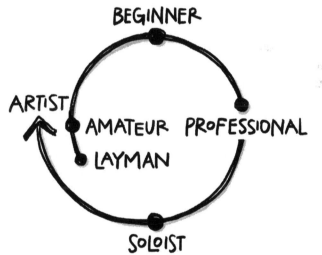

The spiral represents the individual phases in a freelancer's development, as they might tie into each other. Once again it's not a universal model, but I can show certain contrasts through it:

Layman is the default state before heading out on a journey into a particular field. It represents a person's prior personal and professional life and their interests, character, and nature.

An *amateur* is someone who has gone through a certain development, when some activity or profession hooked them enough that they decided to study or engage with it. If they enjoy it and want to improve, one possible road is to go freelance.

A *beginner* is someone who has boldly stepped forth to freelance, either full-time or alongside their studies, employment, or parental leave. But they are still finding their way in business. They finish a few gigs and gradually realize all the things they will still have to learn. They realize that doing business includes both their expertise itself and the ABCs of business – a pile of skills we all must acquire if we were not to be seen as amateurs.

A *professional* is the exact opposite of an amateur. In this advanced stage, the freelancer's business runs smoothly, and often very profitably. By now they have sufficiently mastered both their expertise and business, thus becoming a genuine expert and 100% professional. Business is going well, customers are satisfied and even enthusiastic…what more could one wish for? And so for certain professionals, work eventually stops being fun, and yet they easily come to terms with it, because it all seems natural and adult. This state of things is a sort of extreme when it comes to orderliness and stability. Many people remain in it, believing that their development has reached its end.

A *soloist* is a professional who has made a fundamental turnaround: they have broken free and no longer press on their professional position if it is becoming a brake on their further development. This is the highest stage of evolution, where the freelancer, as a professional, has worked their way to a unique view of their field and is now advancing or even transforming it – and themselves – through their work. The soloist understands that sleek professionalism is only one of the development stages. Their goal is to do unique projects that stand out and that meet their visions and ambitions. Their goal is to approach work as art.

In other words, an *amateur* takes an interest in a given field, a freelance *beginner* seeks a living there, a *professional* fully understands both that field and business, and a *soloist* advances the field in places where no colleague has gone before.

I've borrowed the term *soloist* from an older book called *Soloing* by Harriet Rubin, where she also presents the following table. Note how soloists have basically the opposite tendencies and motivations to freelancers who are just starting out:

Soloists	Freelancers
Work to experiment on their craft	Work to pay the bills
Take on daring clients	Solicit on safe clients
Risk working in fields new to them	Perfect what they already know
See work as an adventure	See work as building stature
Would rather mess up than miss out	Would rather miss out than mess up
Their ideal is being the artist	Their ideal is the professional

So we can imagine the soloist as an expert for whom the golden cage of 100% professionalism has become too narrow and who has decided for a new brave evolutionary step – being freer, keeping the parts of professionalism that suit them, and doing the rest their way, even with some occasional missteps. Why? Because it's an adventure, and because it's fun. A soloist has such a strong professional standing that they can afford it. And an unconventional approach is even expected of them.

Many soloists are recruited from among company (co)owners and top managers who are tired of life in corporations and big institutions. That is, the grand circuit from amateur to freelancer to soloist doesn't always apply. You can end up as a professional soloist through corporate work as well, if it gives you all the needed professional skills. Soloing isn't really imaginable without them. A soloist has mastered these skills, and precisely that fact lets them play and change their style in ways a rigid professional could never risk.

Soloing means professional and business mastery.

You can tell a soloist easily, because they truly stand out and are highly visible and respected. They are generally professionals with superb reputations who influence their field. Their income is so good they are financially independent and can afford to pick and choose orders. They have the reputation of an expert taken at their word, with great insight and scope, as is also clearly shown by their stellar portfolio of successes and projects. They are personalities with a distinct style. Originals. In short, artists.

If a soloist's ideal is to be an artist, what does that mean? That they can approach nearly all of their work or craft like art – with an open mind, a feeling for detail, and an effort to find new ways and not just copy existing solutions – to play and innovate. A soloist strives towards this because they don't want to burn out after doing 100% professional, yet basically identical work for years. So they escape the burnout trap by deliberately deciding to work differently and by treating every order as unique.

That also explains the professional-spiral metaphor I used above. In it, the soloist returns to a mindset similar to what they had as an amateur and beginner. Back then, every job was new and different, each one represented a challenge, and nothing was routine. The soloist has gone a long way, only to return to the heart of the matter – but with much greater professional autonomy and wisdom.

A LONG JOURNEY

Let's make no mistake here. The journey is long, winding, difficult, and full of dangers and dead ends. Every stage brings a different set of challenges, and advancement to the next one is only achieved through titanic efforts:

An *amateur* has to convince themselves that they have the goods and make the leap of faith into the unknown, to freelance. How many manage that? And how many quickly take their leap back? Who would prefer unsure freelance work over a secure job and steady pay?

A *beginner* has to admit that there is more that they don't know and can't do, than what they know and can do. They also have to accept that the free market is to some extent a jungle, where the incapable and the unreliable are rarely given second chances. A freelancer's first run-in with real professionalism is hard on their ego – which will only be bruised further over time. A freelancer may then spend years of hard work fine-tuning their expertise and professionalism. But how many of those who set out on this difficult journey truly work their way to being a top and universally reliable professional? And how many instead get stuck and just settle for less? Most, perhaps, and none can be blamed for it. Not everyone wants to grow and learn. Even an average performance is still a performance, and where there's minimal competition, even an average expert can achieve a good name.

A *100% professional* has gone further than the vast majority, and they are rightfully rewarded with a fantastically running personal business that they can easily operate for the rest of their life. But they can also reach the realization that their formal professionalism is nothing compared to the unrestrained openness of a soloist. Yet, they still have doubts. Why should they want more? Why not spend years doing what works and leave innovation to the young? It demands bravery and an unrelenting inner *calling* for the professional to step out of the crowd and go solo.

The *soloist* consciously rejects comfortable certainty in favor of exciting uncertainty. They go full circle back to their beginnings, because they are willing to admit that everything is open and that the best might still be ahead of them – *if* they embrace change as the prerequisite for further growth. A soloist is a professional with the qualities of an artist, and that makes them very rare and precious goods.

Every soloist is a unique specimen, glowing with genuineness. And because they're not a dull gray, they must be prepared to bear both successes and criticism. An ordinary professional can't handle this public scrutiny, but a soloist is the bearer of strong visions that stand on their own. And a soloist escapes classification by always being a step ahead and thus being in a class of their own.

For beginners, the idea that our priorities can differ so dramatically in different professional-growth phases is unintuitive. But that is how it is, and a freelancer should take it into account when they are choosing their professional role models or listening to someone else's advice.

Looking at it from a distance, the growth I've presented involves fairly large career shifts, and the whole circuit definitely isn't a matter for one year, nor two. It's a slow evolution of professional growth, and its stages aren't very shrinkable, let alone skippable. An amateur can't go straight to being an impeccable professional, just like a beginner can't go straight ahead to being a soloist, because the soloist has learned professional approaches and how to stick to them when needed.

This is also why it's hard for beginners to imitate their professional role models, because these would be much farther along and have completely different priorities. This is also why it's so hard, or even impossible sometimes, to understand the experience and advice of advanced professionals when you are just starting out.

In this book, I've mainly gone over how to start out in business and become a true professional. But I would regret it if you ended up seeing freelancing as a closed track from amateur to professional – that is, as having some kind of clear end.

The end is wonderfully open, and I would even say that the best awaits you right where formally and clearly defined professionalism transitions into the adventurous and exciting uniqueness of the soloist. The latter perceives their business as fully open to changes, the world, and people.

So yes, I have done my best to explain the principles of personal productivity, negotiations, pricing, and building a good name. But only you yourself can make the big decisions – to go international, to submit your work to the world's most prestigious competition, to join groundbreaking research, or maybe even sacrifice a year towards writing a book.

So it's not just about proven know-how; it's also about the courage to do things better, your way. And that, of course, grows with your experience. Flawless professionalism is exceptionally important, but it's not the final goal. Upon achieving (and exceeding) it, you can start to write a much grander story that will lead others on their way, support the development of your field, and perhaps even improve our world.

In this respect, soloing represents a step away from business for the sake of personal profit towards business from which we can all profit. Doing business the freelance way is therefore both an outcome of the freedom we have inherited and a prerequisite for keeping this very freedom safe for future generations.

* * *

A BOOK IS JUST THE BEGINNING

In conclusion, I would like to whole heartily wish you success in free-lancing, and that you will do work that will earn you a living, fulfill you, and help others.

If you have read this whole book and would like to write me how you liked it, or you have ideas for improving future editions, you can email me at **book@vla.ch**. I'll be just as happy to read your posts on Instagram or Twitter mentioning **@robertvlach** or **#FreelanceWay**.

If you haven't found the answers to some important questions in this book and you are looking for advice, don't ask me. I'm not saying this because I wouldn't want to help you – it's just that I'm not a fan of giving out instant advice and quick judgments without understanding the full context. Even when a problem seems simple and clear, a snap judgment can lead to bad advice that overlooks some important fact that only a careful examination would reveal. If you're seeking *good* advice, consider one of these options:

* Approach a more experienced colleague as a mentor and go over it with them.
* Talk to other freelancers about how they would handle the problem.
* Hire a professional consultant.
* Join a professional organization and ask its more experienced members.
* Find a professional group on LinkedIn or Facebook and present your query there.
* Carefully describe your problem at Quora or Reddit and wait to see what kind of responses you get.
* Read some of the books I have recommended, and perhaps also others related to your problem.
* Attend events for your field and bring you question up as a topic for discussion.
* Check if any trustworthy blogs or other websites cover the issue.

Doing business is solving problems, and your first problem won't be your last. Work for the solution, as if it was a test that life itself has placed before you. I'm sure you'll hold on and won't give up. Because there is so much at stake:

Independence. Fulfillment. Freedom.

ACKNOWLEDGMENTS

This book is the result of four years of collaboration between a number of outstanding professionals. First of all, I wouldn't have been able to write this book without the support of my family, especially my dearest Lenka Paprok and my parents Jana and Karel Vlach, who had introduced me to doing business when I was still a teenager. The same goes for my publishers Vit Sebor, Tomas Baranek and all of their colleagues at Jan Melvil Publishing. They are true friends and mentors, who trusted my vision and supported it every step of the way. Most of the heavy lifting on the English edition though was done by two wordsmiths I deeply admire for their work ethic: Erik Piper did the translation and treated my text as his own child, while the editor Scott Hudson spent half a year on these 17 chapters and helped me to refine the final manuscript to perfection. Michal Kasparek, meanwhile, read the whole book several times throughout all its stages and as an experienced editor and book-reviewer pointed out blind spots in my thinking and suggested many smart improvements. Graphic designers Pavel Junk, Radek Petrik, Mira Szkandera and David Dvorak added the visuals and it is only thanks to them that the book looks so great. Then there were professionals from all around the world who I greatly respect and who helped me over the last four years in one way or another to improve the book's contents – namely Steven Pressfield, Adam Grant, Austin Kleon, David H. Hansson, David Allen, Melissa Joulwan, David Humphreys, Katie Perkins, Imre Jernei, Jan de Graaf, Paul Minar, Peter Klymec, Anna Drgova, Adam Zbiejczuk, Daniel Sacha, Daniel Gladis, Vendula Kurkova, Margit Slimakova, Michal Hanych, Jakub Vrana, Dusan Janovsky, Jan Rezac, Mira Vlach, Petr Koubsky, and Dan Moravek – as well as literally hundreds of others who shared their freelance stories and experiences with me over the last 20 years. Thank you all from the bottom of my heart!

BIBLIOGRAPHY

Agassi, Andre. *Open: An Autobiography.* New York: Vintage, 2010.

Allen, David. *Getting Things Done: The Art of Stress-Free Productivity.* New York: Penguin, 2015.

Alter, Adam. *Irresistible: The Rise of Addictive Technology and the Business of Keeping Us Hooked.* New York: Penguin, 2018.

Babauta, Leo. *Focus: A Simplicity Manifesto in the Age of Distraction.* Editorium, 2010.

Babauta, Leo. *Zen To Done: The Ultimate Simple Productivity System.* Seattle: CreateSpace, 2008.

Browder, Bill. *Red Notice: A True Story of High Finance, Murder, and One Man's Fight for Justice.* New York: Simon & Schuster, 2015.

Buffett, Warren. *Berkshire Hathaway: Letters to Shareholders 1965 - 2018.* Mountain View: Explorist Publications, 2018.

Carnegie, Dale. *How to Win Friends and Influence People.* New York: Simon & Schuster, 1981.

Chown, Marcus; Schilling, Govert. *Tweeting the Universe: Tiny Explanations of Very Big Ideas.* London: Faber & Faber, 2013.

Cialdini, Robert. *Influence: The Psychology of Persuasion.* New York: Harper Collins, 2006.

Cialdini, Robert. *Pre-Suasion: A Revolutionary Way to Influence and Persuade.* New York: Simon & Schuster, 2016.

Covey, Stephen; Merrill, Roger A.; Merrill, Rebecca R. *First Things First.* New York: Free Press, 1996.

Currey, Mason. *Daily Rituals: How Artists Work.* New York: Knopf, 2013.

Einhorn, Stefan. *The Art of Being Kind.* New York: Pegasus Books, 2007.

Fears, Rufus J. *A History of Freedom.* [audiobook]. New York: The Teaching Company, 2001. The Great Courses.

Ferriss, Tim. *The 4-Hour Workweek.* New York: Harmony Books, 2009.

Feynman, Richard P. *Surely You're Joking, Mr. Feynman!* New York: W. W. Norton & Co., 1997.

Fisher, Roger; Ury, William L. *Getting to Yes: Negotiating Agreement Without Giving In.* New York: Penguin, 1991.

Freeman, Seth. *The Art of Negotiating the Best Deal.* [audiobook]. New York: The Teaching Company, 2014. The Great Courses.

Fried, Jason; Hansson, David Heinemeier. *Remote: Office Not Required.* New York: Currency, 2013.

Fried, Jason; Hansson, David Heinemeier. *Rework.* New York: Currency, 2010.

Gawande, Atul. *The Checklist Manifesto: How to Get Things Right.* New York: Picador, 2011.

Gladwell, Malcolm. *Outliers: The Story of Success.* New York: Back Bay Books, 2011.

Goodman, Marc. *Future Crimes: Inside the Digital Underground and the Battle for Our Connected World.* New York: Anchor Books, 2016.

Grant, Adam. *Give and Take: Why Helping Others Drives Our Success.* New York: Penguin, 2013.

Horowitz, Sara. *The Freelancer's Bible.* New York: Workman Publishing Company, 2012.

Johnson, Steven. *Where Good Ideas Come From: The Natural History of Innovation.* New York: Riverhead Books, 2011.

Kahneman, Daniel. *Thinking, Fast and Slow.* New York: FSG, 2013.

Kleon, Austin. *Show Your Work!* New York: Workman Publishing Co., 2014.

Krug, Steve. *Don't Make Me Think, Revisited.* San Francisco: New Riders, 2014.

Lewis, Michael. *The Undoing Project: A Friendship That Changed Our Minds.* New York: W.W. Norton & Co., 2017.

Livermore, David. *Customs of the World.* [audiobook]. New York: The Teaching Company, 2013. The Great Courses.

Longo, John M. *The Art of Investing: Lessons from History's Greatest Traders.* [audiobook]. New York: The Teaching Company, 2016.

Mayle, Peter. *Acquired Tastes.* New York: Bantam Books, 1993.

McDougall, Christopher. *Born to Run.* New York: Vintage, 2011.

Murakami, Haruki. *What I Talk About When I Talk About Running: A Memoir.* New York: Vintage, 2009.

Newport, Cal. *Deep Work: Rules for Focused Success in a Distracted World.* New York: Grand Central Publishing, 2016.

Newport, Cal. *Digital Minimalism: Choosing a Focused Life in a Noisy World.* New York: Portfolio, 2019.

Newport, Cal. *So Good They Can't Ignore You: Why Skills Trump Passion in the Quest for Work You Love.* New York: Grand Central Publishing, 2012.

O'Reilly, Tim. *WTF: What's the Future and Why It's Up to Us.* London: Crown Publishing 2017.

Novella, Steven. *Your Deceptive Mind.* [Audiobook]. New York: The Teaching Company, 2013. The Great Courses.

Pressfield, Steven. *The War of Art: Break Through the Blocks and Win Your Inner Creative Battles.* New York: Black Irish Entertainment LLC, 2012.

Pressfield, Steven. *Turning Pro.* New York: Black Irish Entertainment LLC, 2012.

Pink, Daniel. *Free Agent Nation: The Future of Working for Yourself.* New York: Business Plus, 2002.

Pink, Daniel. *To Sell Is Human: The Surprising Truth About Moving Others.* New York: Riverhead Books, 2013.

Pink, Daniel. *When: The Scientific Secrets of Perfect Timing.* New York: Riverhead Books, 2018.

Ratey, John J. *Spark: The Revolutionary New Science of Exercise and the Brain.* Boston: Little, Brown and Co., 2013.

Rath, Tom. *StrengthsFinder 2. 0.* New York: Gallup Press, 2007.

Ries, Eric. *The Lean Startup.* New York: Currency, 2011.

Rubin, Harriet. *Soloing: Realizing Your Life's Ambition.* New York: Harper Business, 1999.

Rohde, Mike. *The Sketchnote Handbook.* San Francisco: Peachpit Press, 2012.

Schwarzenegger, Arnold. *Total Recall: My Unbelievably True Life Story.* New York: Simon & Schuster, 2013.

Seligman, Martin E. P. *Authentic Happiness.* New York: Free Press, 2002.

Steinmetz, Greg. *The Richest Man Who Ever Lived: The Life and Times of Jacob Fugger.* New York: Simon & Schuster, 2015.

Taleb, Nassim Nicholas. *The Black Swan: The Impact of the Highly Improbable.* New York: Random House, 2010.

Voss, Chris. *Never Split the Difference: Negotiating As If Your Life Depended on It.* New York: Harper Business, 2016.

Walker, Matthew. *Why We Sleep: Unlocking the Power of Sleep and Dreams.* New York: Scribner, 2017.

WOULD YOU LIKE TO PUBLISH *THE FREELANCE WAY* IN YOUR COUNTRY?
OR DO YOU KNOW A PUBLISHER THAT MIGHT?

To help as many freelancers as possible, we would love to partner with local publishers arouand the world established in educational and self-help literature for work and business. Our vision is to make this bestseller available to all readers in their native language.

If you want to inquire about the translation rights for *The Freelance Way*, or know a good local publisher, translator or literary agent, who might be interested in the book, send us an email to **rights@janmelvil.com** and we'll be more than happy to write you back.

Vit Sebor & Tomas Baranek
Jan Melvil Publishing

INDEX

A

accountants, accounting, 16, 37–38, 111, 180–181, 326, 419
 – workshops and training, 90, 326
administrative tasks, 16, 38, 101, 131, 150–152
 – client registry, 232–234
 – optimizing administrative tasks, 151–152
 – record keeping, 149, 204–205
Allen, David, 156–157
alphabet of business, 85, 89–91, 292
Android, 163,168–169, 359
 – encryption, 169
 – safety and security, 168
Apple, Macs, 163, 168, 174
 – vs. Google and Microsoft, 163
 – iCloud, 167–168
 – iPhone, 163, 168–169
applications, apps, 151, 163–182, 200–212, 262, 359, 426
audiobooks, 181, 359

B

bad-mouthing clients and colleagues, 60, 90, 185
Basecamp, 78, 96, 110, 200, 262
BATNA (Best Alternative to a Negotiated Agreement), 294–297, 322–323
biorhythms, 143–148
Bit.ly, 360
blogs, blogging, 352–355, 368–370
 – Medium.com, 353
 – themes and templates, 368
 – strategies, 353
 – WordPress, 353, 369–370
brands, branding, 55–57, 390–409
 – company vs. personal, 391, 395
 – personal brand, 55–57, 390–395

Buffett, Warren, 40, 60, 236, 432
building a community, 348, 398
burnout, 44, 53, 74, 140–141, 217, 439
business, 13–16, 19–24
 – as a freelancer, 19–21
 – forms of, 28–32
 – historical overview, 23–24
 – idea of freedom, 25, 442
 – solving problems, 15–16, 443
 – three separate levels of a freelance business, 16
business coaching, see mentors, mentoring
business customs and traditions, 23– 24, 95, 222, 291
business plans, 105–107, 153, 411

C

cafes (as a workspace), 72–73
calendars, 142, 170–182
capital, 21–22, 107
 – personal, 21–22, 47
career changes, 53–54
career strategies, 105–107, 117–133
 – Do What You Love (principle), 119
cash flow, see also finance and financial self-management, 424–431
cash reserve, see also financial reserve 419–423
Chrome (Google), 167, 175
 – secure passwords, 167
chronotype, 144–145
client portfolio, 215–217, 230
clients, see also client portfolio, 215–234
 – client expectations, 95–97, 219–228
 – client registry, 232–234
 – clients vs. inquirers, 220–221
 – loyalty, 223–227
 – problems, 227–230, 324

– professional client care, 221–222
– segmentation, 277
– VIP and premium clients, 221–222
cloud computing, 166–178, 232–233
– applications, cloud based, 172–178, 232–233
– backups, 168
– Dropbox, 176
– G Suite, 171–176
– iCloud, 173
– Office 365, 173
cognitive biases, 102, 104
colleagues, collegiality, 39–42, 69, 86–91
commissions, 190–191
companies and firms, 28–32
– vs. freelancers, 29
confirmation bias, 102
contractors, contracting, *see Freelancers, Freelancing*
– advantages vs. disadvantages, 68–71
– dependence on one big client, 116–117, 215
– independent (self-employed), 20, 68, 116
contracts, 305, 313, 321, 326–328
– RocketLawyer, 38, 339
consultants, consulting, 38, 124–129
circle of competence, 51, 127
coworking, 72–75, 397
– *The Rise of Free Coworking* (article), 72
– training events, 400, 404
creative professionals, creatives, 21, 296–301, 351
critical thinking, 101–102
– vs. intuition, 101
customer-relationship management (CRM), 175, 232–234
– Google Contacts, 175, 233
– Insightly, 232
– Streak CRM, 233
customers, *see clients*
curriculum vitae, CVs, 349, 389–393

D
daily work review, 150–151
debt collection, unpaid claims, 324–329
deep work, 155–156

demand, 30–32
– connection with pricing, 30, 237, 243–246
development projects, 217, 230, 417
digital nomads, 76–78, 129
– perpetual, 78
digital well-being, 359, 376
domains, 170–173, 364–367
Dunning-Kruger effect, 102

E
e-lancers, 26, 58
elevator pitch, 49, 105
email, 95–96, 225–227, 388–389
– *No, You Can't Ignore Email. It's Rude* (article), 226
– professional, 225–227
European Forum for Independent Professionals (EFIP), 21
every day counts (principle), 150
evolution of a professional 437–438
expedition mentality, 200
expertise, 107–109, 117–129
– changing, 53–54
– single vs. double, 107–109
experts, 43–44

F
Facebook, 345–347, 355–360
– Ads, 347
– Groups, 347
– Pages, 347
– Personal Profile, 346–347
– Settings, 346
fast thinking, 102, 126
feedback, 61–62, 100–101
finances, financial planning, *see also risk*, 414–433
– cash flow, 425–430
– debt, 86, 414–416, 424
– Excel spreadsheets, 420, 424
– Google Sheets, 424
– financial overview, 419–424
– financial plan, financial planning, 427–431
– financial reserve, 419–423, 430
– financial self-management, 71, 415–433
– foreign currencies, 425–426
– investing, investments, 431–433

– taxes and mandatory payments, 422
Financial Crisis (2008), 258
financial self-management *see also Finance*, 415–433
– assets and liabilities, 419–427
– monthly revenues, 416–419
– tracking spending, 424–427
fluctuation of income, 70–71, 417–418
freedom, 17, 25, 36–37, 435
Freelance Isn't Free Act, 328
freelancer, freelancing, 16–17, 19–21
– advantages and disadvantages, 68–70
– as a phenomenon, 27
– career strategy, 105, 117–121
– definition, 15, 19–21
– internet and modern technology, 25–27, 78, 96, 162
– literature, 22–27, 86
– preconceptions, 18–20, 84
– vs. employees, 45, 57–58
Freelancers Union, 20–21, 40–41, 122, 258, 331

G
gadgets, 164–166
gatekeeper, 357–362
General Data Protection Regulation (GDPR), 169, 233, 305
Getting Things Done (GTD), 156–158, 178
gig, 15, 29, 99, 110
gig economy, 18–19
Gig Economy Data Hub, 21
GitHub, 351
globalization, 26, 129–130
Gmail, 170–176
– free version, 170–172
– G Suite, 172–176
– losing access to your account, 171
– settings, 175
good name, 43–63, 118, 123, 228–231
– as an advertisement, 45, 377
– as a phenomenon, 55
– better clients, 43–44
– career, 44–46
– cumulative effect, 46
– name changes, 48
– nicknames, 48–49

– vs. personal brand, 56–57
Google, 170–178
– Android, 163, 168–169
– applications, 359
– vs. Apple vs. Microsoft, 163
– Chrome, 167, 175
– Contacts, 233
– Google Analytics, 364
– Google Calendar, 170–175, 368
– Google Drive, 174–178
– Google Hangouts, 299, 314
– Google Keep, 151, 179, 359
– personal info and privacy, 175
grammar of business, 90
Grant, Adam, 59, 226, 301
grouping tasks, 151–152
growth, 52, 186, 195, 239, 257, 435–441
– career, 118, 437
– professional, 52, 186, 195, 239, 257

H
Hansson, David Heinemeier, 78, 110
happy accidents, 131–133
health, 143–148, 163–165
healthy work environment, 164–166
– healthy hardware, 166
– ventilation and air quality, 164–165
– working at a standing desk, 165–166
Hollywood Model, 23
home office, working from home, 71–74
Horowitz, Sara, 41, 86, 99, 122, 215, 231

I
Impact HUB, 72
increasing scale of business complexity, 28
independent professional, *see also Freelancer*, 21–24
individualism, 25
– *The Century of the Self* (BBC Documentary), 25
influencers, 241, 408
information technology, 162–181
inquiries, 220–221, 237, 243, 322
intake of commitments, 132

intellectual marketing, 407–409
internet *see also social media*, 343–344,
  362–364
  – online presence (findability),
    343–344
  – quality web content, 343
  – search engines, 362–364
intuition, 101–102
investments, investing, 431–433
invoices, invoicing, 37, 180–182, 186
  – applications, 180–181
IPSE (Association of Independent
  Professionals and the Self Employed),
  20, 75, 398
irreplaceability, 75–76
IT security and safety, 166–170
  – antivirus programs, 167–167
  – backing up data, 168
  – encryption, 169
  – free programs, 167
  – Gmail, 170–176
  – legal knowledge, 169–170
  – secure passwords and password
    management, 167
  – two-factor authentication, 2FA,
    167, 176

K
know-how, 33–39, 288–304
  – accounting, 37
  – mentors and mentoring, 37–39
  – negotiating and negotiating
    strategies, 288–304
  – specialization and niche
    freelancing, 33
knowledge workers, 22, 101

L
late adopters (principle), 168
late payers, *see also non-payers*, 328–329
Lateral Action (blog), 34
liberalism, 25
licensing, 264–265
LinkedIn *see also Social Media*, 349–350
  – Groups, 349
  – Recommendations, 349
little bets *see also small bets*, 109–112
location, 397–398
logos *see also brands, branding*,
  396–397
  – cost(s), 397

  – visual style, 396
luck, 130–132

M
Mailchimp, 370
marketing, 55, 377–409
  – advertising campaigns, 409
  – business cards, 387–388
  – career statistics, 389–390
  – clothing and appearance, 395–396
  – community involvement, 382–383
  – intellectual marketing, 407–409
  – marketing plan, 409
  – marketing strategies, 377–378
  – networking, 380–382
  – personal branding, 390–396
  – personal marketing, 380–381
  – public speaking and events, 399–401
  – recommending colleagues, 385
  – social media, 345–350, 388–389
  – testimonials and written
    recommendations, 362, 383–384
McGuinness, Mark, 34
media, 401–404
mentors, mentoring, 37–39
  – vs. consultants, 38–39
Microsoft, 163, 166, 173–174, 178
  – vs. Apple vs. Google, 163
  – Office, 173
microservices, *see personal assistance*
mind maps, 149, 154
minimalism, 156
misclassification, 19, 116
mistakes, 195–197
motivational best–sellers, 83, 137

N
negotiation process, 306–322
  – email follow-up, 312–318
  – initial phone call, 307–312
  – optimizing negotiations, 306–322
  – orders, 321–322
  – personal meetings, 318–321
negotiations, 288–304
  – BATNA (best alternative to
    a negotiated agreement), 294–296
  – consultative negotiators, 290–292
  – contractual penalties, *see also
    NDAs*, 304–306
  – distributive bargaining, 296–298
  – exclusivity and price, 304

– hard negotiators, 289
– preparations, 292–294
– principled negotiation, 292
– soft negotiators, 289
Newport, Cal, 119, 121, 141, 155–156, 343
newsletters, 274, 368, 370
non-disclosure agreements, NDAs, 304–305
non–payers, *see also late payers*, 324–340
– balance payments, 336–337
– collecting debts, 331
– legal awareness, 326–327
– researching prospective clients, 330–334
– risk of non-payment, 324–326
– safe approaches, 339–340
– upfront payments, 334–336
– warning signs, 327–330
note-taking, 154–155, 178–179
– Bullet Journal, 154
– Evernote, 178
– G Suite Drive, 178
– Moleskine, 154
– Rocketbook, 154
– Sketchnotes, 154

O

online portfolios, 351–352, 377

P

parentrepreneurs, 74–75
– mompreneurs and dadpreneurs, 74–75
passive aggressive behavior, 187–189, 308
passwords, 168–171
– forgotten passwords, 170–171
password management, 168–169
pay per click, PPC advertisements, 363–364, 409
permanent temps, perma-temps, 318
personal assistance, personal assistants, 158–160
– housekeepers and home helpers, 159–160
– microservices, 160
– virtual, 158–160
personal branding, 55–57, 390–396
– brand totality, 391

– building a brand, 392–393
– *Case Against Personal Brands* (article), 391
– consultants, 395–396
– foundation of personal branding, 393–394
– sins and pitfalls, 390–392
– touchpoints, 392–393
– vs. a good name, 56–57
personal calling, 122–123, 133
personal IT, 162–163
– cloud based applications, 172–176
– gadgets, 164–166
– smartphones, 163–169
personal marketing *see also marketing*, 378–381
– elevator pitch, 49, 105
– vs. company marketing, 377
personal productivity, 137
– impact on income, 137
– internal resistance, 138–140
– practical aids, 154–155
– priorities, prioritizing, 141–143
Pink, Daniel, 27, 144, 146, 379
planning fallacy, 102
podcasts, podcasting, 356–357
power user (principle), 168
Pressfield, Steven, 95, 121, 138–139
prices, pricing, 236–261, 283–287
– determines profits, 237–238
– discounts, 285–286
– fixed, 260
– "good price," 258–260
– how to define, 283–285
– individual rates, 251–254
– price jumps, 254–257
– raising prices, 246–251
– setting prices, 238–246
pricing methods, 261–283
– author's fees and royalties, 264–265
– based on a client's budget, 268–269
– customer segmentation, 273–275
– day rate, 266
– flat rates, 269–270
– hourly rates, 261–263
– hourly super-packages, 278–280
– introductory rates, 283
– job rates, 263–264
– pre-sales, 280–281

- price lists, 260
- price packages, 271
- price-per-unit, 265–266
- product prices, 266–268
- satisfaction fees and success fees, 281–283
- service as a product, 271–273
- variant pricing, 275–278
problematic customers, 309, 324–326
- prevention, 339–340
processes, 202–205
- diagrams, 202
- the point of freelance processes, 203–205
- vs. projects, 197–198
process management, 205–211
- analyzing processes, 207–208
- applications, 212–213
- delegation, 209–210
- evaluation of processes, 210
- mapping processes, 206–207
- meta-processes, 211
- process audits, 211–212
- process optimization, 208–209
- reporting processes, 210–211
- subprocesses, 211
professional calling, *see also personal calling*, 122–124
professional growth, 186, 195, 435–441
- growth + expertise vs. price, 254
project management, 157, 191, 198–202
- applications (for support), 200
- competencies, 198–200
- project managers, 201–202
public courses, online courses, 404–407
- agencies, 405
- as a product, 405
- financial considerations, 405
- framework for preparation, 406–407
- online courses, 354–356, 407
public intellectuals, 407
public speaking, 100–101, 399–401

R
raising prices, 246–251
reliability, 91–98
- as a prerequisite for success, 91–92
- communication, 92–93
- explicit vs. implicit, 92

- 5-level scale of reliability, 97
remote work, working remotely, 73–78, 129–130
reports, studies and surveys,
- *Accenture Technology Vision 2017*, 26
- *Deloitte Millennial Survey 2017*, 27
- *Evolving Workforce*, 68
- *Exploring the UK Freelance Workforce (2016)*, 20, 398
- *Field Nation Freelance Study (2016)*, 68
- *Freelance Industry Report (2012)*, 241
- *Freelancing in America 2017*, 71, 416
- *Freelancing in America 2018*, 20, 62, 85, 240
- *Independent Work* (McKinsey Global Institute), 21, 67
- *Independents United Report*, 21
- *The New Freelancers Report*, 26
- *PwC Work-life 3.0*, 27
- *The State of Independence in American 2018*, 240
- *State of Remote Work 2019*, 73
reputation, *see also good name*, 43–60
reputation bonus, 57–59
- employees vs. freelancers, 57
reputation penalty, 58
research, 225, 308, 331–334
resumes, 349, 389
retention offers for clients (model), 256–257
resistance, internal, 138–140
risk, 411–415
- aversion, 413
- downplaying future risk, 412
- protection against risk, 414–415
- mapping and prevention, 413–414

S
savings, *see financial self-management*
search engines, 362–364
Search Engine Optimization (SEO), 363
self-determination theory, 67
self-employed, *see also freelancer*, 19–20
shadow career, 120–121
shadow economy, 26
side jobs, 15, 19, 52, 109–112

– little and small bets, 109–112
Skype, 96, 176, 299
slander, *see also bad-mouthing*, 90, 343
small bets *see little Bets*
social media, 342–362
– aggression and disinhibition
   effect, 361
– blogs, blogging, 352–354
– cyberbullying, 361
– Facebook, 345–347
– Instagram, 348
– LinkedIn, 349–350
– online portfolios, 351–352
– podcasts, 356–357
– trolls, 361–362
– Twitter, 350–351
– videoblogs, vlogs, 354–356
– Vimeo, 354
– YouTube, 354–356
spec work, 300–301, 325
specialization, 51–54
step-by-step management, 152–154
strategic partnerships, 194
stress, 78–80
subcontractors, subcontracting, 189–190
– sub-deliveries, 191–192
success, 82–103
– foundations for, 85–87
– model for success (for beginning
   freelancers), 85
– personal prerequisites, 91–103
– salesman of success, 82–84
survivorship bias, 102
Swiss approach to business, 88

T

taxes, taxation, 326, 422
temporary workers, 20
testimonials, 383–384
time (keeping track of), 149, 179–180
– Taptile, 180
– Toggl, 180, 262
Toastmasters, 100

to-do lists, 142, 150–152, 178–179
– Todoist, 151, 179
– Trello, 179, 200
– Wunderlist, 179
touch typing, 176–178
traditions of small business, 23–24
turning down work, 30, 99
Twitter, 350–351
two-factor authentication, 2FA, 167,
   176

U

Udemy, 356
uncertainty, 69–70, 78–80
– connection to stress, 79
unwritten rules of email, 96
upselling, 274

V

videoblogs, vlogs, 354–356
VIP and premium clients, 268–276,
   288

W

web consultants, 153, 372
web pages, 343–344, 367–375
– as a business card, 367
– choosing a domain name, 364–367
– content sites, 369–370
– longreads, 371
– microsites (single page sites), 367
– role and selection of web designer,
   374–375
– turnkey sites, 370–372
weirdo hypothesis, 243, 309
WeWork, 72
WordPress, 353, 369–370
work-life balance, 71–75
working vacations, 76–77
working for free, 109, 113–115

Y

YearCompass, 142
YouTube, 354–356

THE FREELANCE WAY
Best Business Practices, Tools & Strategies for Freelancers
Robert Vlach

Author: Robert Vlach
Translation: Erik Piper
Copy editing: Scott Hudson
Proofreading: Katie Perkins
Illustrations: Radek Petrik, Miroslav Szkandera
Design and composition: David Dvorak
Cover art: Pavel Junk

Published by Jan Melvil Publishing
Roubalova 13
602 00 Brno
Czech Republic
European Union
www.janmelvil.com

Discuss the book online: **#FreelanceWay**
Follow updates, or buy the e-book: **www.freelanceway.eu**
Report typos and other errors: **erratum@janmelvil.com**
Inquiries for translation rights or bulk orders: **rights@janmelvil.com**
Reviews, feedback and comments for the author: **book@vla.ch**

ISBN 978-80-7555-079-8

Made in the USA
Middletown, DE
24 November 2019